Dr.STONE

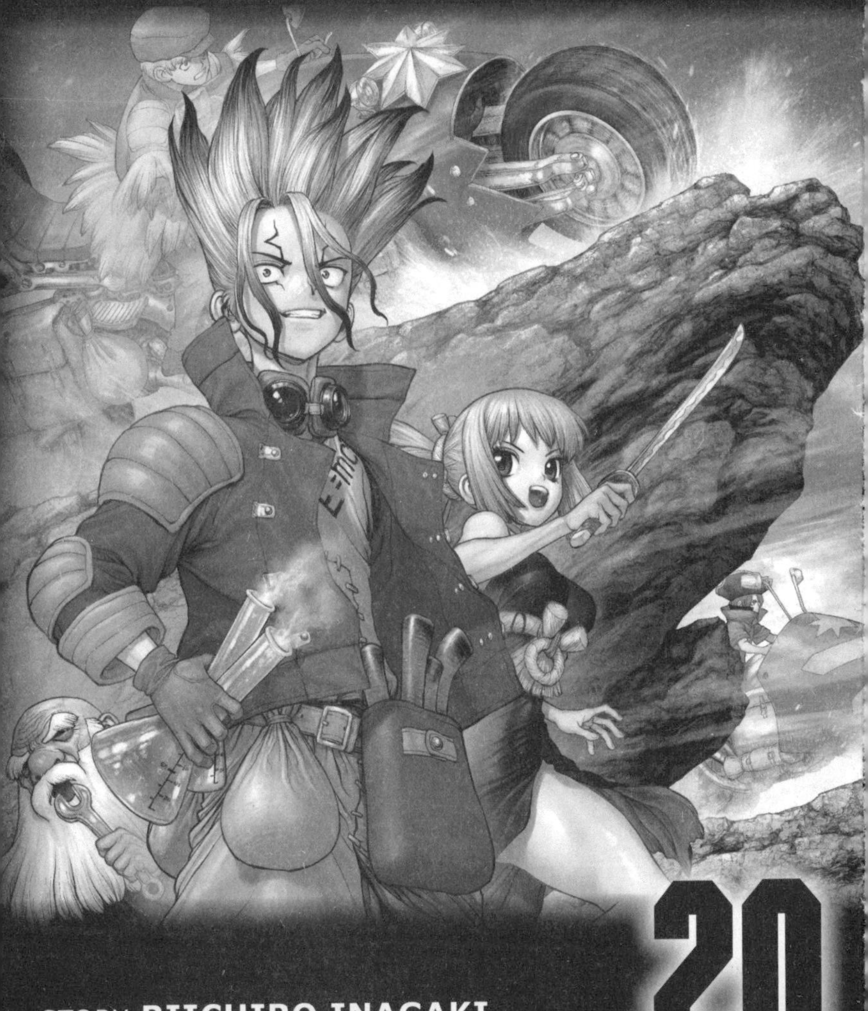

20

MEDUSA MECHANISM

STORY **RIICHIRO INAGAKI**
ART **BOICHI**

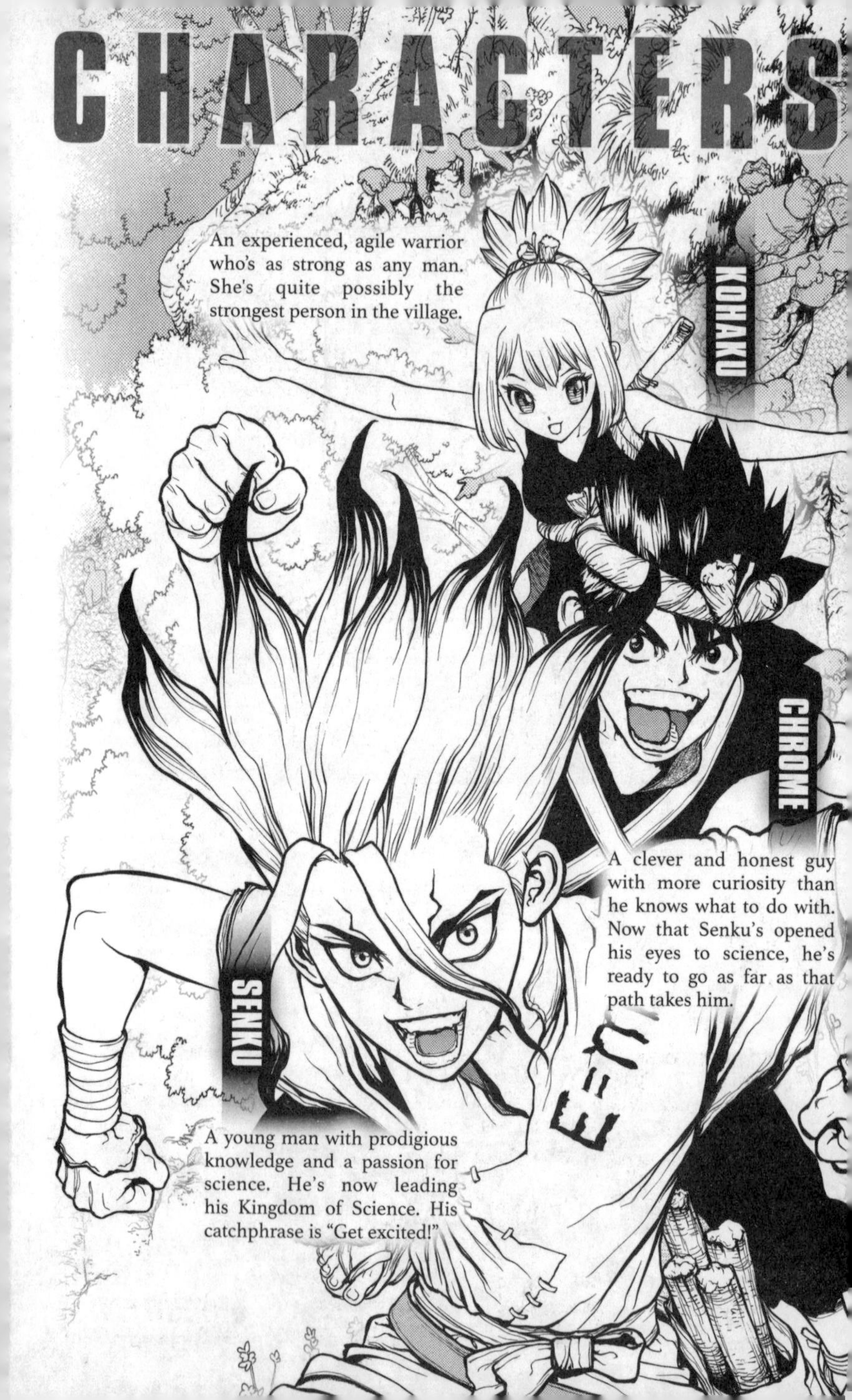
CHARACTERS
KOHAKU
An experienced, agile warrior who's as strong as any man. She's quite possibly the strongest person in the village.
CHROME
A clever and honest guy with more curiosity than he knows what to do with. Now that Senku's opened his eyes to science, he's ready to go as far as that path takes him.
SENKU
A young man with prodigious knowledge and a passion for science. He's now leading his Kingdom of Science. His catchphrase is "Get excited!"

Dr.STONE

STORY

Every human on earth is turned to stone by a mysterious phenomenon, including high school student Taiju. Nearly 3,700 years later, Taiju awakens and finds his friend Senku, who revived a bit earlier. Together, they vow to restore civilization, but Tsukasa, once considered the strongest high schooler alive, nearly kills Senku in order to put a stop to his scientific plans.

After being secretly revived by his friends, Senku arrives at Ishigami Village. But when word of Senku's survival gets back to Tsukasa, the war between the two forces begins! Eventually, the two factions make peace. After acquiring a petrification device on Treasure Island, Senku heads for the U.S.A. to find corn, and encounters another science kingdom!

The science kingdoms are battling for supremacy over land, air, and sea! The enemy submarine attacks, allowing Stanley and his people to take over the *Perseus*, but Chrome's team manages to nab Dr. Xeno! The crew is now on its way to the petri-beam's origin in South America with Stanley in hot pursuit!

LUNA **STANLEY** **DR. XENO**

TAIJU **RYUSUI** **TSUKASA** **GEN ASAGIRI**

CONTENTS

20
MEDUSA MECHANISM

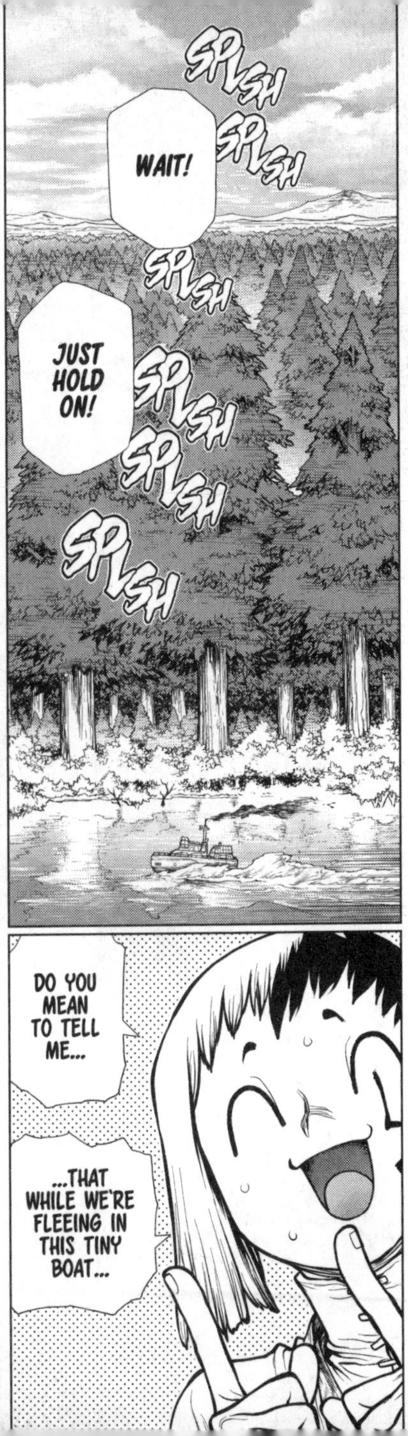
SPLSH
SPLSH
WAIT!
SPLSH
JUST HOLD ON!
SPLSH
SPLSH
SPLSH
DO YOU MEAN TO TELL ME...
...THAT WHILE WE'RE FLEEING IN THIS TINY BOAT...

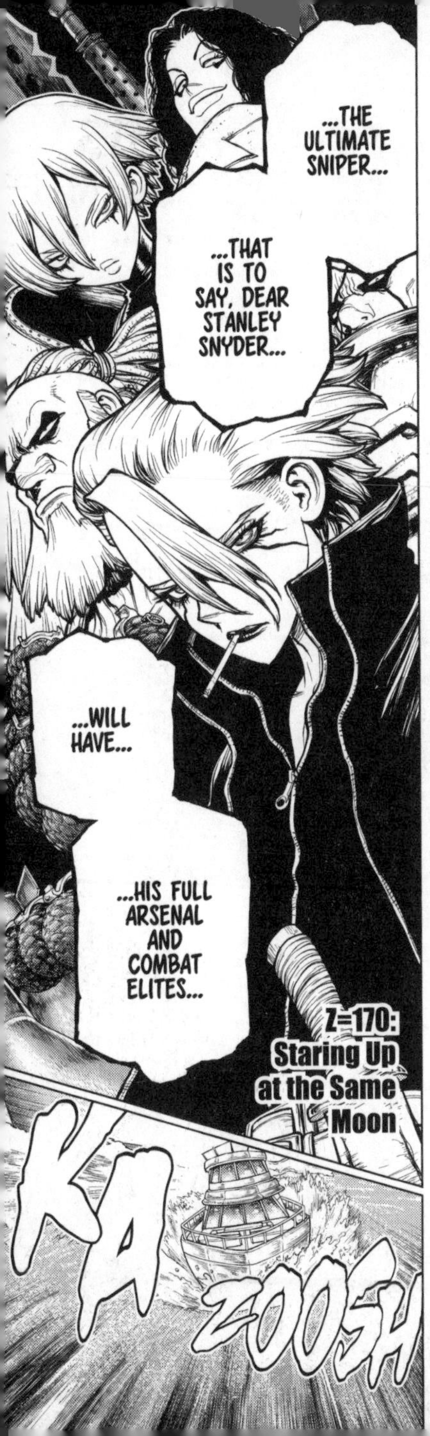
...THE ULTIMATE SNIPER...
...THAT IS TO SAY, DEAR STANLEY SNYDER...
...WILL HAVE...
...HIS FULL ARSENAL AND COMBAT ELITES...
Z=170: Staring Up at the Same Moon
KA ZOOSH

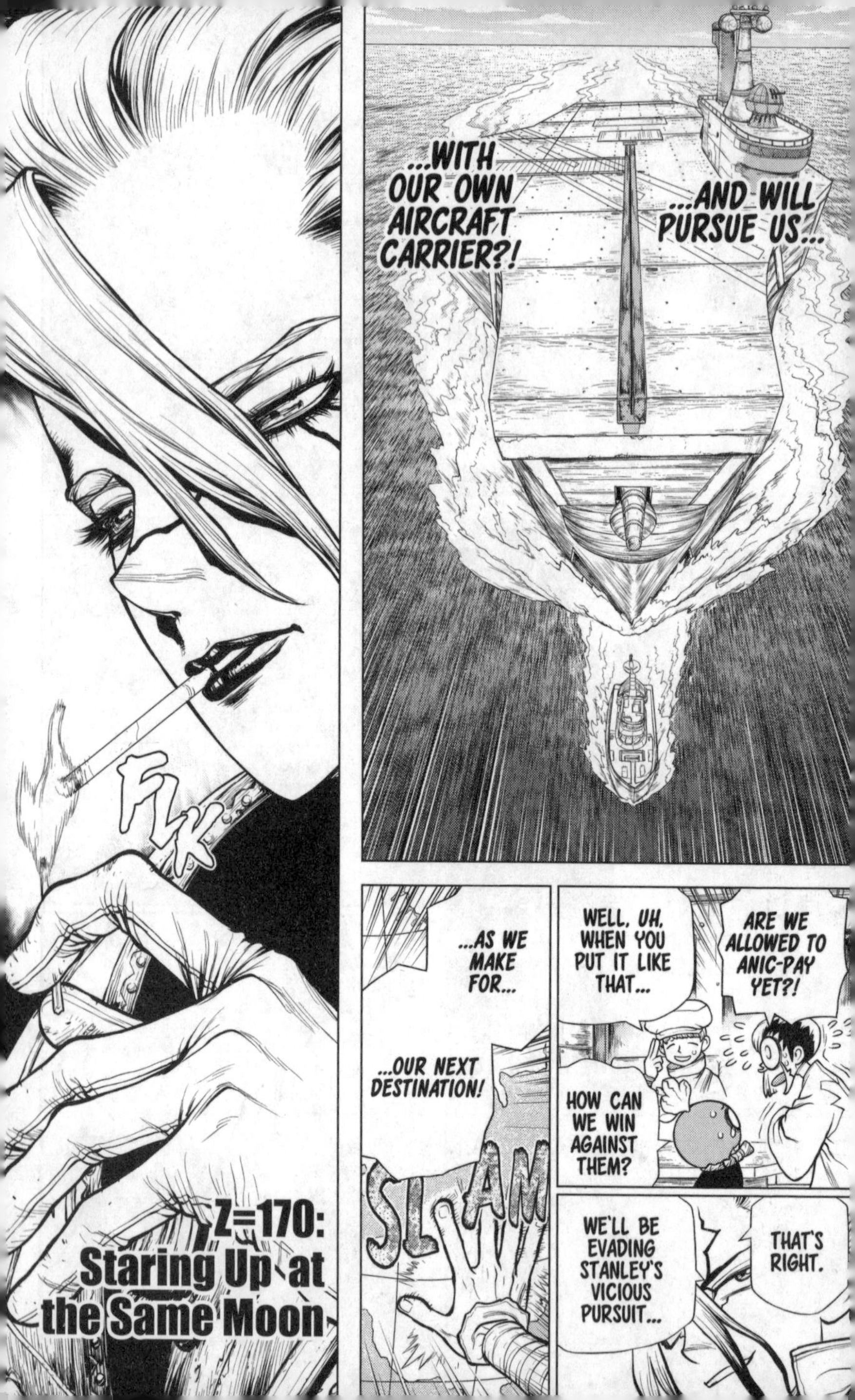
...AND WILL PURSUE US...
...WITH OUR OWN AIRCRAFT CARRIER?!
ARE WE ALLOWED TO ANIC-PAY YET?!
WELL, UH, WHEN YOU PUT IT LIKE THAT...
HOW CAN WE WIN AGAINST THEM?
THAT'S RIGHT.
WE'LL BE EVADING STANLEY'S VICIOUS PURSUIT...
...AS WE MAKE FOR...
...OUR NEXT DESTINATION!
SLAM
FLK
Z=170: Staring Up at the Same Moon

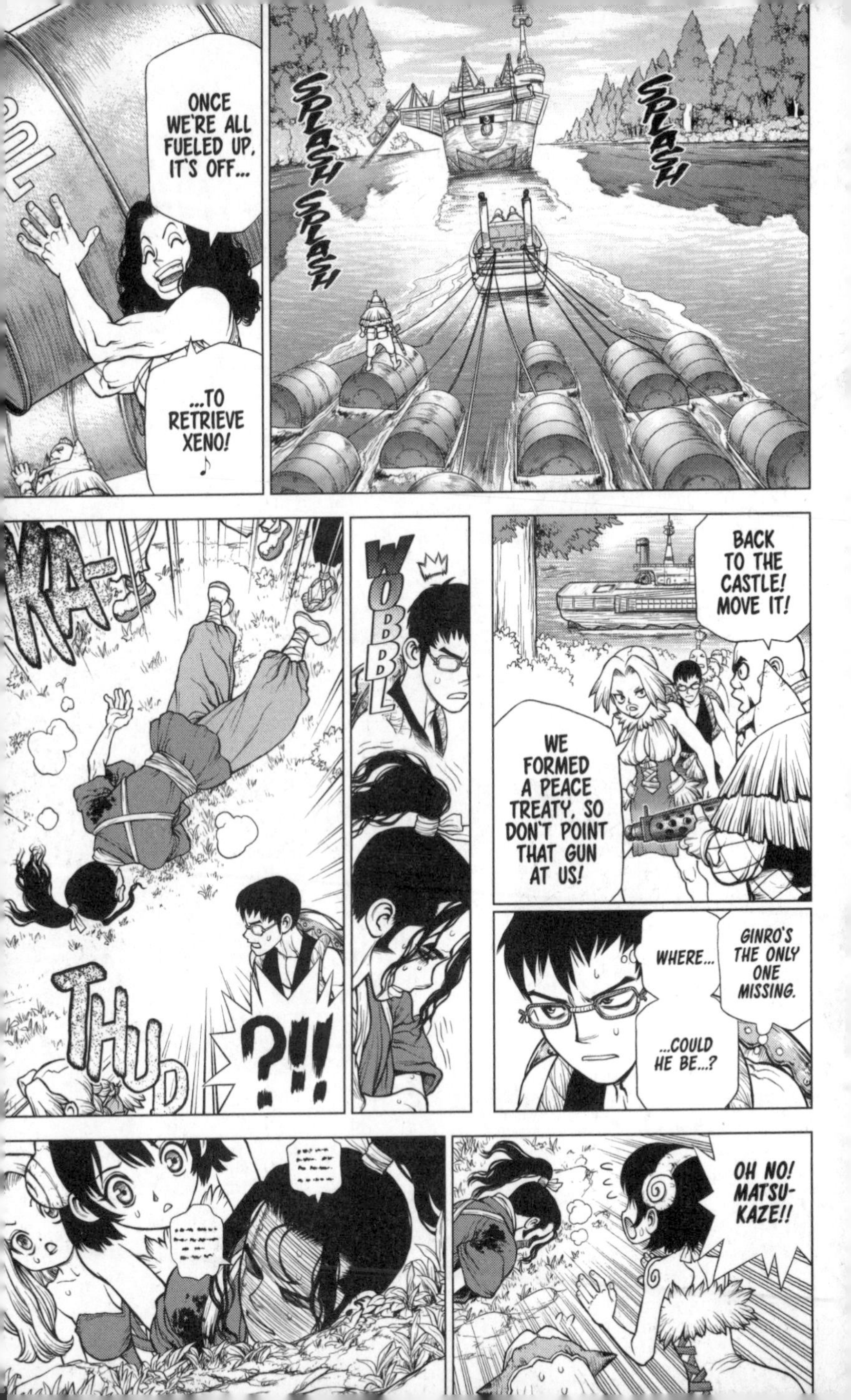
SPLASH
SPLASH SPLASH
ONCE WE'RE ALL FUELED UP, IT'S OFF...
...TO RETRIEVE XENO! ♪
BACK TO THE CASTLE! MOVE IT!
WE FORMED A PEACE TREATY, SO DON'T POINT THAT GUN AT US!
GINRO'S THE ONLY ONE MISSING.
WHERE...
...COULD HE BE...?
WOBBL
KA-
THUD
?!!
OH NO! MATSU-KAZE!!

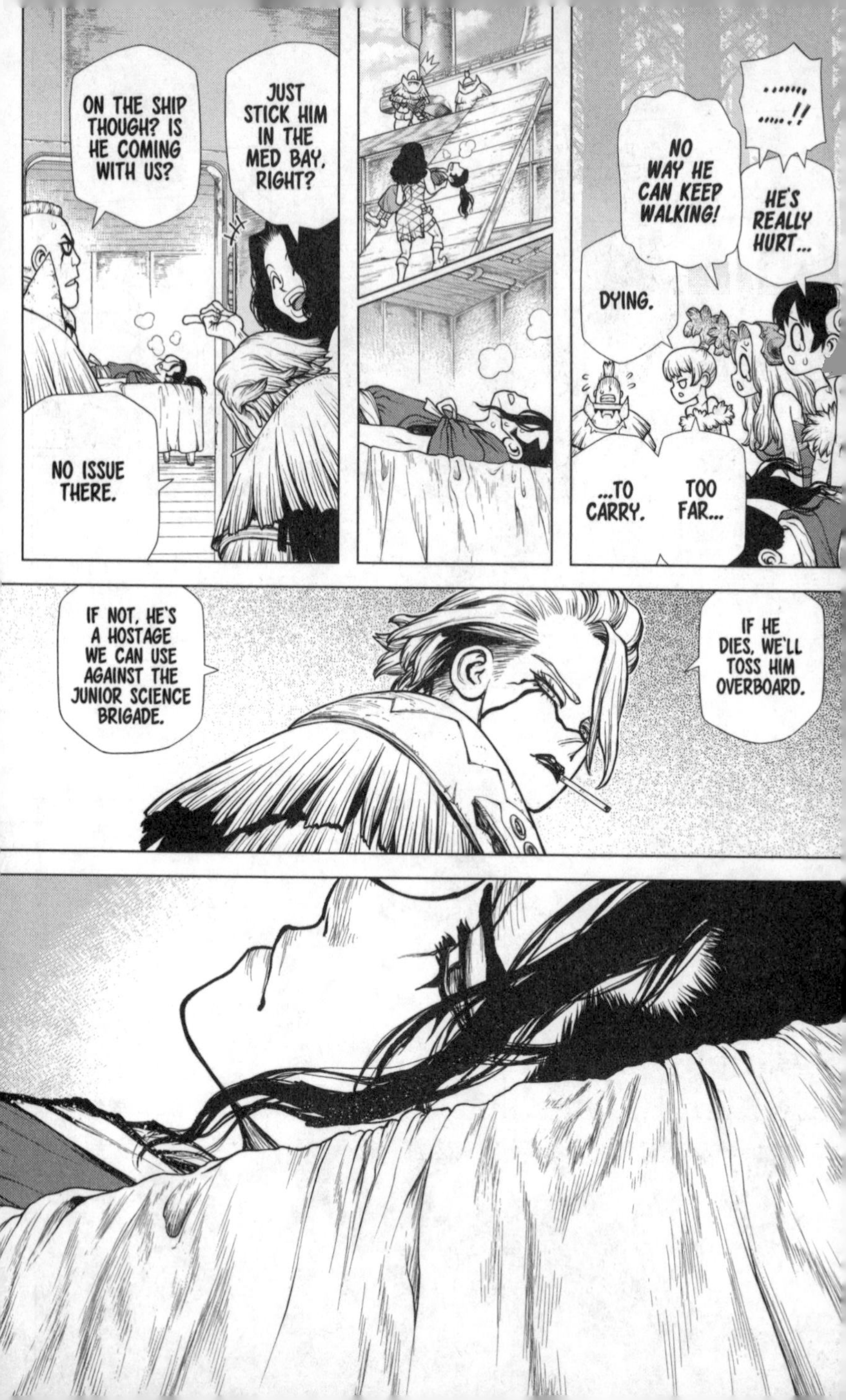
......,
......!!
HE'S REALLY HURT...
NO WAY HE CAN KEEP WALKING!
DYING.
TOO FAR...
...TO CARRY.
JUST STICK HIM IN THE MED BAY, RIGHT?
ON THE SHIP THOUGH? IS HE COMING WITH US?
NO ISSUE THERE.
IF HE DIES, WE'LL TOSS HIM OVERBOARD.
IF NOT, HE'S A HOSTAGE WE CAN USE AGAINST THE JUNIOR SCIENCE BRIGADE.

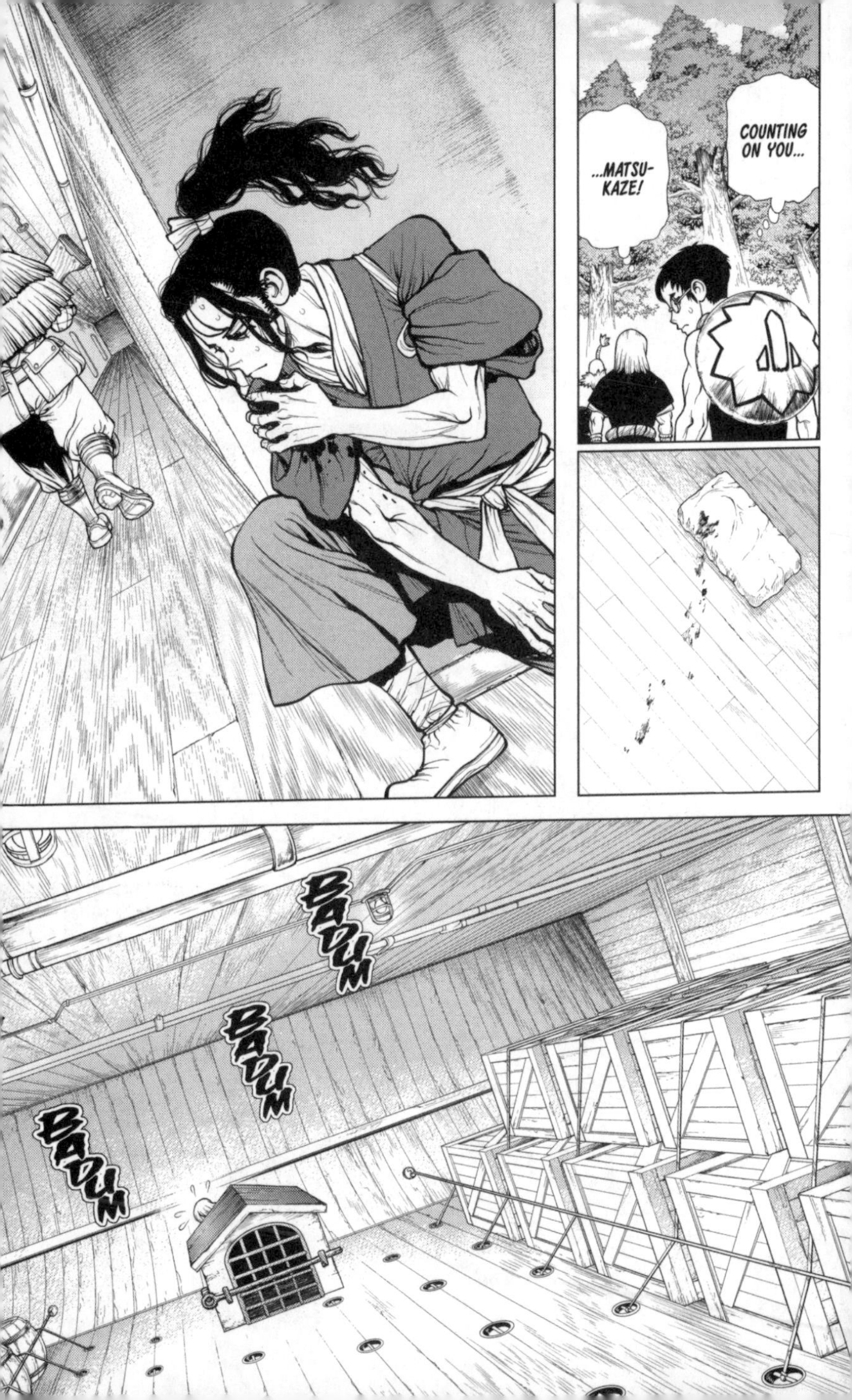
COUNTING ON YOU...
...MATSU-KAZE!
BADUM
BADUM
BADUM

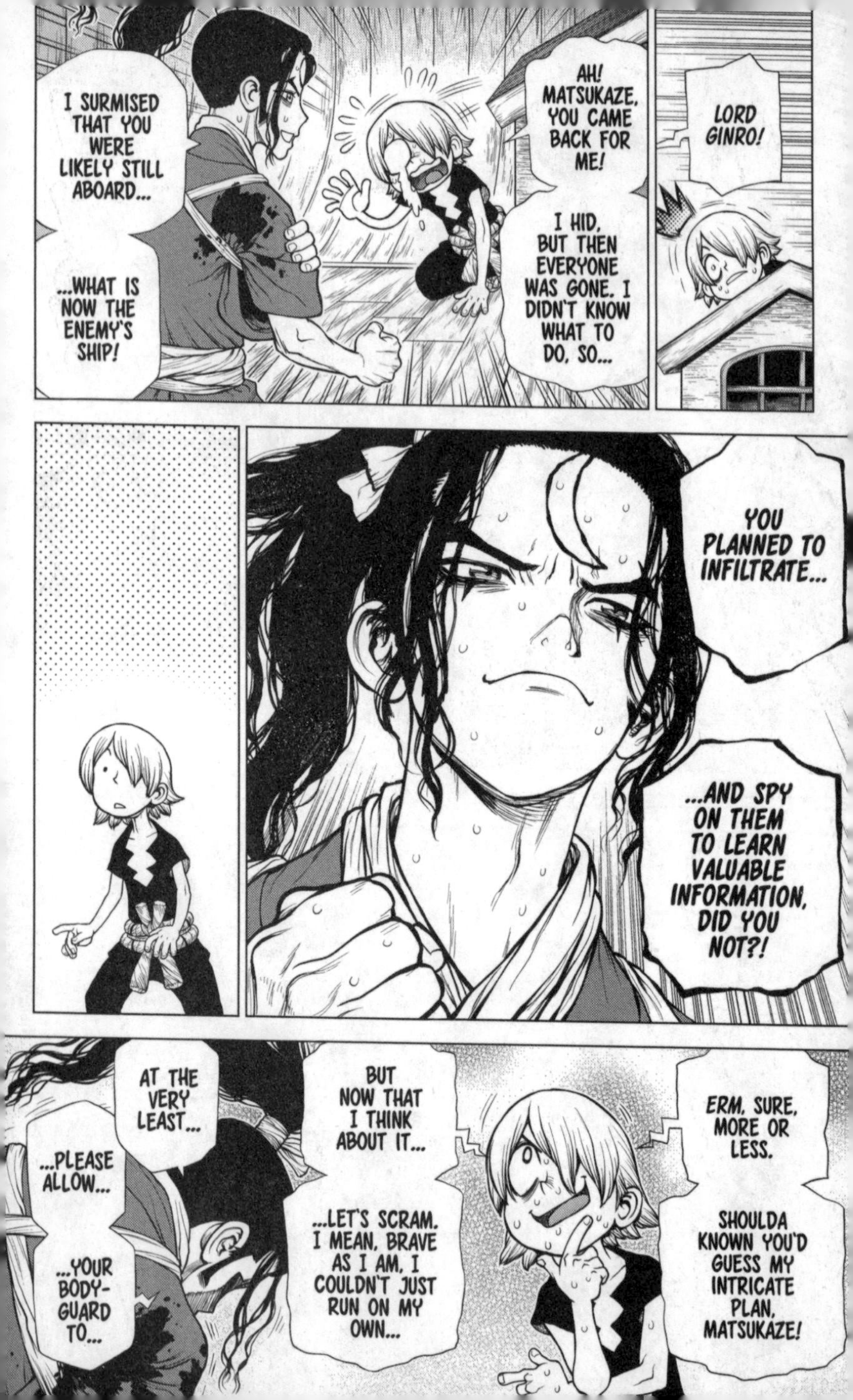
LORD GINRO!
AH! MATSUKAZE, YOU CAME BACK FOR ME!
I HID, BUT THEN EVERYONE WAS GONE. I DIDN'T KNOW WHAT TO DO, SO...
I SURMISED THAT YOU WERE LIKELY STILL ABOARD...
...WHAT IS NOW THE ENEMY'S SHIP!
YOU PLANNED TO INFILTRATE...
...AND SPY ON THEM TO LEARN VALUABLE INFORMATION, DID YOU NOT?!
ERM, SURE, MORE OR LESS.
SHOULDA KNOWN YOU'D GUESS MY INTRICATE PLAN, MATSUKAZE!
BUT NOW THAT I THINK ABOUT IT...
...LET'S SCRAM. I MEAN, BRAVE AS I AM, I COULDN'T JUST RUN ON MY OWN...
AT THE VERY LEAST...
...PLEASE ALLOW...
...YOUR BODY-GUARD TO...

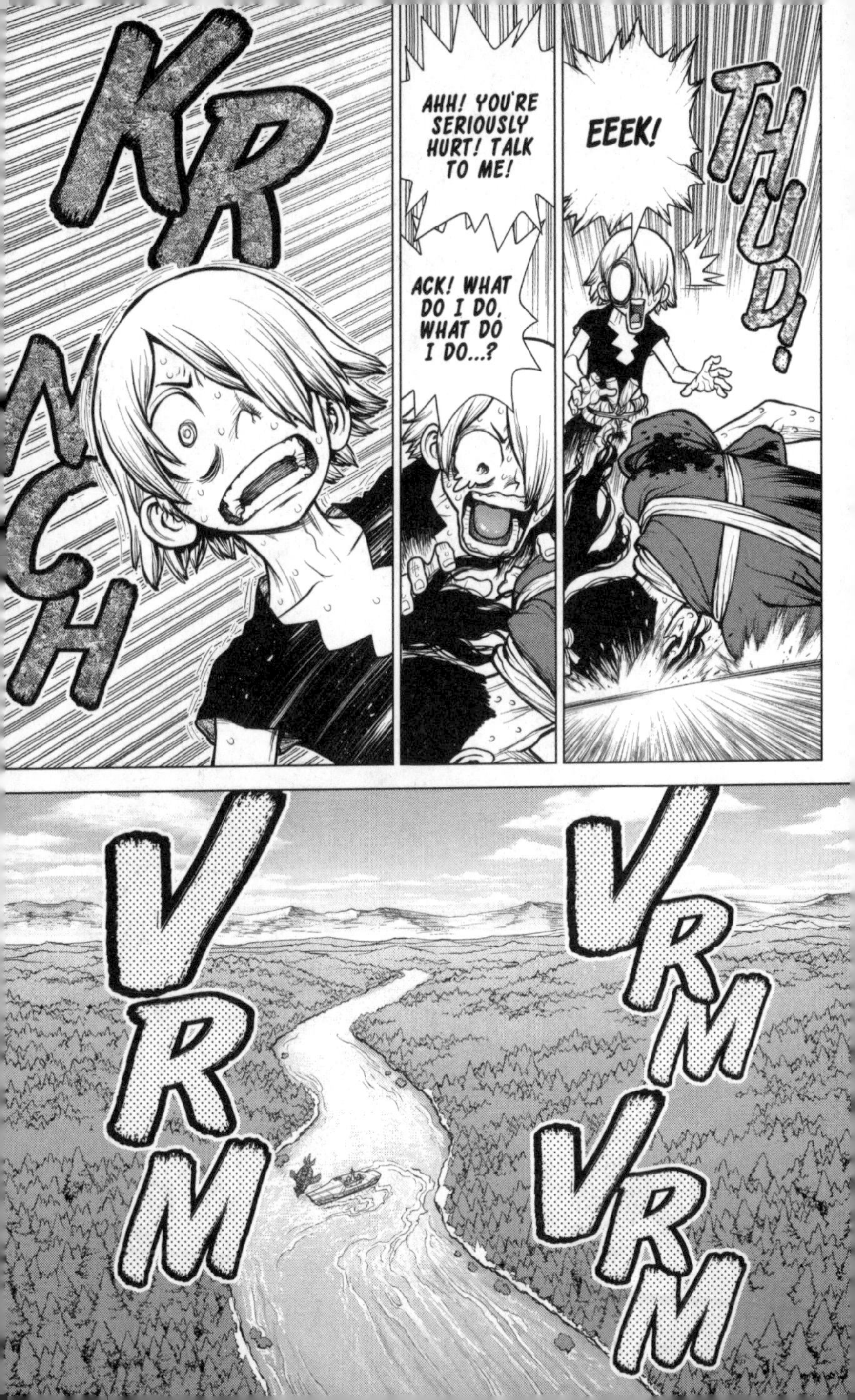
EEEK!
THUD!
AHH! YOU'RE SERIOUSLY HURT! TALK TO ME!
ACK! WHAT DO I DO, WHAT DO I DO...?
KRNCH
VRM VRM
VRM

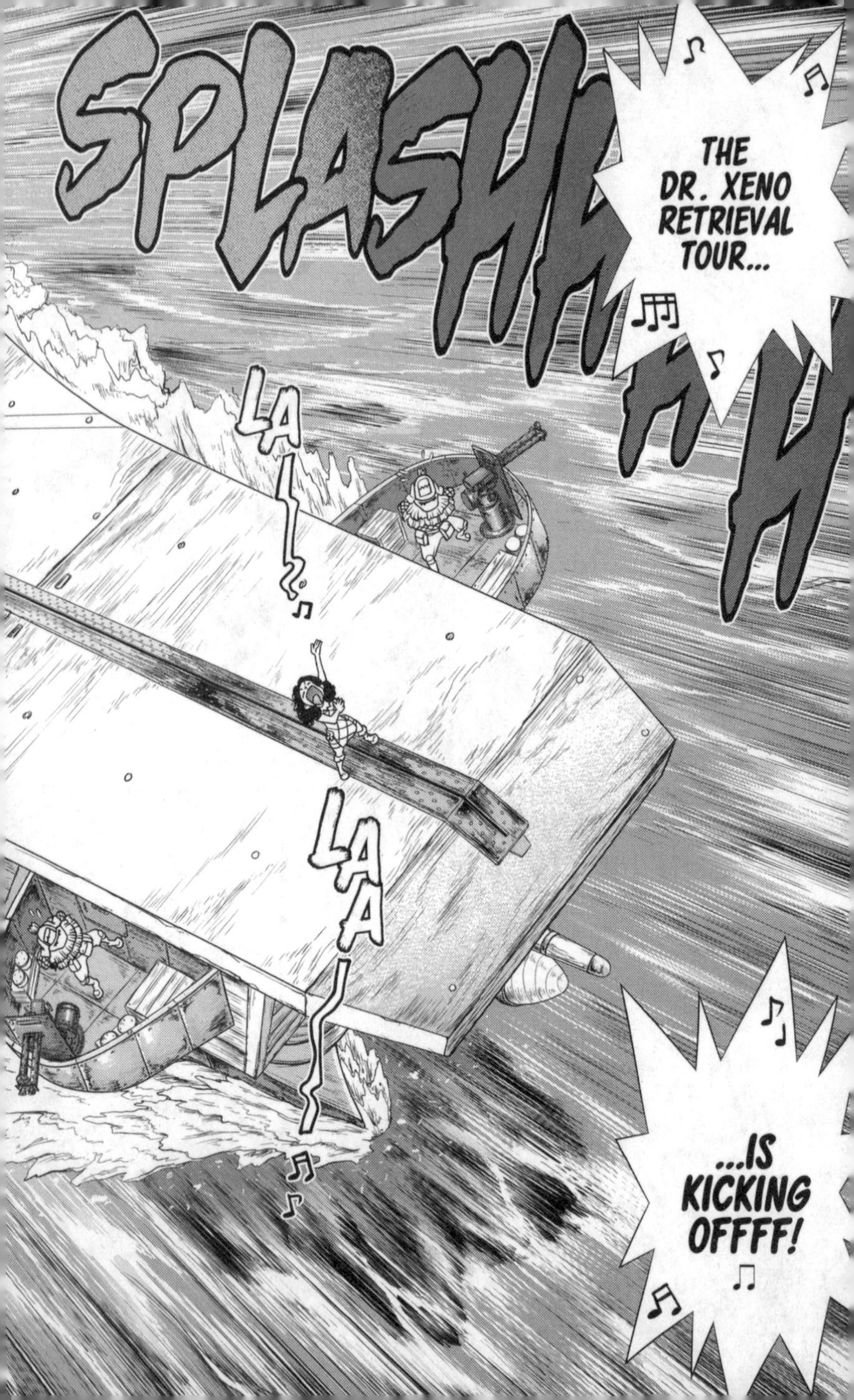
SPLASHHH
THE DR. XENO RETRIEVAL TOUR...
LA~
LAA~
...IS KICKING OFFFF!

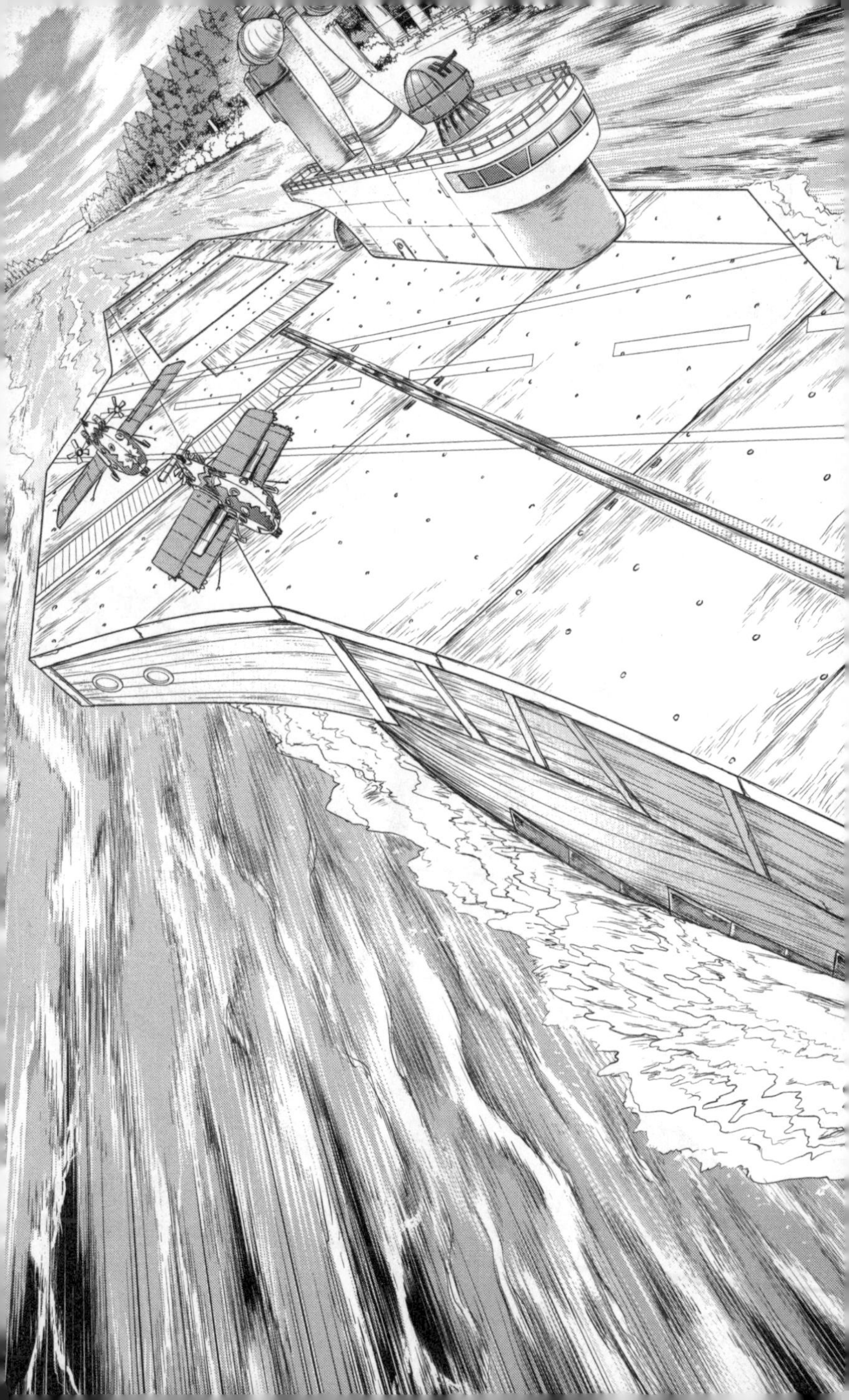

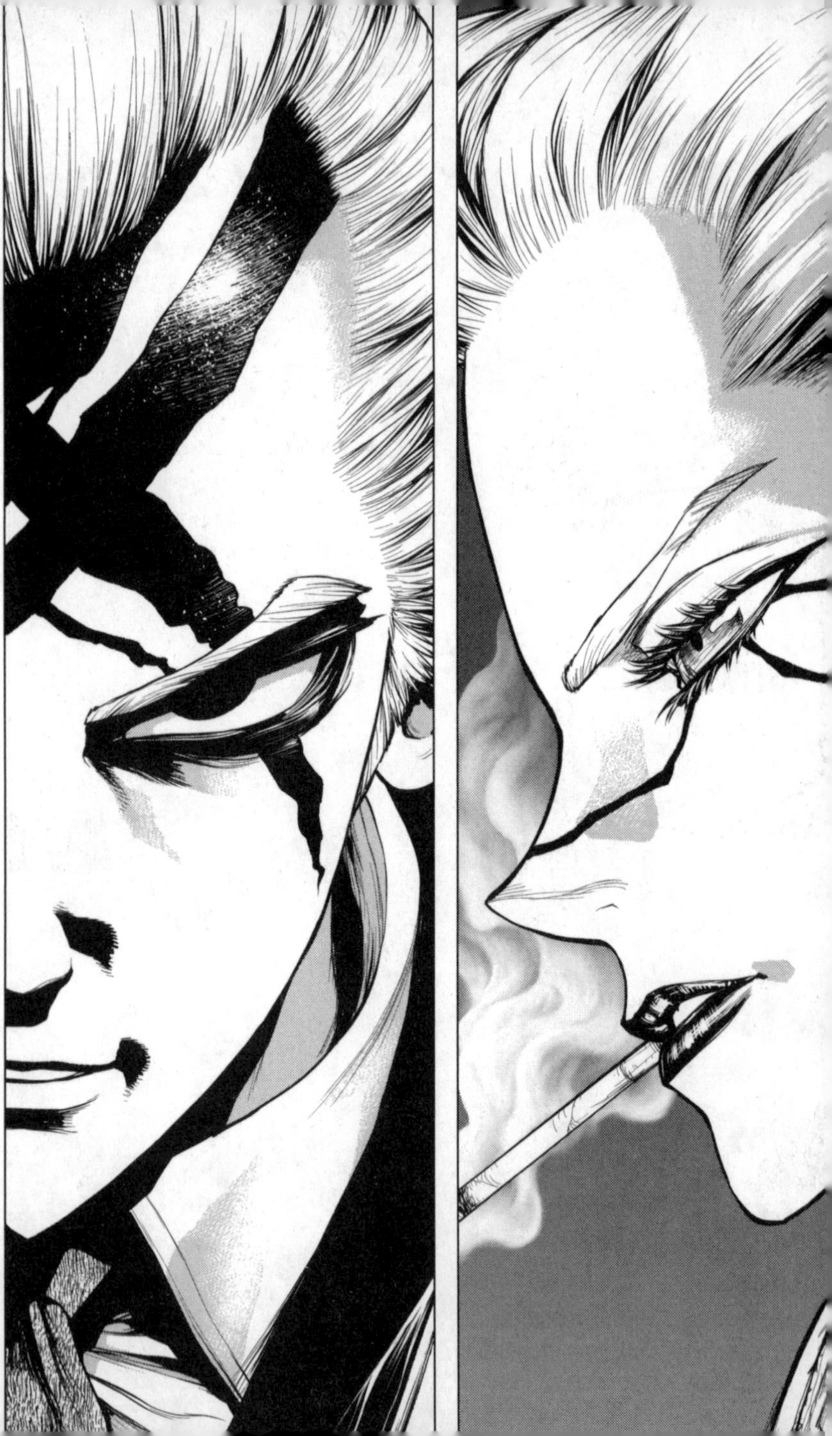

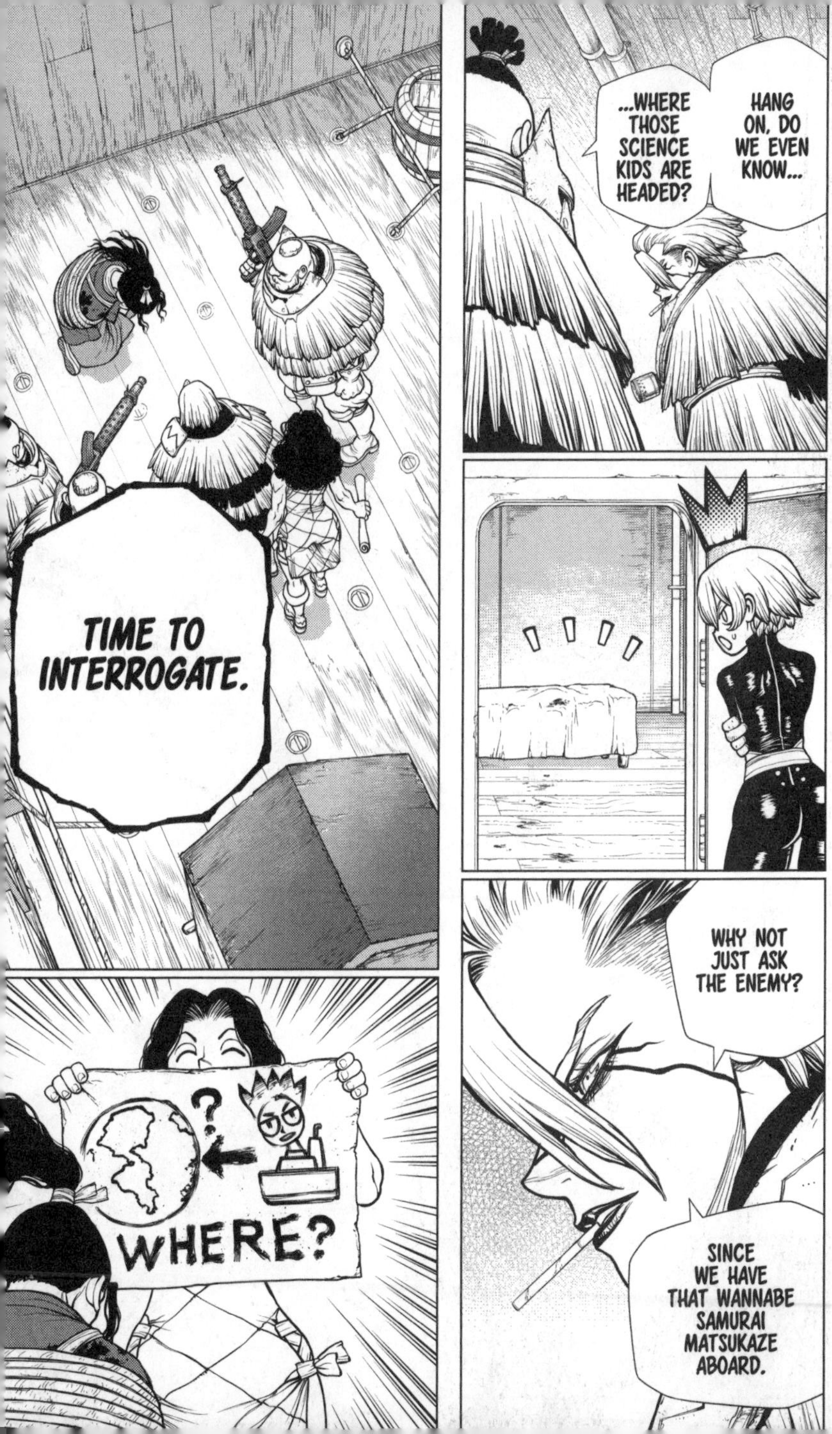
HANG ON, DO WE EVEN KNOW...
...WHERE THOSE SCIENCE KIDS ARE HEADED?
WHY NOT JUST ASK THE ENEMY?
SINCE WE HAVE THAT WANNABE SAMURAI MATSUKAZE ABOARD.
TIME TO INTERROGATE.
WHERE?

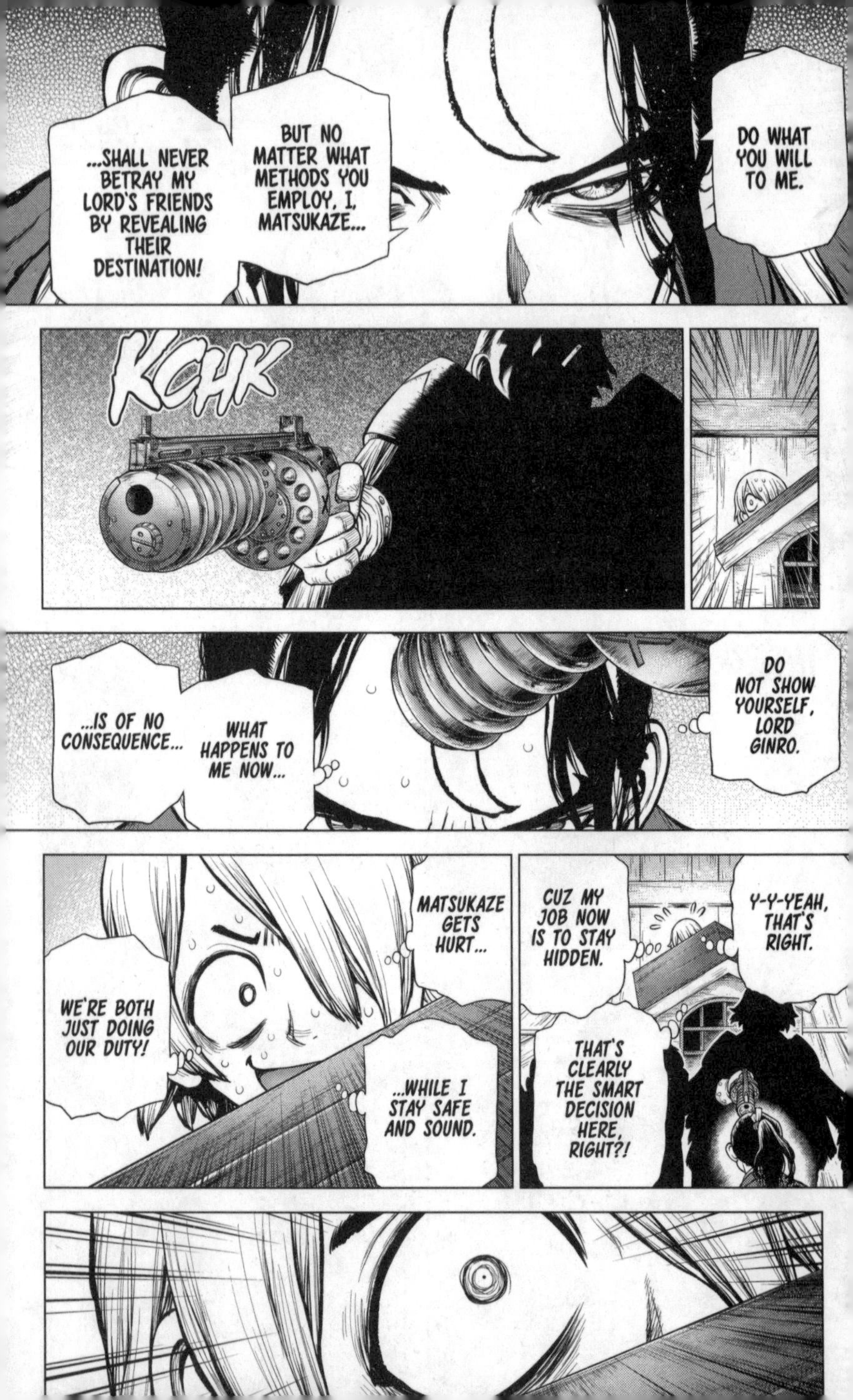
DO WHAT YOU WILL TO ME.
BUT NO MATTER WHAT METHODS YOU EMPLOY, I, MATSUKAZE...
...SHALL NEVER BETRAY MY LORD'S FRIENDS BY REVEALING THEIR DESTINATION!
KCHK
DO NOT SHOW YOURSELF, LORD GINRO.
WHAT HAPPENS TO ME NOW...
...IS OF NO CONSEQUENCE...
Y-Y-YEAH, THAT'S RIGHT.
CUZ MY JOB NOW IS TO STAY HIDDEN.
THAT'S CLEARLY THE SMART DECISION HERE, RIGHT?!
MATSUKAZE GETS HURT...
...WHILE I STAY SAFE AND SOUND.
WE'RE BOTH JUST DOING OUR DUTY!

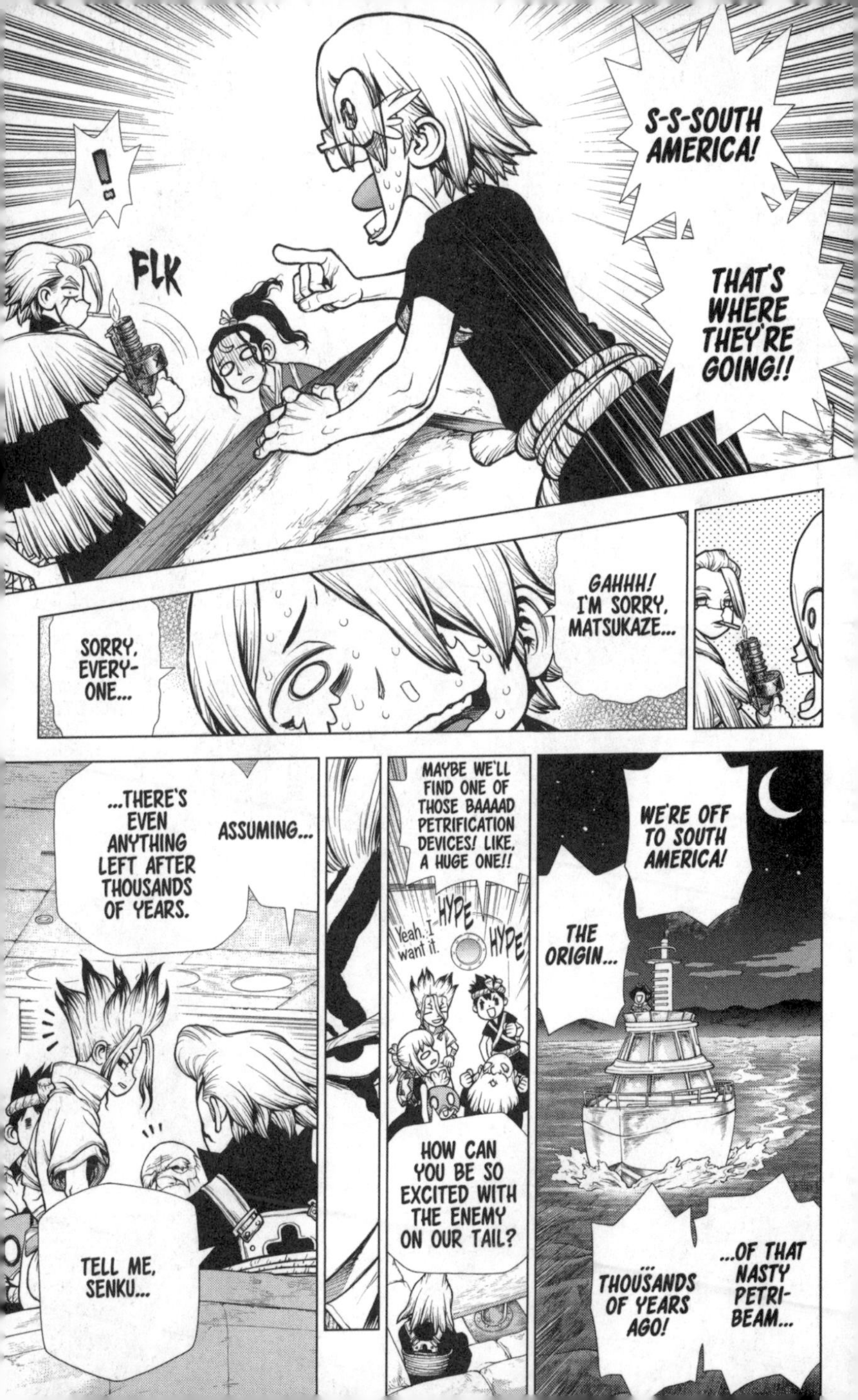
S-S-SOUTH AMERICA!
THAT'S WHERE THEY'RE GOING!!
!
FLK
GAHHH! I'M SORRY, MATSUKAZE...
SORRY, EVERY-ONE...
WE'RE OFF TO SOUTH AMERICA!
THE ORIGIN...
...OF THAT NASTY PETRI-BEAM...
... THOUSANDS OF YEARS AGO!
MAYBE WE'LL FIND ONE OF THOSE BAAAAD PETRIFICATION DEVICES! LIKE, A HUGE ONE!!
HYPE
HYPE
Yeah, I want it.
HOW CAN YOU BE SO EXCITED WITH THE ENEMY ON OUR TAIL?
ASSUMING...
...THERE'S EVEN ANYTHING LEFT AFTER THOUSANDS OF YEARS.
TELL ME, SENKU...

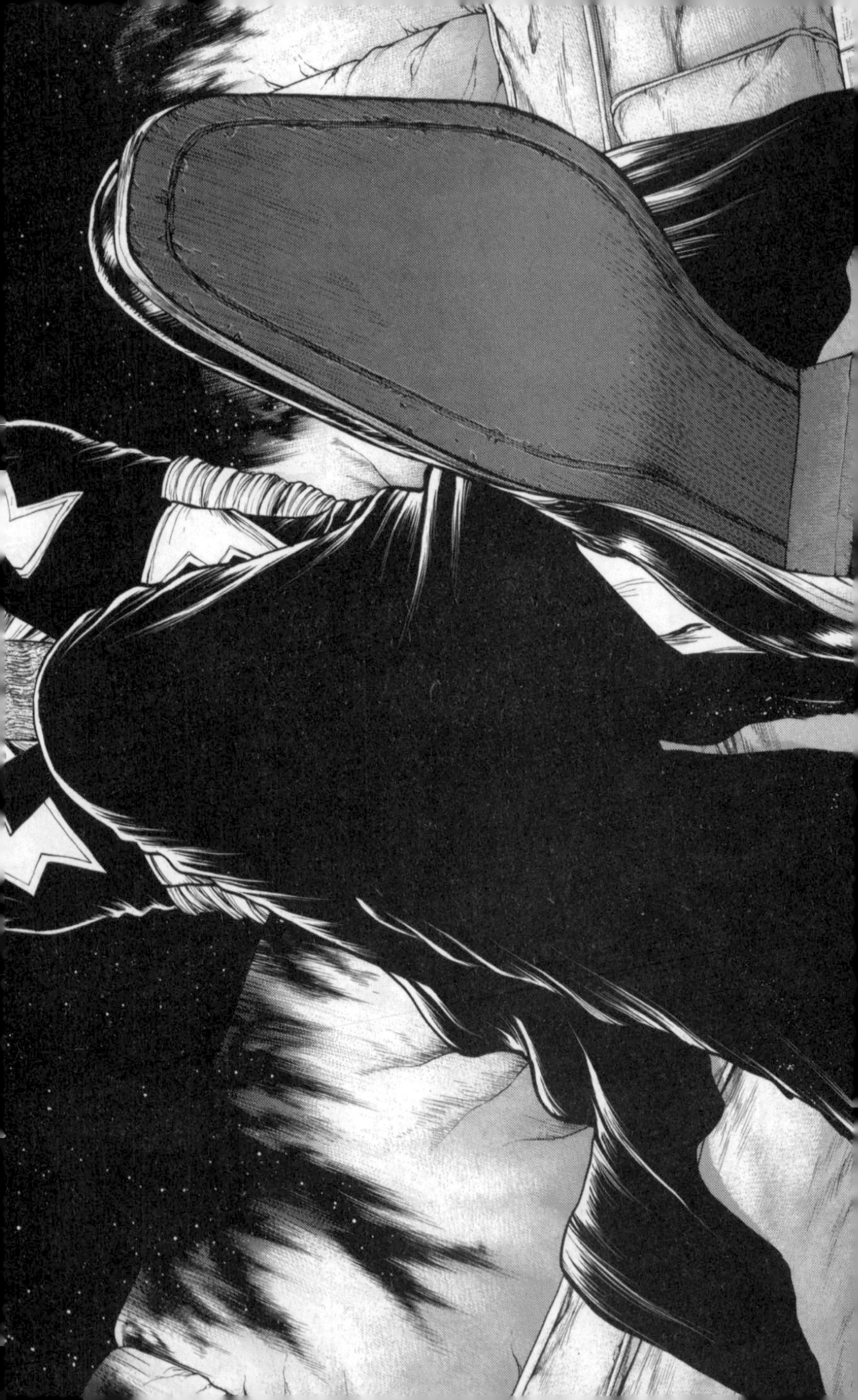

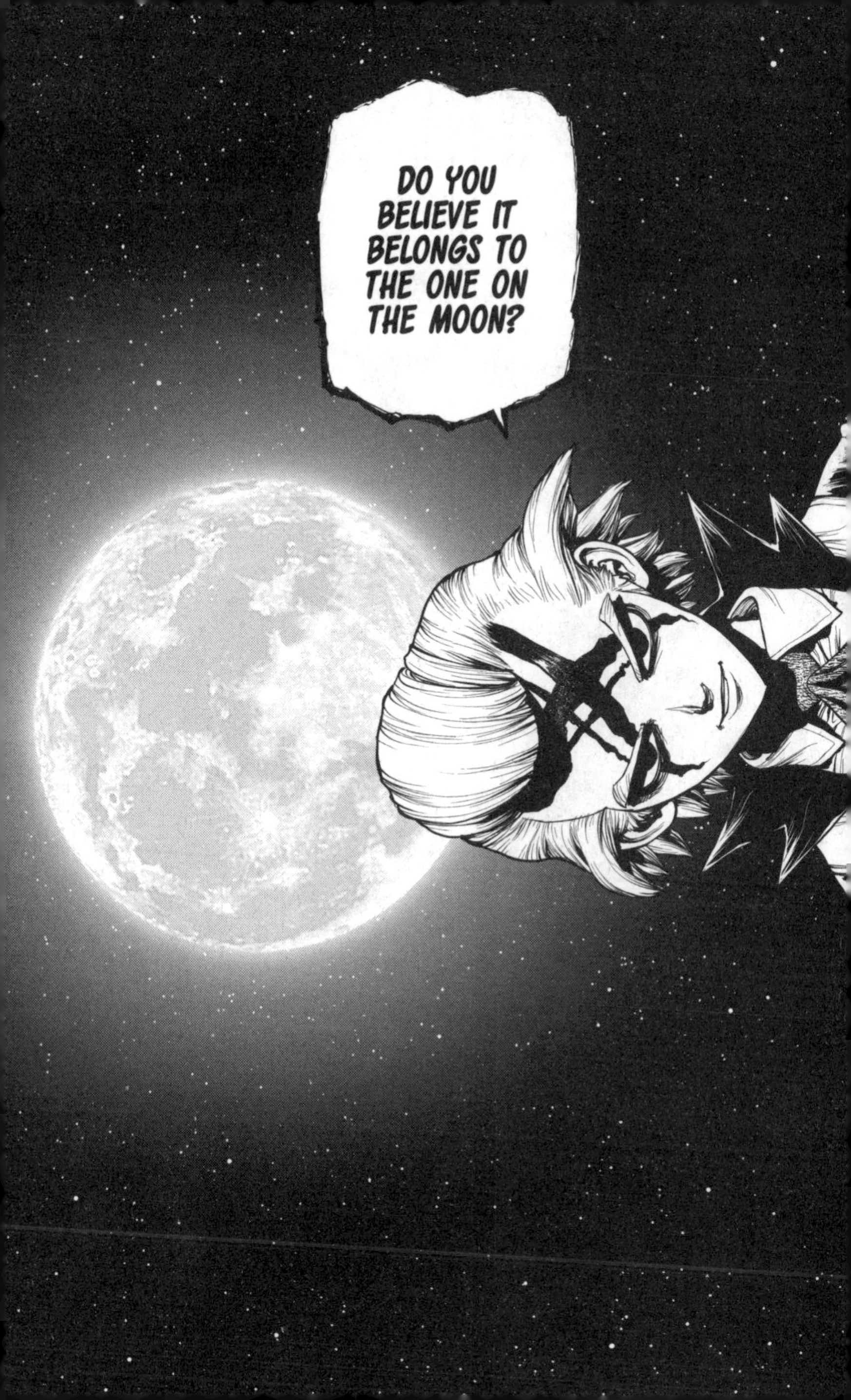
DO YOU BELIEVE IT BELONGS TO THE ONE ON THE MOON?

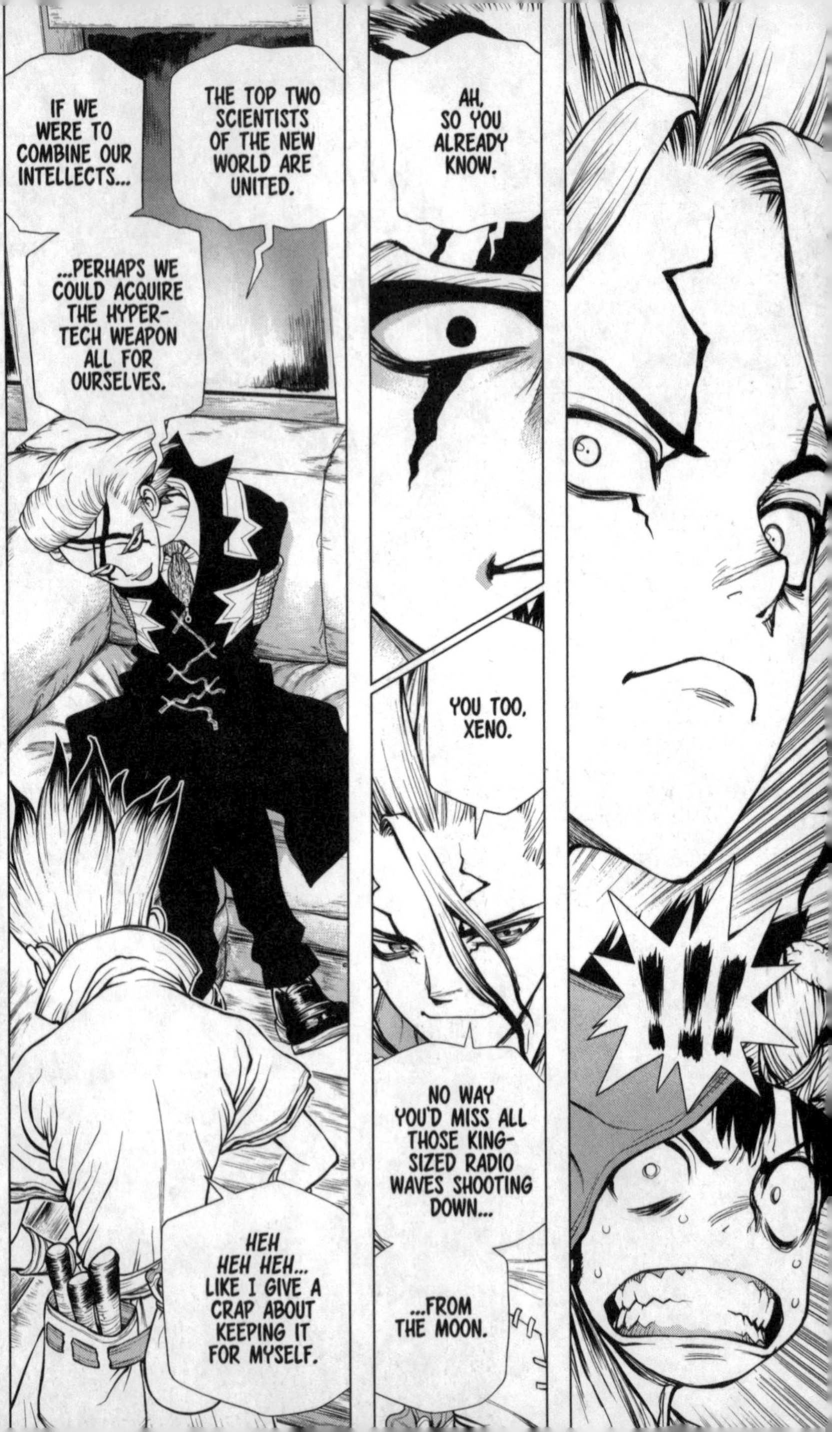
!!
AH, SO YOU ALREADY KNOW.
YOU TOO, XENO.
NO WAY YOU'D MISS ALL THOSE KING-SIZED RADIO WAVES SHOOTING DOWN...
...FROM THE MOON.
THE TOP TWO SCIENTISTS OF THE NEW WORLD ARE UNITED.
IF WE WERE TO COMBINE OUR INTELLECTS...
...PERHAPS WE COULD ACQUIRE THE HYPER-TECH WEAPON ALL FOR OURSELVES.
HEH HEH HEH... LIKE I GIVE A CRAP ABOUT KEEPING IT FOR MYSELF.

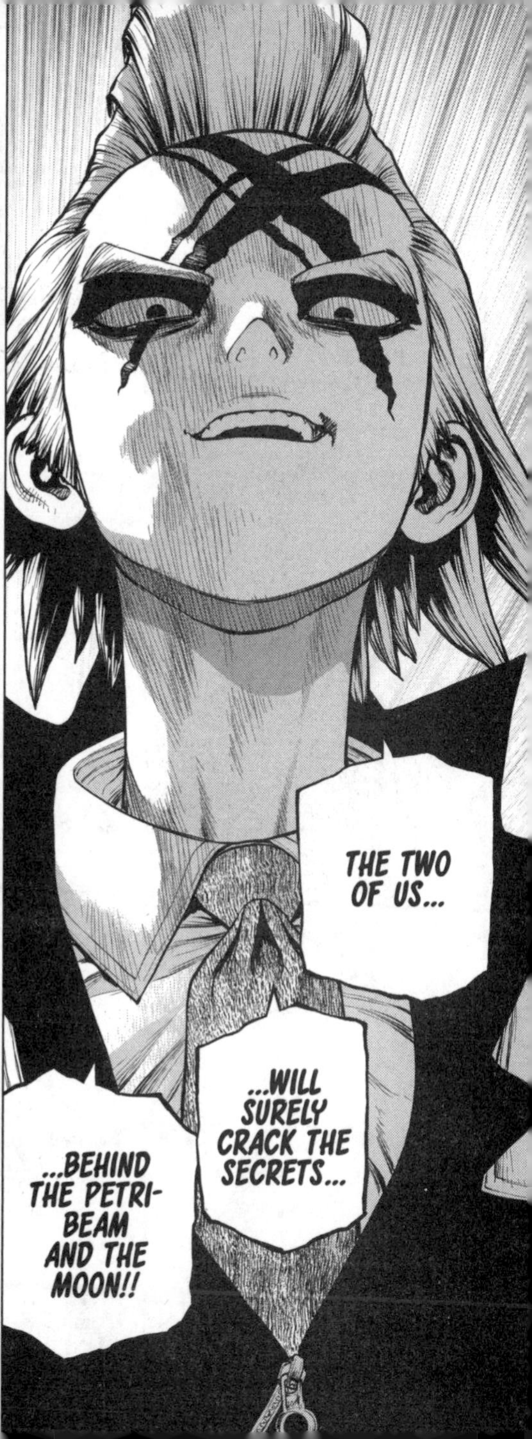
THE TWO OF US...
...WILL SURELY CRACK THE SECRETS...
...BEHIND THE PETRI-BEAM AND THE MOON!!

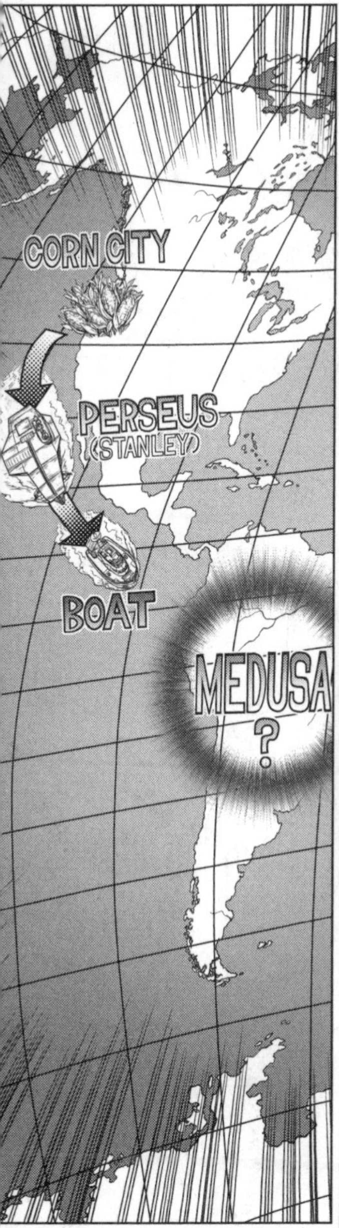
CORN CITY
PERSEUS (STANLEY)
BOAT
MEDUSA ?

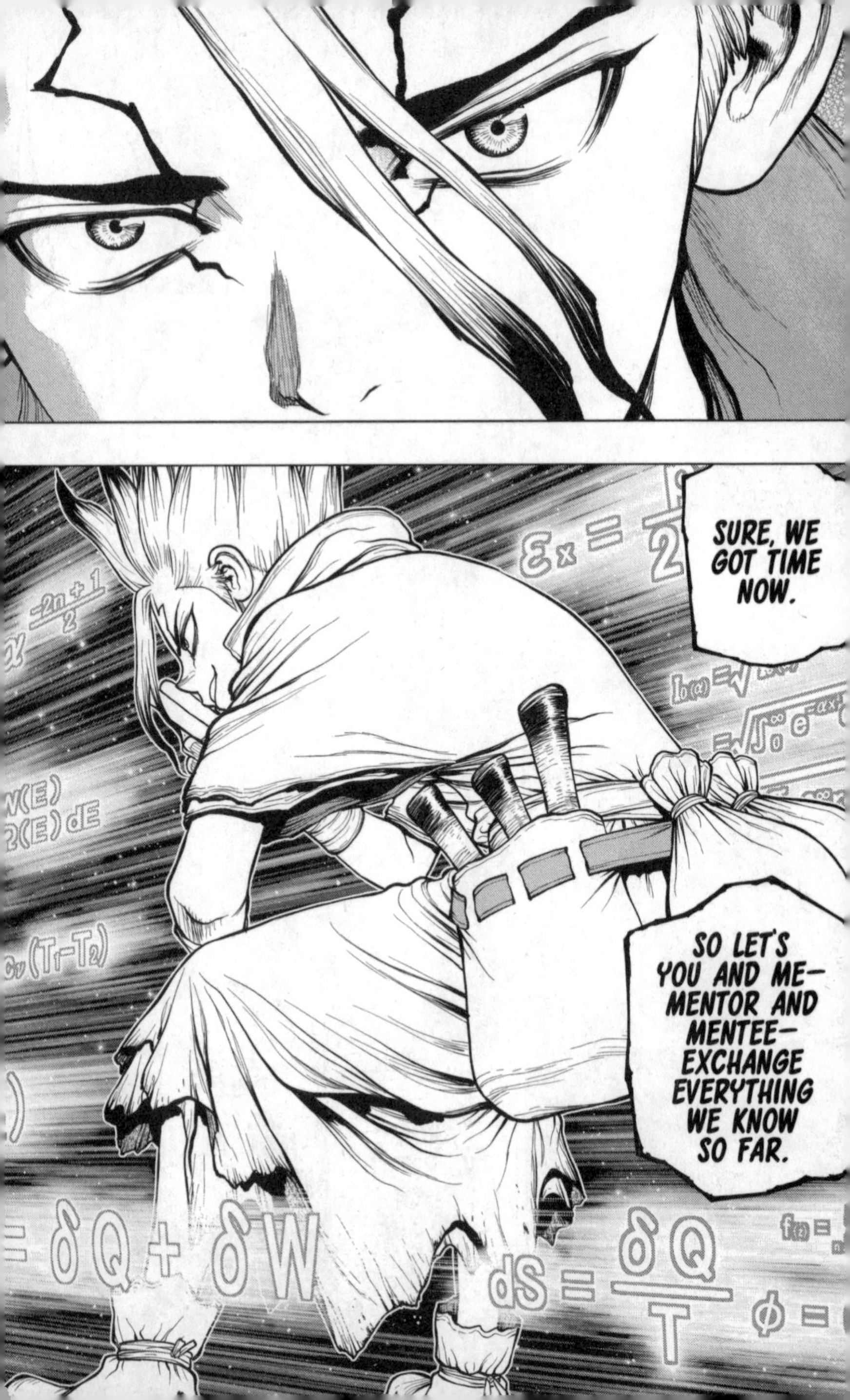
SURE, WE GOT TIME NOW.
SO LET'S YOU AND ME—MENTOR AND MENTEE—EXCHANGE EVERYTHING WE KNOW SO FAR.

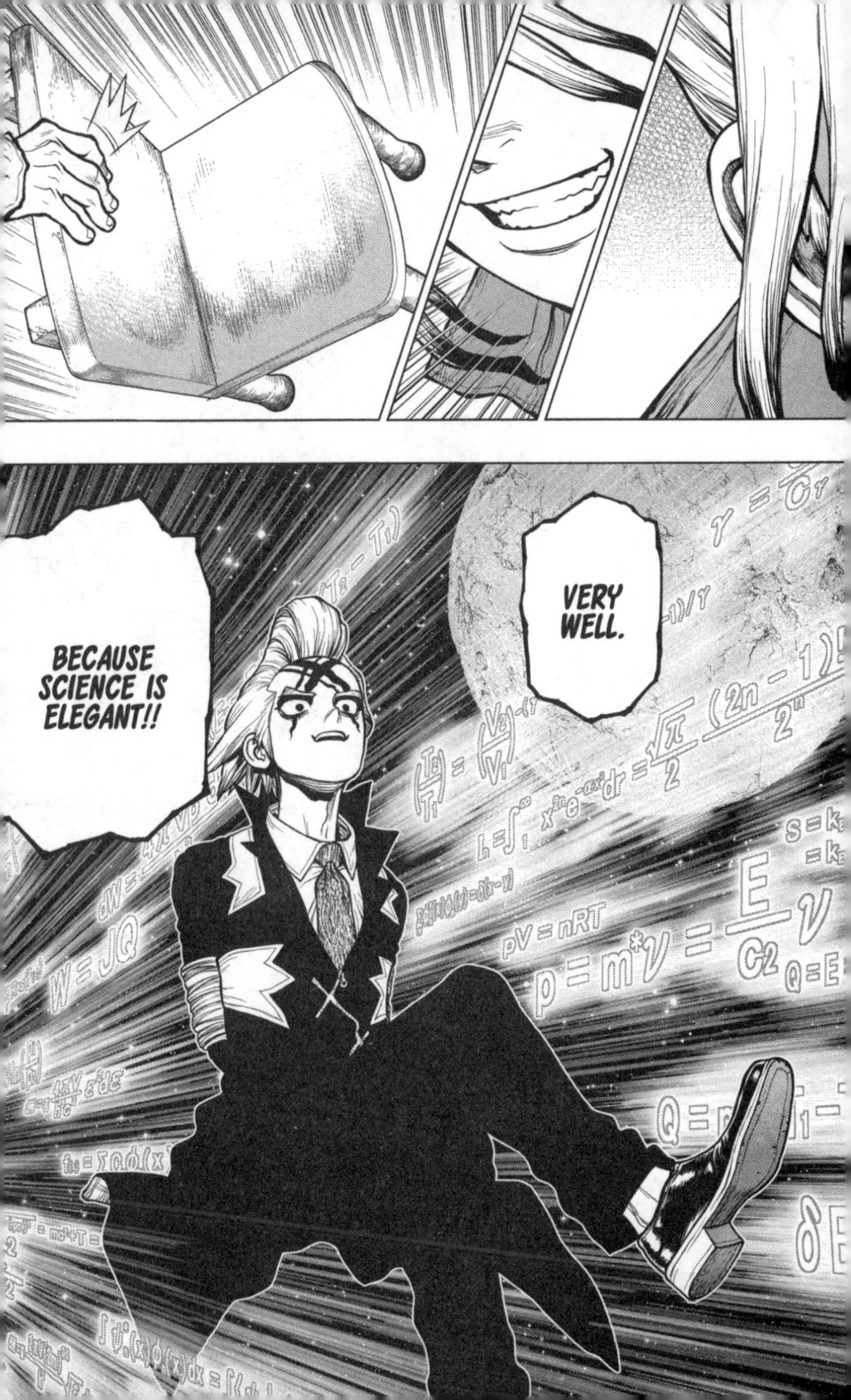
VERY WELL.
BECAUSE SCIENCE IS ELEGANT!!

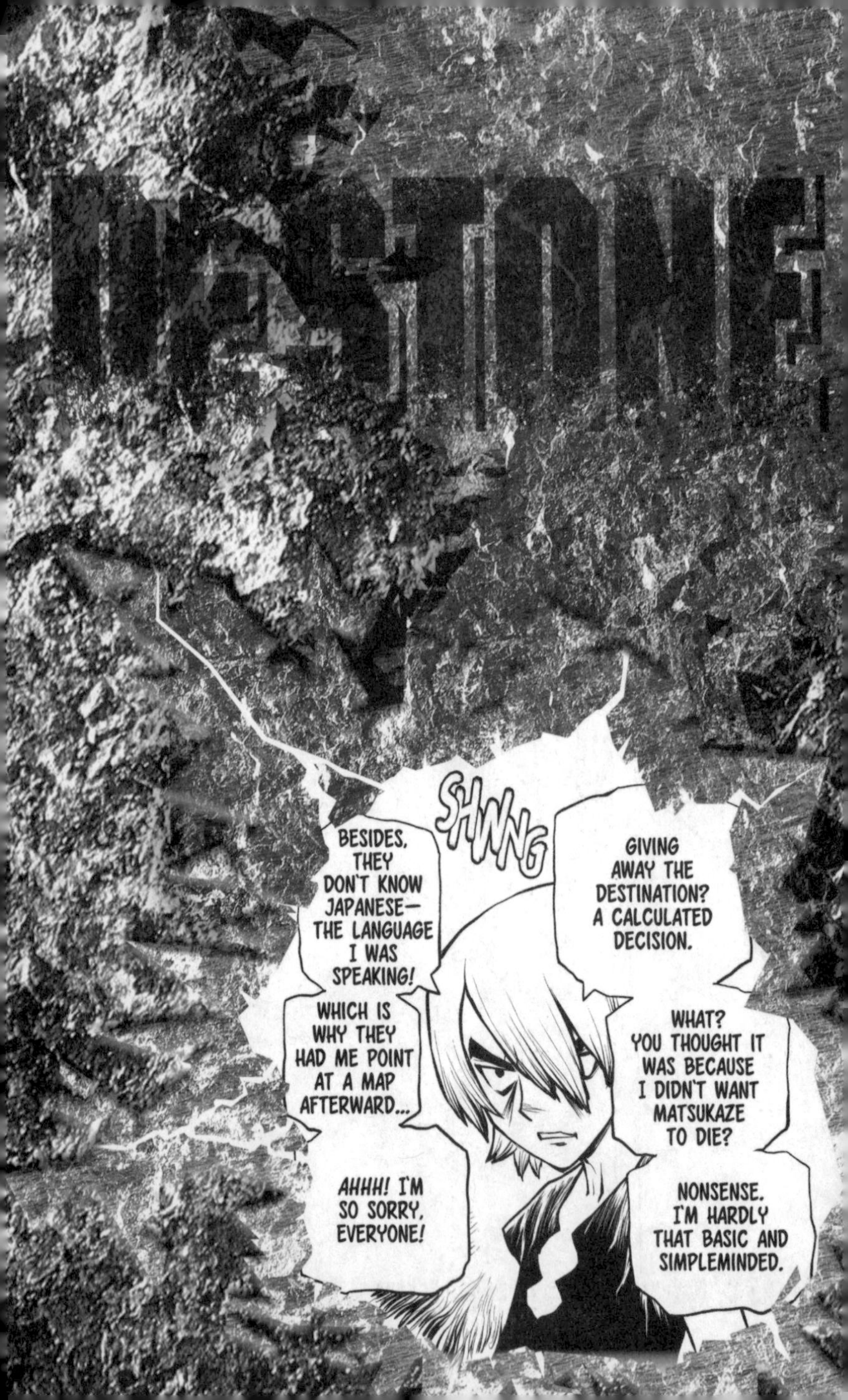
DR.STONE
SHWNG
GIVING AWAY THE DESTINATION? A CALCULATED DECISION.
WHAT? YOU THOUGHT IT WAS BECAUSE I DIDN'T WANT MATSUKAZE TO DIE?
NONSENSE. I'M HARDLY THAT BASIC AND SIMPLEMINDED.
BESIDES, THEY DON'T KNOW JAPANESE—THE LANGUAGE I WAS SPEAKING!
WHICH IS WHY THEY HAD ME POINT AT A MAP AFTERWARD...
AHHH! I'M SO SORRY, EVERYONE!

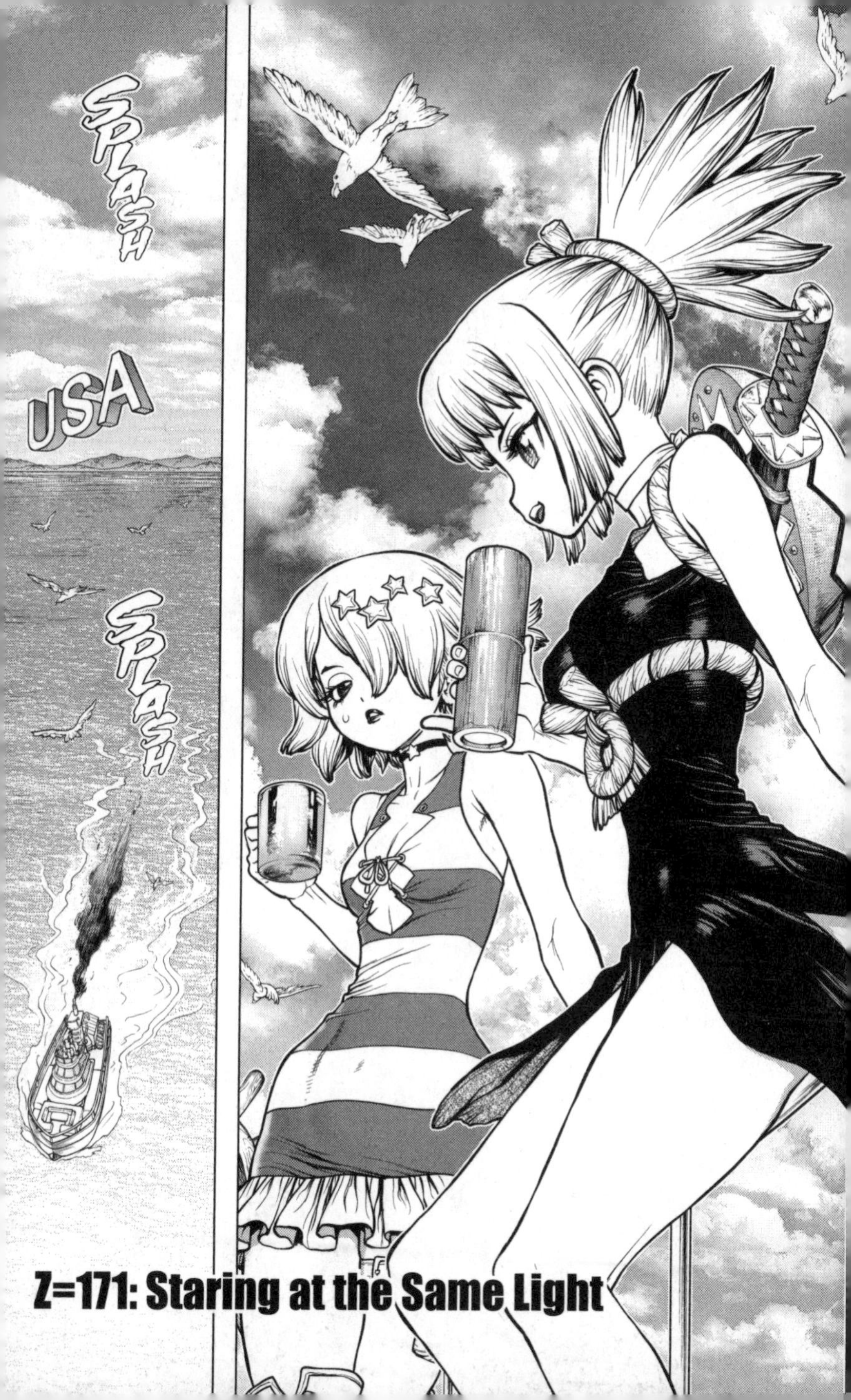
SPLASH
USA
SPLASH

Z=171: Staring at the Same Light

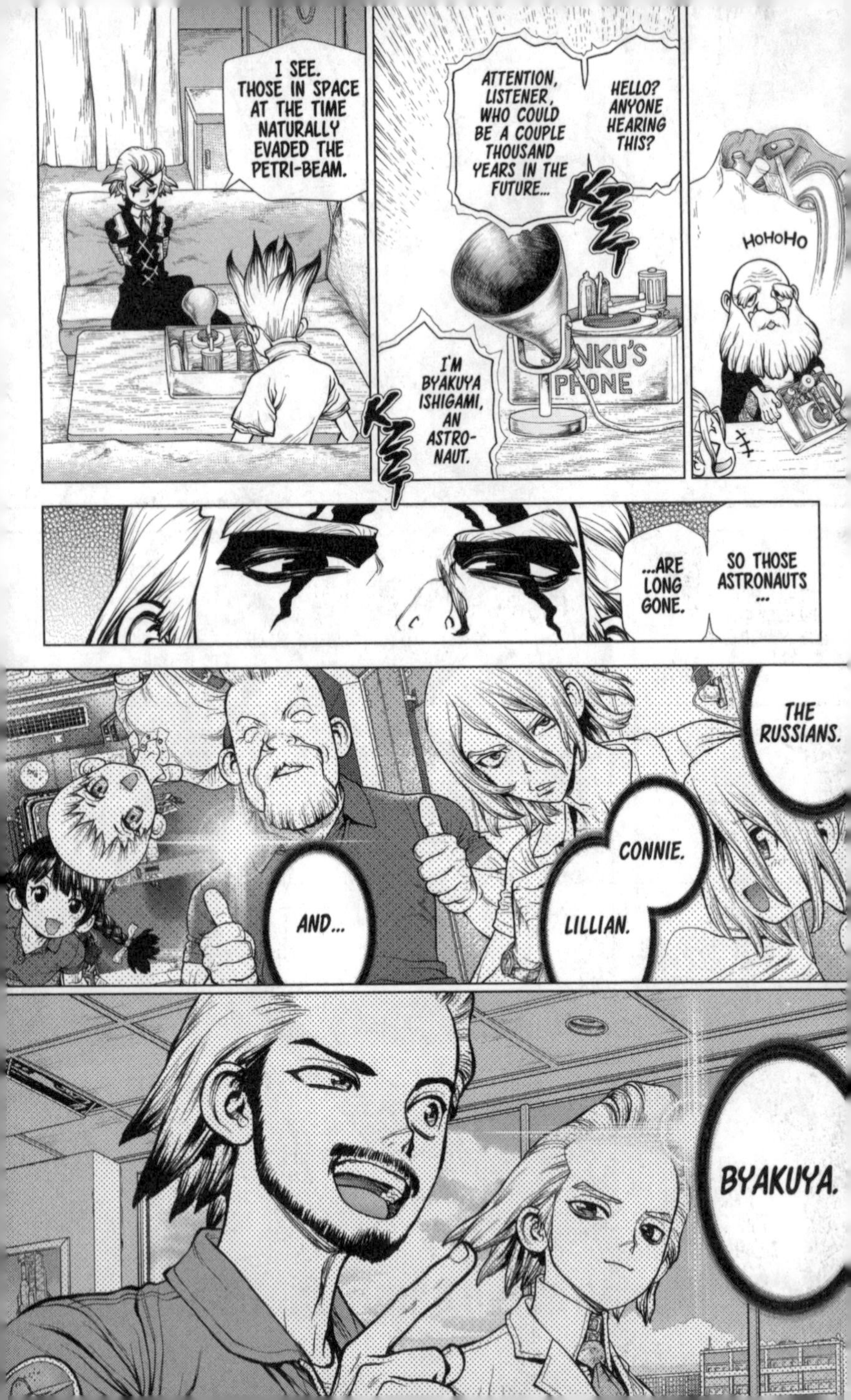
HOHOHO
HELLO? ANYONE HEARING THIS?
ATTENTION, LISTENER, WHO COULD BE A COUPLE THOUSAND YEARS IN THE FUTURE...
KZZT
I'M BYAKUYA ISHIGAMI, AN ASTRONAUT.
KZZT
I SEE. THOSE IN SPACE AT THE TIME NATURALLY EVADED THE PETRI-BEAM.
SO THOSE ASTRONAUTS...
...ARE LONG GONE.
THE RUSSIANS.
CONNIE.
LILLIAN.
AND...
BYAKUYA.

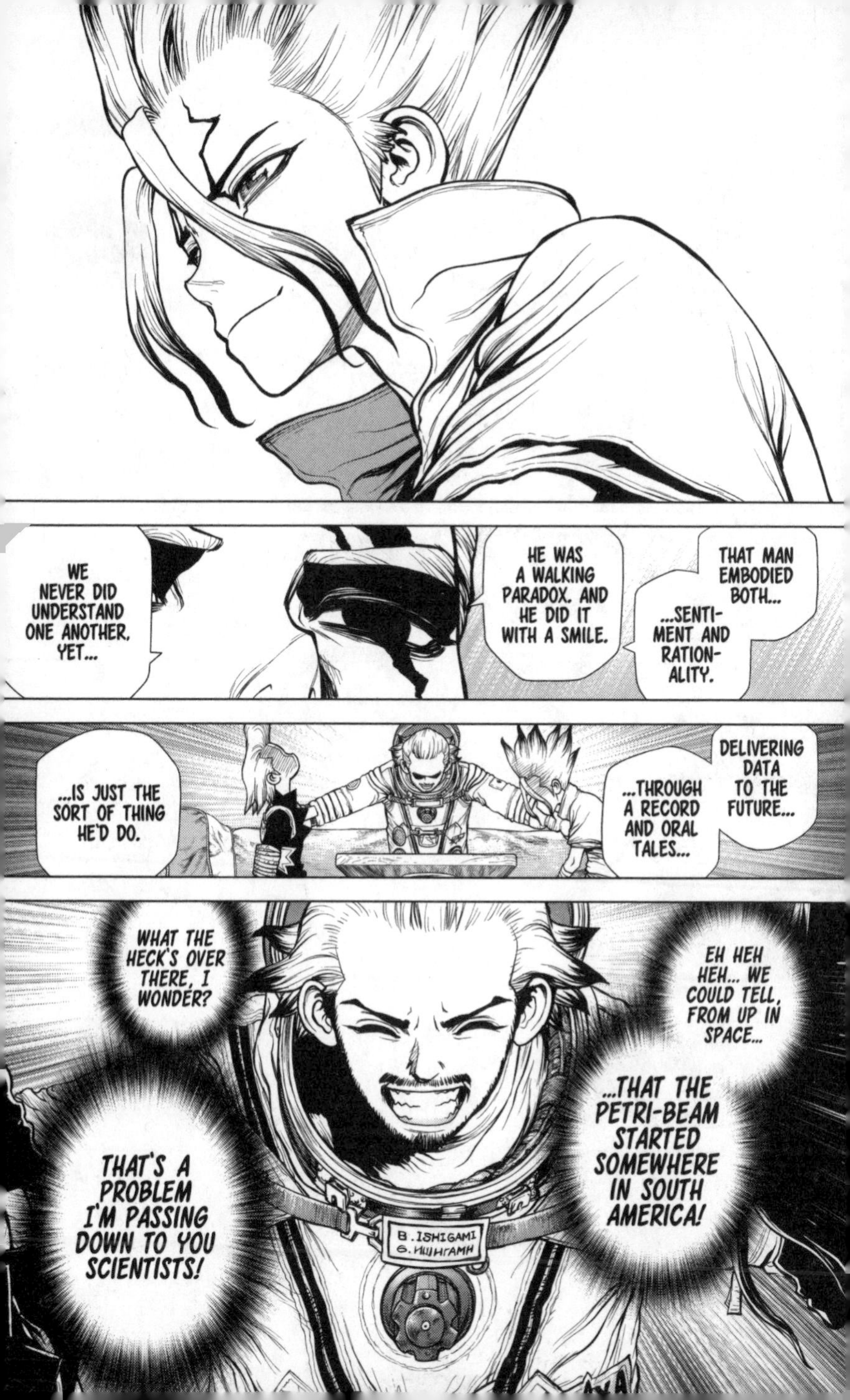
THAT MAN EMBODIED BOTH...
...SENTIMENT AND RATIONALITY.
HE WAS A WALKING PARADOX. AND HE DID IT WITH A SMILE.
WE NEVER DID UNDERSTAND ONE ANOTHER. YET...
DELIVERING DATA TO THE FUTURE...
...THROUGH A RECORD AND ORAL TALES...
...IS JUST THE SORT OF THING HE'D DO.
EH HEH HEH... WE COULD TELL, FROM UP IN SPACE...
...THAT THE PETRI-BEAM STARTED SOMEWHERE IN SOUTH AMERICA!
WHAT THE HECK'S OVER THERE, I WONDER?
THAT'S A PROBLEM I'M PASSING DOWN TO YOU SCIENTISTS!
B. ISHIGAMI
Б. ИШИГАМИ

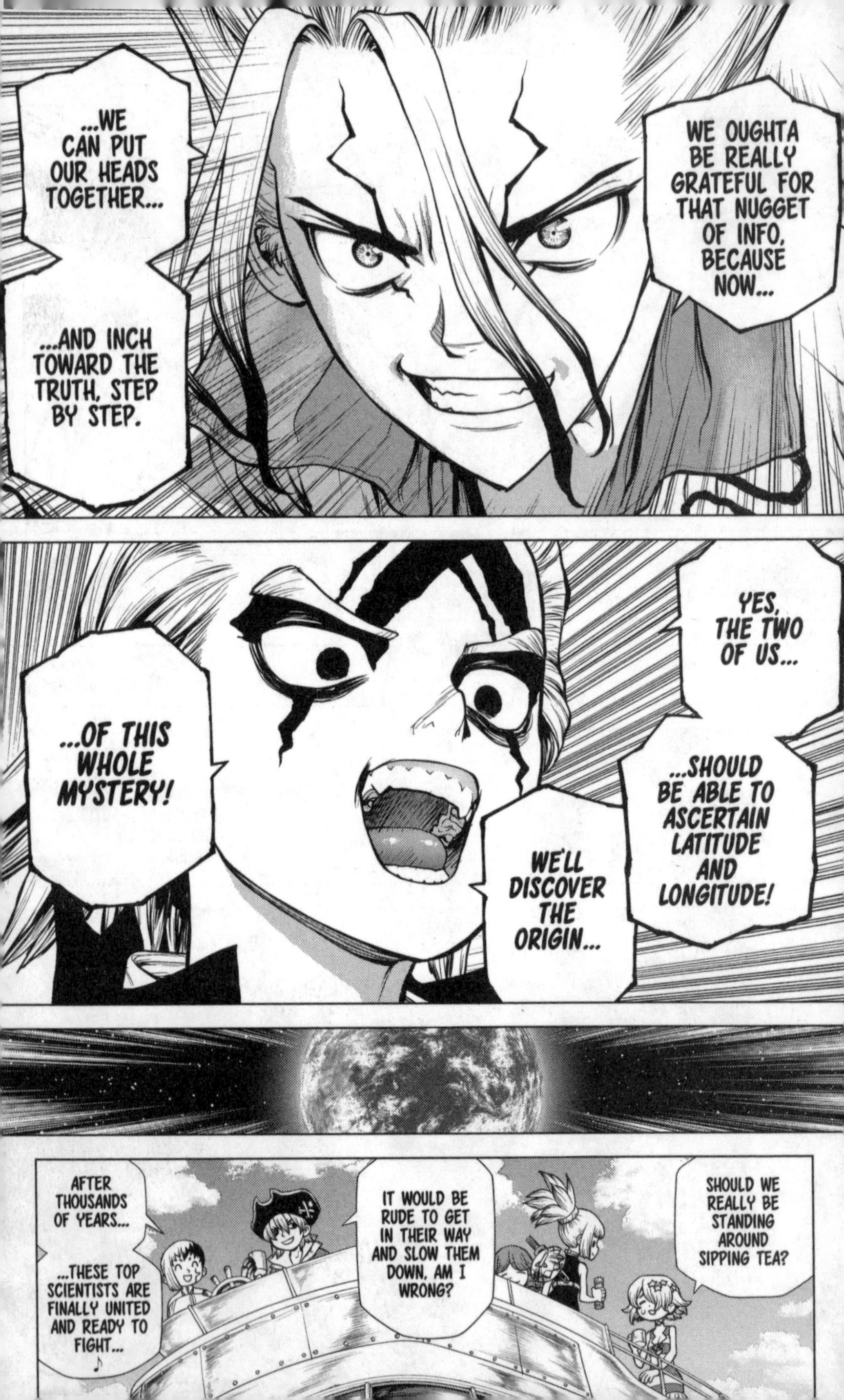
WE OUGHTA BE REALLY GRATEFUL FOR THAT NUGGET OF INFO, BECAUSE NOW...
...WE CAN PUT OUR HEADS TOGETHER...
...AND INCH TOWARD THE TRUTH, STEP BY STEP.
YES, THE TWO OF US...
...SHOULD BE ABLE TO ASCERTAIN LATITUDE AND LONGITUDE!
WE'LL DISCOVER THE ORIGIN...
...OF THIS WHOLE MYSTERY!
SHOULD WE REALLY BE STANDING AROUND SIPPING TEA?
IT WOULD BE RUDE TO GET IN THEIR WAY AND SLOW THEM DOWN, AM I WRONG?
AFTER THOUSANDS OF YEARS...
...THESE TOP SCIENTISTS ARE FINALLY UNITED AND READY TO FIGHT... ♪

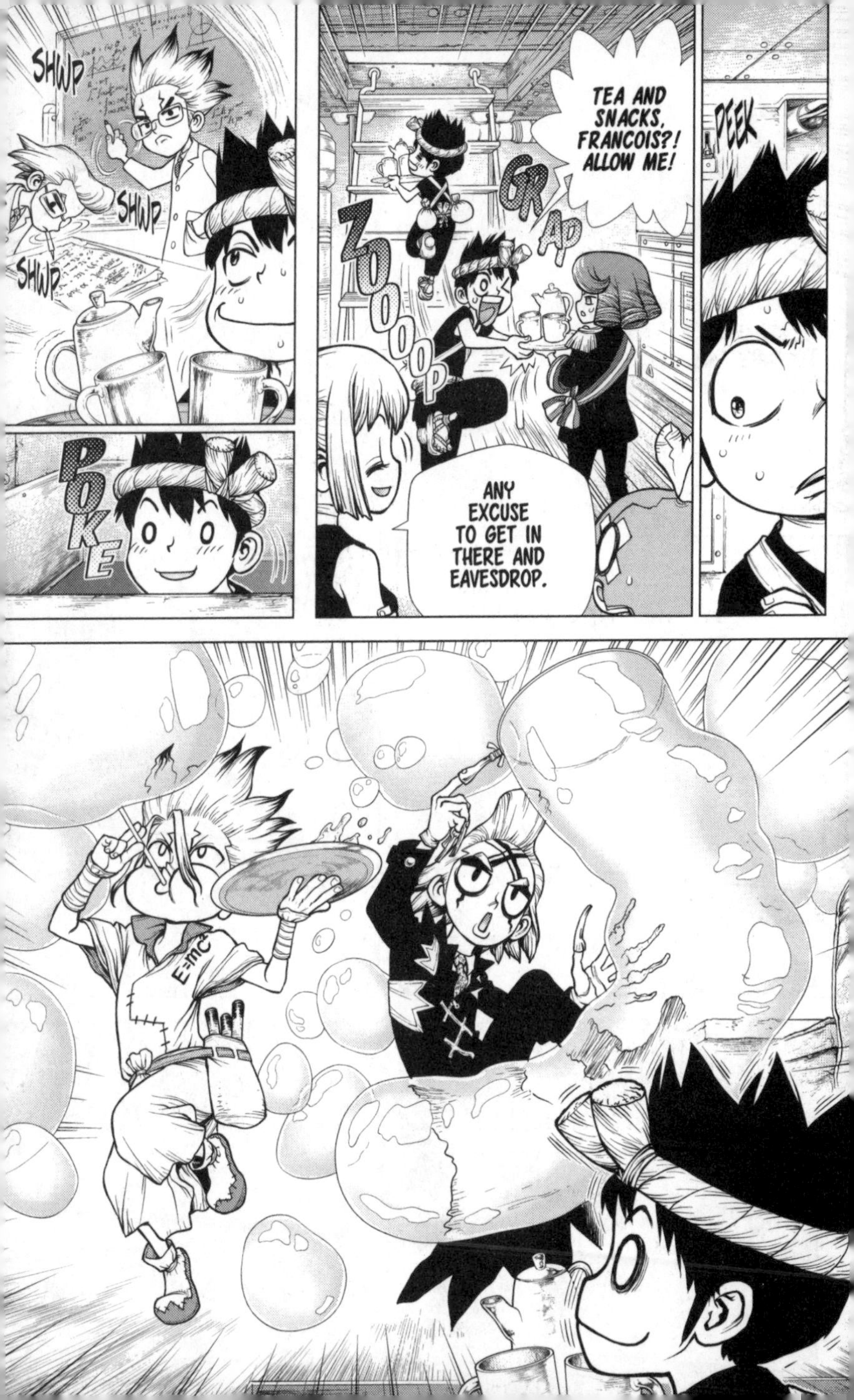
PEEK
TEA AND SNACKS, FRANCOIS?! ALLOW ME!
GRAP
ZOOOOP
ANY EXCUSE TO GET IN THERE AND EAVESDROP.
SHWP
SHWP
SHWP
POKE
E=mc²

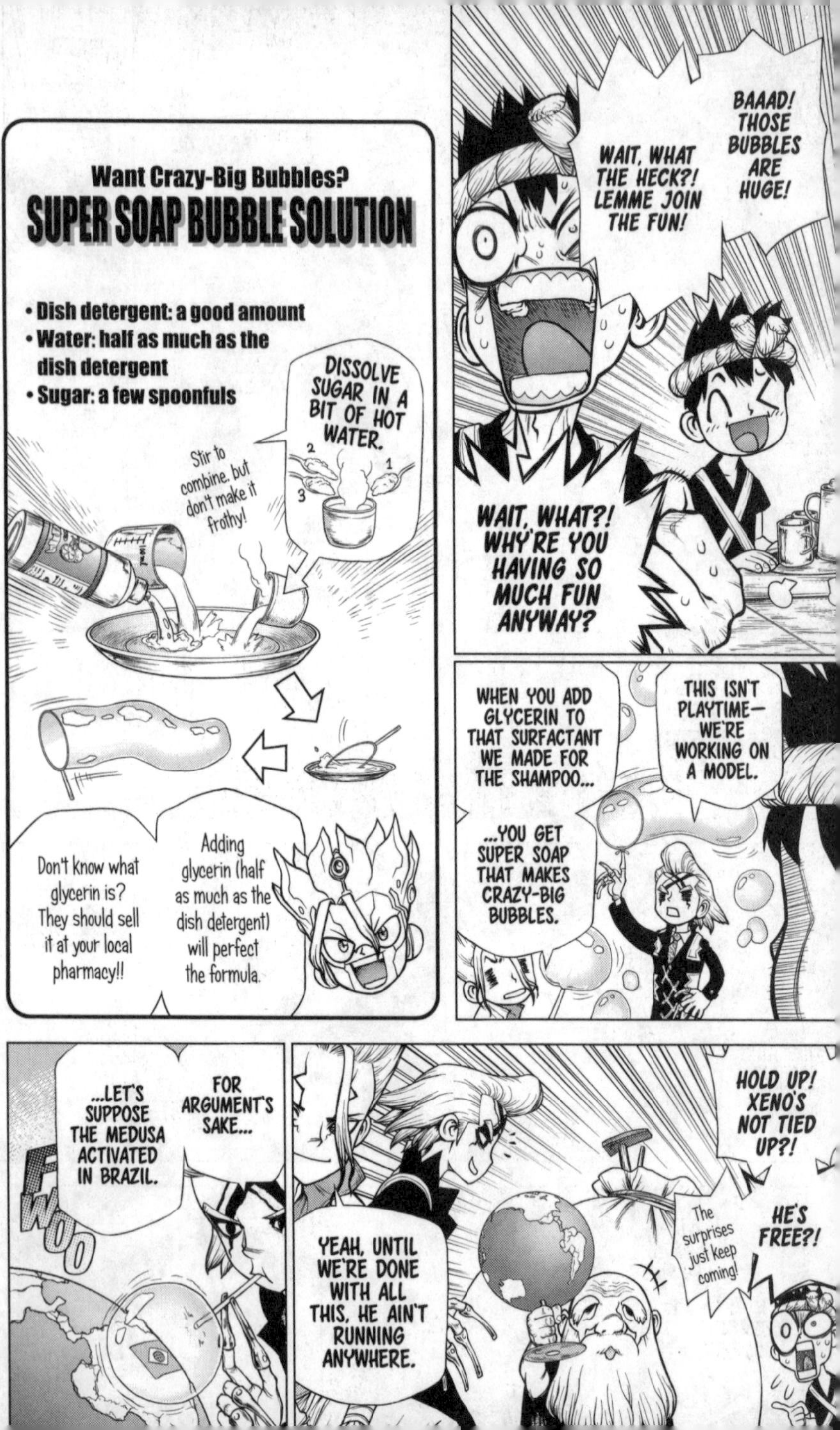
BAAAD! THOSE BUBBLES ARE HUGE!
WAIT, WHAT THE HECK?! LEMME JOIN THE FUN!
WAIT, WHAT?! WHY'RE YOU HAVING SO MUCH FUN ANYWAY?
THIS ISN'T PLAYTIME— WE'RE WORKING ON A MODEL.
WHEN YOU ADD GLYCERIN TO THAT SURFACTANT WE MADE FOR THE SHAMPOO...
...YOU GET SUPER SOAP THAT MAKES CRAZY-BIG BUBBLES.
Want Crazy-Big Bubbles?
SUPER SOAP BUBBLE SOLUTION
• Dish detergent: a good amount
• Water: half as much as the dish detergent
• Sugar: a few spoonfuls
DISSOLVE SUGAR IN A BIT OF HOT WATER.
Stir to combine, but don't make it frothy!
Adding glycerin (half as much as the dish detergent) will perfect the formula.
Don't know what glycerin is? They should sell it at your local pharmacy!!
HOLD UP! XENO'S NOT TIED UP?!
HE'S FREE?!
The surprises just keep coming!
YEAH, UNTIL WE'RE DONE WITH ALL THIS, HE AIN'T RUNNING ANYWHERE.
FOR ARGUMENT'S SAKE...
...LET'S SUPPOSE THE MEDUSA ACTIVATED IN BRAZIL.
FWOO

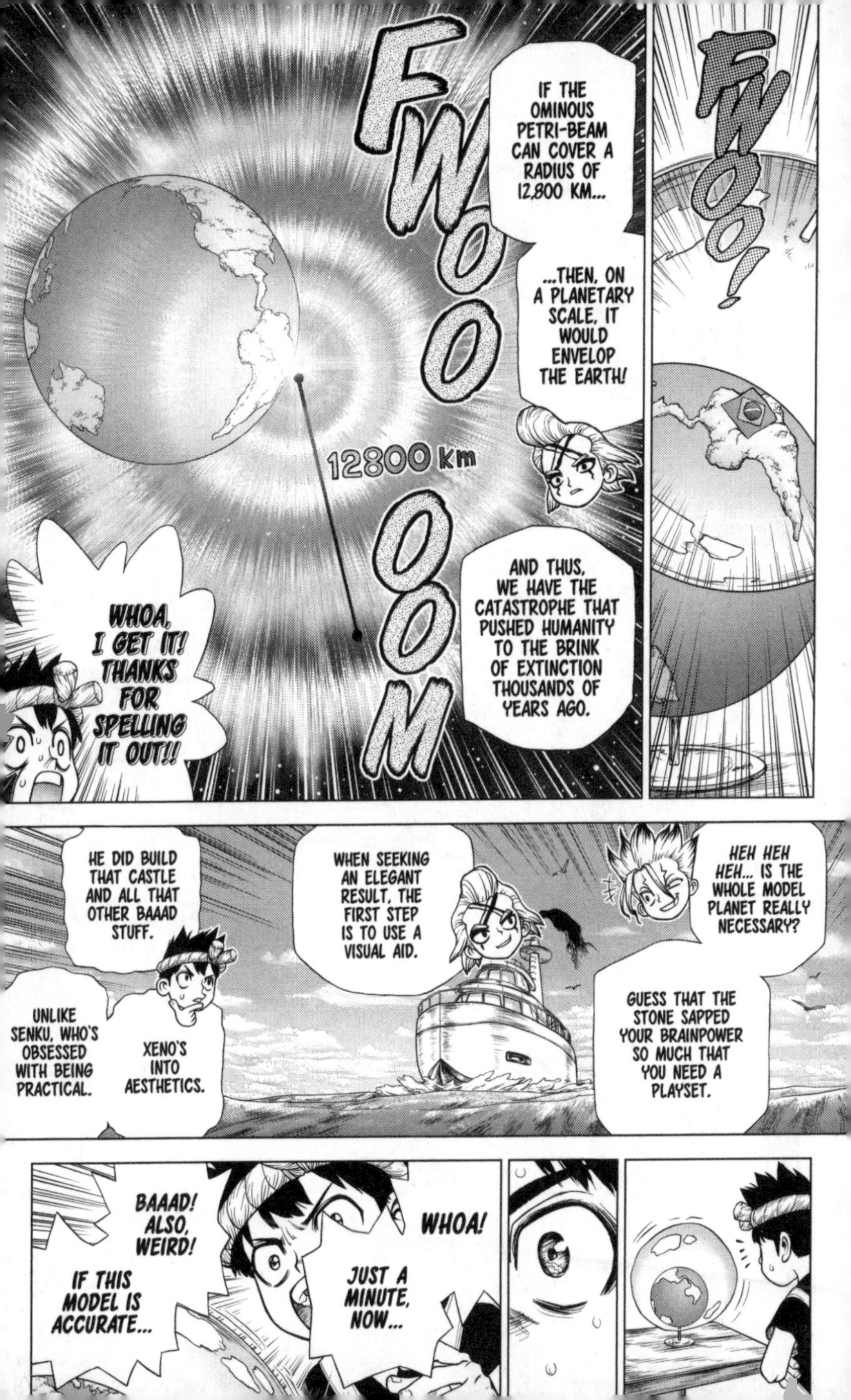
FWOOO!
IF THE OMINOUS PETRI-BEAM CAN COVER A RADIUS OF 12,800 KM...
...THEN, ON A PLANETARY SCALE, IT WOULD ENVELOP THE EARTH!
FWOOOOOOM
12800 km
AND THUS, WE HAVE THE CATASTROPHE THAT PUSHED HUMANITY TO THE BRINK OF EXTINCTION THOUSANDS OF YEARS AGO.
WHOA, I GET IT! THANKS FOR SPELLING IT OUT!!
HEH HEH HEH... IS THE WHOLE MODEL PLANET REALLY NECESSARY?
GUESS THAT THE STONE SAPPED YOUR BRAINPOWER SO MUCH THAT YOU NEED A PLAYSET.
WHEN SEEKING AN ELEGANT RESULT, THE FIRST STEP IS TO USE A VISUAL AID.
HE DID BUILD THAT CASTLE AND ALL THAT OTHER BAAAD STUFF.
XENO'S INTO AESTHETICS.
UNLIKE SENKU, WHO'S OBSESSED WITH BEING PRACTICAL.
WHOA!
JUST A MINUTE, NOW...
BAAAD! ALSO, WEIRD!
IF THIS MODEL IS ACCURATE...

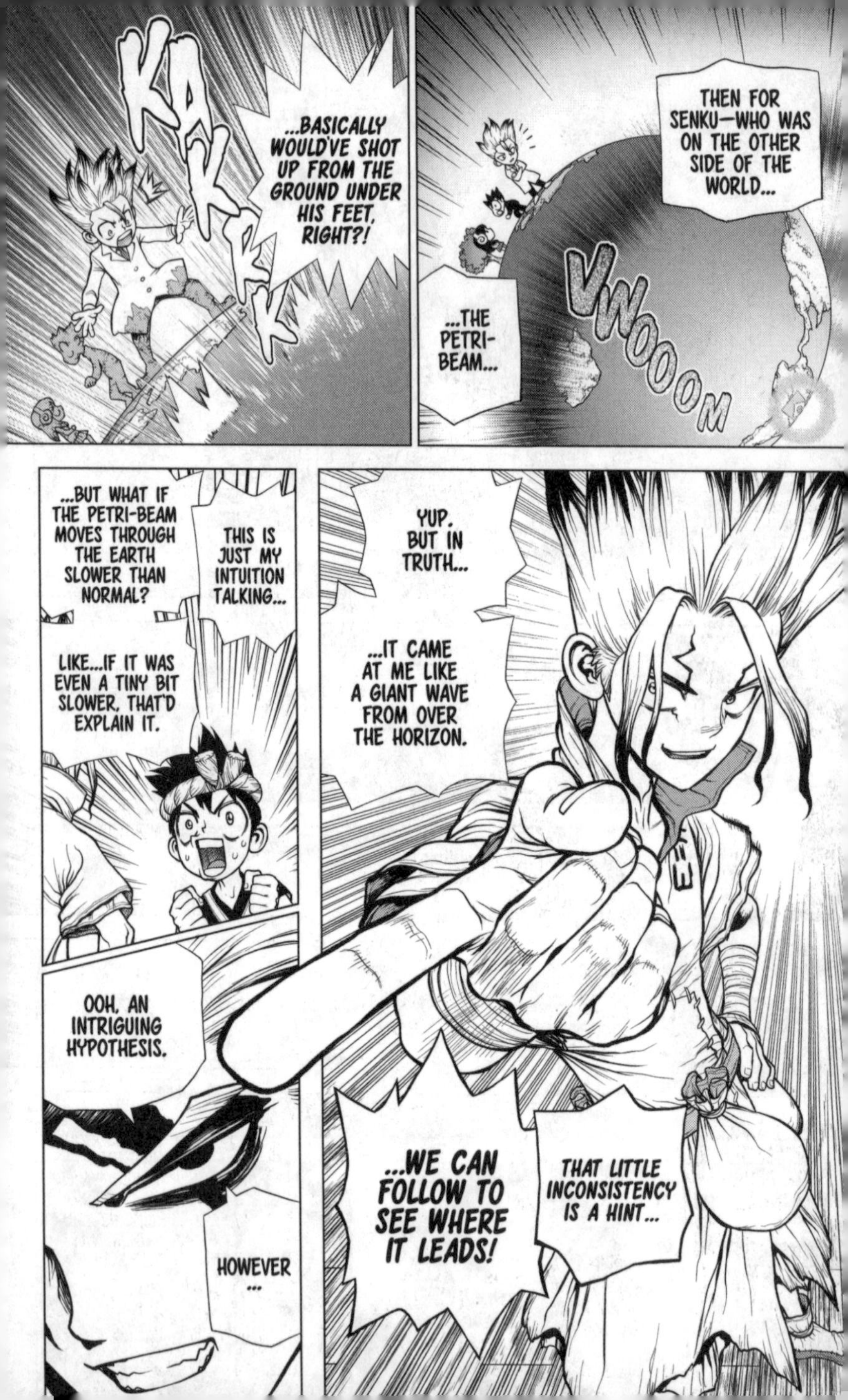
THEN FOR SENKU—WHO WAS ON THE OTHER SIDE OF THE WORLD...
...THE PETRI-BEAM...
VWOOOOM
...BASICALLY WOULD'VE SHOT UP FROM THE GROUND UNDER HIS FEET, RIGHT?!
YUP. BUT IN TRUTH...
...IT CAME AT ME LIKE A GIANT WAVE FROM OVER THE HORIZON.
THAT LITTLE INCONSISTENCY IS A HINT...
...WE CAN FOLLOW TO SEE WHERE IT LEADS!
THIS IS JUST MY INTUITION TALKING...
...BUT WHAT IF THE PETRI-BEAM MOVES THROUGH THE EARTH SLOWER THAN NORMAL?
LIKE...IF IT WAS EVEN A TINY BIT SLOWER, THAT'D EXPLAIN IT.
OOH, AN INTRIGUING HYPOTHESIS.
HOWEVER ...

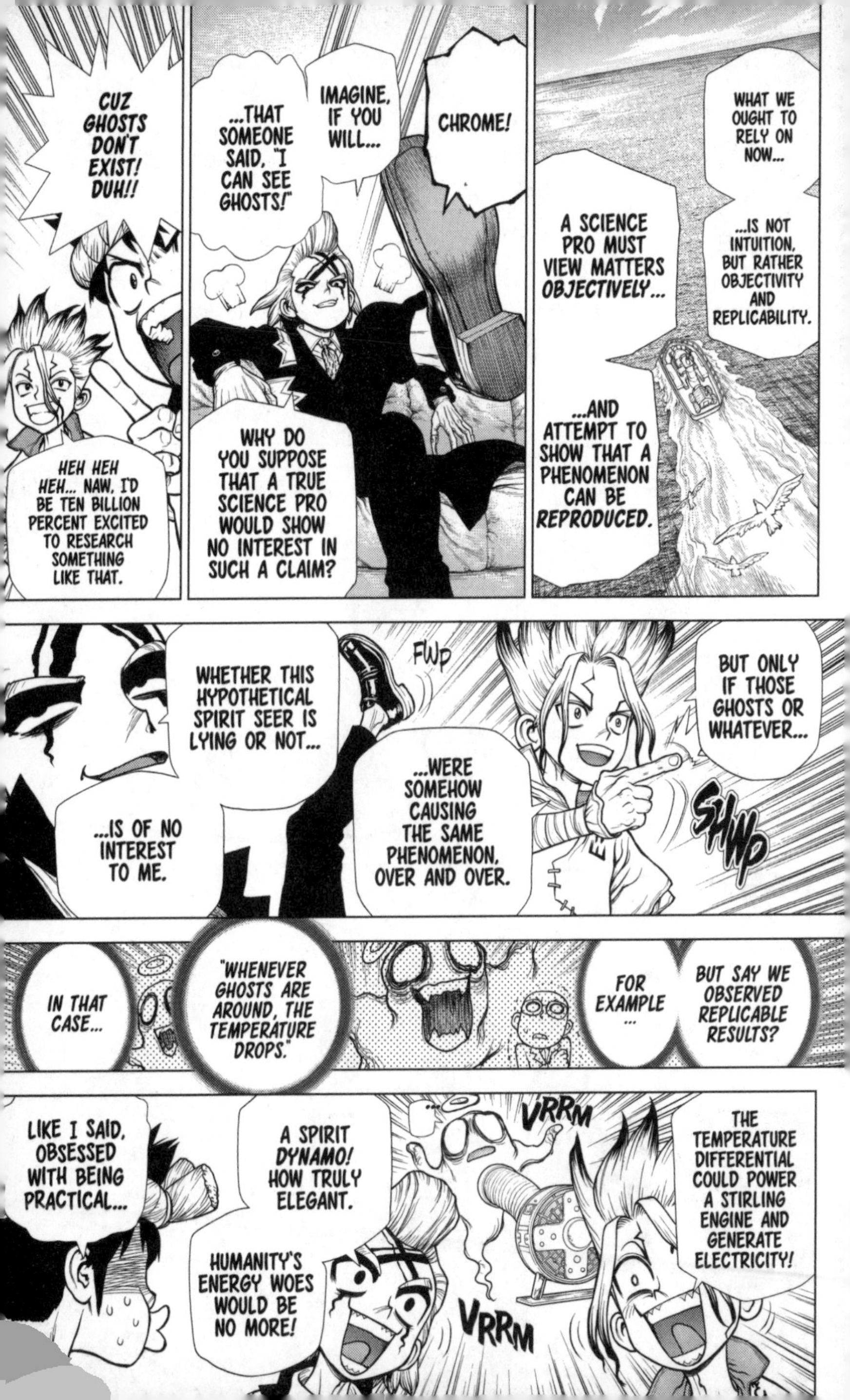
WHAT WE OUGHT TO RELY ON NOW...
...IS NOT INTUITION, BUT RATHER OBJECTIVITY AND REPLICABILITY.
A SCIENCE PRO MUST VIEW MATTERS OBJECTIVELY...
...AND ATTEMPT TO SHOW THAT A PHENOMENON CAN BE REPRODUCED.
CHROME!
IMAGINE, IF YOU WILL...
...THAT SOMEONE SAID, "I CAN SEE GHOSTS!"
WHY DO YOU SUPPOSE THAT A TRUE SCIENCE PRO WOULD SHOW NO INTEREST IN SUCH A CLAIM?
CUZ GHOSTS DON'T EXIST! DUH!!
HEH HEH HEH... NAW, I'D BE TEN BILLION PERCENT EXCITED TO RESEARCH SOMETHING LIKE THAT.
BUT ONLY IF THOSE GHOSTS OR WHATEVER...
SHWP
...WERE SOMEHOW CAUSING THE SAME PHENOMENON, OVER AND OVER.
FWP
WHETHER THIS HYPOTHETICAL SPIRIT SEER IS LYING OR NOT...
...IS OF NO INTEREST TO ME.
BUT SAY WE OBSERVED REPLICABLE RESULTS?
FOR EXAMPLE...
"WHENEVER GHOSTS ARE AROUND, THE TEMPERATURE DROPS."
IN THAT CASE...
THE TEMPERATURE DIFFERENTIAL COULD POWER A STIRLING ENGINE AND GENERATE ELECTRICITY!
VRRM
VRRM
A SPIRIT DYNAMO! HOW TRULY ELEGANT.
HUMANITY'S ENERGY WOES WOULD BE NO MORE!
LIKE I SAID, OBSESSED WITH BEING PRACTICAL...

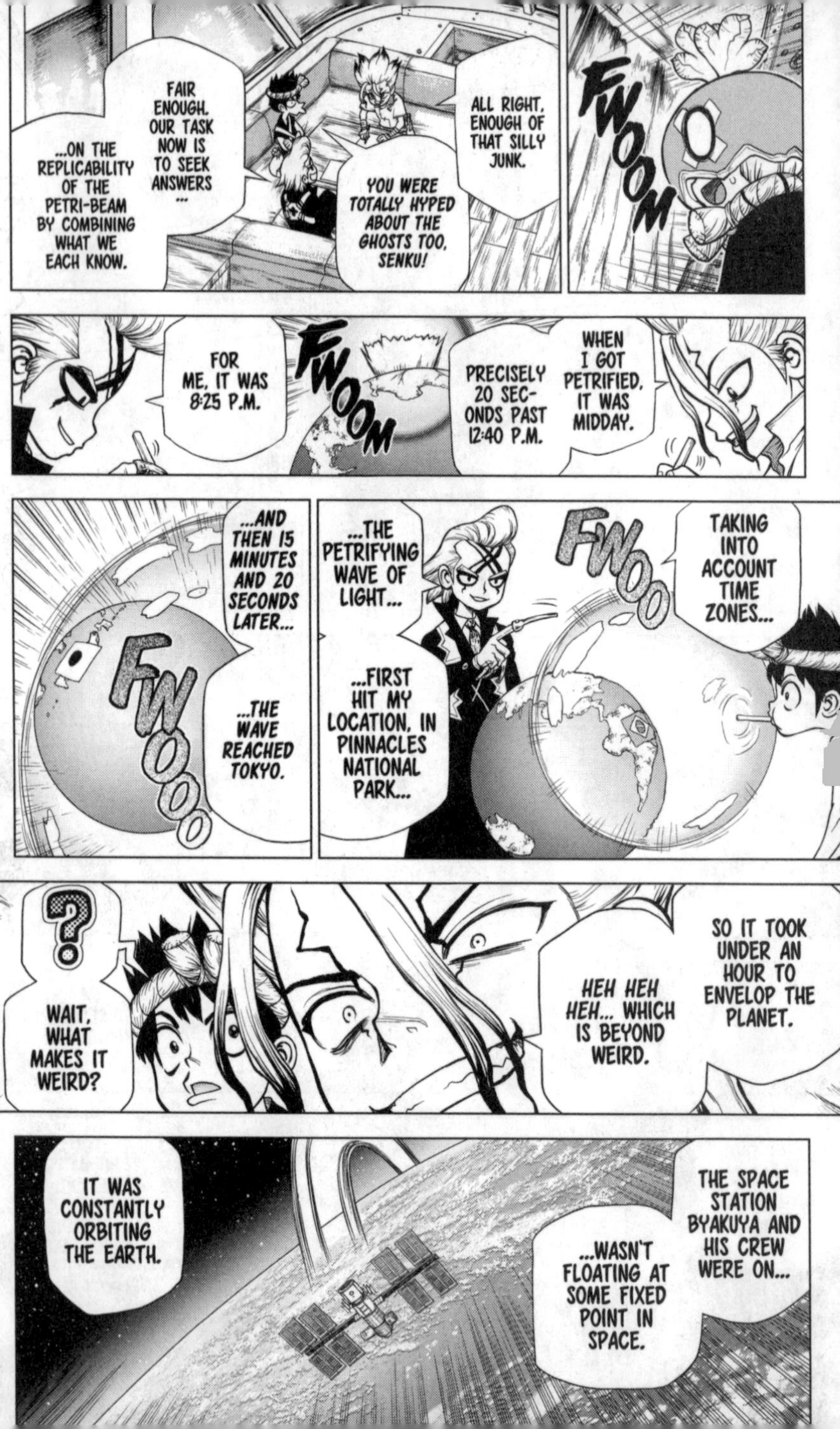
FWOOM
ALL RIGHT, ENOUGH OF THAT SILLY JUNK.
YOU WERE TOTALLY HYPED ABOUT THE GHOSTS TOO, SENKU!
FAIR ENOUGH. OUR TASK NOW IS TO SEEK ANSWERS...
...ON THE REPLICABILITY OF THE PETRI-BEAM BY COMBINING WHAT WE EACH KNOW.
WHEN I GOT PETRIFIED, IT WAS MIDDAY.
PRECISELY 20 SECONDS PAST 12:40 P.M.
FWOOM
FOR ME, IT WAS 8:25 P.M.
TAKING INTO ACCOUNT TIME ZONES...
FWOO
...THE PETRIFYING WAVE OF LIGHT...
...FIRST HIT MY LOCATION, IN PINNACLES NATIONAL PARK...
...AND THEN 15 MINUTES AND 20 SECONDS LATER...
FWOOO
...THE WAVE REACHED TOKYO.
SO IT TOOK UNDER AN HOUR TO ENVELOP THE PLANET.
HEH HEH HEH... WHICH IS BEYOND WEIRD.
?
WAIT, WHAT MAKES IT WEIRD?
THE SPACE STATION BYAKUYA AND HIS CREW WERE ON...
...WASN'T FLOATING AT SOME FIXED POINT IN SPACE.
IT WAS CONSTANTLY ORBITING THE EARTH.

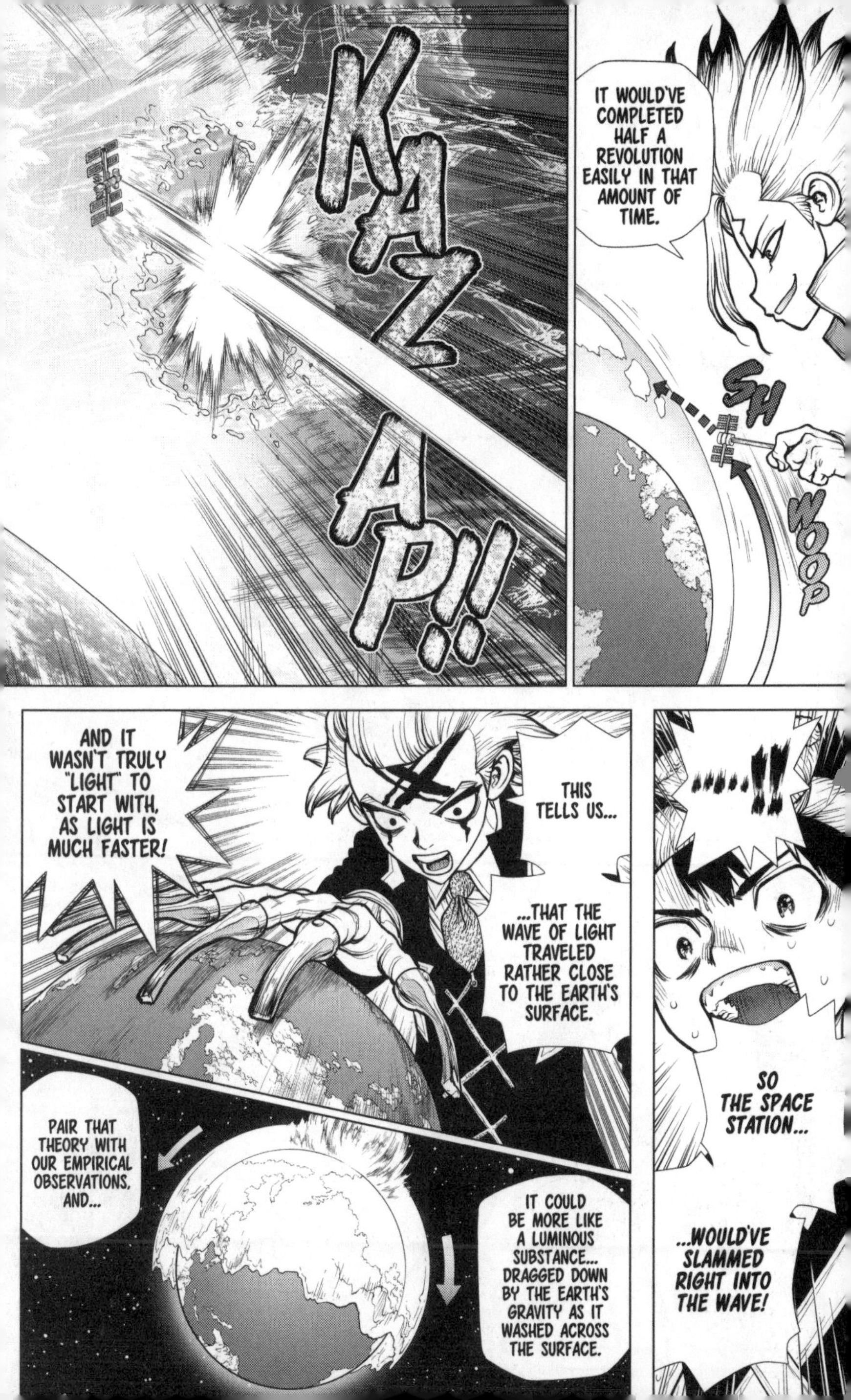

IT WOULD'VE COMPLETED HALF A REVOLUTION EASILY IN THAT AMOUNT OF TIME.
SH
WOOP
KAZAP!!
.....!!
SO THE SPACE STATION...
...WOULD'VE SLAMMED RIGHT INTO THE WAVE!
THIS TELLS US...
...THAT THE WAVE OF LIGHT TRAVELED RATHER CLOSE TO THE EARTH'S SURFACE.
AND IT WASN'T TRULY "LIGHT" TO START WITH, AS LIGHT IS MUCH FASTER!
PAIR THAT THEORY WITH OUR EMPIRICAL OBSERVATIONS, AND...
IT COULD BE MORE LIKE A LUMINOUS SUBSTANCE... DRAGGED DOWN BY THE EARTH'S GRAVITY AS IT WASHED ACROSS THE SURFACE.

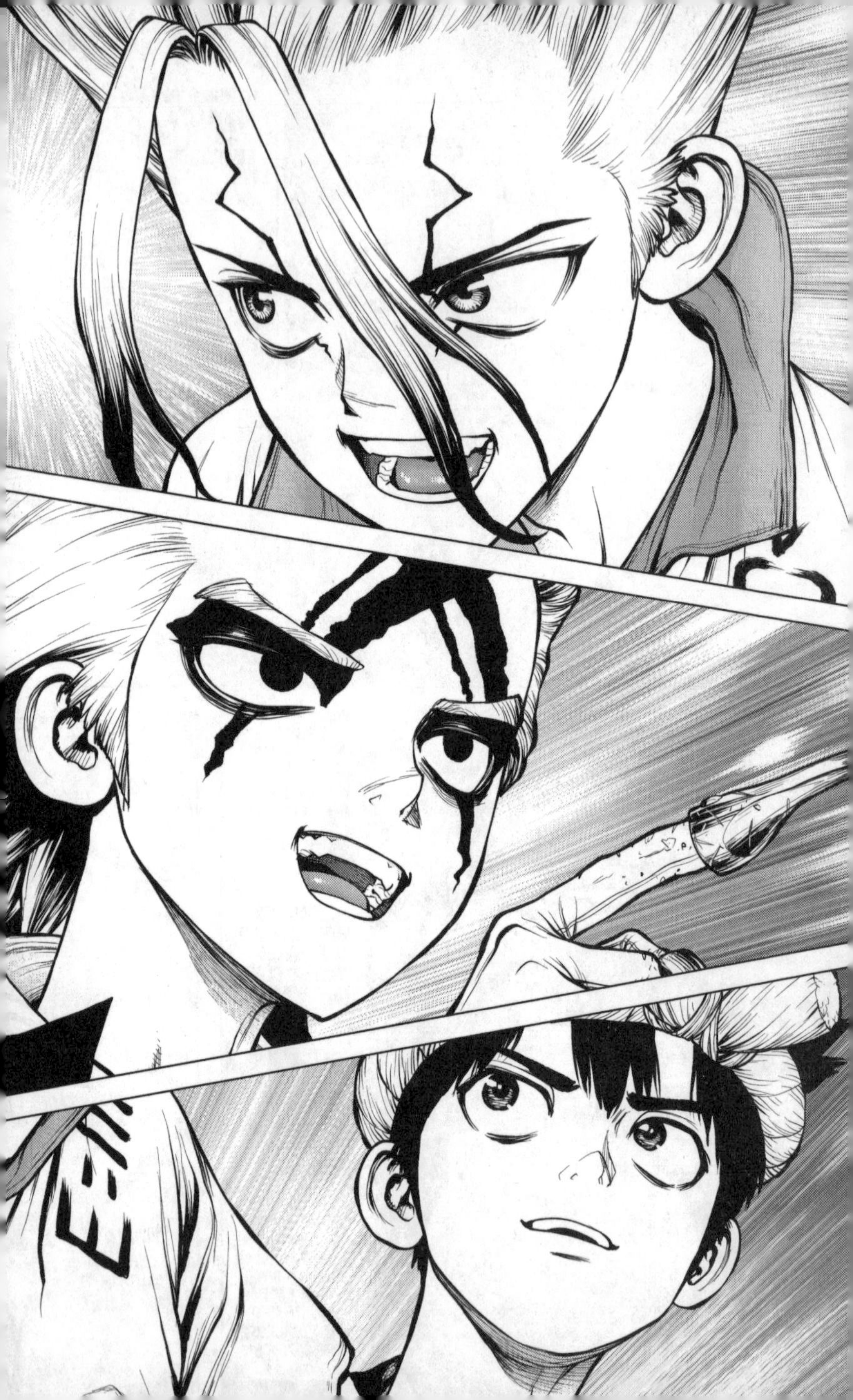

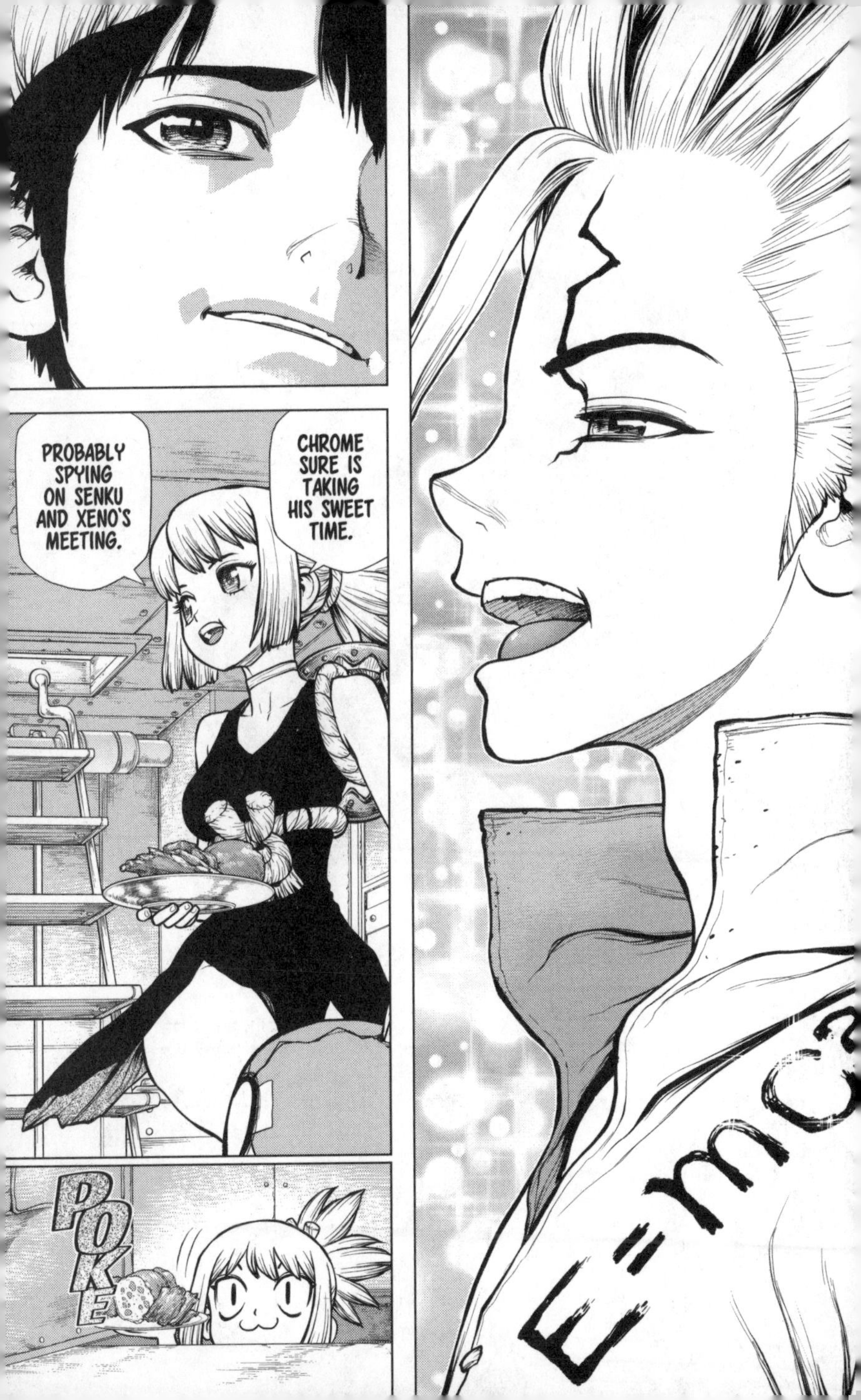
E=mc
CHROME SURE IS TAKING HIS SWEET TIME.
PROBABLY SPYING ON SENKU AND XENO'S MEETING.
POKE

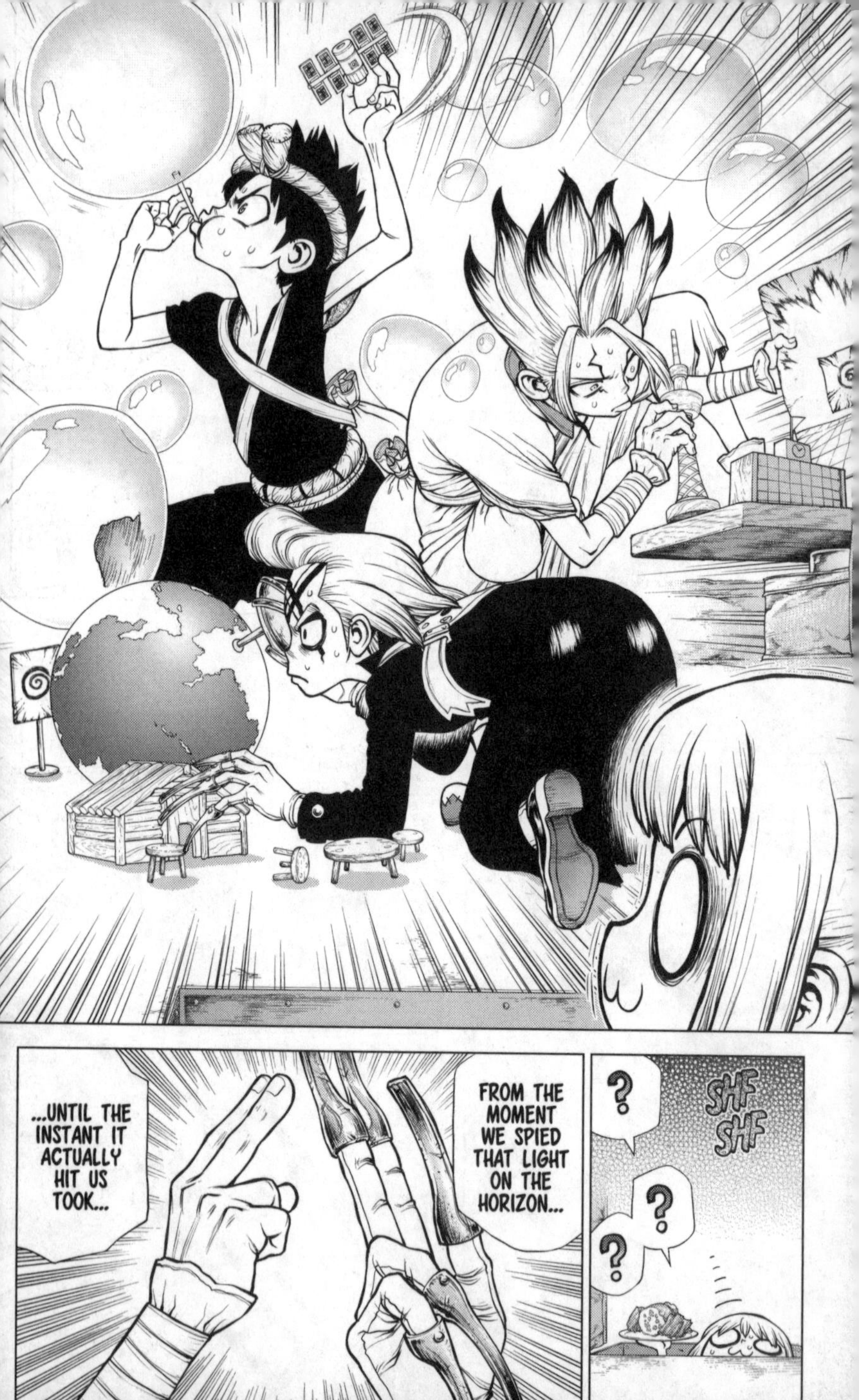
?
SHF SHF
?
?
FROM THE MOMENT WE SPIED THAT LIGHT ON THE HORIZON...
...UNTIL THE INSTANT IT ACTUALLY HIT US TOOK...

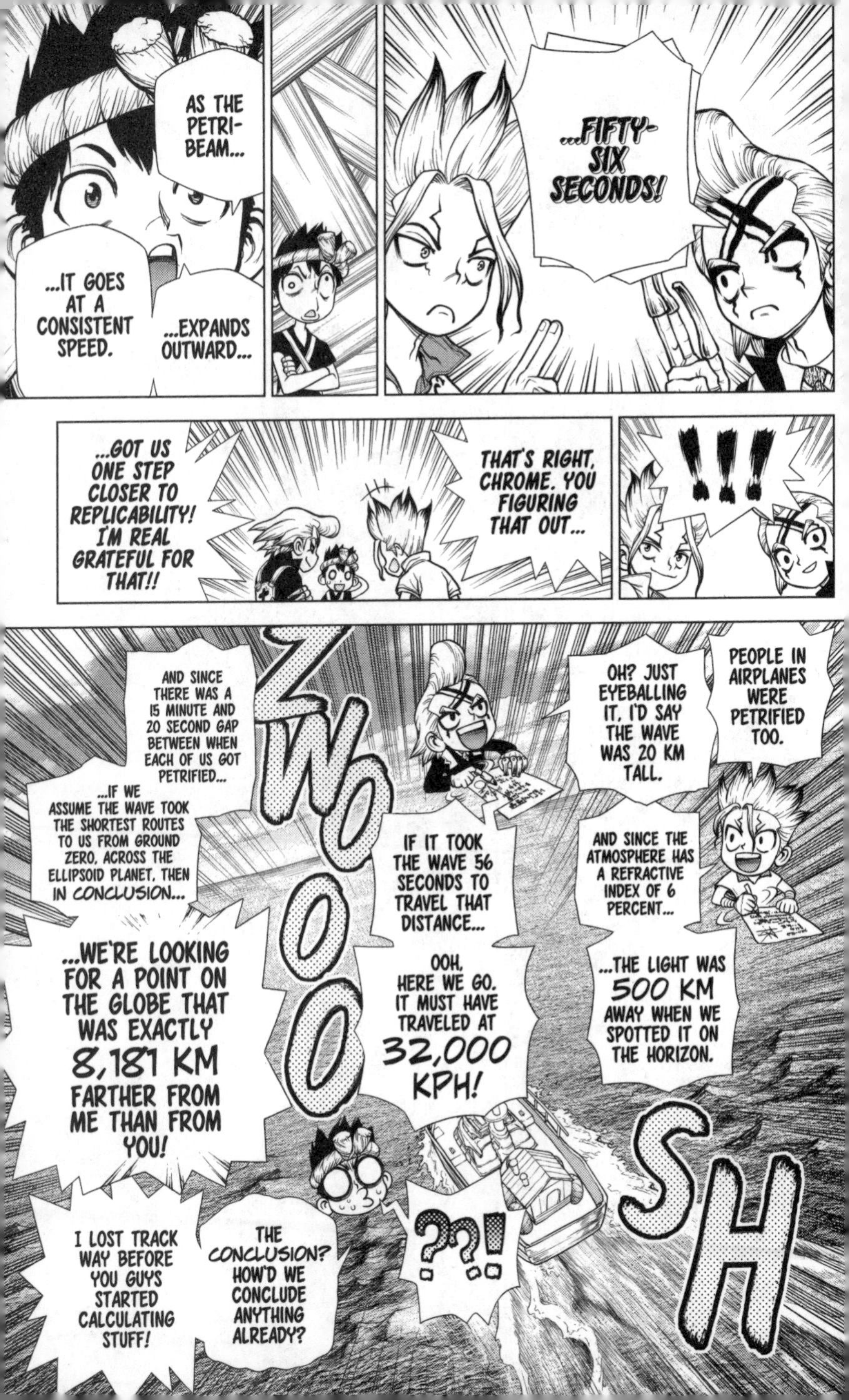
...FIFTY-SIX SECONDS!
AS THE PETRI-BEAM...
...EXPANDS OUTWARD...
...IT GOES AT A CONSISTENT SPEED.
!!!
THAT'S RIGHT, CHROME. YOU FIGURING THAT OUT...
...GOT US ONE STEP CLOSER TO REPLICABILITY! I'M REAL GRATEFUL FOR THAT!!
PEOPLE IN AIRPLANES WERE PETRIFIED TOO.
OH? JUST EYEBALLING IT, I'D SAY THE WAVE WAS 20 KM TALL.
AND SINCE THE ATMOSPHERE HAS A REFRACTIVE INDEX OF 6 PERCENT...
...THE LIGHT WAS 500 KM AWAY WHEN WE SPOTTED IT ON THE HORIZON.
IF IT TOOK THE WAVE 56 SECONDS TO TRAVEL THAT DISTANCE...
OOH, HERE WE GO. IT MUST HAVE TRAVELED AT 32,000 KPH!
AND SINCE THERE WAS A 15 MINUTE AND 20 SECOND GAP BETWEEN WHEN EACH OF US GOT PETRIFIED...
...IF WE ASSUME THE WAVE TOOK THE SHORTEST ROUTES TO US FROM GROUND ZERO, ACROSS THE ELLIPSOID PLANET, THEN IN CONCLUSION...
...WE'RE LOOKING FOR A POINT ON THE GLOBE THAT WAS EXACTLY 8,181 KM FARTHER FROM ME THAN FROM YOU!
ZWOOOSH
??!
THE CONCLUSION? HOW'D WE CONCLUDE ANYTHING ALREADY?
I LOST TRACK WAY BEFORE YOU GUYS STARTED CALCULATING STUFF!

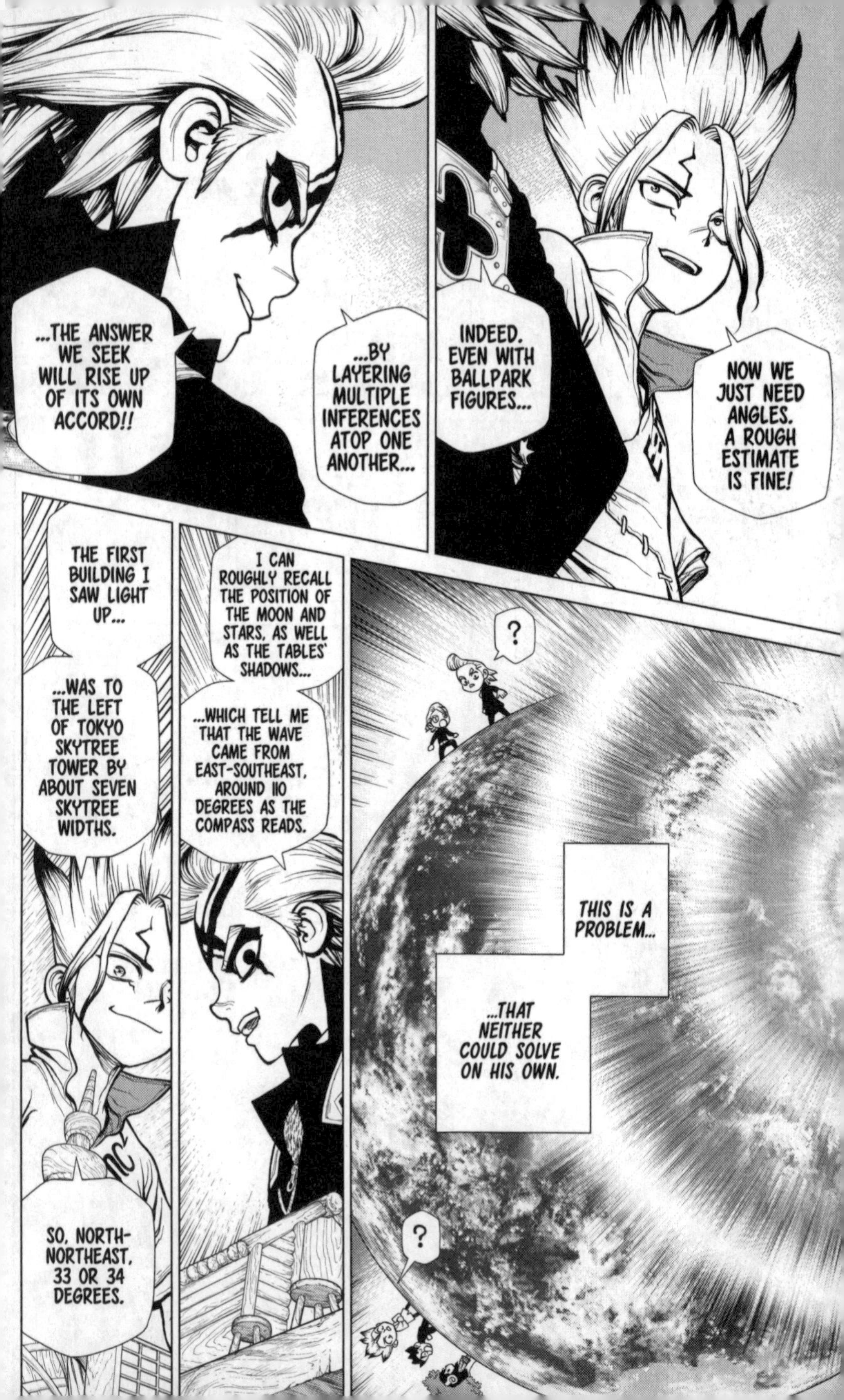
NOW WE JUST NEED ANGLES. A ROUGH ESTIMATE IS FINE!
INDEED. EVEN WITH BALLPARK FIGURES...
...BY LAYERING MULTIPLE INFERENCES ATOP ONE ANOTHER...
...THE ANSWER WE SEEK WILL RISE UP OF ITS OWN ACCORD!!
?
THIS IS A PROBLEM...
...THAT NEITHER COULD SOLVE ON HIS OWN.
?
I CAN ROUGHLY RECALL THE POSITION OF THE MOON AND STARS, AS WELL AS THE TABLES' SHADOWS...
...WHICH TELL ME THAT THE WAVE CAME FROM EAST-SOUTHEAST, AROUND 110 DEGREES AS THE COMPASS READS.
THE FIRST BUILDING I SAW LIGHT UP...
...WAS TO THE LEFT OF TOKYO SKYTREE TOWER BY ABOUT SEVEN SKYTREE WIDTHS.
SO, NORTH-NORTHEAST, 33 OR 34 DEGREES.

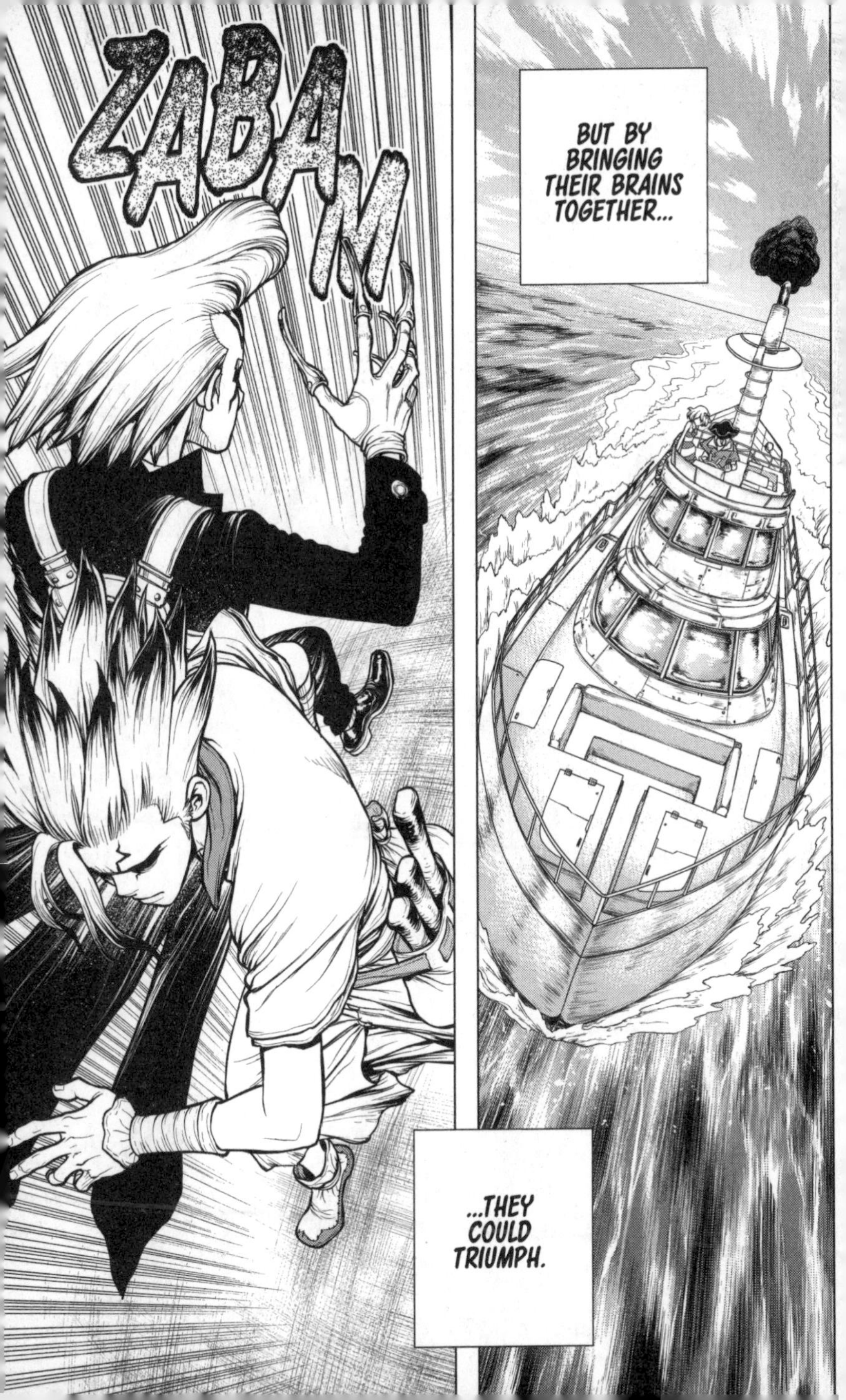
BUT BY BRINGING THEIR BRAINS TOGETHER...
...THEY COULD TRIUMPH.
ZABAM

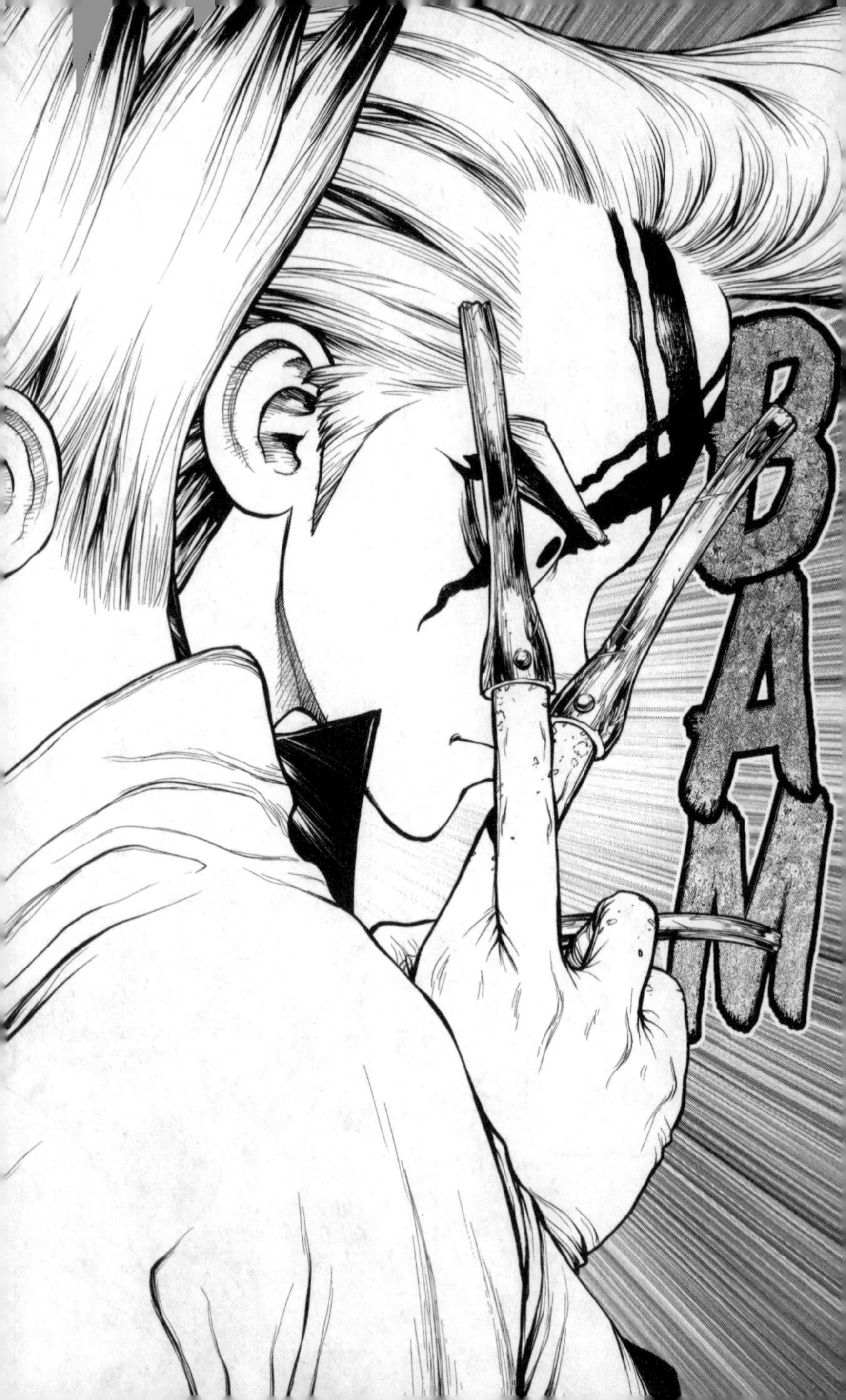
BAM

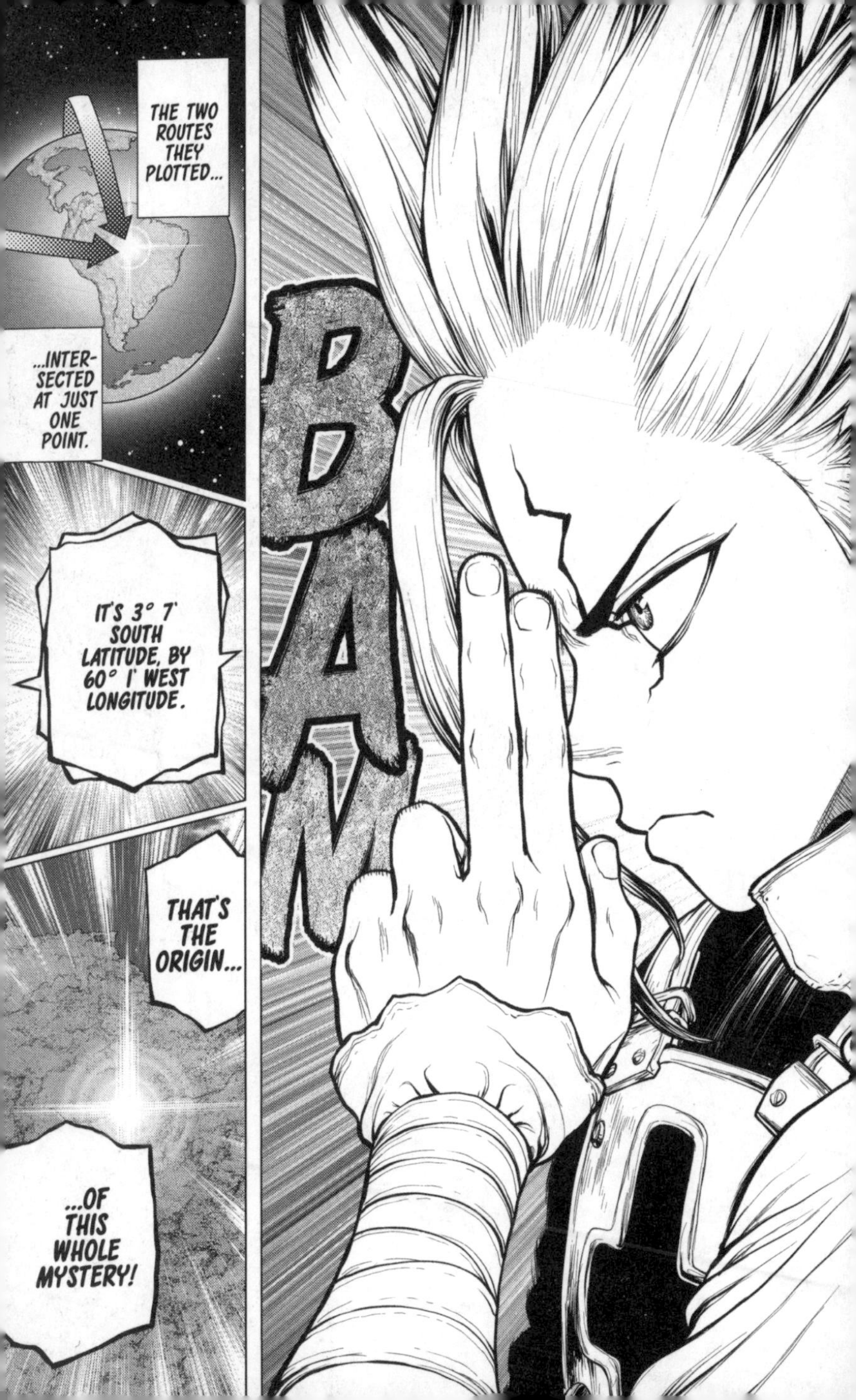
BAM
THE TWO ROUTES THEY PLOTTED...
...INTER-SECTED AT JUST ONE POINT.
IT'S 3° 7' SOUTH LATITUDE, BY 60° 1' WEST LONGITUDE.
THAT'S THE ORIGIN...
...OF THIS WHOLE MYSTERY!

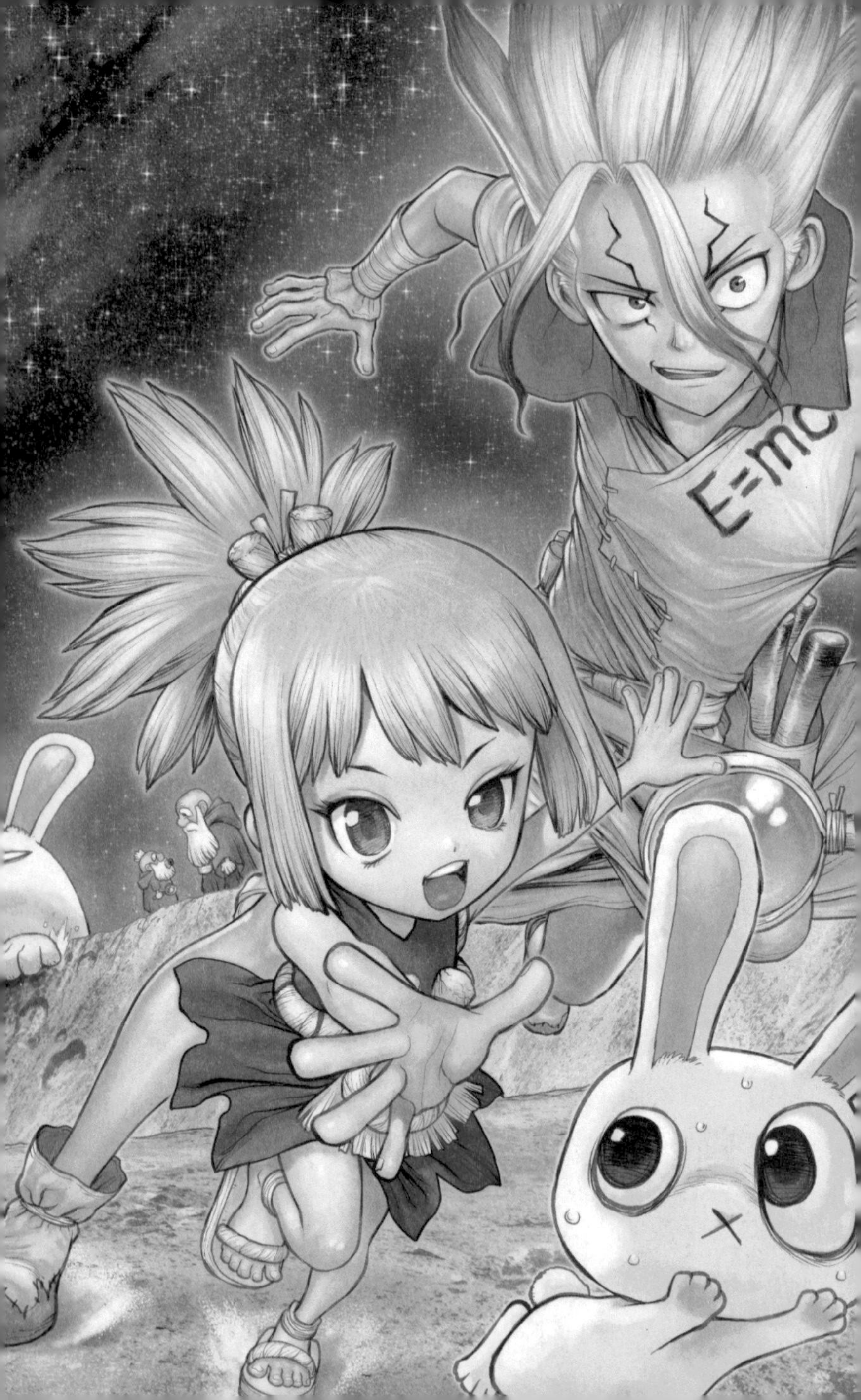
E=mc

Z=172: Marked with an "X" of Wisdom

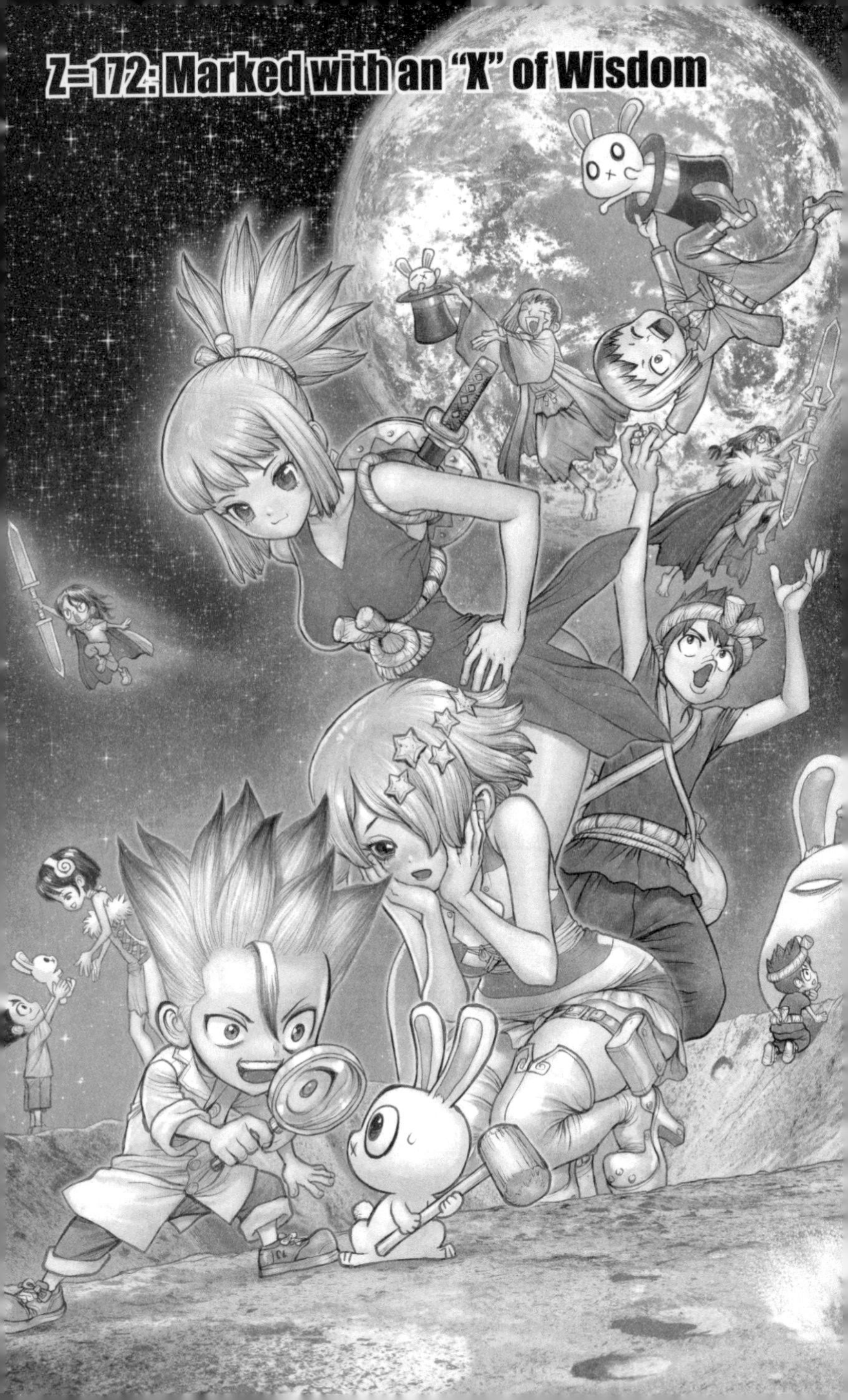

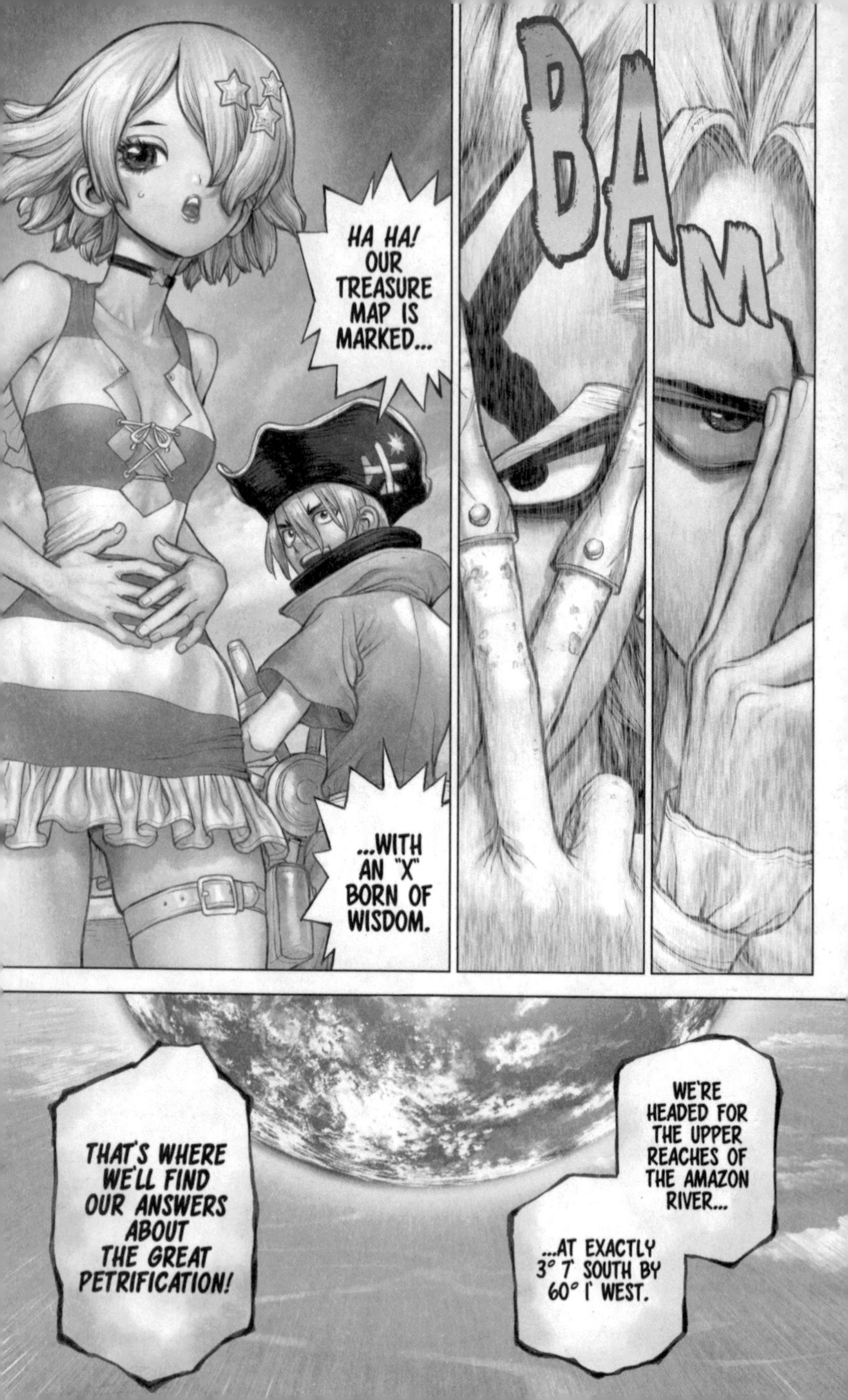
BAM
HA HA! OUR TREASURE MAP IS MARKED...
...WITH AN "X" BORN OF WISDOM.
WE'RE HEADED FOR THE UPPER REACHES OF THE AMAZON RIVER...
...AT EXACTLY 3° 7' SOUTH BY 60° 1' WEST.
THAT'S WHERE WE'LL FIND OUR ANSWERS ABOUT THE GREAT PETRIFICATION!

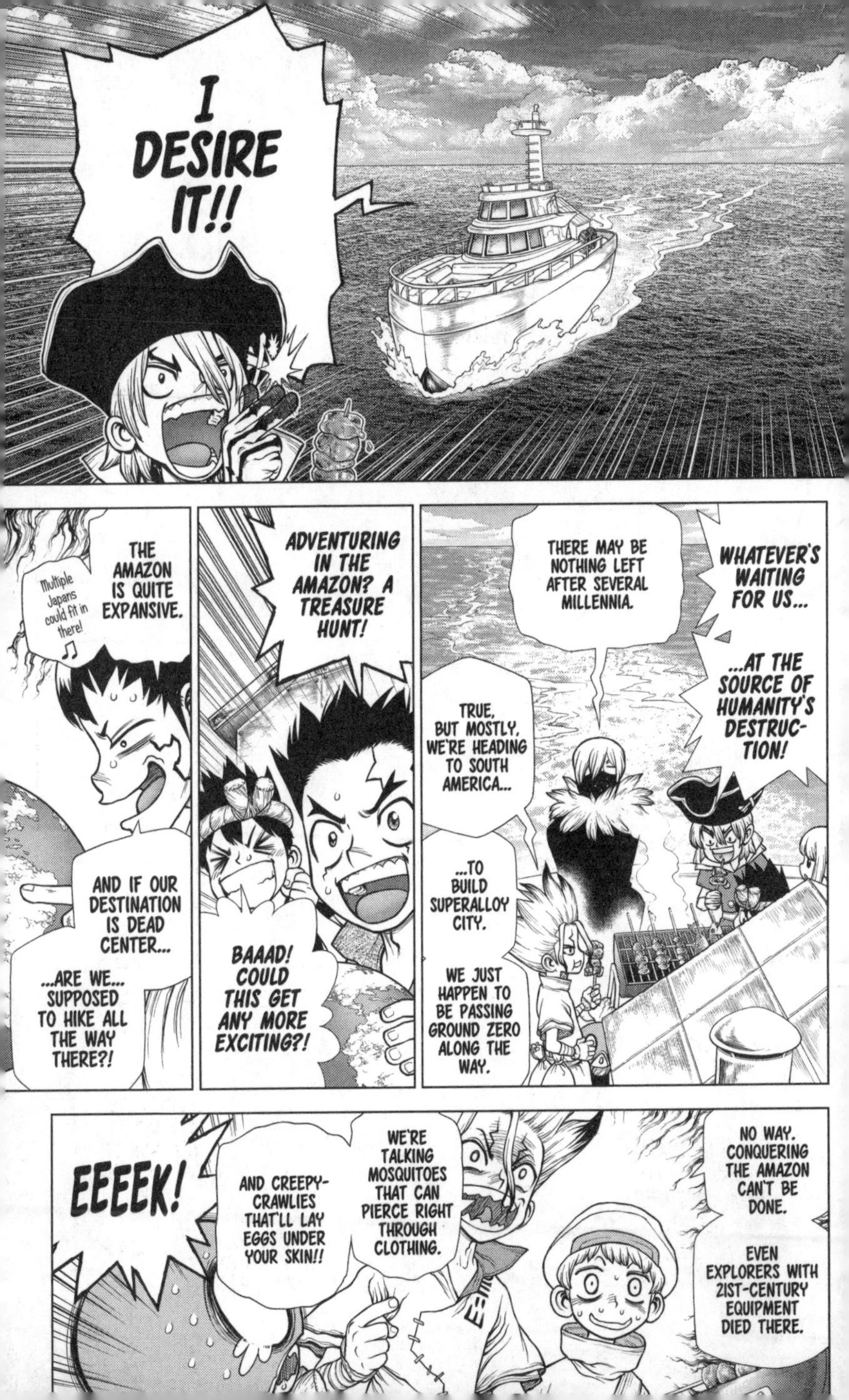
I DESIRE IT!!
WHATEVER'S WAITING FOR US...
...AT THE SOURCE OF HUMANITY'S DESTRUCTION!
THERE MAY BE NOTHING LEFT AFTER SEVERAL MILLENNIA.
TRUE, BUT MOSTLY, WE'RE HEADING TO SOUTH AMERICA...
...TO BUILD SUPERALLOY CITY.
WE JUST HAPPEN TO BE PASSING GROUND ZERO ALONG THE WAY.
ADVENTURING IN THE AMAZON? A TREASURE HUNT!
BAAAD! COULD THIS GET ANY MORE EXCITING?!
THE AMAZON IS QUITE EXPANSIVE.
Multiple Japans could fit in there! ♫
AND IF OUR DESTINATION IS DEAD CENTER...
...ARE WE... SUPPOSED TO HIKE ALL THE WAY THERE?!
NO WAY. CONQUERING THE AMAZON CAN'T BE DONE.
EVEN EXPLORERS WITH 21ST-CENTURY EQUIPMENT DIED THERE.
WE'RE TALKING MOSQUITOES THAT CAN PIERCE RIGHT THROUGH CLOTHING.
AND CREEPY-CRAWLIES THAT'LL LAY EGGS UNDER YOUR SKIN!!
EEEEK!

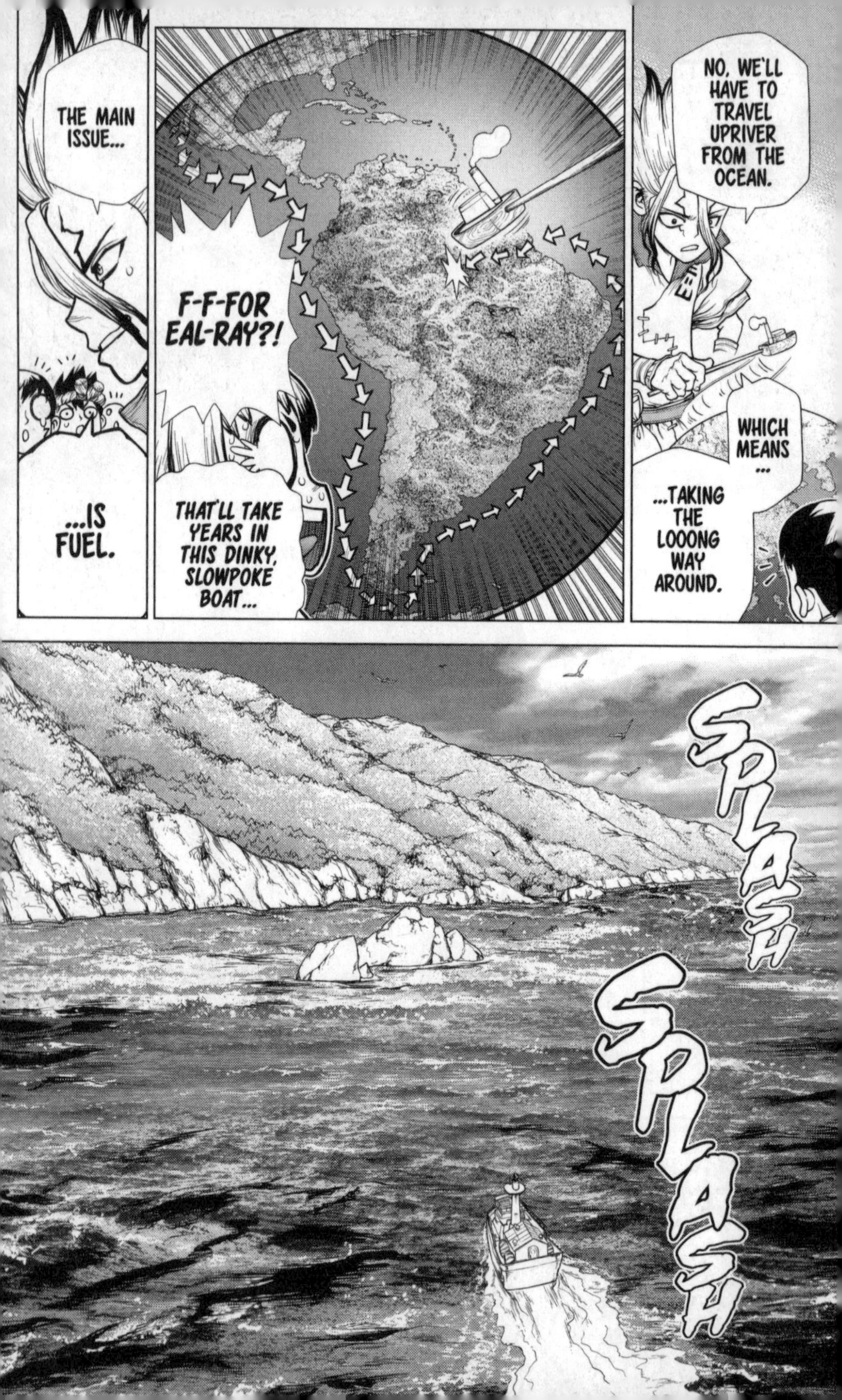
NO, WE'LL HAVE TO TRAVEL UPRIVER FROM THE OCEAN.
WHICH MEANS...
...TAKING THE LOOONG WAY AROUND.
F-F-FOR EAL-RAY?!
THAT'LL TAKE YEARS IN THIS DINKY, SLOWPOKE BOAT...
THE MAIN ISSUE...
...IS FUEL.
SPLASH
SPLASH

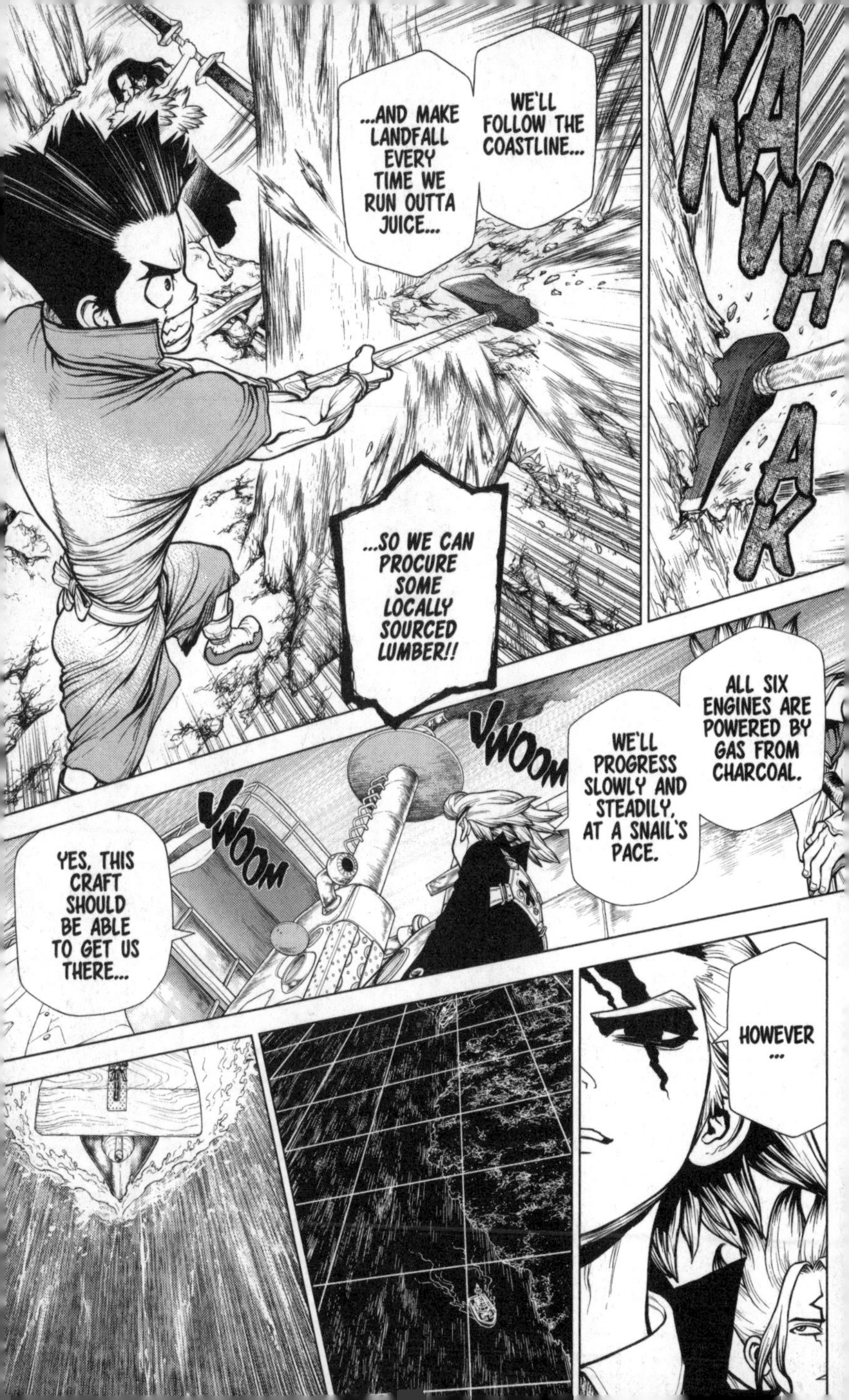
KAWHAK
WE'LL FOLLOW THE COASTLINE...
...AND MAKE LANDFALL EVERY TIME WE RUN OUTTA JUICE...
...SO WE CAN PROCURE SOME LOCALLY SOURCED LUMBER!!
ALL SIX ENGINES ARE POWERED BY GAS FROM CHARCOAL.
WE'LL PROGRESS SLOWLY AND STEADILY, AT A SNAIL'S PACE.
VWOOM
VWOOM
YES, THIS CRAFT SHOULD BE ABLE TO GET US THERE...
HOWEVER ...

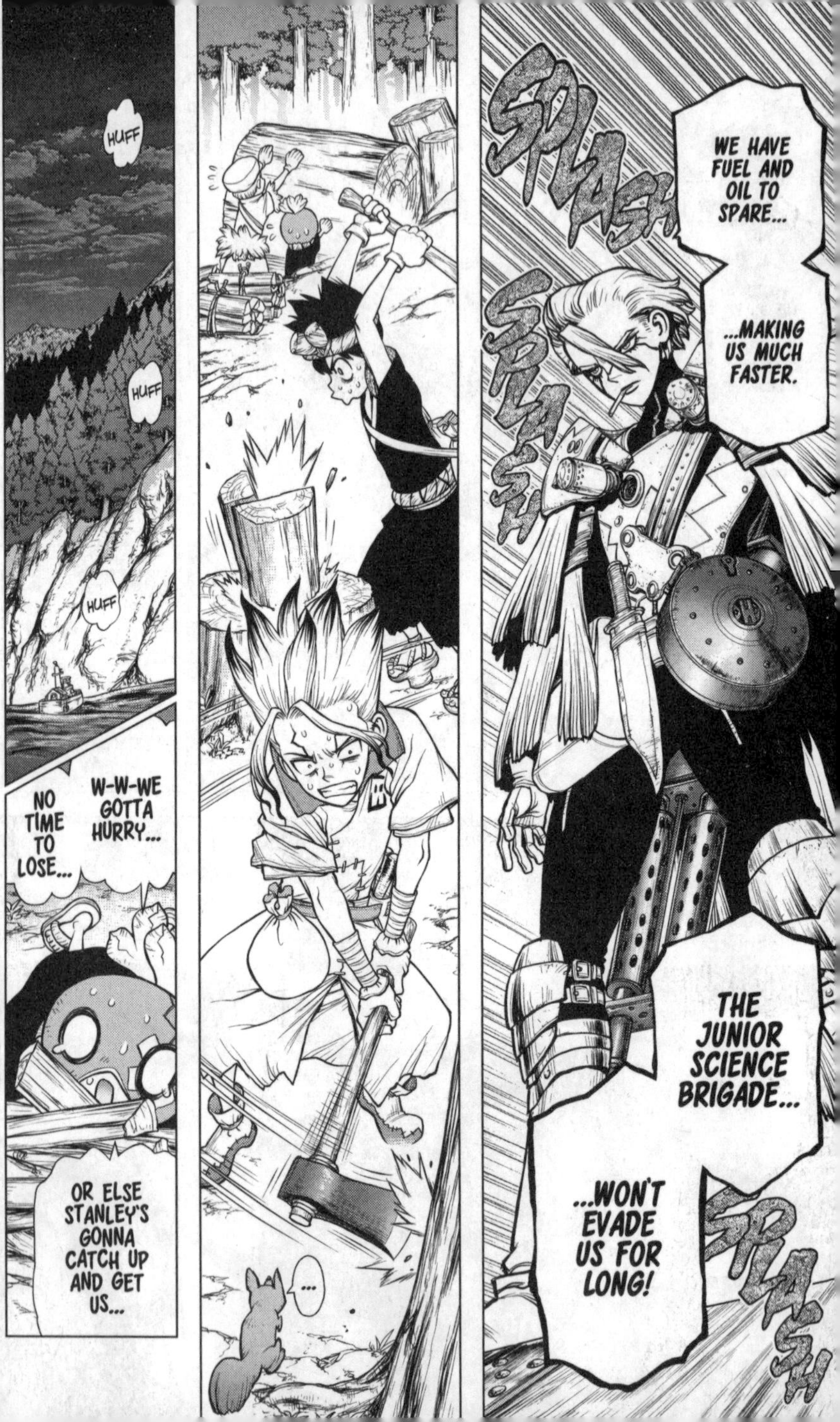
SPLASH
WE HAVE FUEL AND OIL TO SPARE...
SPLASH
...MAKING US MUCH FASTER.
THE JUNIOR SCIENCE BRIGADE...
...WON'T EVADE US FOR LONG!
SPLASH
...
HUFF
HUFF
HUFF
W-W-WE GOTTA HURRY...
NO TIME TO LOSE...
OR ELSE STANLEY'S GONNA CATCH UP AND GET US...

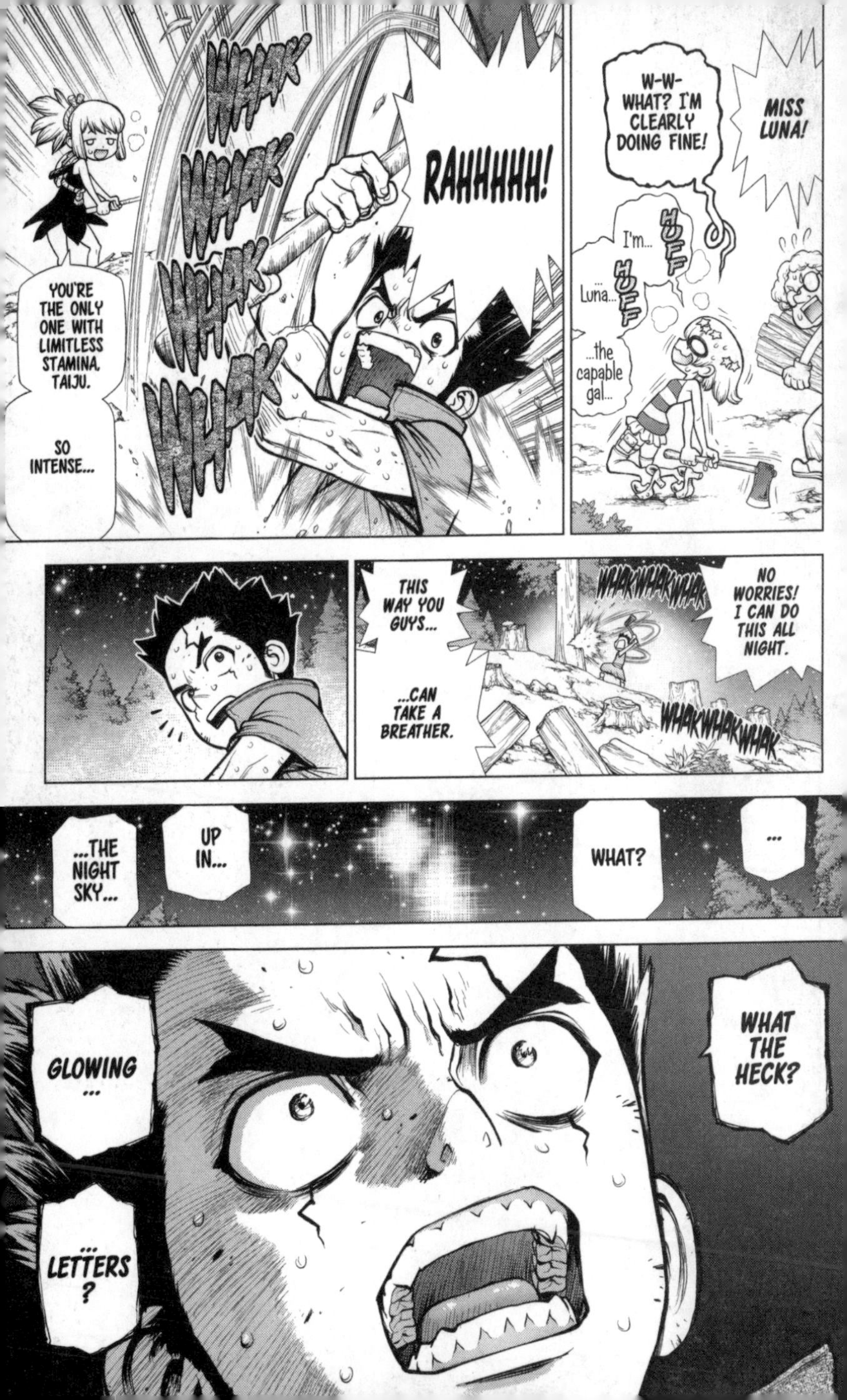
MISS LUNA!
W-W-WHAT? I'M CLEARLY DOING FINE!
I'm...
HUFF
...Luna...
HUFF
...the capable gal...
RAHHHHH!
WHAK
WHAK
WHAK
WHAK
YOU'RE THE ONLY ONE WITH LIMITLESS STAMINA, TAIJU.
SO INTENSE...
NO WORRIES! I CAN DO THIS ALL NIGHT.
WHAKWHAKWHAK
WHAKWHAKWHAK
THIS WAY YOU GUYS...
...CAN TAKE A BREATHER.
...
WHAT?
UP IN...
...THE NIGHT SKY...
WHAT THE HECK?
GLOWING...
...LETTERS?

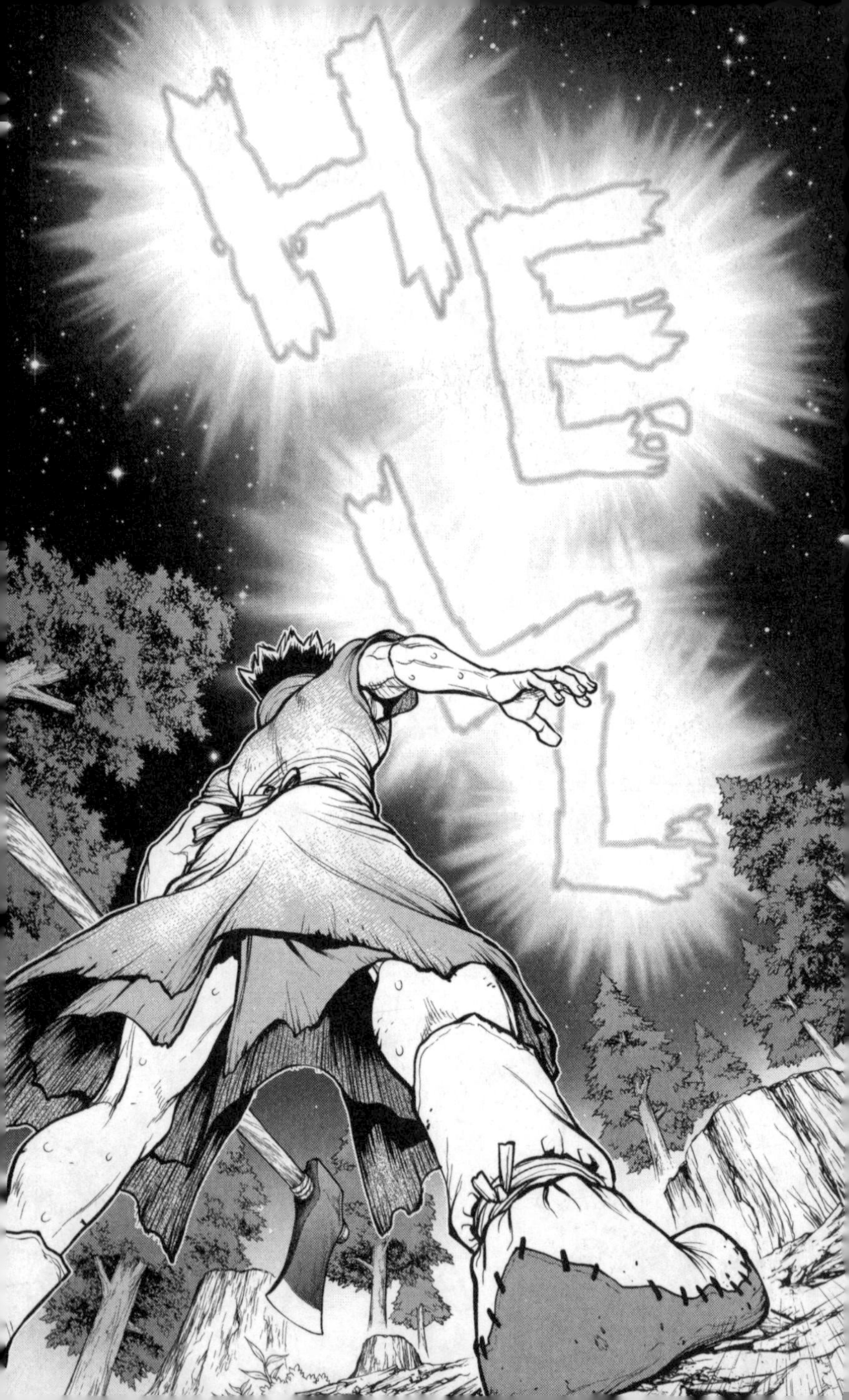
HELL

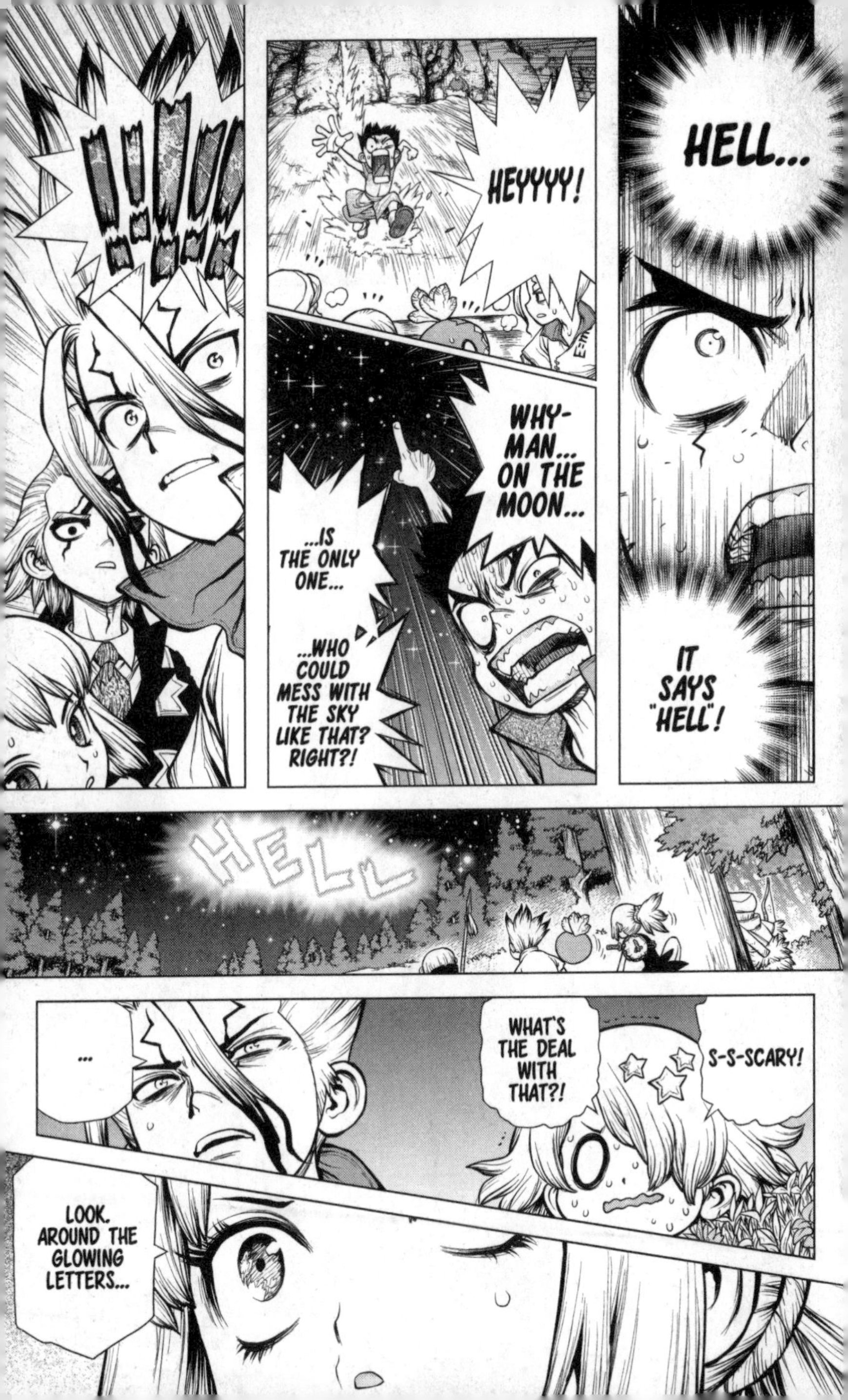
HELL...
IT SAYS "HELL"!
HEYYYY!
WHY-MAN... ON THE MOON...
...IS THE ONLY ONE...
...WHO COULD MESS WITH THE SKY LIKE THAT? RIGHT?!
HELL
S-S-SCARY!
WHAT'S THE DEAL WITH THAT?!
...
LOOK. AROUND THE GLOWING LETTERS...

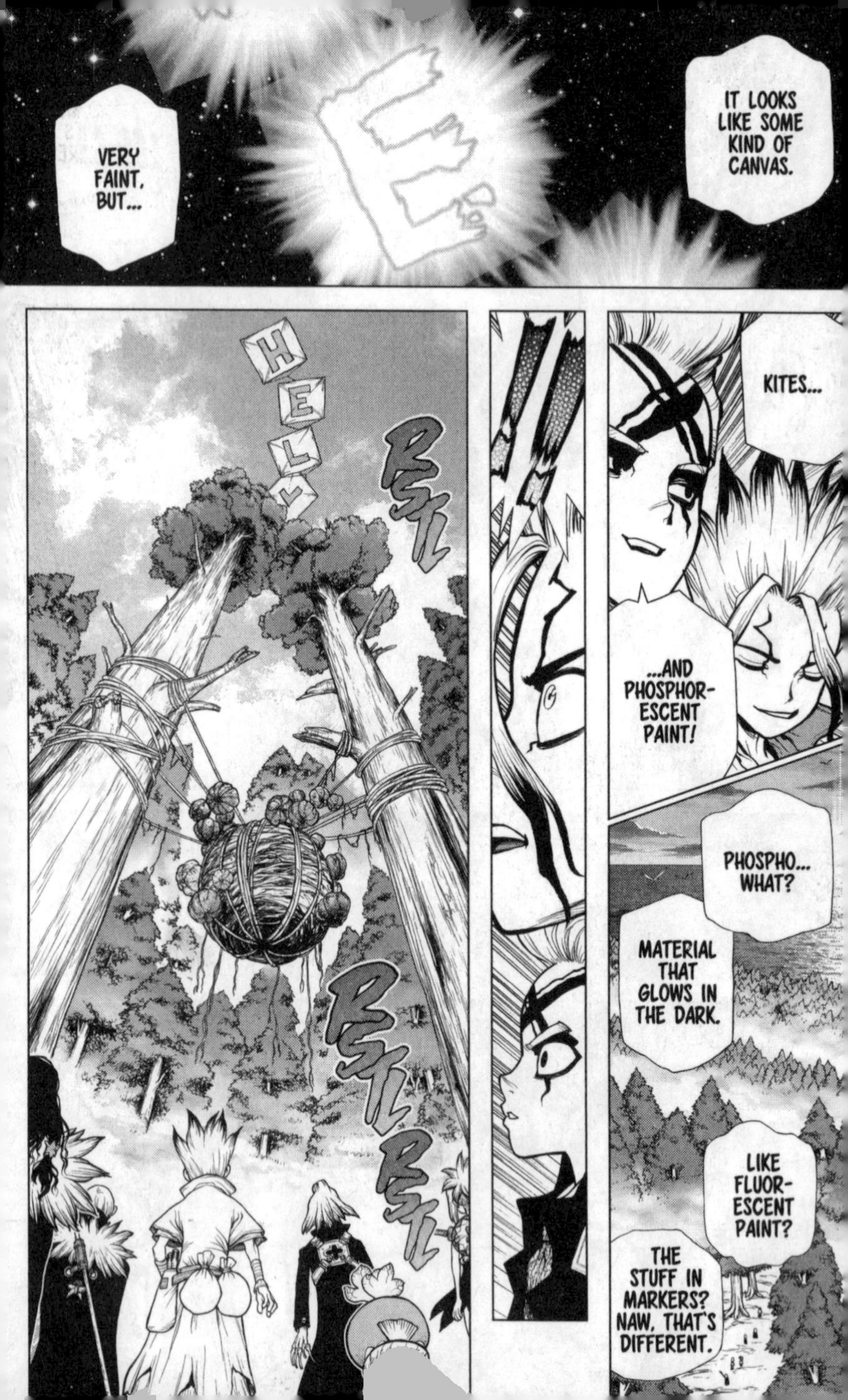
IT LOOKS LIKE SOME KIND OF CANVAS.
VERY FAINT, BUT...
KITES...
...AND PHOSPHOR-ESCENT PAINT!
PHOSPHO... WHAT?
MATERIAL THAT GLOWS IN THE DARK.
LIKE FLUOR-ESCENT PAINT?
THE STUFF IN MARKERS? NAW, THAT'S DIFFERENT.
HEL
RSTL
RSTL RSTL

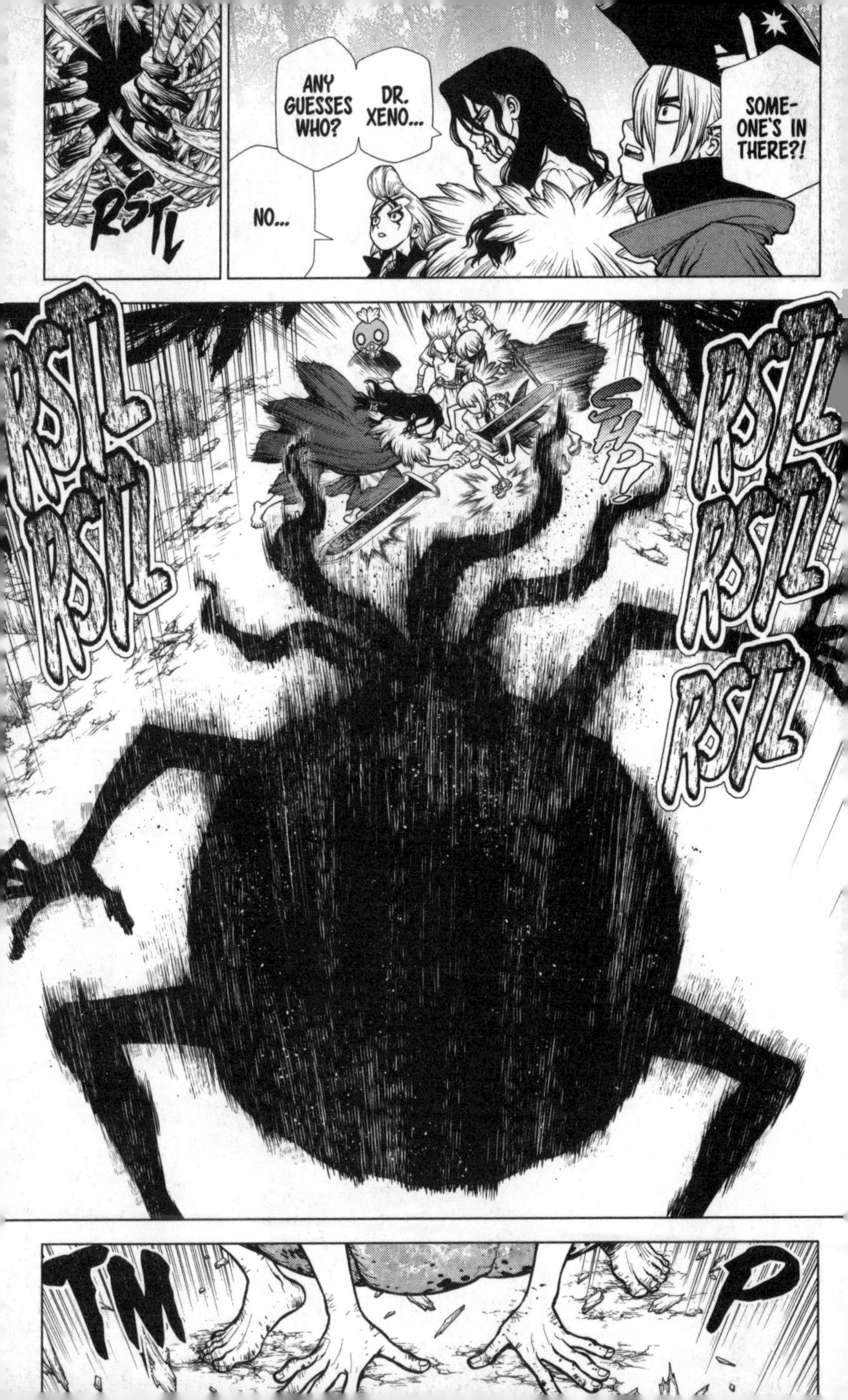
SOME-ONE'S IN THERE?!
DR. XENO...
ANY GUESSES WHO?
NO...
RSTL
RSTL RSTL RSTL
SHP!
RSTL RSTL
TMP

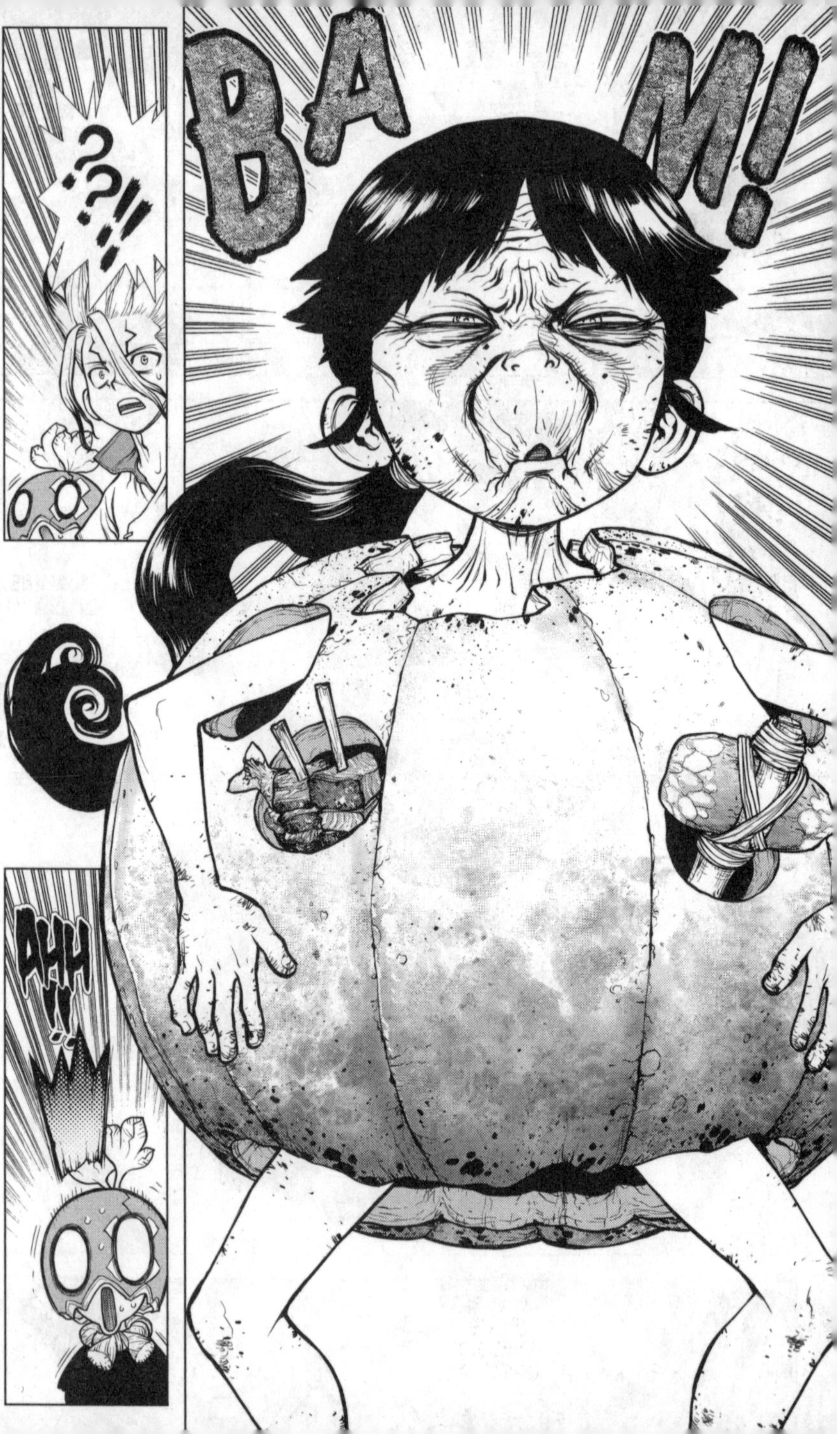
BAM!
??!!
AHH!!

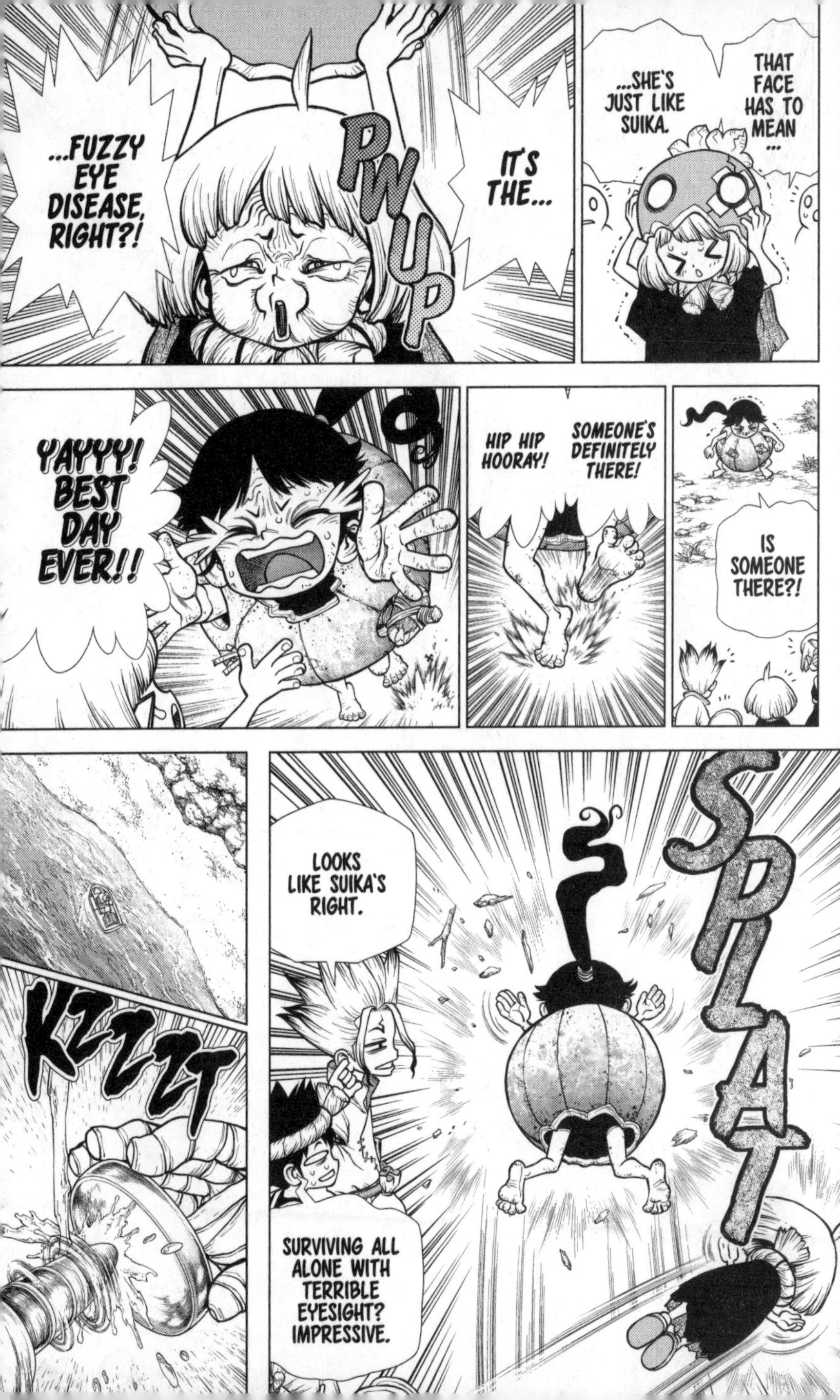
THAT FACE HAS TO MEAN...
...SHE'S JUST LIKE SUIKA.
IT'S THE...
...FUZZY EYE DISEASE, RIGHT?!
PWUP
IS SOMEONE THERE?!
SOMEONE'S DEFINITELY THERE!
HIP HIP HOORAY!
YAYYY! BEST DAY EVER!!
SPLAT
LOOKS LIKE SUIKA'S RIGHT.
SURVIVING ALL ALONE WITH TERRIBLE EYESIGHT? IMPRESSIVE.
KZZZT

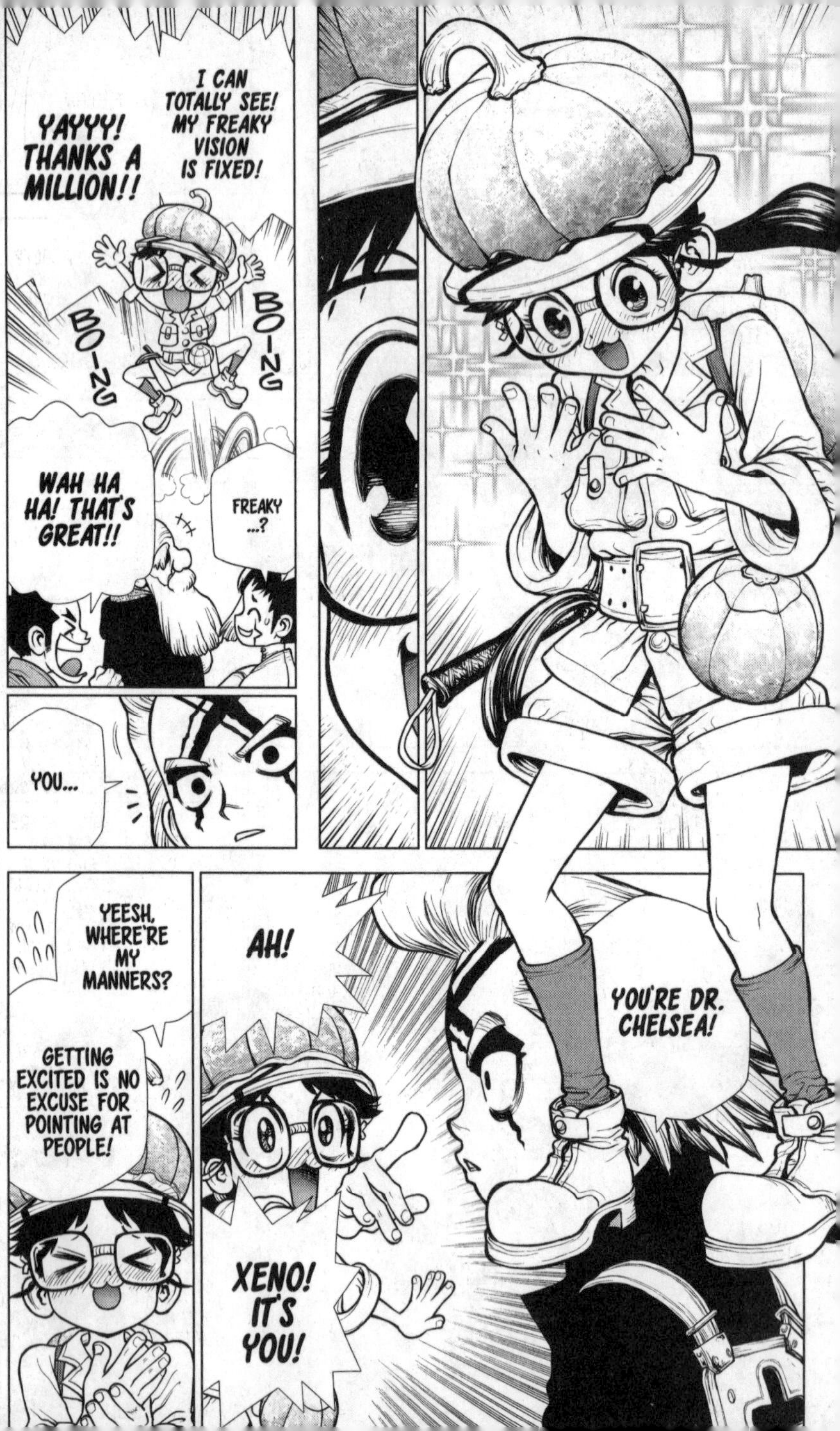
I CAN TOTALLY SEE! MY FREAKY VISION IS FIXED!
YAYYY! THANKS A MILLION!!
BOING
BOING
FREAKY ...?
WAH HA HA! THAT'S GREAT!!
YOU...
YOU'RE DR. CHELSEA!
AH!
XENO! IT'S YOU!
YEESH, WHERE'RE MY MANNERS?
GETTING EXCITED IS NO EXCUSE FOR POINTING AT PEOPLE!

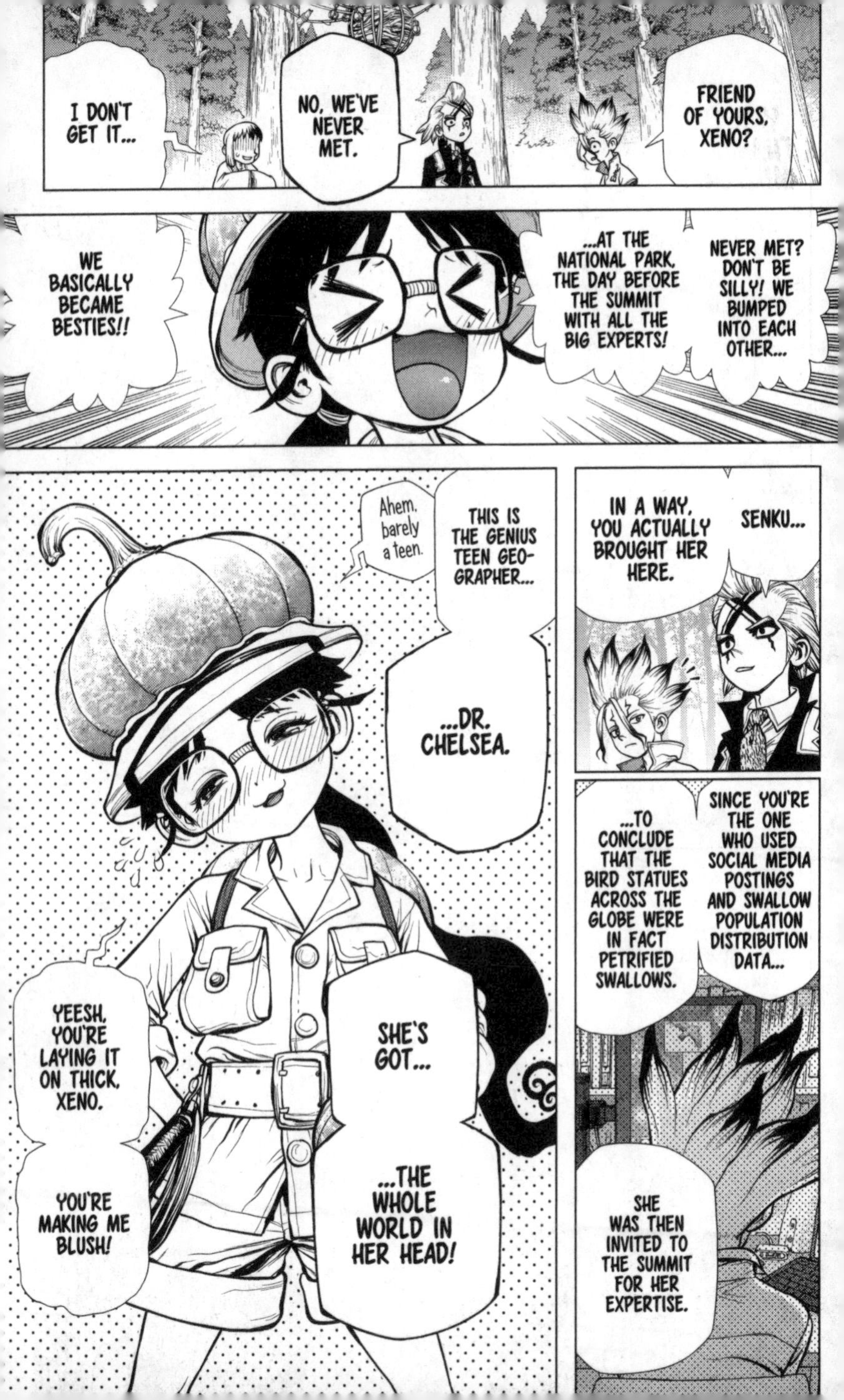
FRIEND OF YOURS, XENO?
NO, WE'VE NEVER MET.
I DON'T GET IT...
NEVER MET? DON'T BE SILLY! WE BUMPED INTO EACH OTHER...
...AT THE NATIONAL PARK, THE DAY BEFORE THE SUMMIT WITH ALL THE BIG EXPERTS!
WE BASICALLY BECAME BESTIES!!
SENKU...
IN A WAY, YOU ACTUALLY BROUGHT HER HERE.
SINCE YOU'RE THE ONE WHO USED SOCIAL MEDIA POSTINGS AND SWALLOW POPULATION DISTRIBUTION DATA...
...TO CONCLUDE THAT THE BIRD STATUES ACROSS THE GLOBE WERE IN FACT PETRIFIED SWALLOWS.
SHE WAS THEN INVITED TO THE SUMMIT FOR HER EXPERTISE.
THIS IS THE GENIUS TEEN GEO-GRAPHER...
Ahem, barely a teen.
...DR. CHELSEA.
SHE'S GOT...
...THE WHOLE WORLD IN HER HEAD!
YEESH, YOU'RE LAYING IT ON THICK, XENO.
YOU'RE MAKING ME BLUSH!

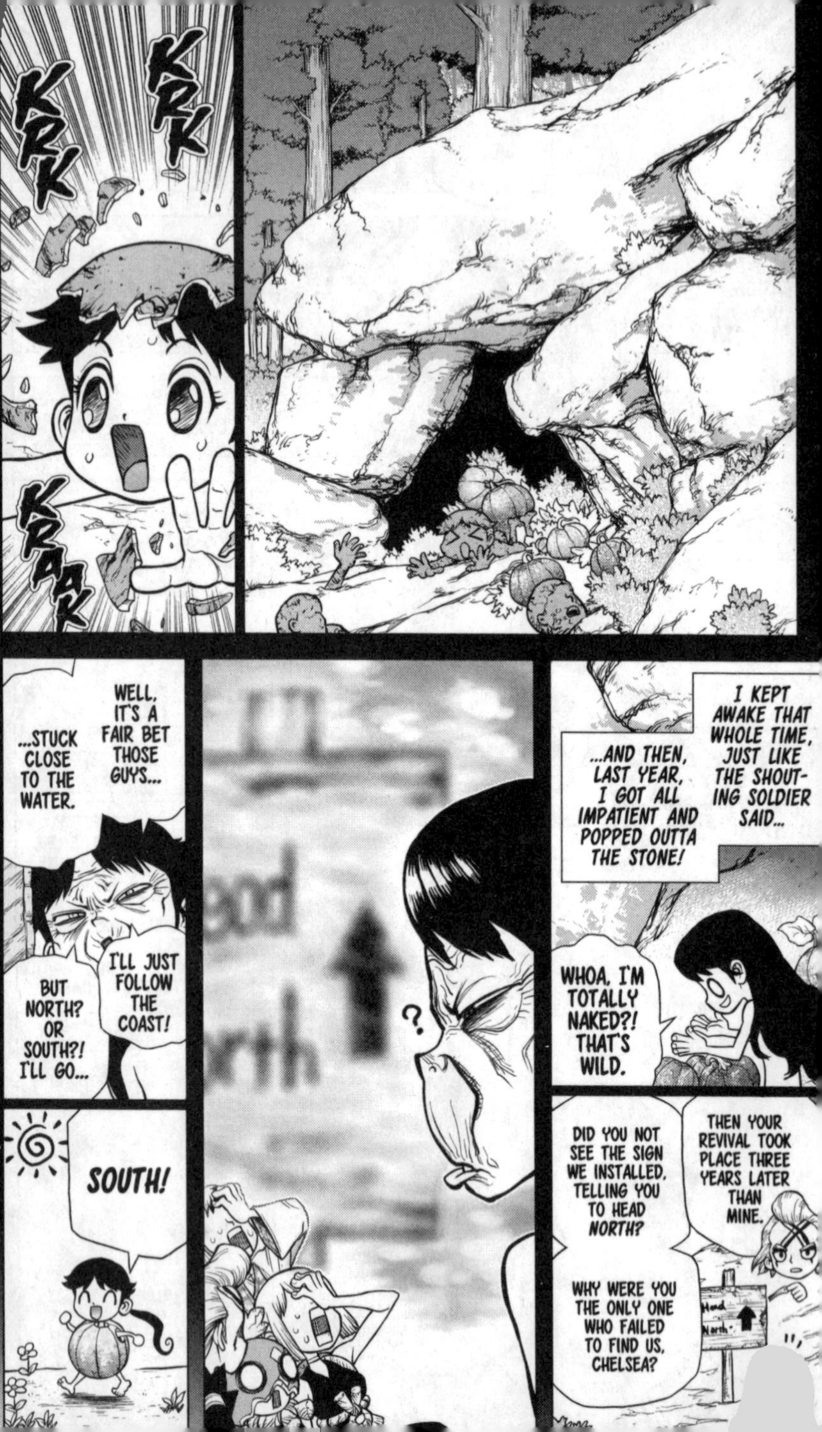
KRK
KRK
KRAAK
I KEPT AWAKE THAT WHOLE TIME, JUST LIKE THE SHOUTING SOLDIER SAID...
...AND THEN, LAST YEAR, I GOT ALL IMPATIENT AND POPPED OUTTA THE STONE!
WHOA, I'M TOTALLY NAKED?! THAT'S WILD.
THEN YOUR REVIVAL TOOK PLACE THREE YEARS LATER THAN MINE.
DID YOU NOT SEE THE SIGN WE INSTALLED, TELLING YOU TO HEAD NORTH?
WHY WERE YOU THE ONLY ONE WHO FAILED TO FIND US, CHELSEA?
Head North
?
WELL, IT'S A FAIR BET THOSE GUYS...
...STUCK CLOSE TO THE WATER.
I'LL JUST FOLLOW THE COAST!
BUT NORTH? OR SOUTH?! I'LL GO...
SOUTH!

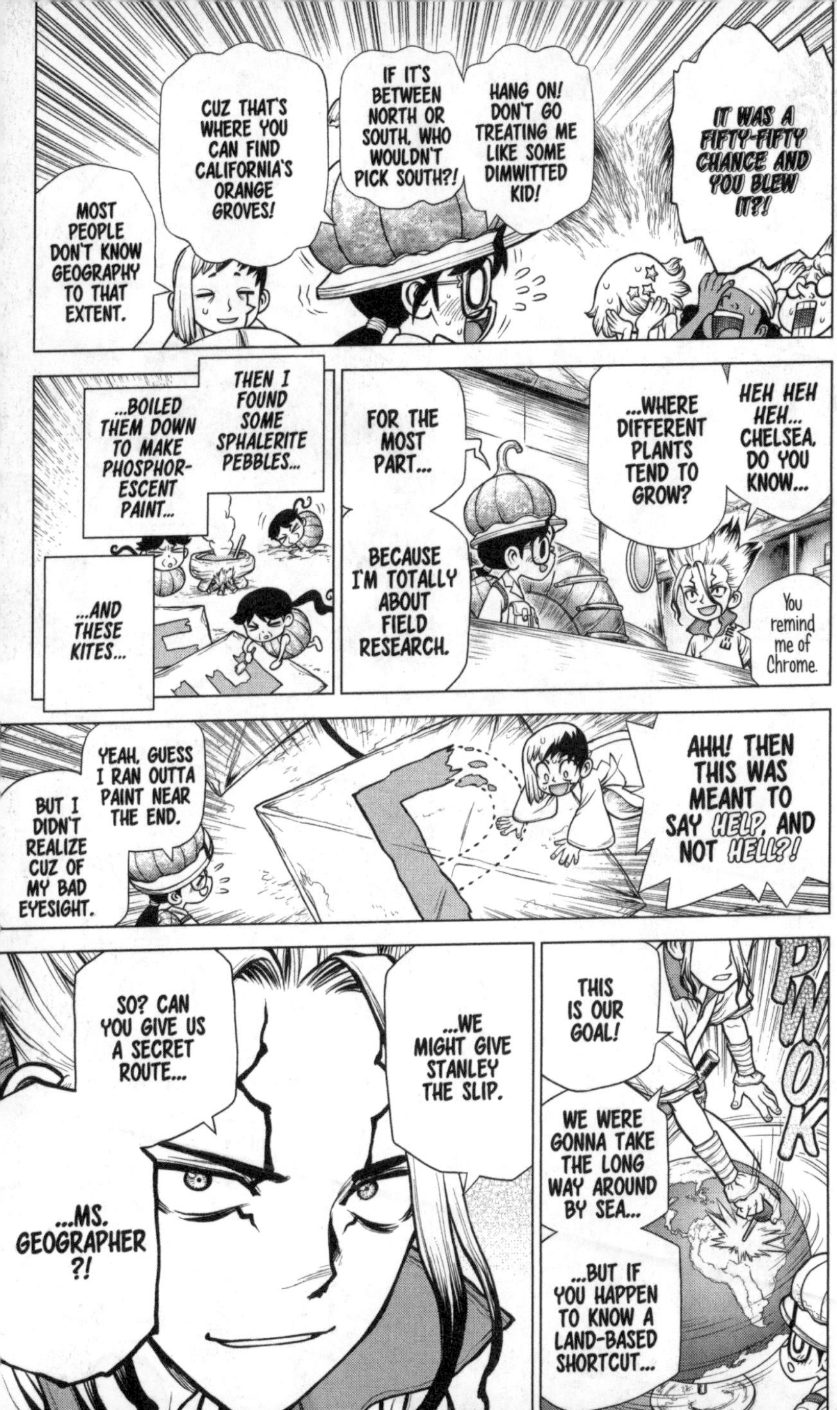
IT WAS A FIFTY-FIFTY CHANCE AND YOU BLEW IT?!
HANG ON! DON'T GO TREATING ME LIKE SOME DIMWITTED KID!
IF IT'S BETWEEN NORTH OR SOUTH, WHO WOULDN'T PICK SOUTH?!
CUZ THAT'S WHERE YOU CAN FIND CALIFORNIA'S ORANGE GROVES!
MOST PEOPLE DON'T KNOW GEOGRAPHY TO THAT EXTENT.
HEH HEH HEH... CHELSEA, DO YOU KNOW...
...WHERE DIFFERENT PLANTS TEND TO GROW?
You remind me of Chrome.
FOR THE MOST PART...
BECAUSE I'M TOTALLY ABOUT FIELD RESEARCH.
THEN I FOUND SOME SPHALERITE PEBBLES...
...BOILED THEM DOWN TO MAKE PHOSPHOR-ESCENT PAINT...
...AND THESE KITES...
AHH! THEN THIS WAS MEANT TO SAY HELP, AND NOT HELL?!
YEAH, GUESS I RAN OUTTA PAINT NEAR THE END.
BUT I DIDN'T REALIZE CUZ OF MY BAD EYESIGHT.
PWOK
THIS IS OUR GOAL!
WE WERE GONNA TAKE THE LONG WAY AROUND BY SEA...
...BUT IF YOU HAPPEN TO KNOW A LAND-BASED SHORTCUT...
...WE MIGHT GIVE STANLEY THE SLIP.
SO? CAN YOU GIVE US A SECRET ROUTE...
...MS. GEOGRAPHER?!

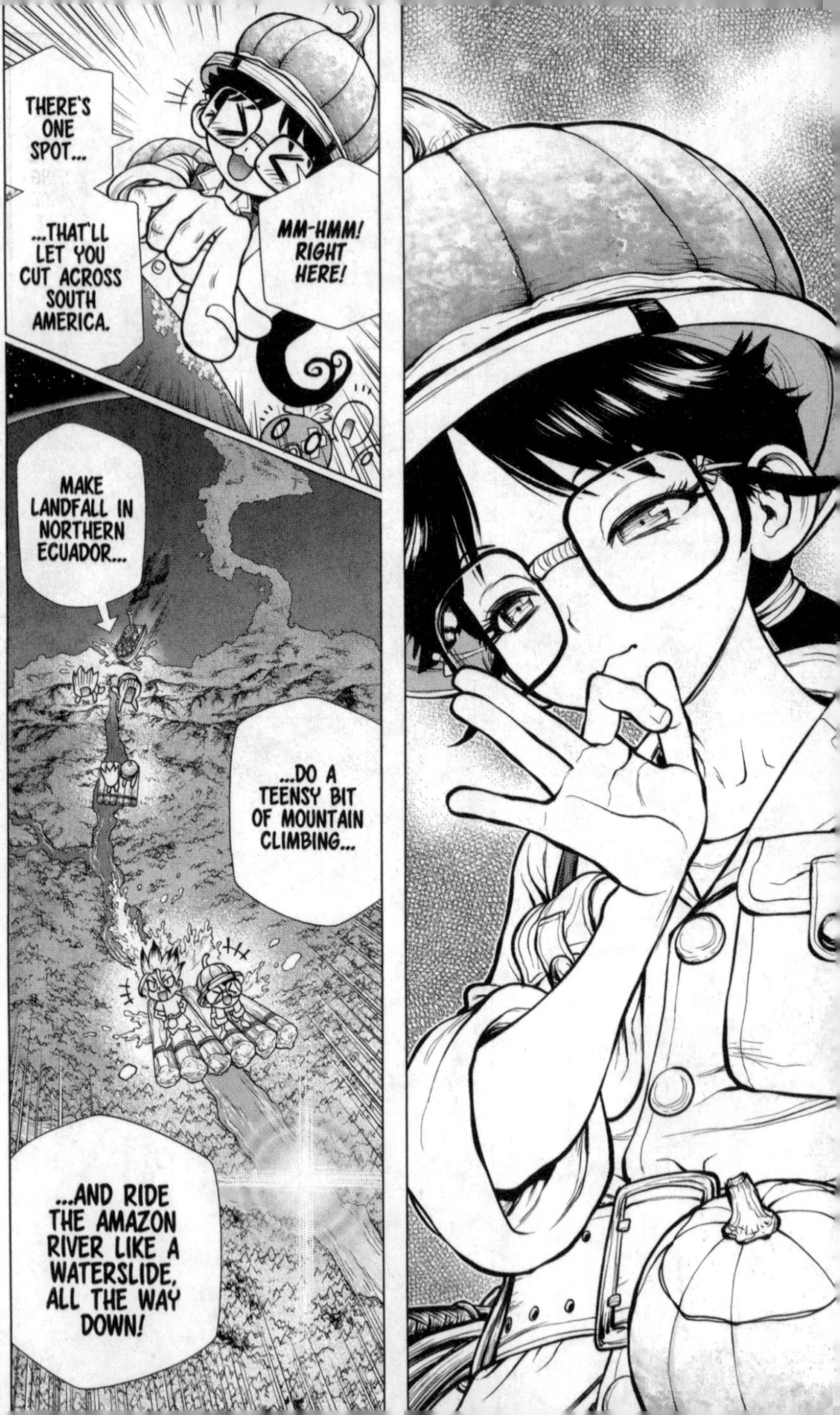
THERE'S ONE SPOT...
...THAT'LL LET YOU CUT ACROSS SOUTH AMERICA.
MM-HMM! RIGHT HERE!
MAKE LANDFALL IN NORTHERN ECUADOR...
...DO A TEENSY BIT OF MOUNTAIN CLIMBING...
...AND RIDE THE AMAZON RIVER LIKE A WATERSLIDE, ALL THE WAY DOWN!

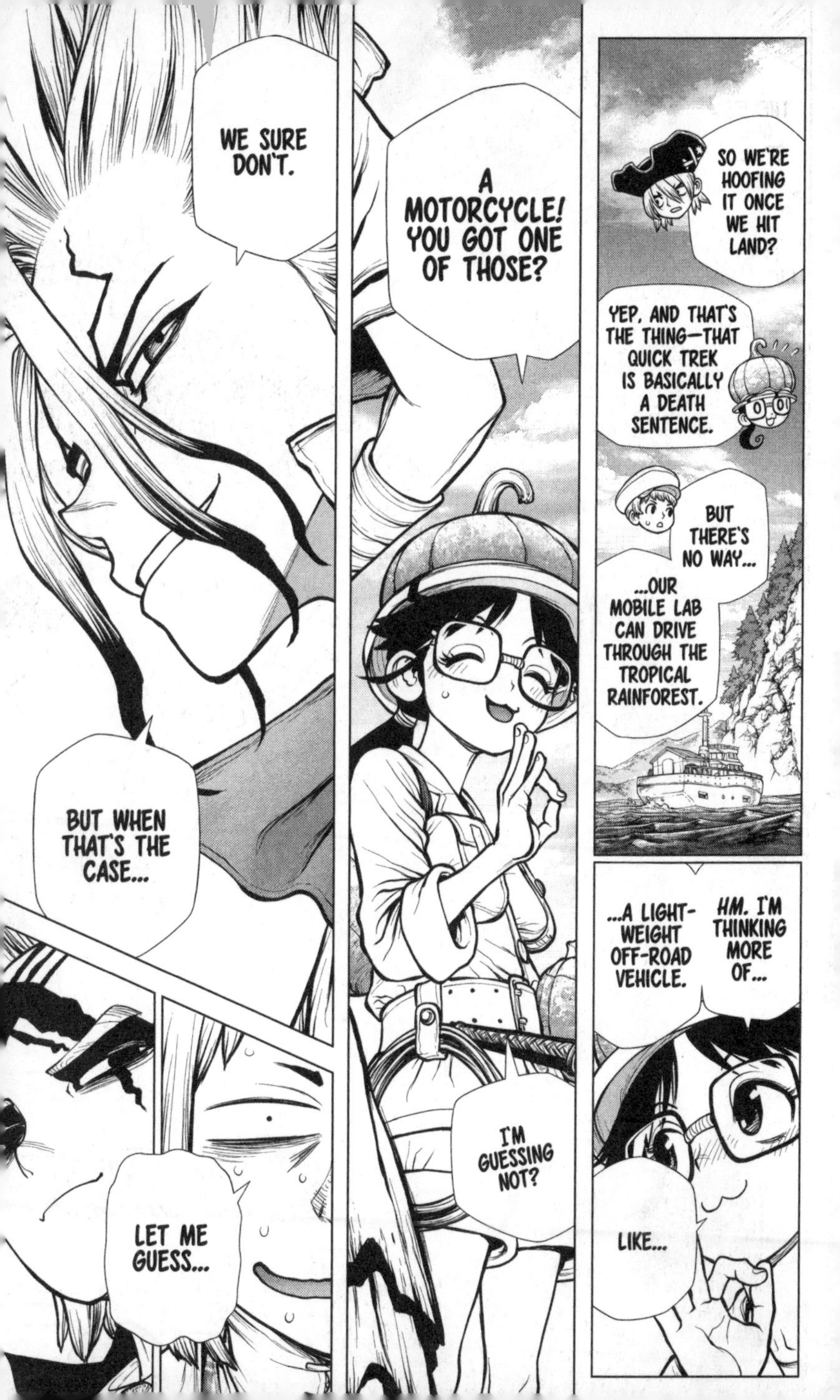
SO WE'RE HOOFING IT ONCE WE HIT LAND?
YEP, AND THAT'S THE THING—THAT QUICK TREK IS BASICALLY A DEATH SENTENCE.
BUT THERE'S NO WAY...
...OUR MOBILE LAB CAN DRIVE THROUGH THE TROPICAL RAINFOREST.
HM. I'M THINKING MORE OF...
...A LIGHT-WEIGHT OFF-ROAD VEHICLE.
LIKE...
A MOTORCYCLE! YOU GOT ONE OF THOSE?
I'M GUESSING NOT?
WE SURE DON'T.
BUT WHEN THAT'S THE CASE...
LET ME GUESS...

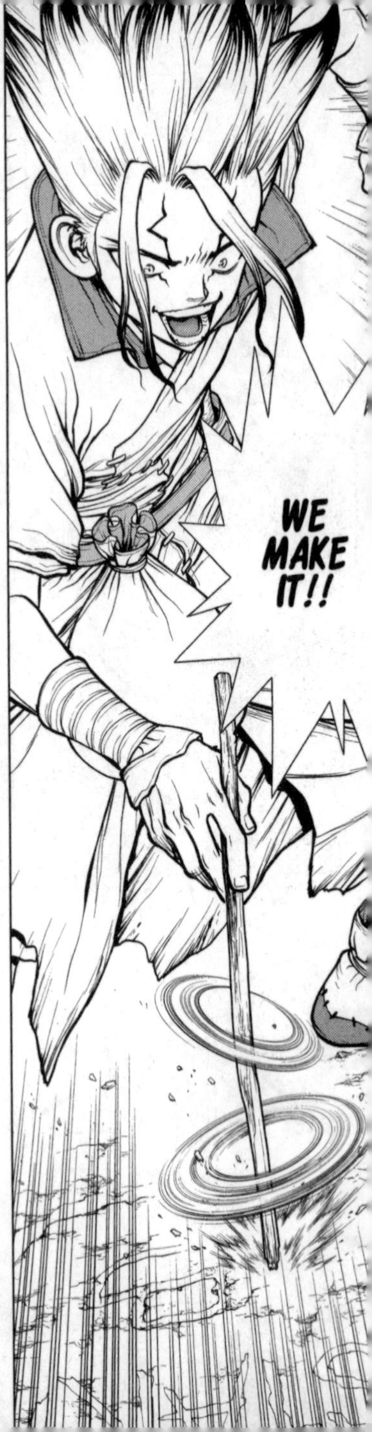
WE MAKE IT!!

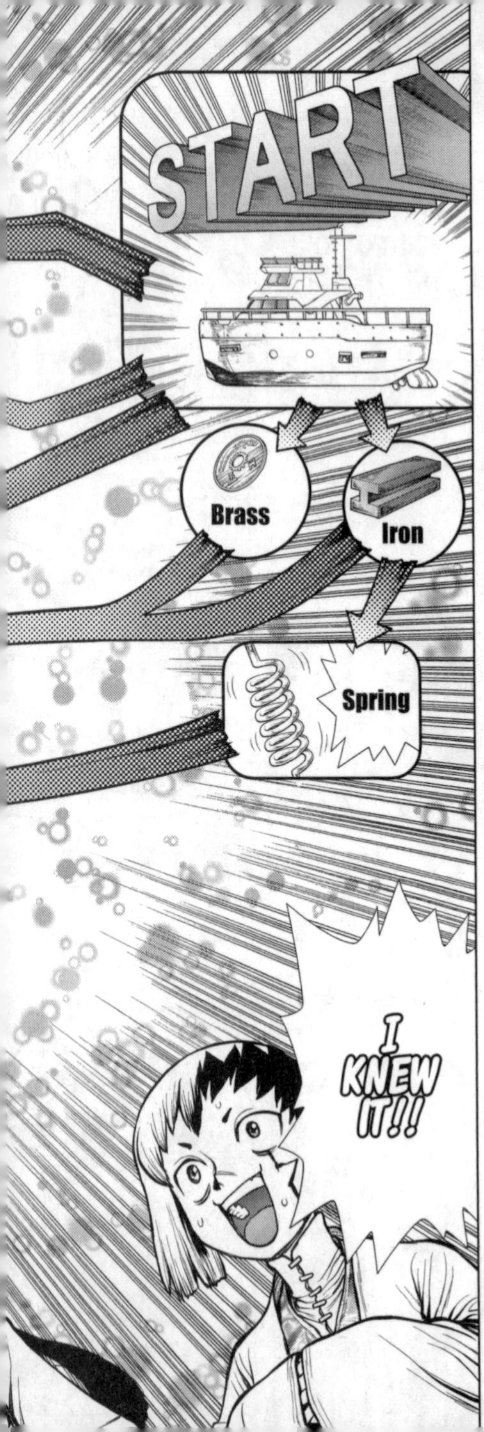
START
Brass
Iron
Spring
I KNEW IT!!

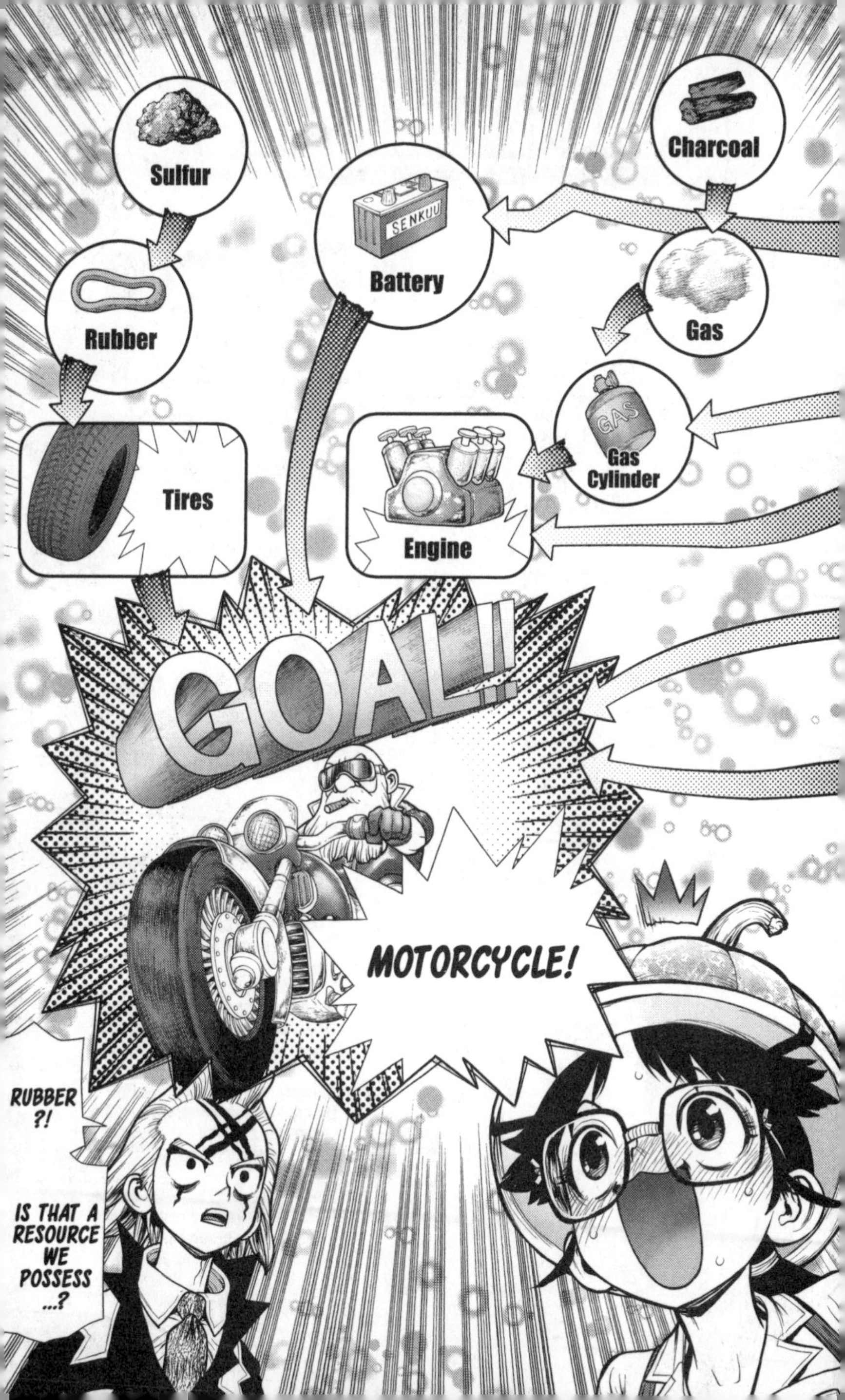
Charcoal
Gas
Gas Cylinder
GAS
Battery
SENKUU
Sulfur
Rubber
Engine
Tires
GOAL!!
MOTORCYCLE!
RUBBER ?!
IS THAT A RESOURCE WE POSSESS ...?

Kingdom of Science

WORKER FILE ⑨

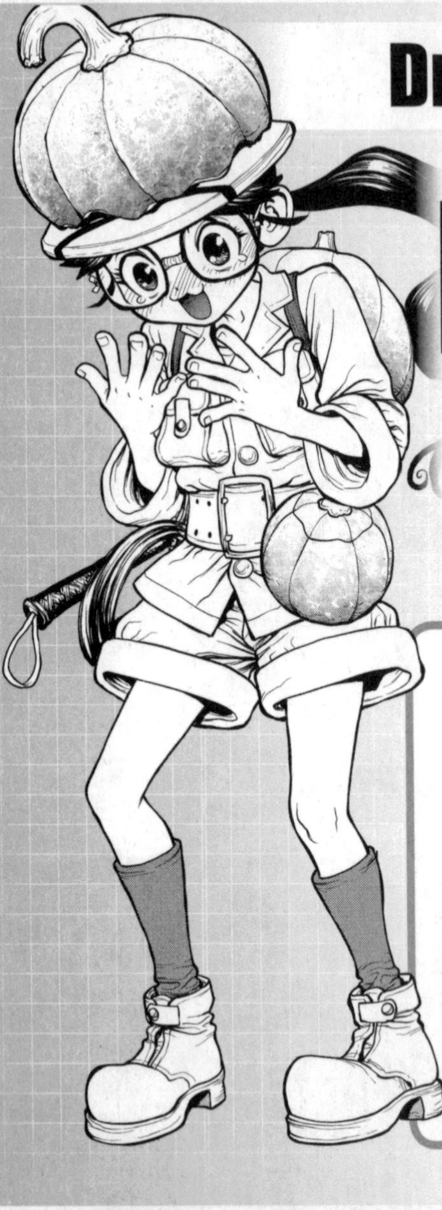

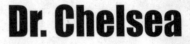

Dr. Chelsea

Geography:	★★★★★
Exploration:	★★★★
Tact:	★

Full Name: Chelsea Childe

Height: 148 cm

Job in Kingdom: Geographer

Chelsea loves using her own two feet to get out there and do field research! She can draw a topographic map of the entire world purely from memory.

Even her research papers are peppered with her unique speech quirks, but it's such high-level stuff that nobody dares to complain.

Since she treats everyone with the same flippant approach—and never out of ill will—it's hard to hold it against her.

That overly causal behavior comes from her belief that once you're introduced to someone, that automatically makes you pals!

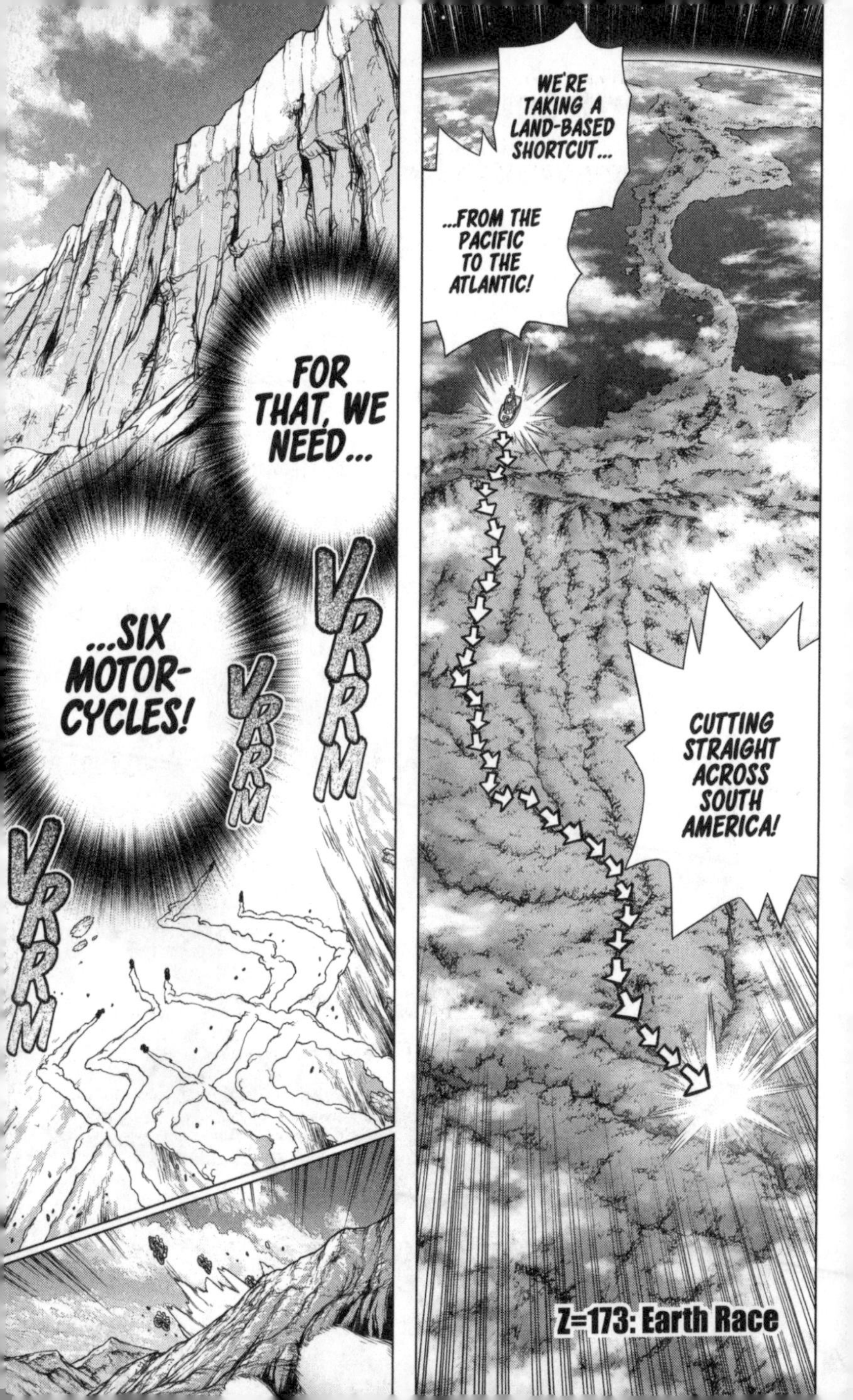
WE'RE TAKING A LAND-BASED SHORTCUT...
...FROM THE PACIFIC TO THE ATLANTIC!
CUTTING STRAIGHT ACROSS SOUTH AMERICA!
Z=173: Earth Race
FOR THAT, WE NEED...
...SIX MOTOR-CYCLES!
VRRM
VRRM
VRRM

Z=173: Earth Race

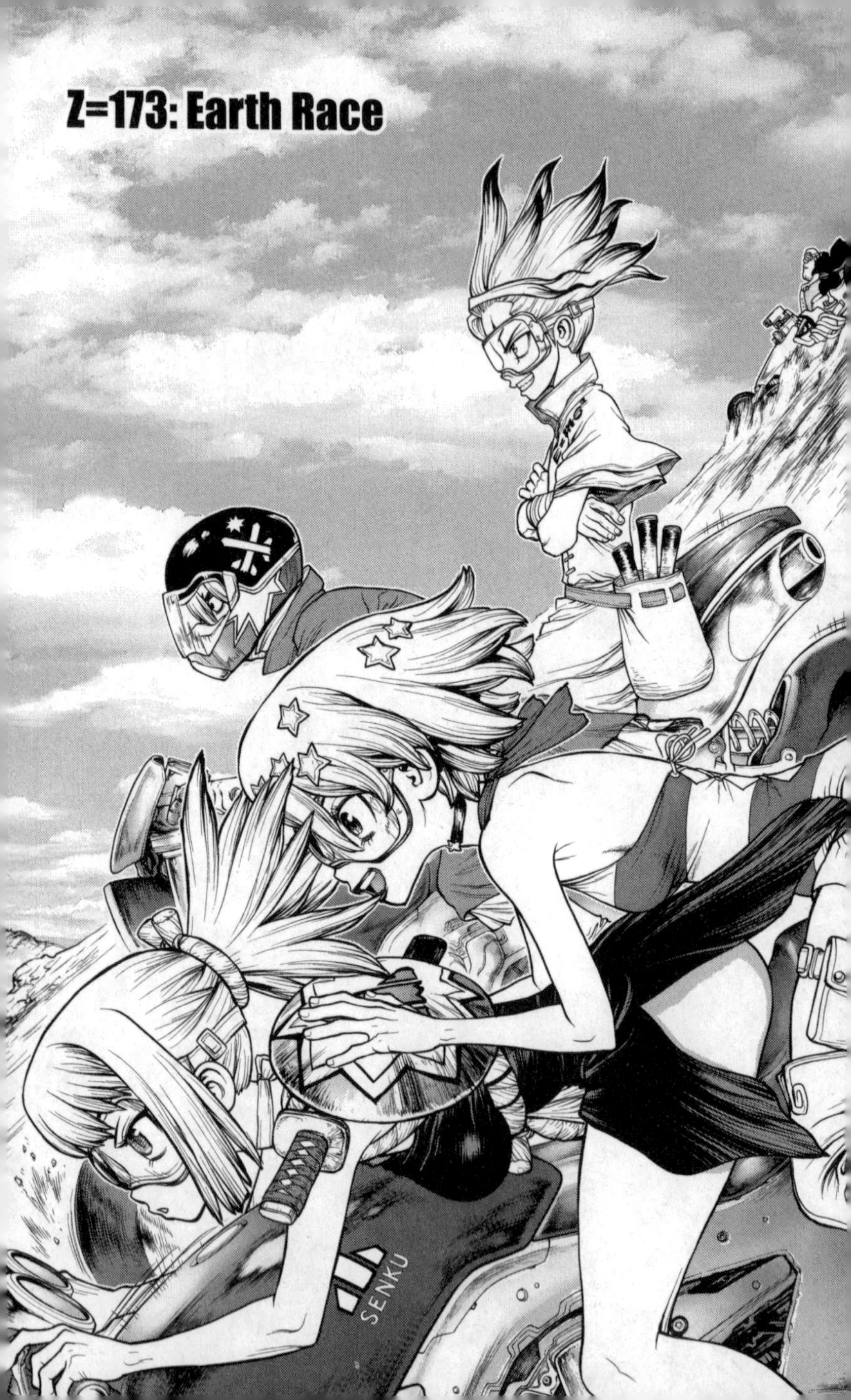
SENKU

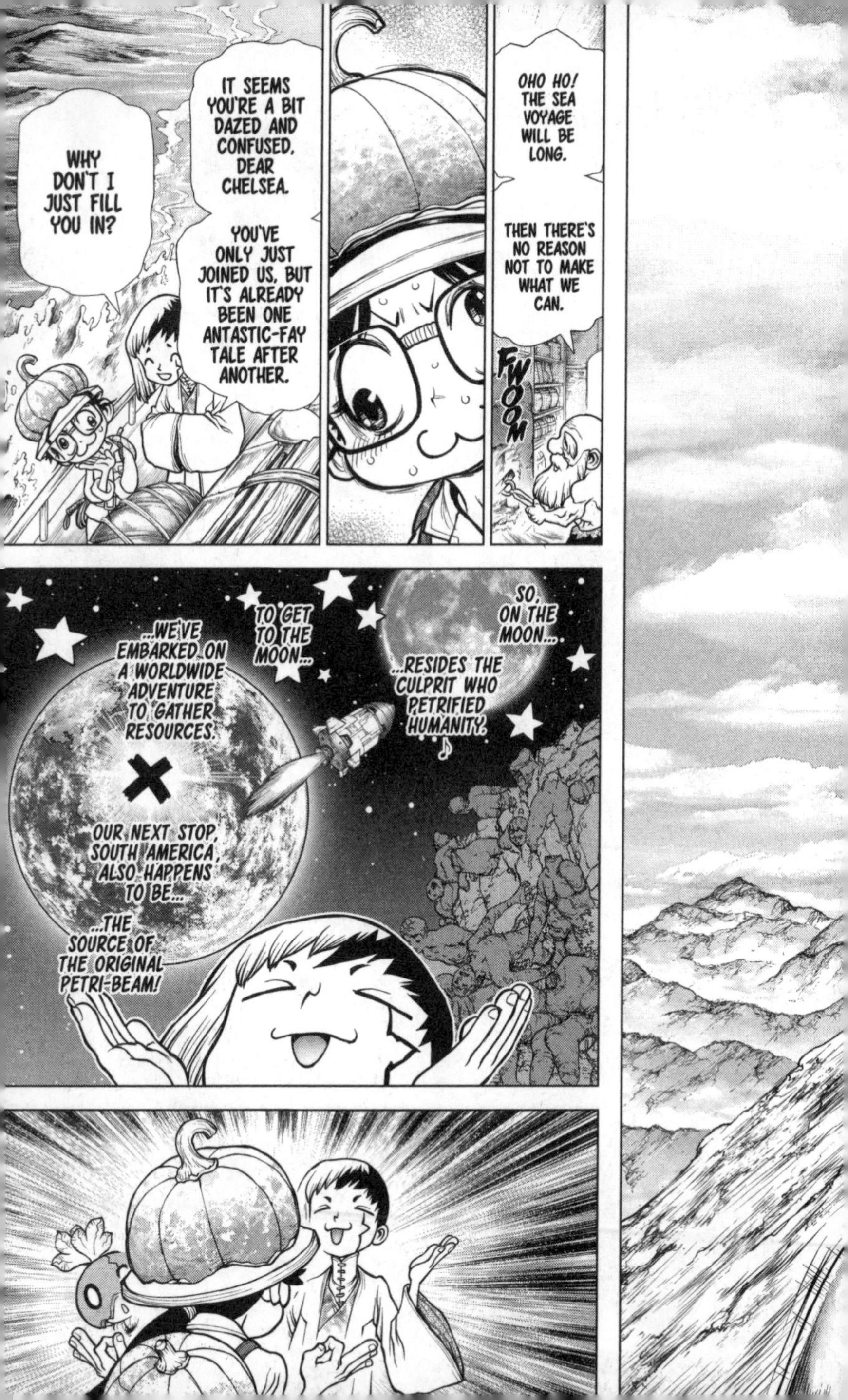
OHO HO! THE SEA VOYAGE WILL BE LONG.
THEN THERE'S NO REASON NOT TO MAKE WHAT WE CAN.
FWOOM
IT SEEMS YOU'RE A BIT DAZED AND CONFUSED, DEAR CHELSEA.
YOU'VE ONLY JUST JOINED US, BUT IT'S ALREADY BEEN ONE ANTASTIC-FAY TALE AFTER ANOTHER.
WHY DON'T I JUST FILL YOU IN?
SO, ON THE MOON...
...RESIDES THE CULPRIT WHO PETRIFIED HUMANITY.
TO GET TO THE MOON...
...WE'VE EMBARKED ON A WORLDWIDE ADVENTURE TO GATHER RESOURCES.
OUR NEXT STOP, SOUTH AMERICA, ALSO HAPPENS TO BE...
...THE SOURCE OF THE ORIGINAL PETRI-BEAM!

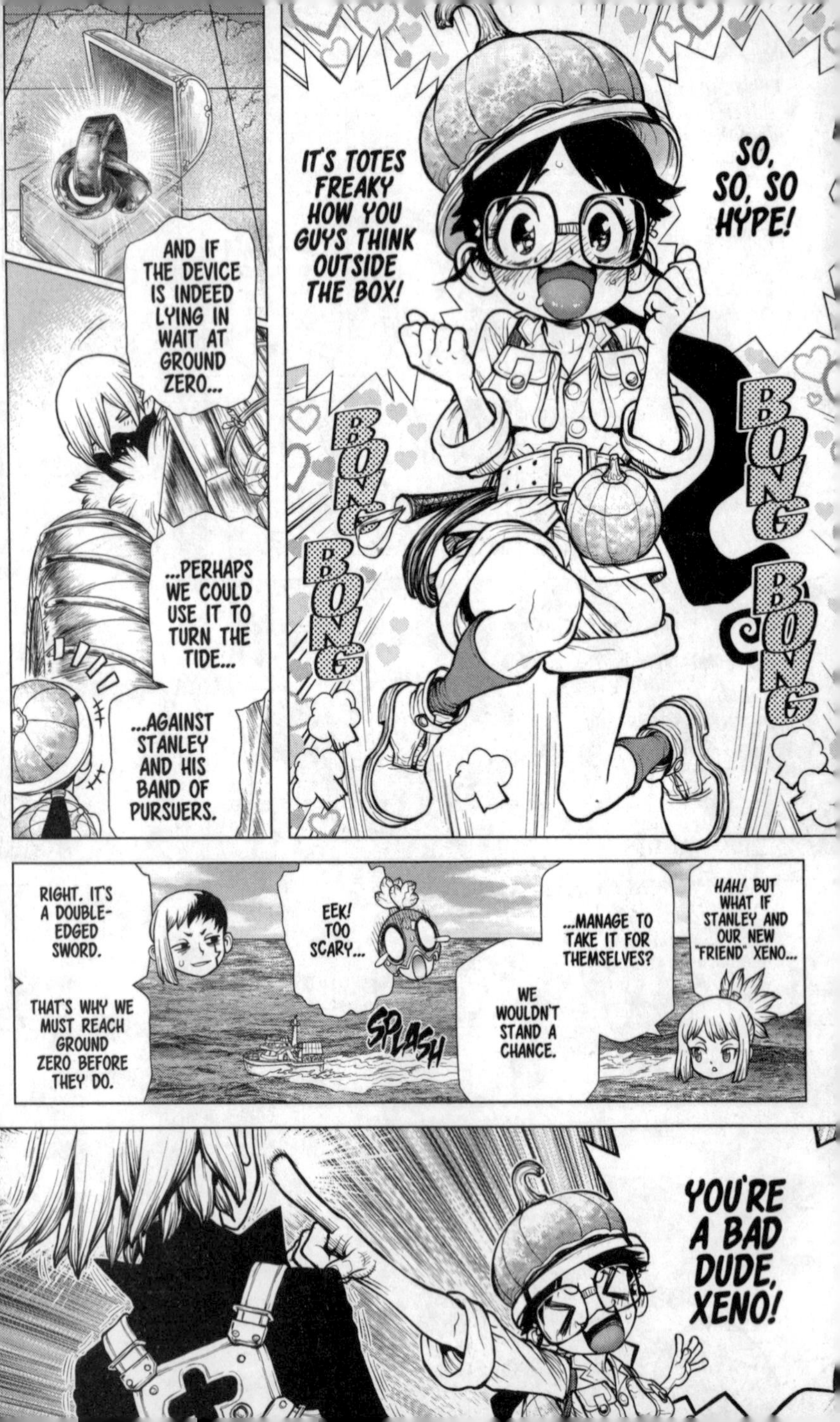
SO, SO, SO HYPE!
BONG BONG
BONG BONG
IT'S TOTES FREAKY HOW YOU GUYS THINK OUTSIDE THE BOX!
AND IF THE DEVICE IS INDEED LYING IN WAIT AT GROUND ZERO...
...PERHAPS WE COULD USE IT TO TURN THE TIDE...
...AGAINST STANLEY AND HIS BAND OF PURSUERS.
HAH! BUT WHAT IF STANLEY AND OUR NEW "FRIEND" XENO...
...MANAGE TO TAKE IT FOR THEMSELVES?
WE WOULDN'T STAND A CHANCE.
EEK! TOO SCARY...
SPLASH
RIGHT. IT'S A DOUBLE-EDGED SWORD.
THAT'S WHY WE MUST REACH GROUND ZERO BEFORE THEY DO.
YOU'RE A BAD DUDE, XENO!

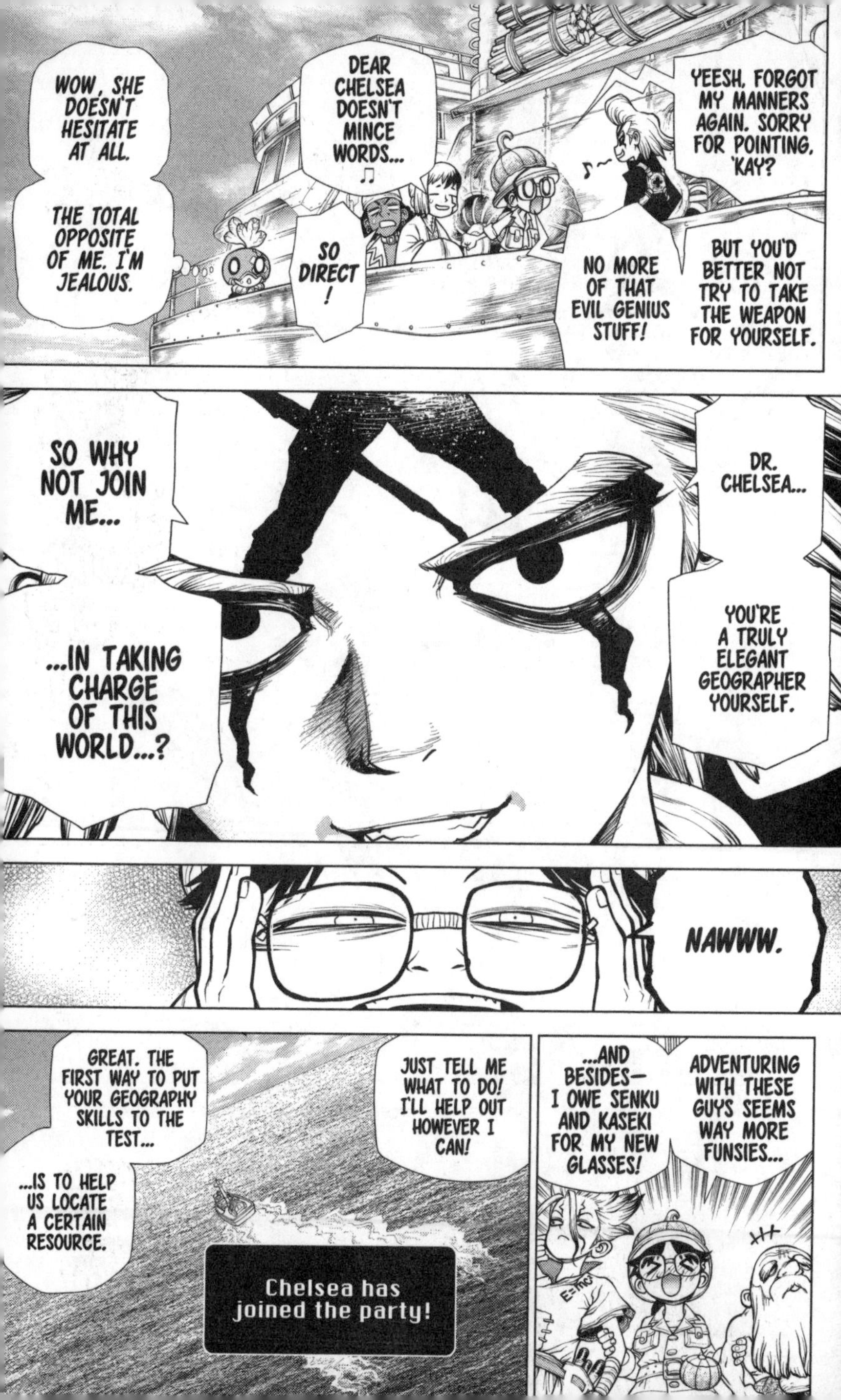
YEESH, FORGOT MY MANNERS AGAIN. SORRY FOR POINTING, 'KAY?
BUT YOU'D BETTER NOT TRY TO TAKE THE WEAPON FOR YOURSELF.
NO MORE OF THAT EVIL GENIUS STUFF!
DEAR CHELSEA DOESN'T MINCE WORDS... ♫
SO DIRECT!
WOW, SHE DOESN'T HESITATE AT ALL.
THE TOTAL OPPOSITE OF ME. I'M JEALOUS.
DR. CHELSEA...
YOU'RE A TRULY ELEGANT GEOGRAPHER YOURSELF.
SO WHY NOT JOIN ME...
...IN TAKING CHARGE OF THIS WORLD...?
NAWWW.
ADVENTURING WITH THESE GUYS SEEMS WAY MORE FUNSIES...
...AND BESIDES— I OWE SENKU AND KASEKI FOR MY NEW GLASSES!
E=mc²
JUST TELL ME WHAT TO DO! I'LL HELP OUT HOWEVER I CAN!
GREAT. THE FIRST WAY TO PUT YOUR GEOGRAPHY SKILLS TO THE TEST...
...IS TO HELP US LOCATE A CERTAIN RESOURCE.
Chelsea has joined the party!

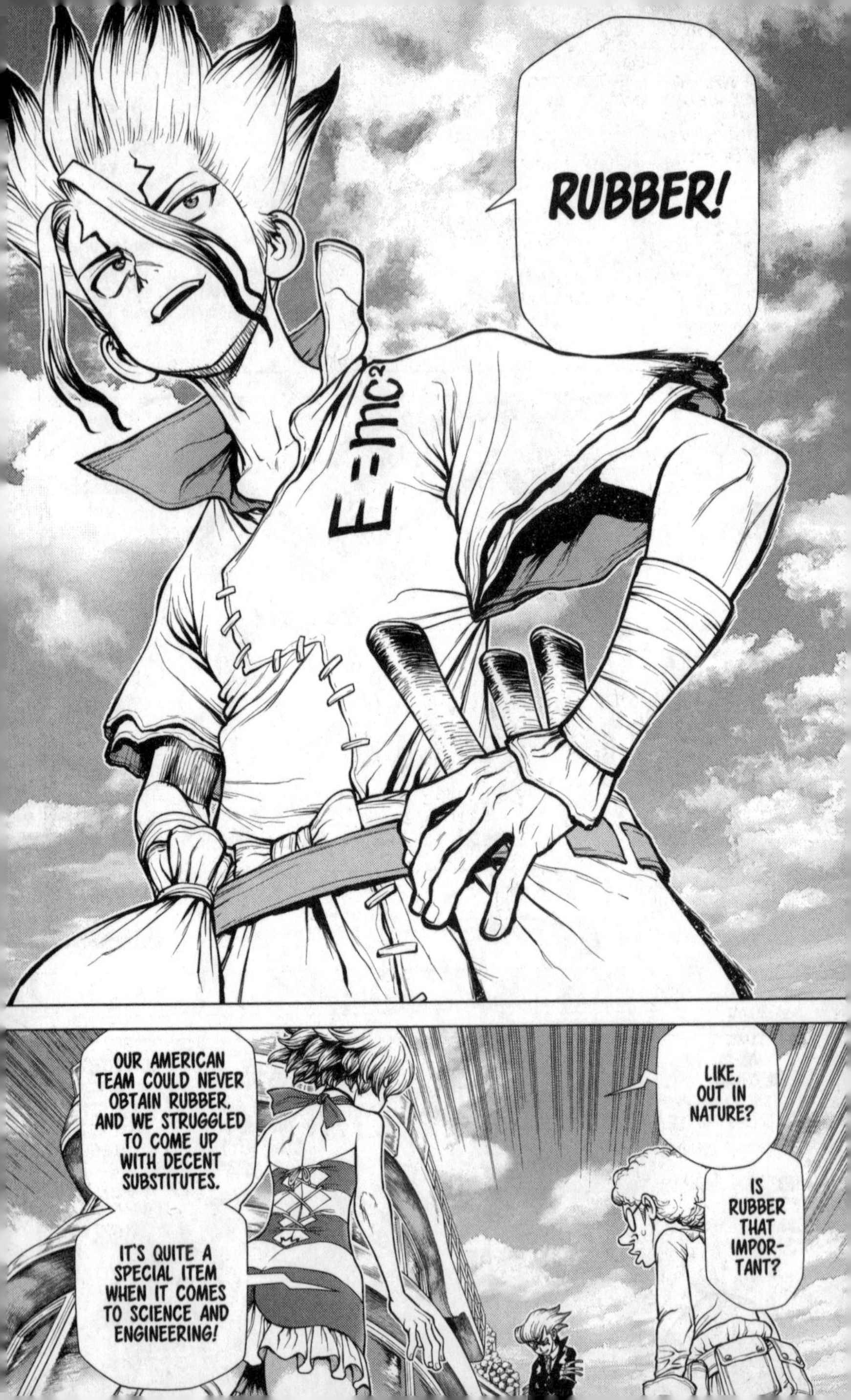
RUBBER!
$E=mc^2$
LIKE, OUT IN NATURE?
IS RUBBER THAT IMPORTANT?
OUR AMERICAN TEAM COULD NEVER OBTAIN RUBBER, AND WE STRUGGLED TO COME UP WITH DECENT SUBSTITUTES.
IT'S QUITE A SPECIAL ITEM WHEN IT COMES TO SCIENCE AND ENGINEERING!

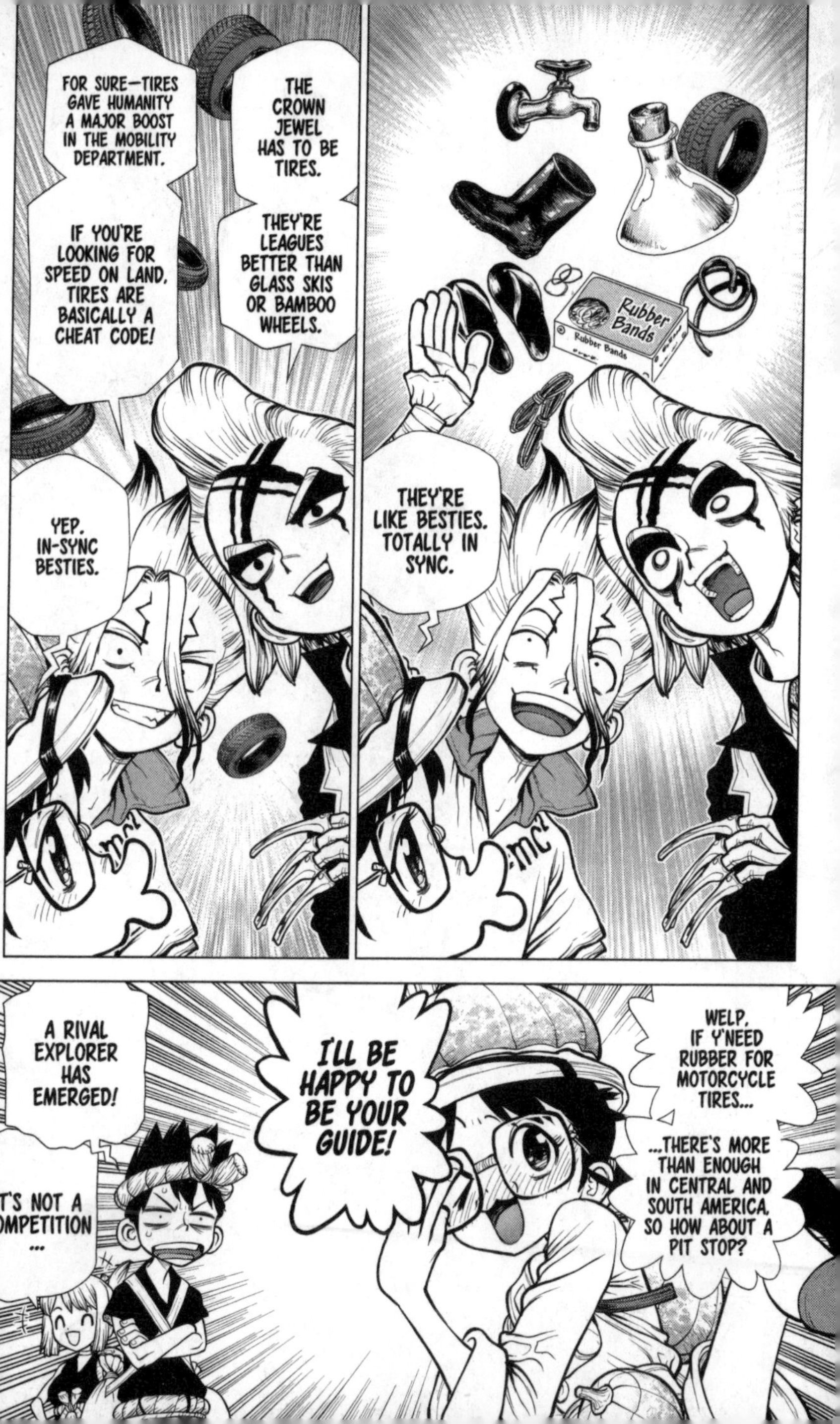
Rubber Bands
Rubber Bands
THEY'RE LIKE BESTIES. TOTALLY IN SYNC.
THE CROWN JEWEL HAS TO BE TIRES.
THEY'RE LEAGUES BETTER THAN GLASS SKIS OR BAMBOO WHEELS.
FOR SURE—TIRES GAVE HUMANITY A MAJOR BOOST IN THE MOBILITY DEPARTMENT.
IF YOU'RE LOOKING FOR SPEED ON LAND, TIRES ARE BASICALLY A CHEAT CODE!
YEP. IN-SYNC BESTIES.
WELP, IF Y'NEED RUBBER FOR MOTORCYCLE TIRES...
...THERE'S MORE THAN ENOUGH IN CENTRAL AND SOUTH AMERICA, SO HOW ABOUT A PIT STOP?
I'LL BE HAPPY TO BE YOUR GUIDE!
A RIVAL EXPLORER HAS EMERGED!
IT'S NOT A COMPETITION...

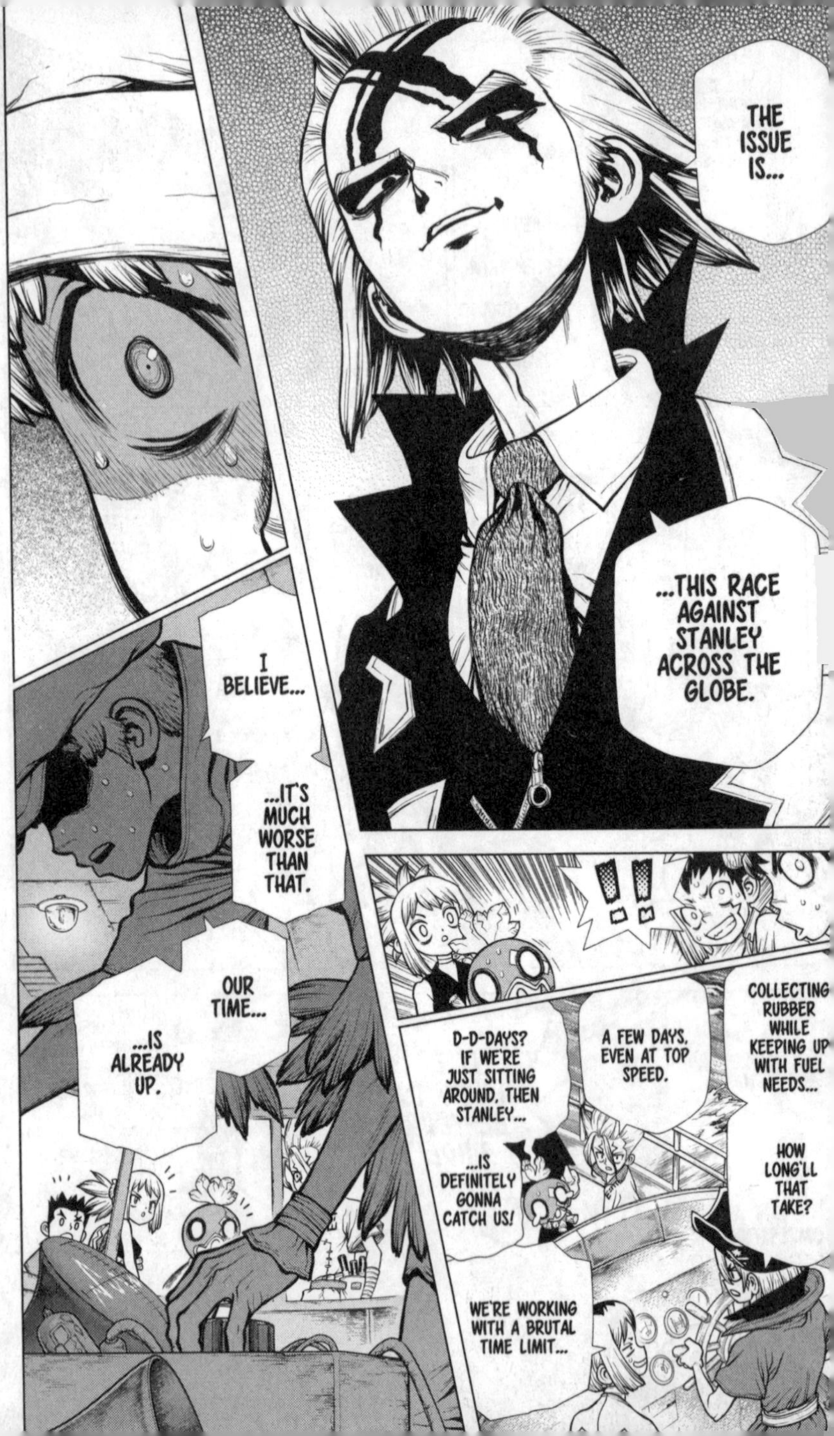
THE ISSUE IS...
...THIS RACE AGAINST STANLEY ACROSS THE GLOBE.
!!
COLLECTING RUBBER WHILE KEEPING UP WITH FUEL NEEDS...
HOW LONG'LL THAT TAKE?
A FEW DAYS, EVEN AT TOP SPEED.
D-D-DAYS? IF WE'RE JUST SITTING AROUND, THEN STANLEY...
...IS DEFINITELY GONNA CATCH US!
WE'RE WORKING WITH A BRUTAL TIME LIMIT...
I BELIEVE...
...IT'S MUCH WORSE THAN THAT.
OUR TIME...
...IS ALREADY UP.

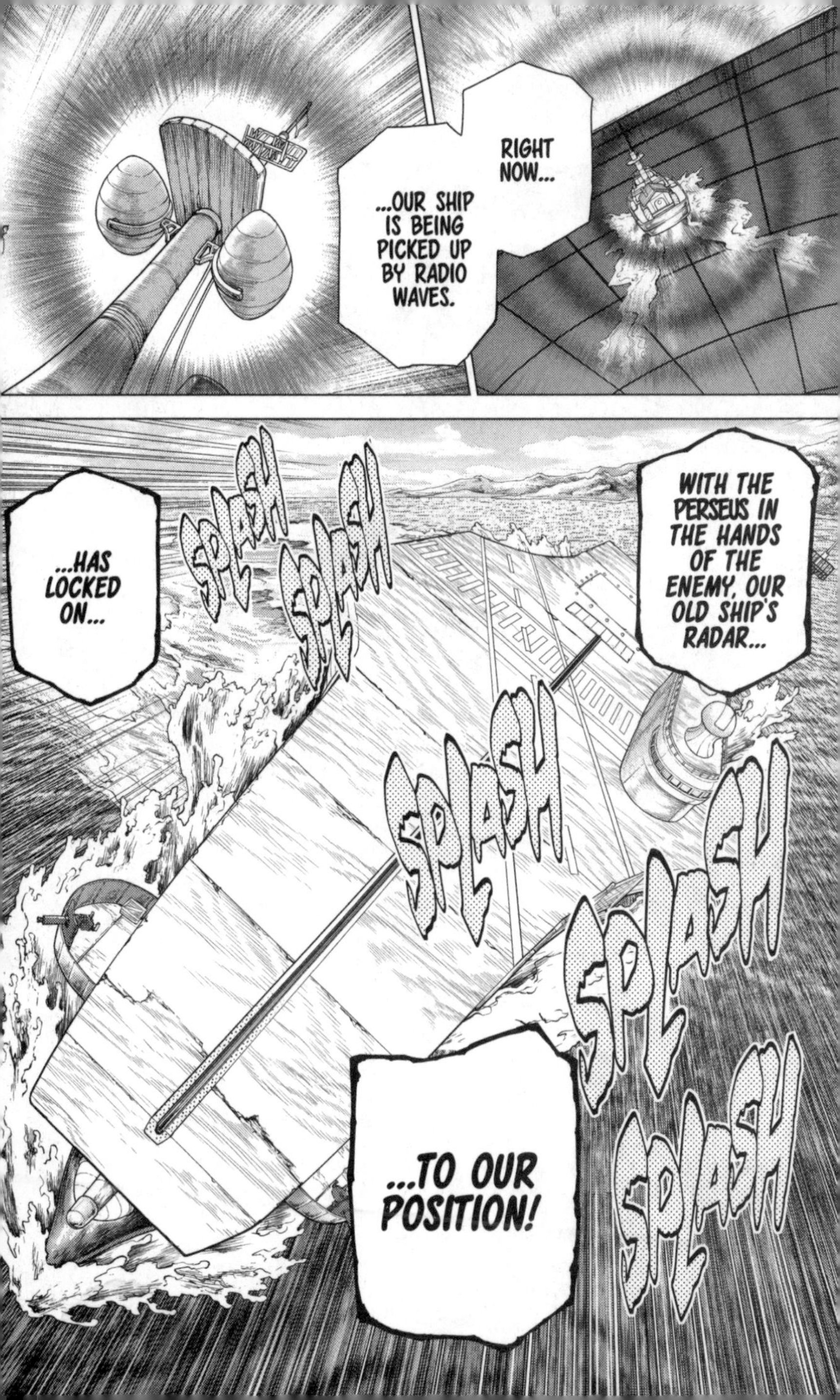
RIGHT NOW...
...OUR SHIP IS BEING PICKED UP BY RADIO WAVES.
WITH THE PERSEUS IN THE HANDS OF THE ENEMY, OUR OLD SHIP'S RADAR...
SPLASH
SPLASH
...HAS LOCKED ON...
SPLASH
SPLASH
SPLASH
SPLASH
...TO OUR POSITION!

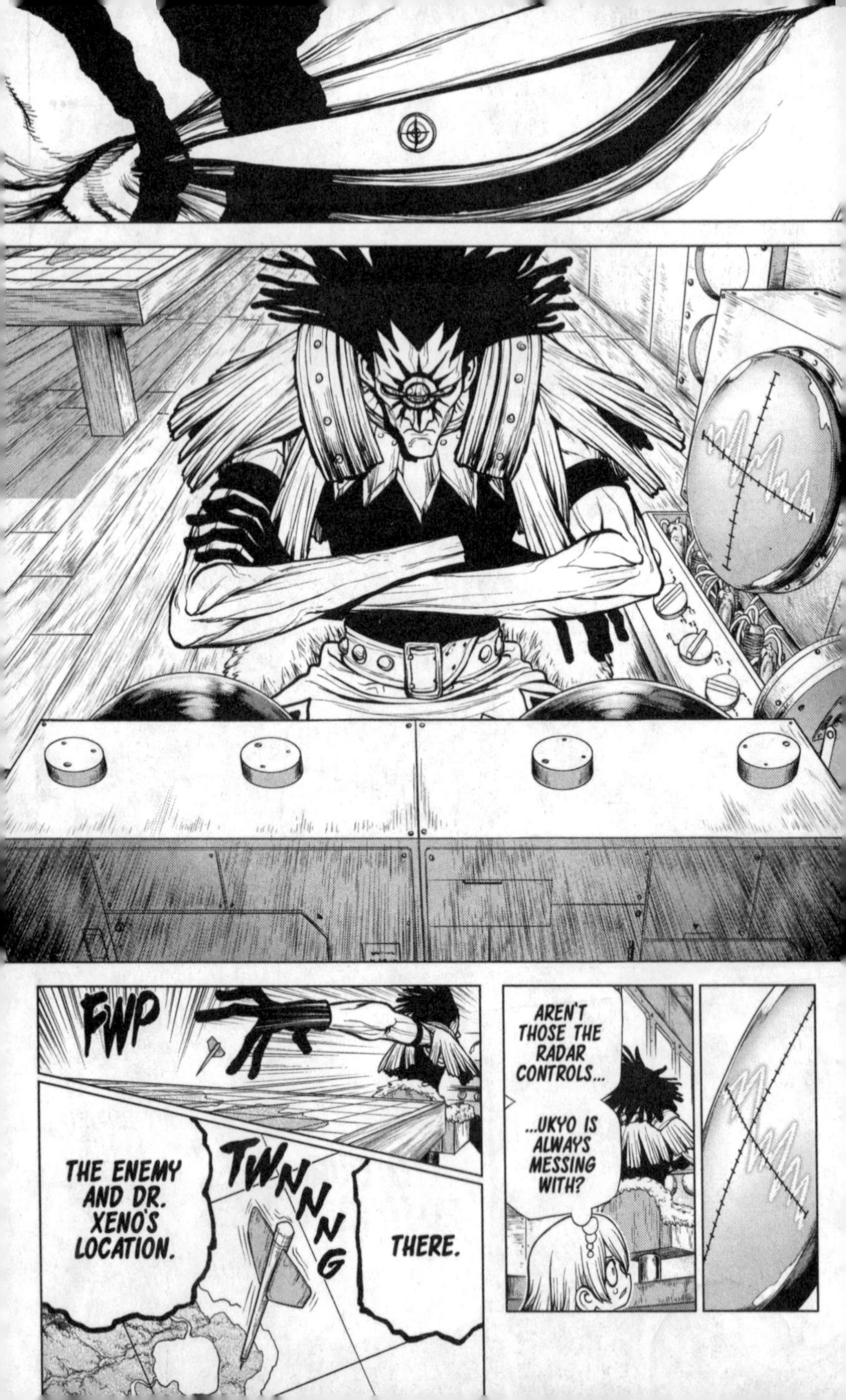
AREN'T THOSE THE RADAR CONTROLS...
...UKYO IS ALWAYS MESSING WITH?
FWP
TWNNNG
THERE.
THE ENEMY AND DR. XENO'S LOCATION.

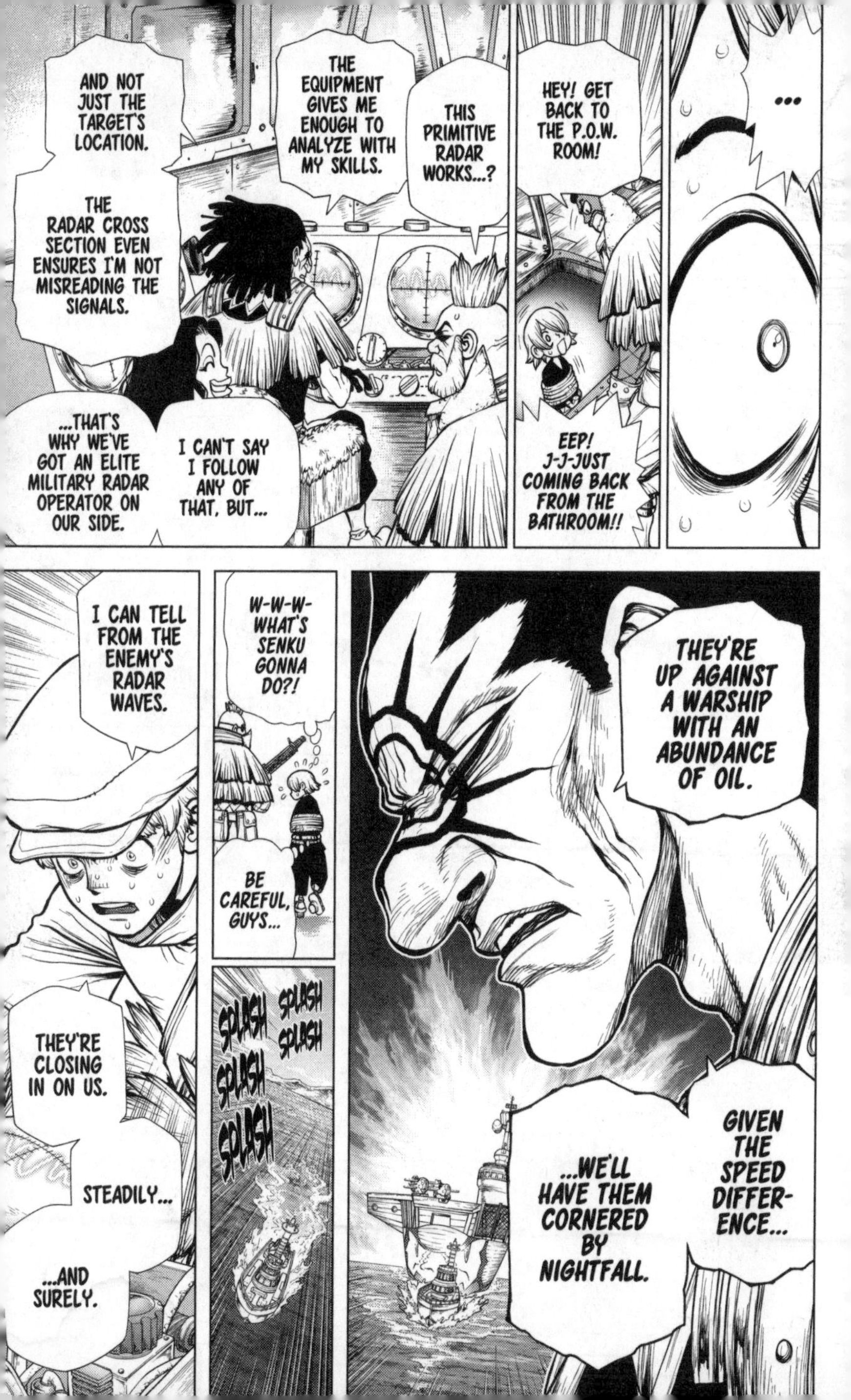
...
HEY! GET BACK TO THE P.O.W. ROOM!
EEP! J-J-JUST COMING BACK FROM THE BATHROOM!!
THIS PRIMITIVE RADAR WORKS...?
THE EQUIPMENT GIVES ME ENOUGH TO ANALYZE WITH MY SKILLS.
AND NOT JUST THE TARGET'S LOCATION.
THE RADAR CROSS SECTION EVEN ENSURES I'M NOT MISREADING THE SIGNALS.
I CAN'T SAY I FOLLOW ANY OF THAT, BUT...
...THAT'S WHY WE'VE GOT AN ELITE MILITARY RADAR OPERATOR ON OUR SIDE.
THEY'RE UP AGAINST A WARSHIP WITH AN ABUNDANCE OF OIL.
GIVEN THE SPEED DIFFERENCE...
...WE'LL HAVE THEM CORNERED BY NIGHTFALL.
W-W-W-WHAT'S SENKU GONNA DO?!
BE CAREFUL, GUYS...
SPLASH SPLASH
SPLASH SPLASH
SPLASH
I CAN TELL FROM THE ENEMY'S RADAR WAVES.
THEY'RE CLOSING IN ON US.
STEADILY...
...AND SURELY.

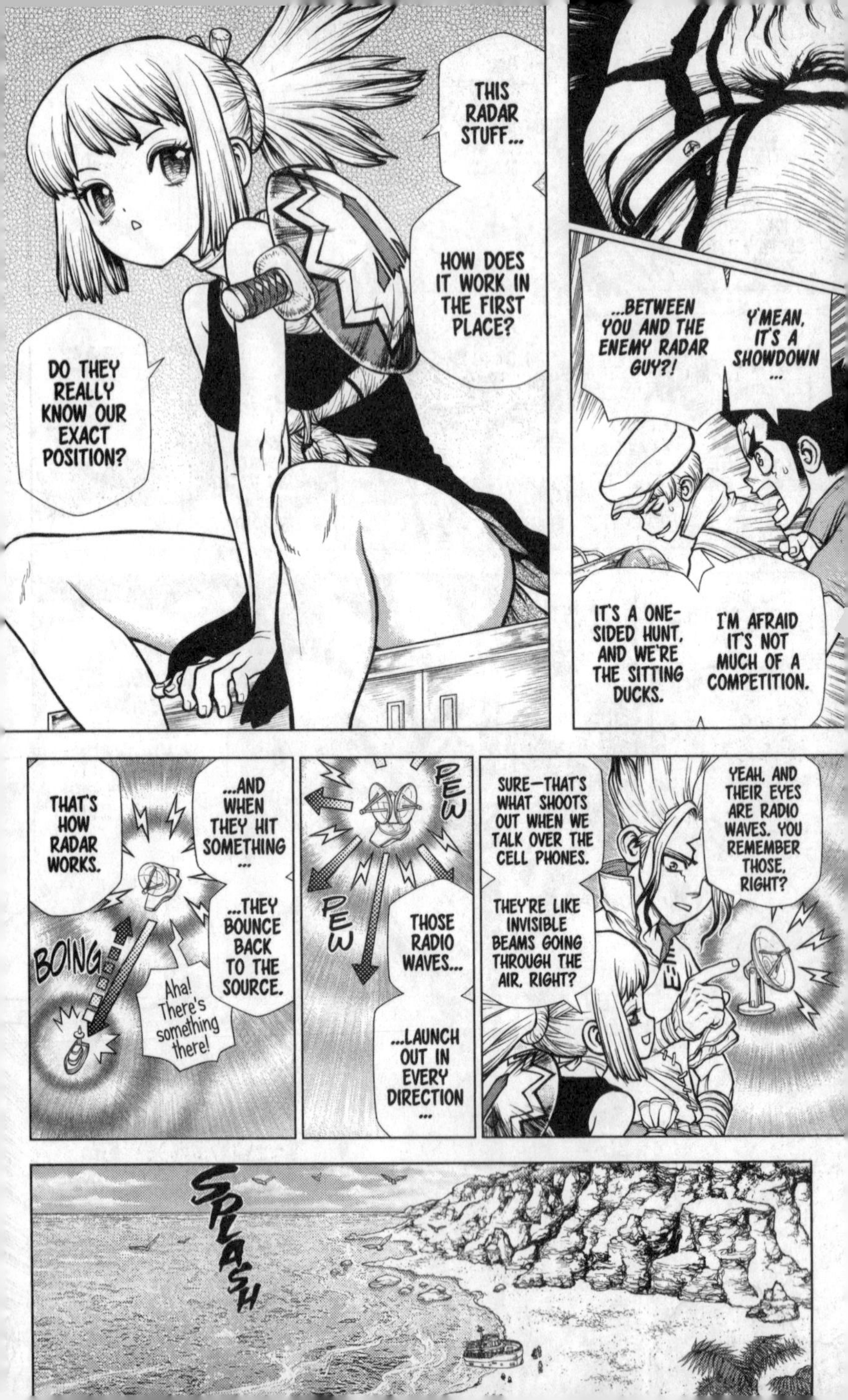
Y'MEAN, IT'S A SHOWDOWN...
...BETWEEN YOU AND THE ENEMY RADAR GUY?!
I'M AFRAID IT'S NOT MUCH OF A COMPETITION.
IT'S A ONE-SIDED HUNT, AND WE'RE THE SITTING DUCKS.
THIS RADAR STUFF...
HOW DOES IT WORK IN THE FIRST PLACE?
DO THEY REALLY KNOW OUR EXACT POSITION?
YEAH, AND THEIR EYES ARE RADIO WAVES. YOU REMEMBER THOSE, RIGHT?
SURE—THAT'S WHAT SHOOTS OUT WHEN WE TALK OVER THE CELL PHONES.
THEY'RE LIKE INVISIBLE BEAMS GOING THROUGH THE AIR, RIGHT?
PEW
PEW
THOSE RADIO WAVES...
...LAUNCH OUT IN EVERY DIRECTION...
...AND WHEN THEY HIT SOMETHING...
...THEY BOUNCE BACK TO THE SOURCE.
THAT'S HOW RADAR WORKS.
BOING
Aha! There's something there!
SPLASH

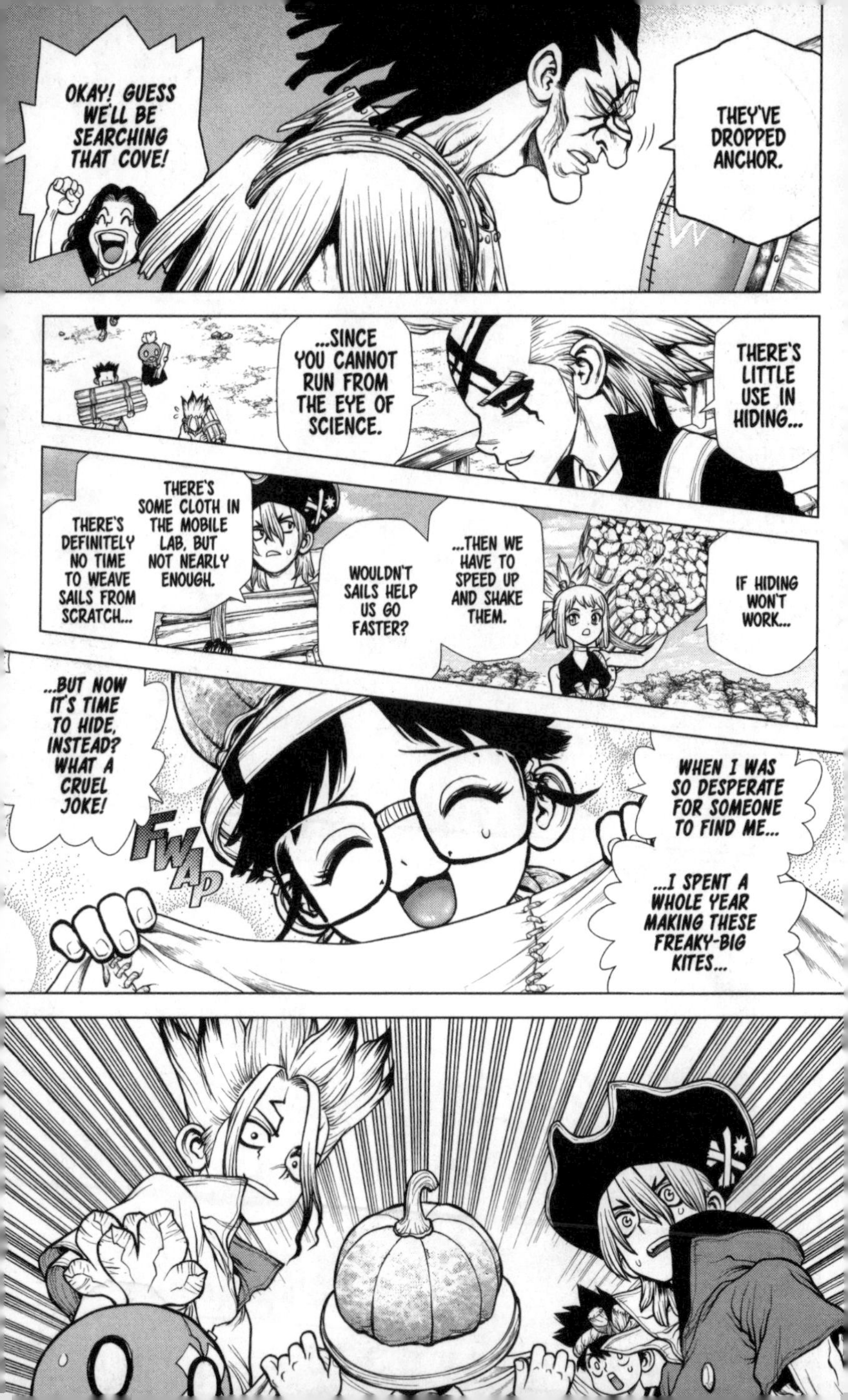
THEY'VE DROPPED ANCHOR.
OKAY! GUESS WE'LL BE SEARCHING THAT COVE!
THERE'S LITTLE USE IN HIDING...
...SINCE YOU CANNOT RUN FROM THE EYE OF SCIENCE.
IF HIDING WON'T WORK...
...THEN WE HAVE TO SPEED UP AND SHAKE THEM.
WOULDN'T SAILS HELP US GO FASTER?
THERE'S SOME CLOTH IN THE MOBILE LAB, BUT NOT NEARLY ENOUGH.
THERE'S DEFINITELY NO TIME TO WEAVE SAILS FROM SCRATCH...
WHEN I WAS SO DESPERATE FOR SOMEONE TO FIND ME...
...I SPENT A WHOLE YEAR MAKING THESE FREAKY-BIG KITES...
...BUT NOW IT'S TIME TO HIDE, INSTEAD? WHAT A CRUEL JOKE!
FWAP

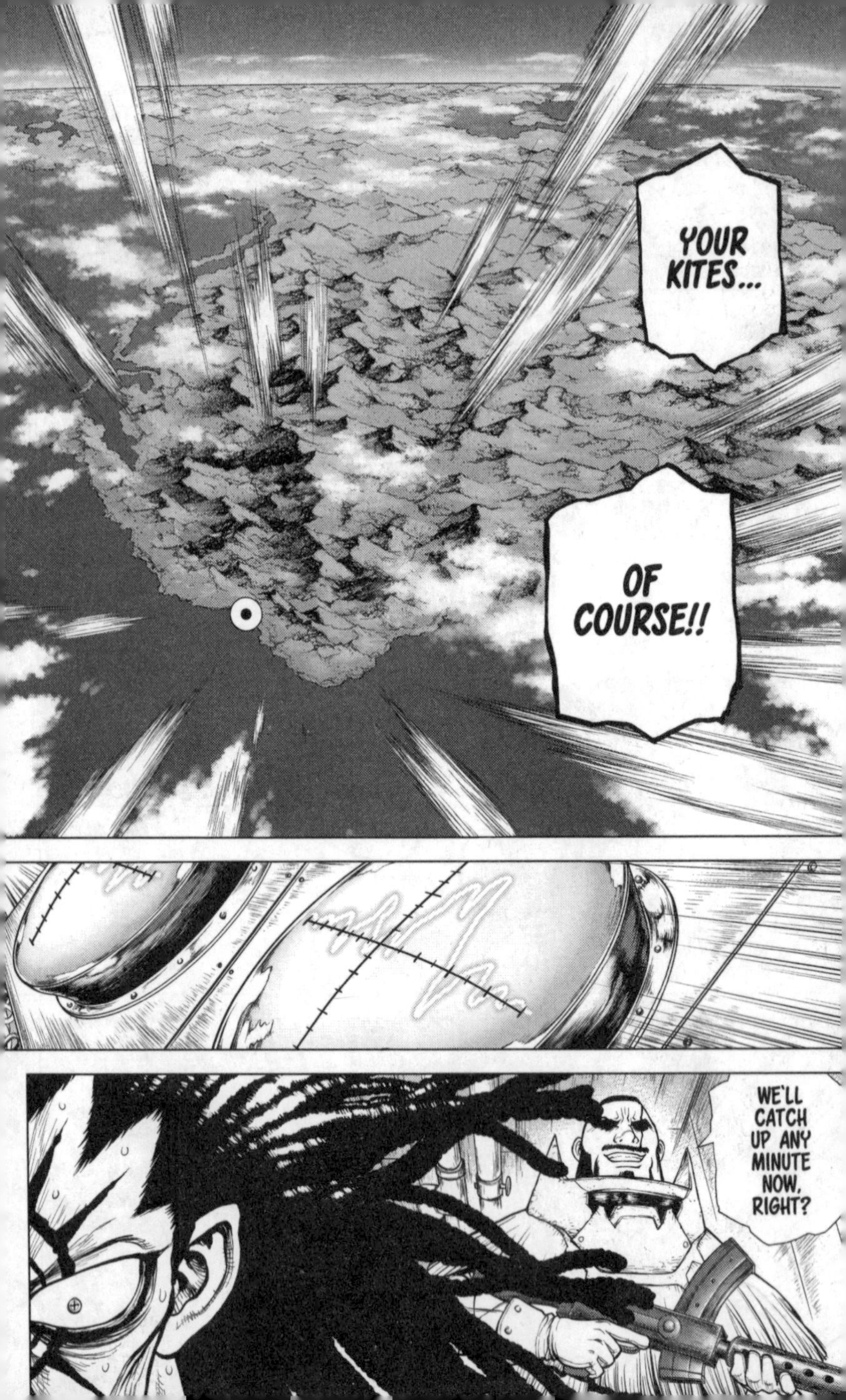
YOUR KITES...
OF COURSE!!
WE'LL CATCH UP ANY MINUTE NOW, RIGHT?

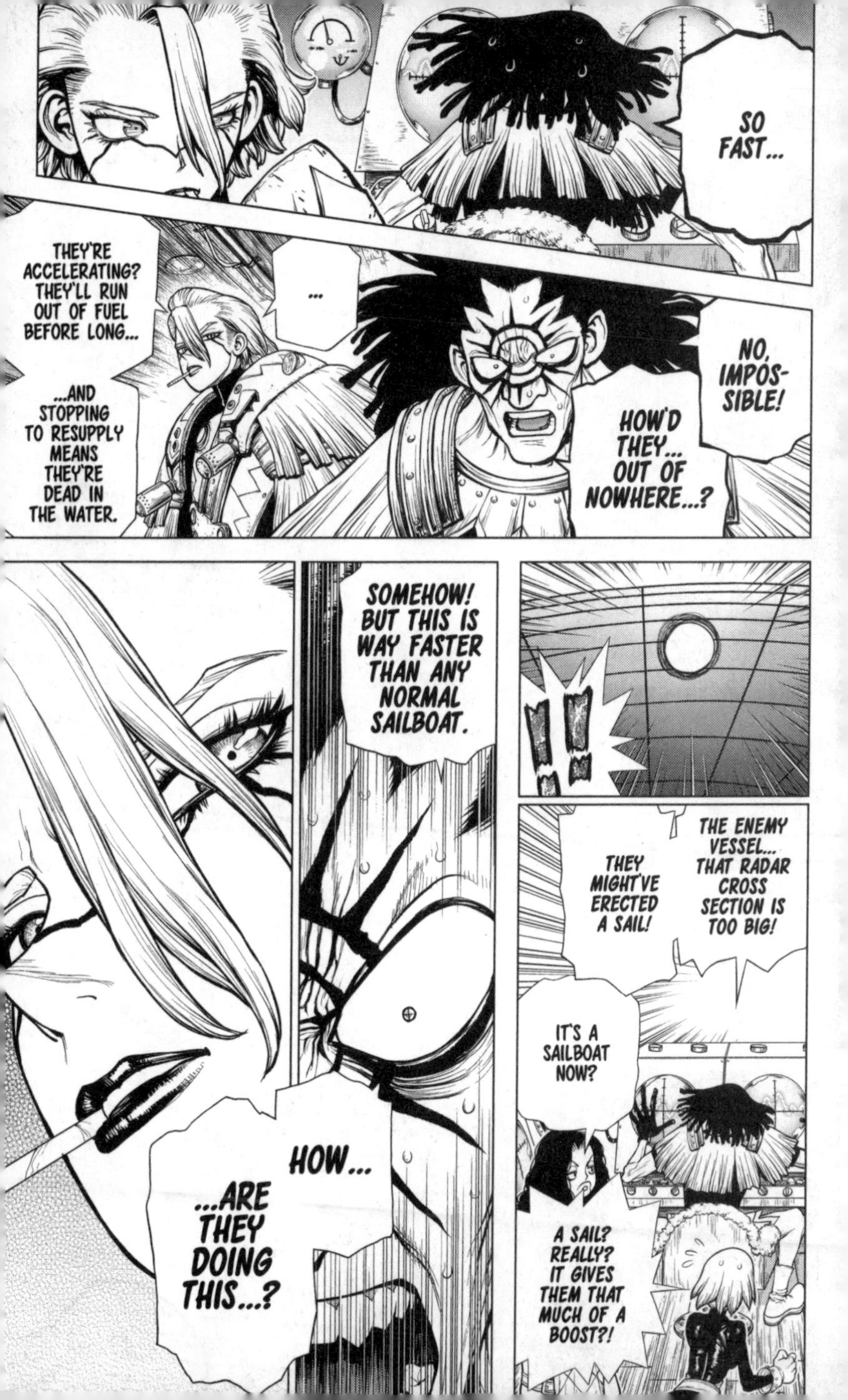
SO FAST...
NO, IMPOS-SIBLE!
HOW'D THEY... OUT OF NOWHERE...?
...
THEY'RE ACCELERATING? THEY'LL RUN OUT OF FUEL BEFORE LONG...
...AND STOPPING TO RESUPPLY MEANS THEY'RE DEAD IN THE WATER.
!!
THE ENEMY VESSEL... THAT RADAR CROSS SECTION IS TOO BIG!
THEY MIGHT'VE ERECTED A SAIL!
IT'S A SAILBOAT NOW?
A SAIL? REALLY? IT GIVES THEM THAT MUCH OF A BOOST?!
SOMEHOW! BUT THIS IS WAY FASTER THAN ANY NORMAL SAILBOAT.
HOW...
...ARE THEY DOING THIS...?

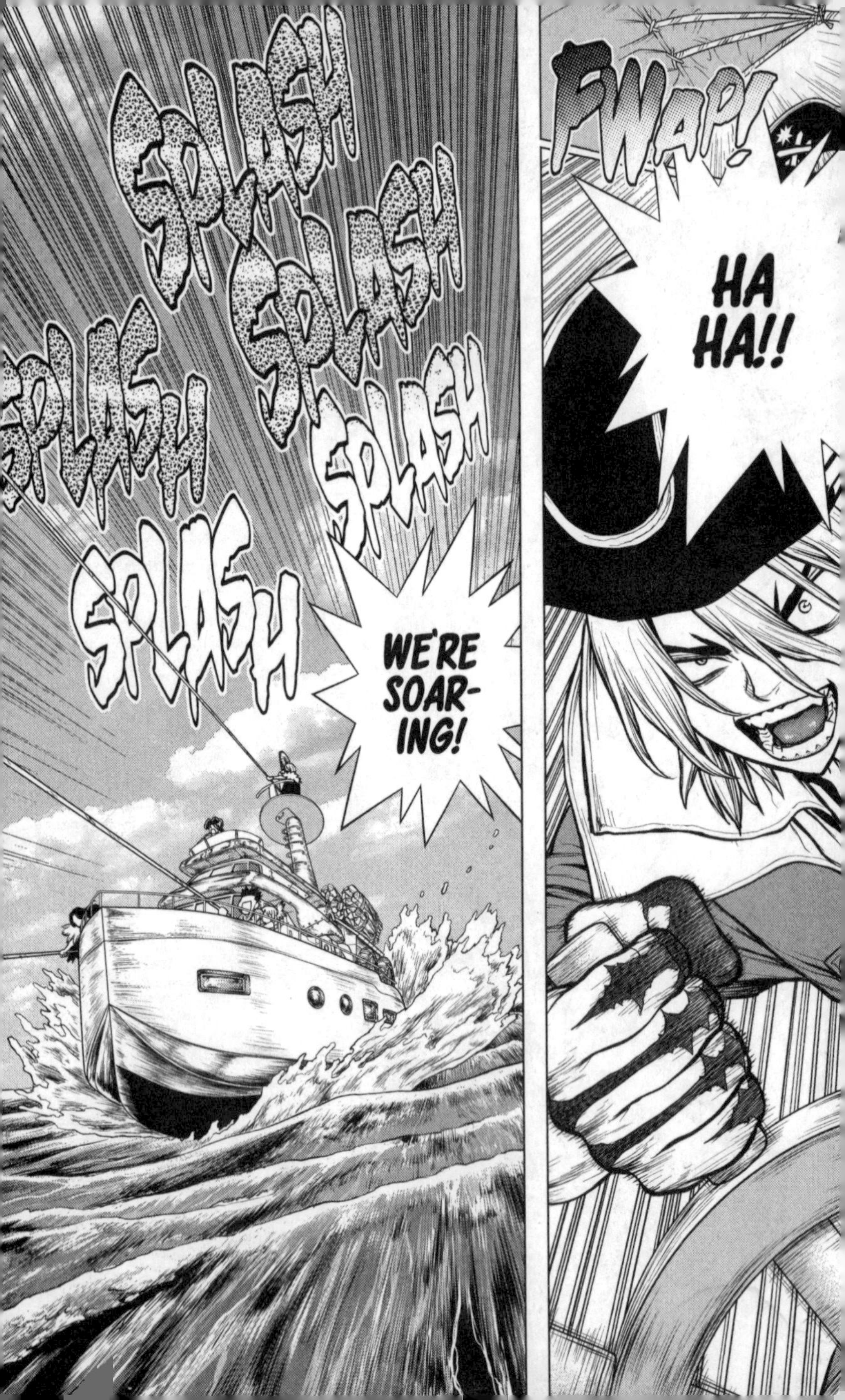
FWAP!
HA HA!!
SPLASH
SPLASH
SPLASH
SPLASH
SPLASH
WE'RE SOARING!

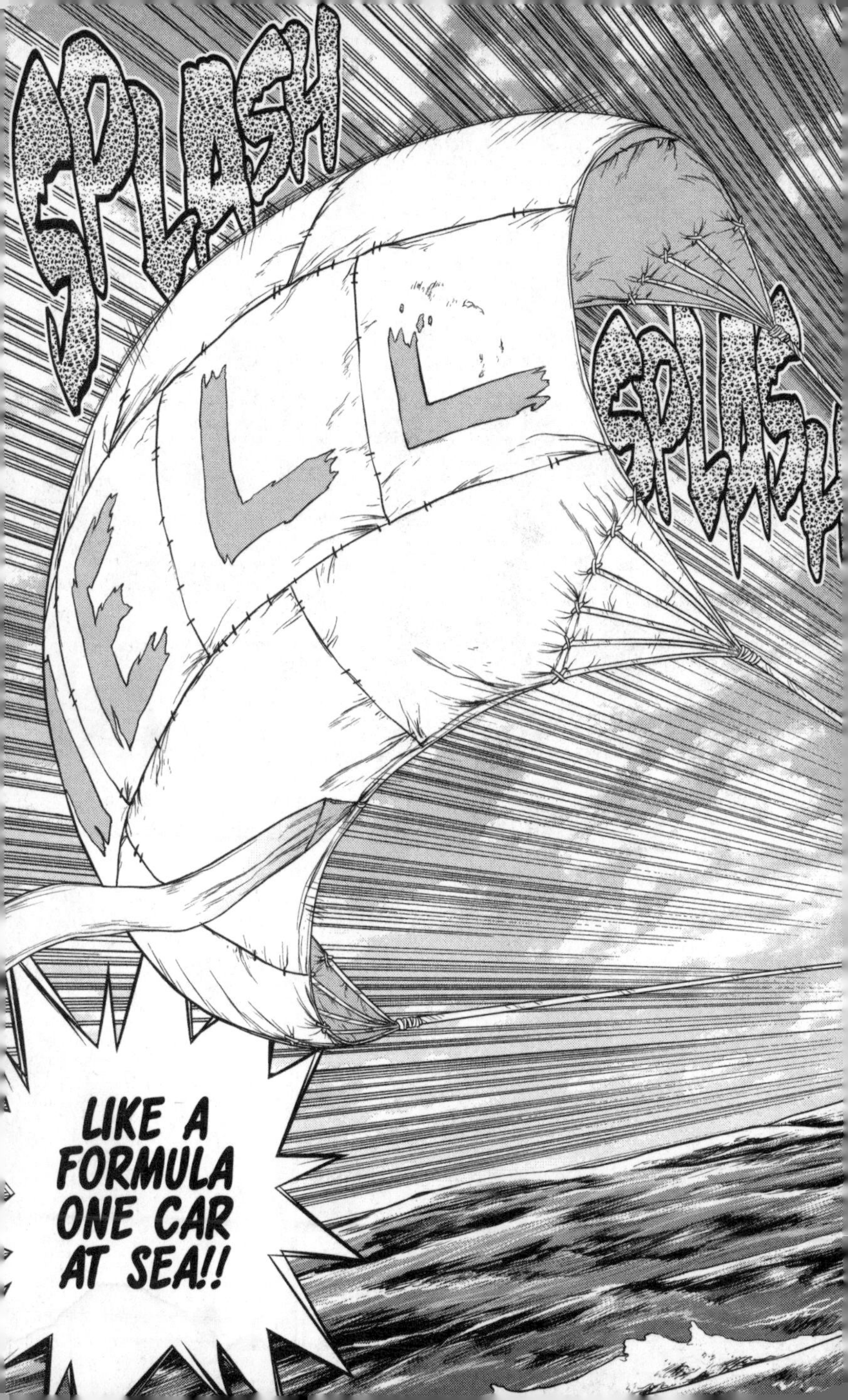
SPLASH
SPLASH
LIKE A FORMULA ONE CAR AT SEA!!

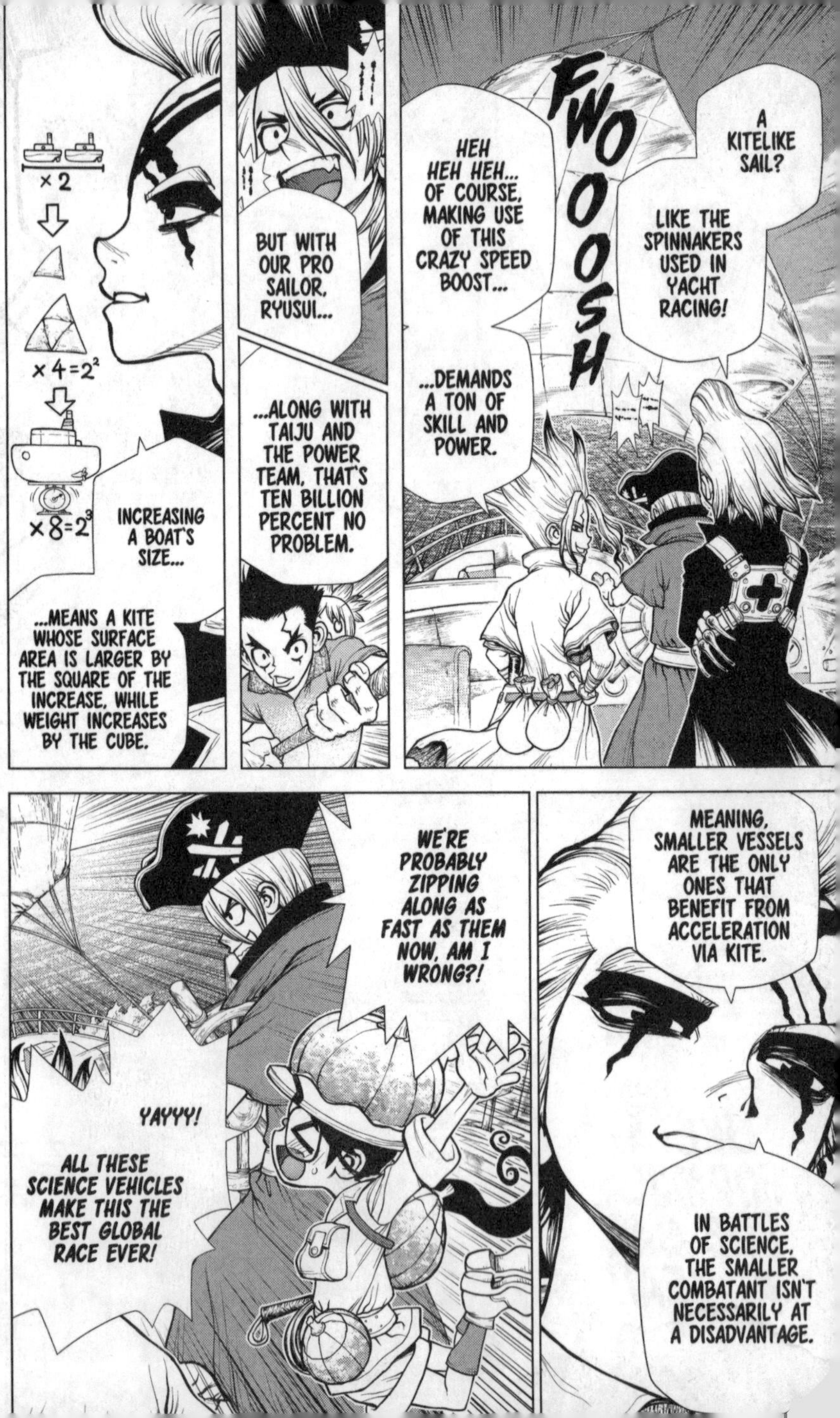
A KITELIKE SAIL?
LIKE THE SPINNAKERS USED IN YACHT RACING!
FWOOOSH
HEH HEH HEH... OF COURSE, MAKING USE OF THIS CRAZY SPEED BOOST...
...DEMANDS A TON OF SKILL AND POWER.
BUT WITH OUR PRO SAILOR, RYUSUI...
...ALONG WITH TAIJU AND THE POWER TEAM, THAT'S TEN BILLION PERCENT NO PROBLEM.
×2
$\times 4=2^2$
$\times 8=2^3$
INCREASING A BOAT'S SIZE...
...MEANS A KITE WHOSE SURFACE AREA IS LARGER BY THE SQUARE OF THE INCREASE, WHILE WEIGHT INCREASES BY THE CUBE.
MEANING, SMALLER VESSELS ARE THE ONLY ONES THAT BENEFIT FROM ACCELERATION VIA KITE.
IN BATTLES OF SCIENCE, THE SMALLER COMBATANT ISN'T NECESSARILY AT A DISADVANTAGE.
WE'RE PROBABLY ZIPPING ALONG AS FAST AS THEM NOW, AM I WRONG?!
YAYYY!
ALL THESE SCIENCE VEHICLES MAKE THIS THE BEST GLOBAL RACE EVER!

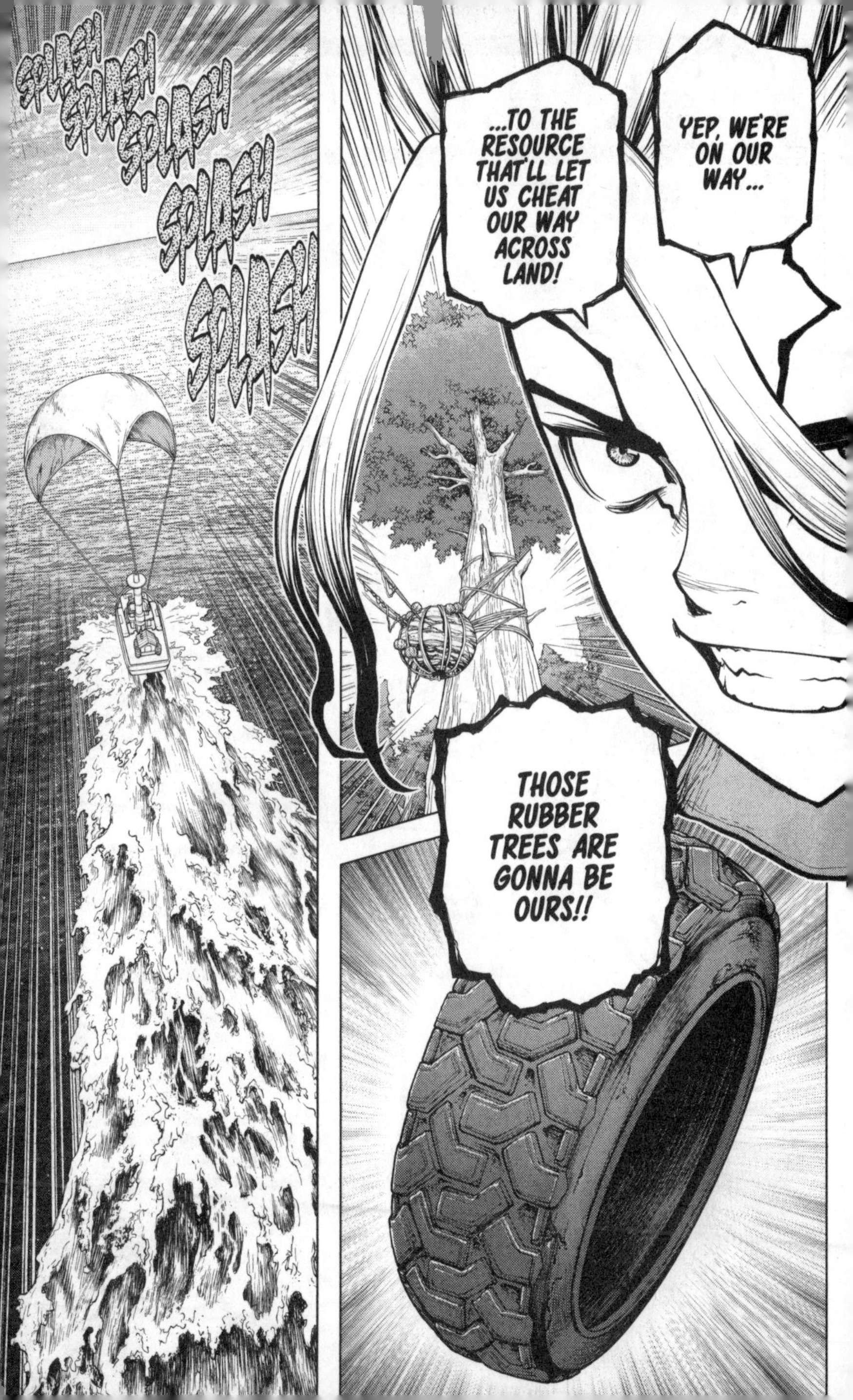
YEP, WE'RE ON OUR WAY...
...TO THE RESOURCE THAT'LL LET US CHEAT OUR WAY ACROSS LAND!
THOSE RUBBER TREES ARE GONNA BE OURS!!
SPLASH
SPLASH
SPLASH
SPLASH
SPLASH

Xeno's Science Kingdom

KNIGHT FILE 7

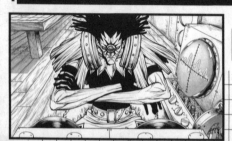

Radar Man

Practical Experience: ★★★★★

Mental Math: ★★★★★

Caution: ★★★★

■ Full Name: Leonard Maxwell

■ Height: 184 cm

■ Profession: Operations Specialist (radarman in American military)

"Electromagnetic waves reveal all—even a person's soul." That's Leonard's favorite saying.

Radio waves, X-rays, and even light may come in different wavelengths, but they're all fundamentally the same thing—electromagnetic waves.

Radar carries a tremendous amount of raw data that would normally be analyzed by a computer, but Leonard is experienced enough to interpret it through sheer instinct.

Knowing that data is enough for him to draw a picture of the target in his mind, as if he were viewing it with his own two eyes.

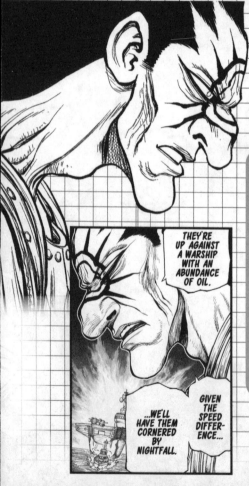

THEY'RE UP AGAINST A WARSHIP WITH AN ABUNDANCE OF OIL.
GIVEN THE SPEED DIFFERENCE...
...WE'LL HAVE THEM CORNERED BY NIGHTFALL.

Z=174: The Specter of the Panama Canal

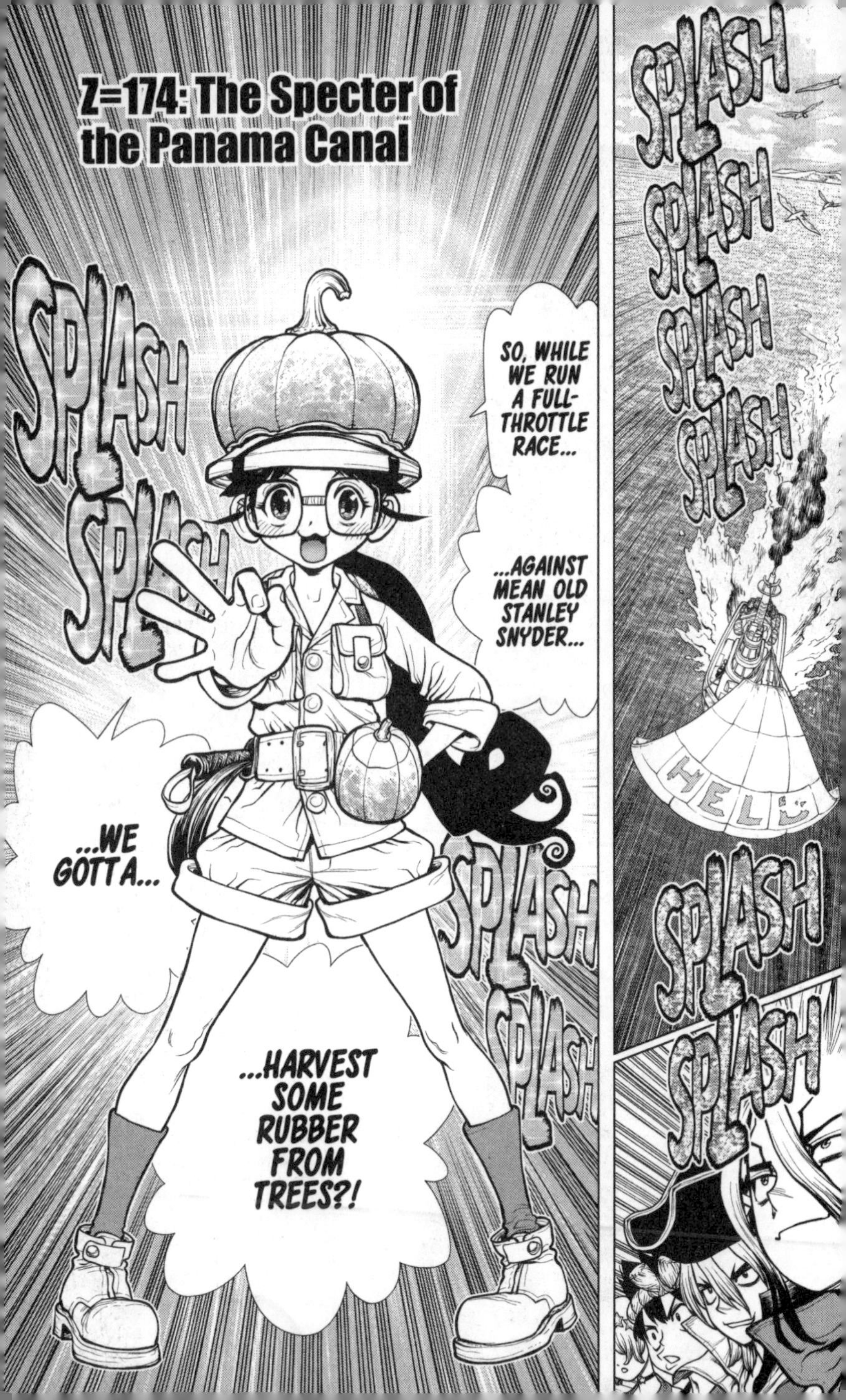
SPLASH
SPLASH
SPLASH
SPLASH
SPLASH
SPLASH
SPLASH
SPLASH
SO, WHILE WE RUN A FULL-THROTTLE RACE...
...AGAINST MEAN OLD STANLEY SNYDER...
...WE GOTTA...
...HARVEST SOME RUBBER FROM TREES?!
SPLASH
SPLASH

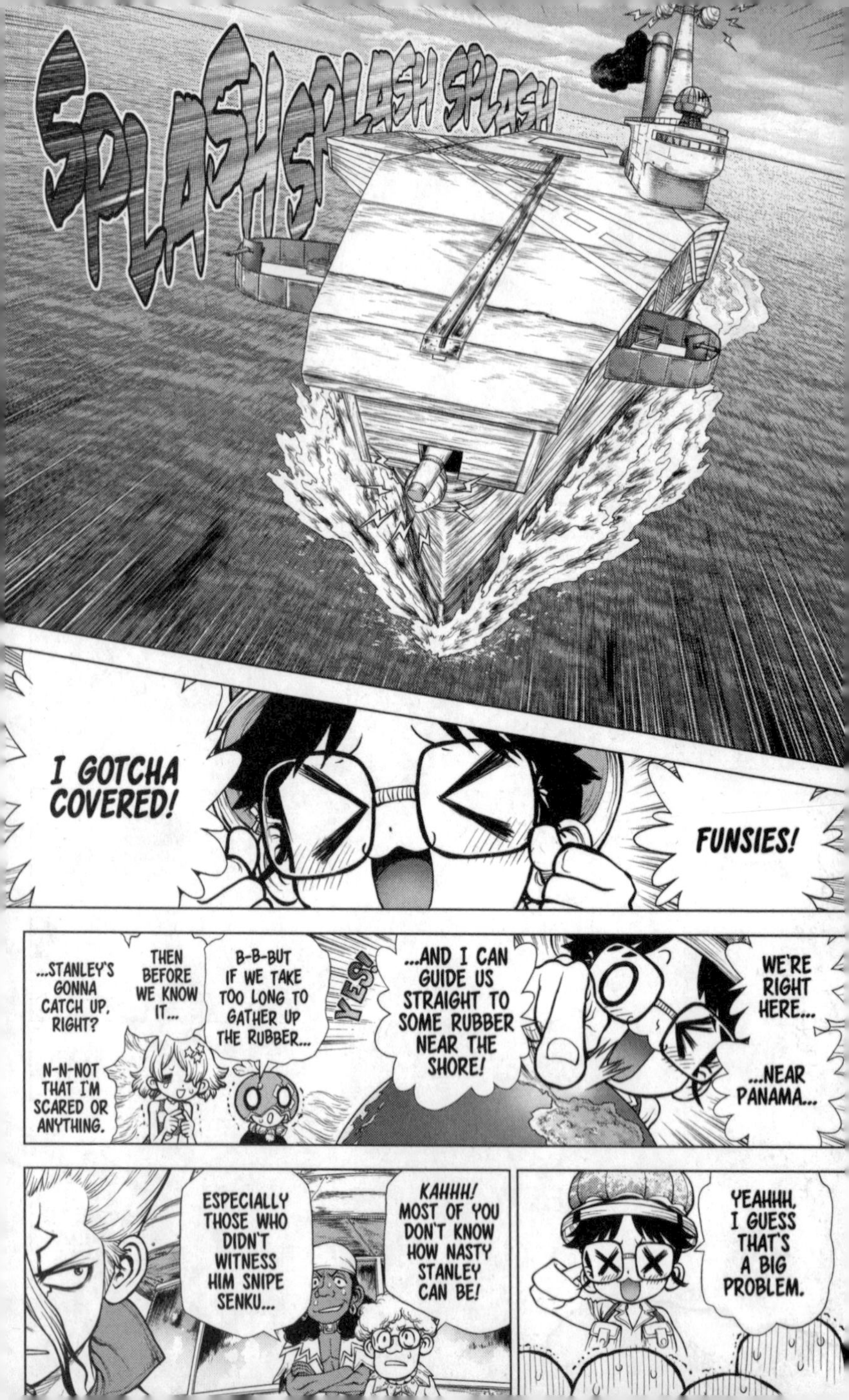

SPLASH SPLASH SPLASH SPLASH
FUNSIES!
I GOTCHA COVERED!
WE'RE RIGHT HERE...
...NEAR PANAMA...
...AND I CAN GUIDE US STRAIGHT TO SOME RUBBER NEAR THE SHORE!
YES!
B-B-BUT IF WE TAKE TOO LONG TO GATHER UP THE RUBBER...
THEN BEFORE WE KNOW IT...
...STANLEY'S GONNA CATCH UP, RIGHT?
N-N-NOT THAT I'M SCARED OR ANYTHING.
YEAHHH, I GUESS THAT'S A BIG PROBLEM.
KAHHH! MOST OF YOU DON'T KNOW HOW NASTY STANLEY CAN BE!
ESPECIALLY THOSE WHO DIDN'T WITNESS HIM SNIPE SENKU...

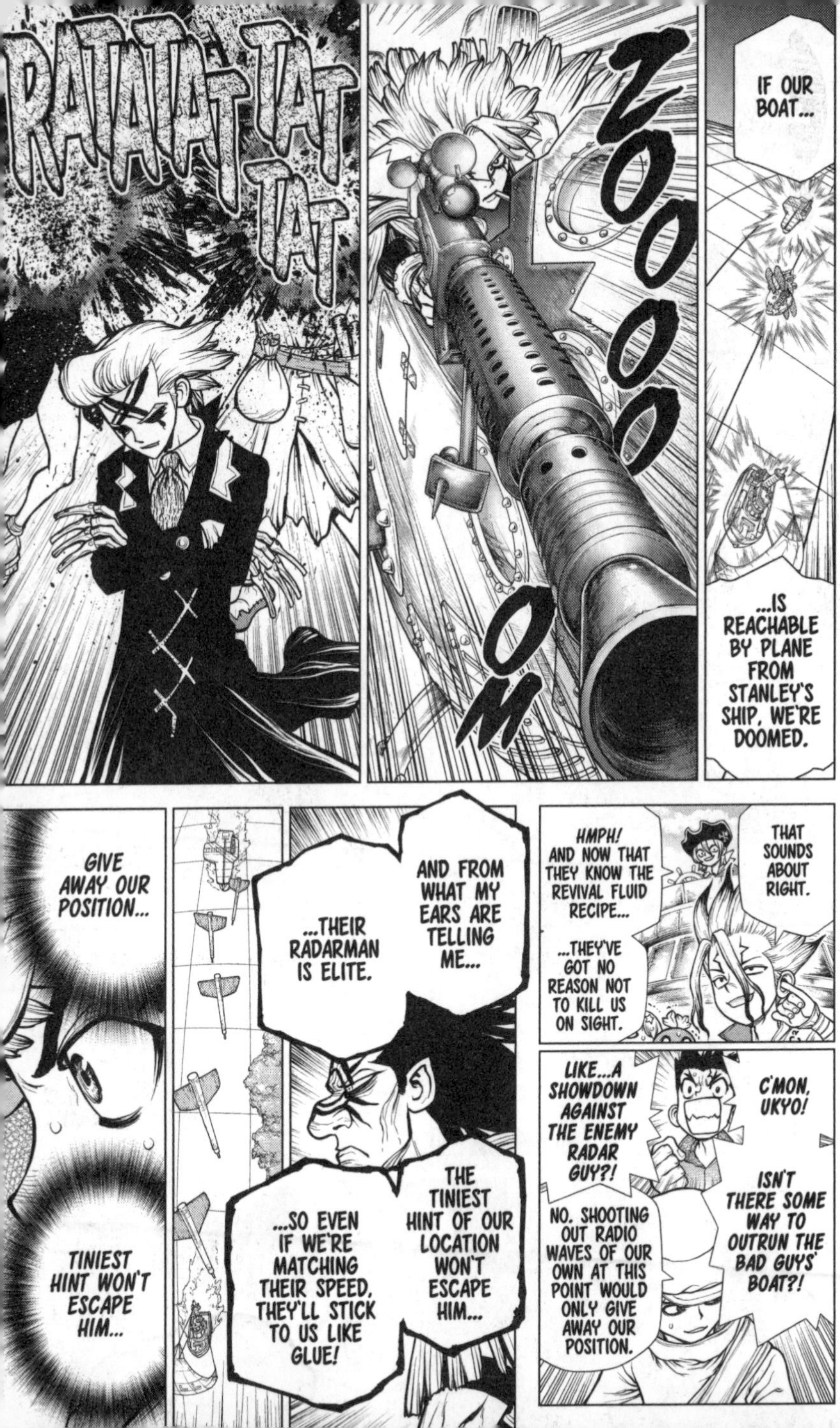
IF OUR BOAT...
...IS REACHABLE BY PLANE FROM STANLEY'S SHIP, WE'RE DOOMED.
ZOOOOOOM
RATATAT-TAT TAT
THAT SOUNDS ABOUT RIGHT.
HMPH! AND NOW THAT THEY KNOW THE REVIVAL FLUID RECIPE...
...THEY'VE GOT NO REASON NOT TO KILL US ON SIGHT.
C'MON, UKYO!
ISN'T THERE SOME WAY TO OUTRUN THE BAD GUYS' BOAT?!
LIKE...A SHOWDOWN AGAINST THE ENEMY RADAR GUY?!
NO. SHOOTING OUT RADIO WAVES OF OUR OWN AT THIS POINT WOULD ONLY GIVE AWAY OUR POSITION.
AND FROM WHAT MY EARS ARE TELLING ME...
...THEIR RADARMAN IS ELITE.
THE TINIEST HINT OF OUR LOCATION WON'T ESCAPE HIM...
...SO EVEN IF WE'RE MATCHING THEIR SPEED, THEY'LL STICK TO US LIKE GLUE!
GIVE AWAY OUR POSITION...
TINIEST HINT WON'T ESCAPE HIM...

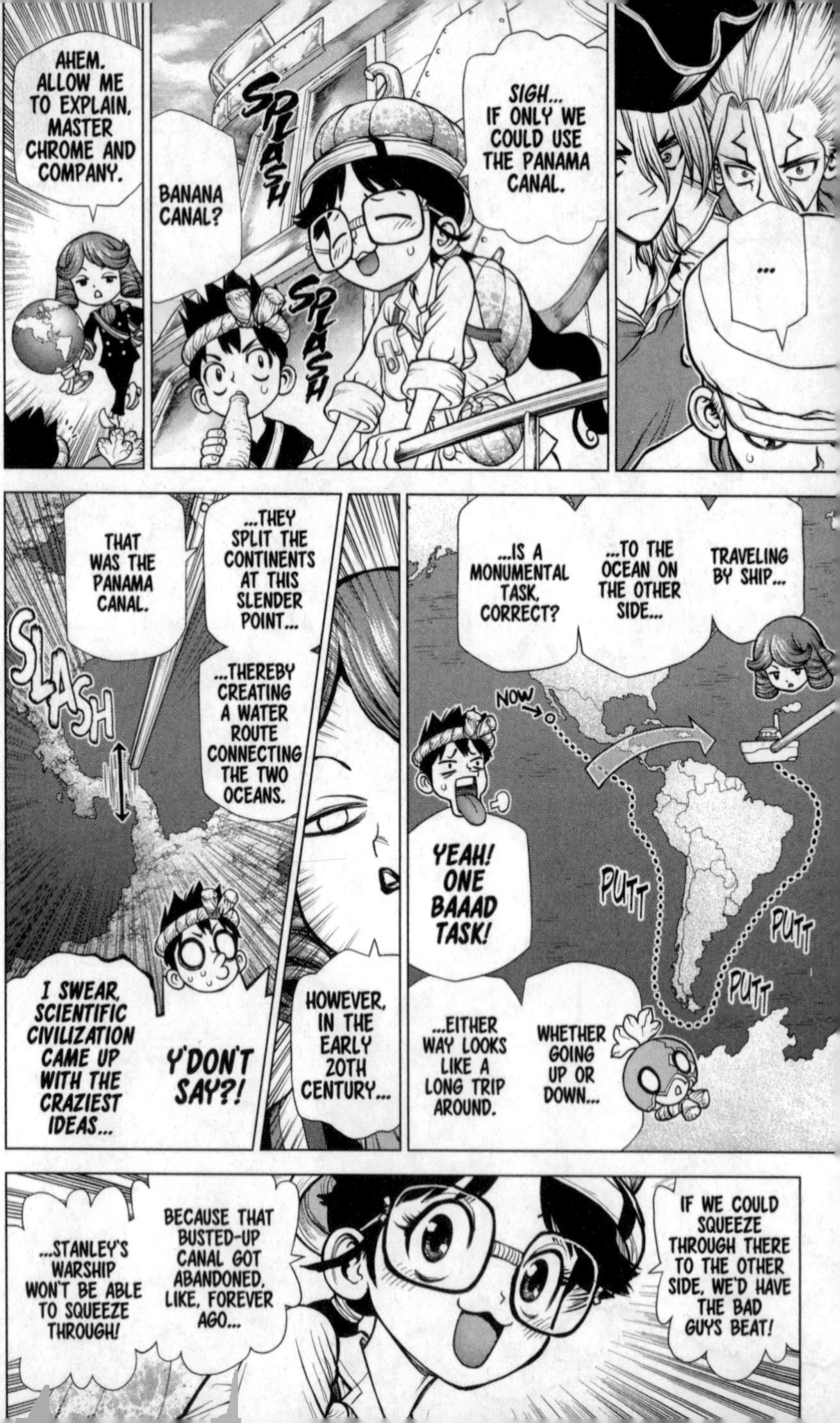
...
SIGH... IF ONLY WE COULD USE THE PANAMA CANAL.
SPLASH
SPLASH
BANANA CANAL?
AHEM. ALLOW ME TO EXPLAIN, MASTER CHROME AND COMPANY.
TRAVELING BY SHIP...
...TO THE OCEAN ON THE OTHER SIDE...
...IS A MONUMENTAL TASK, CORRECT?
NOW
YEAH! ONE BAAAD TASK!
PUTT
PUTT
PUTT
WHETHER GOING UP OR DOWN...
...EITHER WAY LOOKS LIKE A LONG TRIP AROUND.
HOWEVER, IN THE EARLY 20TH CENTURY...
...THEY SPLIT THE CONTINENTS AT THIS SLENDER POINT...
...THEREBY CREATING A WATER ROUTE CONNECTING THE TWO OCEANS.
THAT WAS THE PANAMA CANAL.
SLASH
Y'DON'T SAY?!
I SWEAR, SCIENTIFIC CIVILIZATION CAME UP WITH THE CRAZIEST IDEAS...
IF WE COULD SQUEEZE THROUGH THERE TO THE OTHER SIDE, WE'D HAVE THE BAD GUYS BEAT!
BECAUSE THAT BUSTED-UP CANAL GOT ABANDONED, LIKE, FOREVER AGO...
...STANLEY'S WARSHIP WON'T BE ABLE TO SQUEEZE THROUGH!

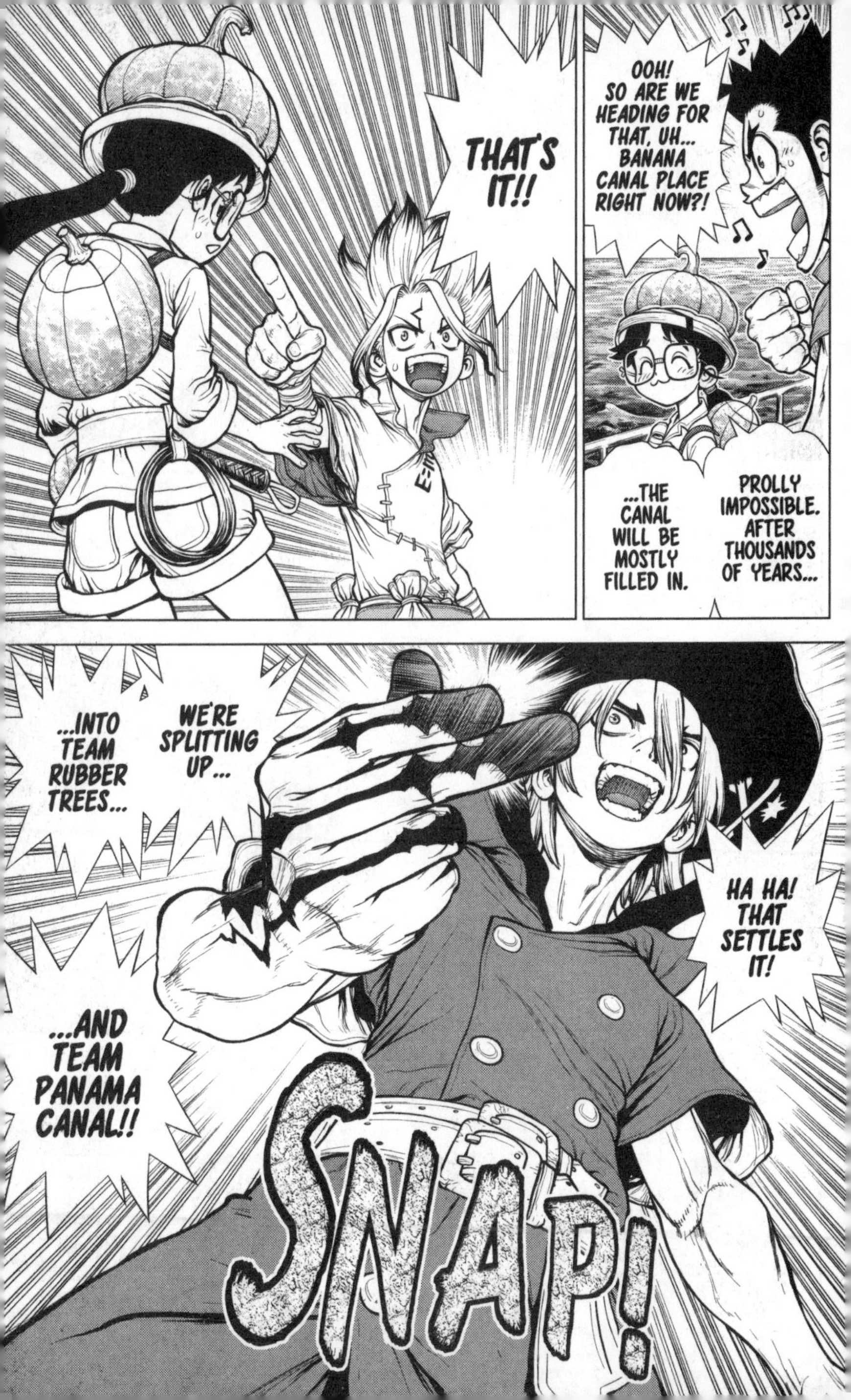
OOH! SO ARE WE HEADING FOR THAT, UH... BANANA CANAL PLACE RIGHT NOW?!
PROLLY IMPOSSIBLE. AFTER THOUSANDS OF YEARS...
...THE CANAL WILL BE MOSTLY FILLED IN.
THAT'S IT!!
HA HA! THAT SETTLES IT!
WE'RE SPLITTING UP...
...INTO TEAM RUBBER TREES...
...AND TEAM PANAMA CANAL!!
SNAP!

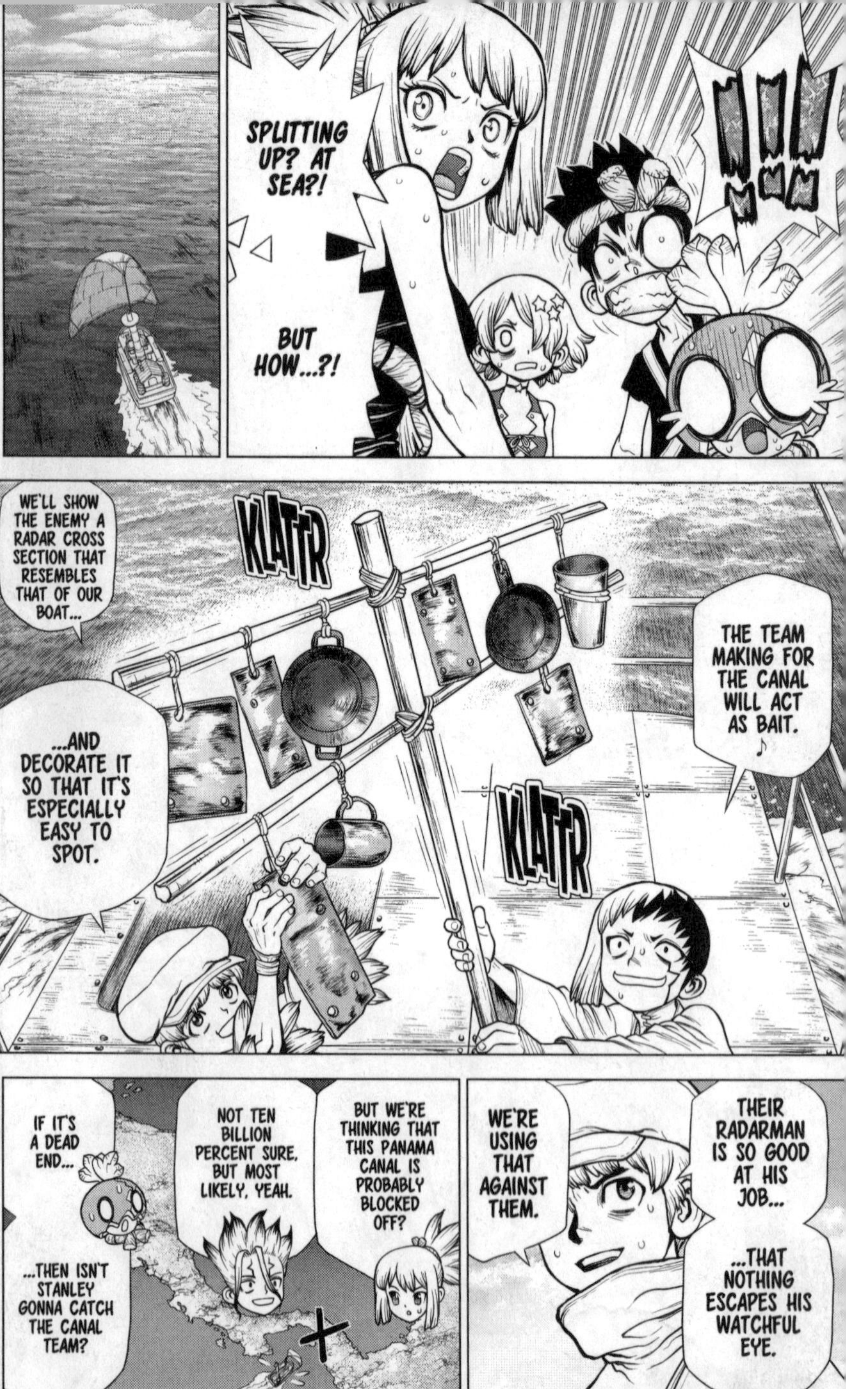
SPLITTING UP? AT SEA?!
BUT HOW...?!
THE TEAM MAKING FOR THE CANAL WILL ACT AS BAIT. ♪
KLATTR
WE'LL SHOW THE ENEMY A RADAR CROSS SECTION THAT RESEMBLES THAT OF OUR BOAT...
KLATTR
...AND DECORATE IT SO THAT IT'S ESPECIALLY EASY TO SPOT.
THEIR RADARMAN IS SO GOOD AT HIS JOB...
...THAT NOTHING ESCAPES HIS WATCHFUL EYE.
WE'RE USING THAT AGAINST THEM.
BUT WE'RE THINKING THAT THIS PANAMA CANAL IS PROBABLY BLOCKED OFF?
NOT TEN BILLION PERCENT SURE, BUT MOST LIKELY, YEAH.
IF IT'S A DEAD END...
...THEN ISN'T STANLEY GONNA CATCH THE CANAL TEAM?

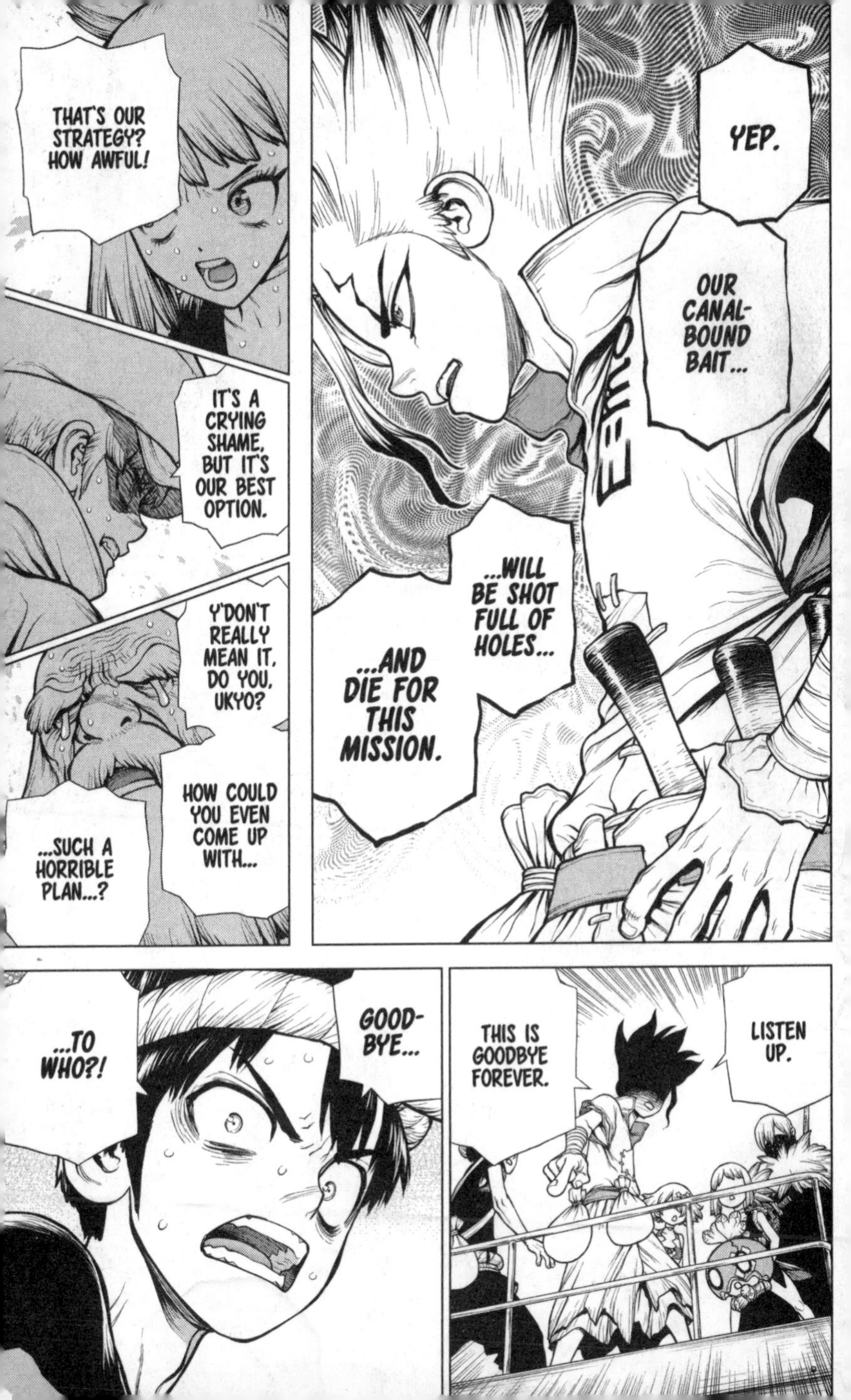
YEP.
OUR CANAL-BOUND BAIT...
...WILL BE SHOT FULL OF HOLES...
...AND DIE FOR THIS MISSION.
THAT'S OUR STRATEGY? HOW AWFUL!
IT'S A CRYING SHAME, BUT IT'S OUR BEST OPTION.
Y'DON'T REALLY MEAN IT, DO YOU, UKYO?
HOW COULD YOU EVEN COME UP WITH...
...SUCH A HORRIBLE PLAN...?
LISTEN UP.
THIS IS GOODBYE FOREVER.
GOOD-BYE...
...TO WHO?!

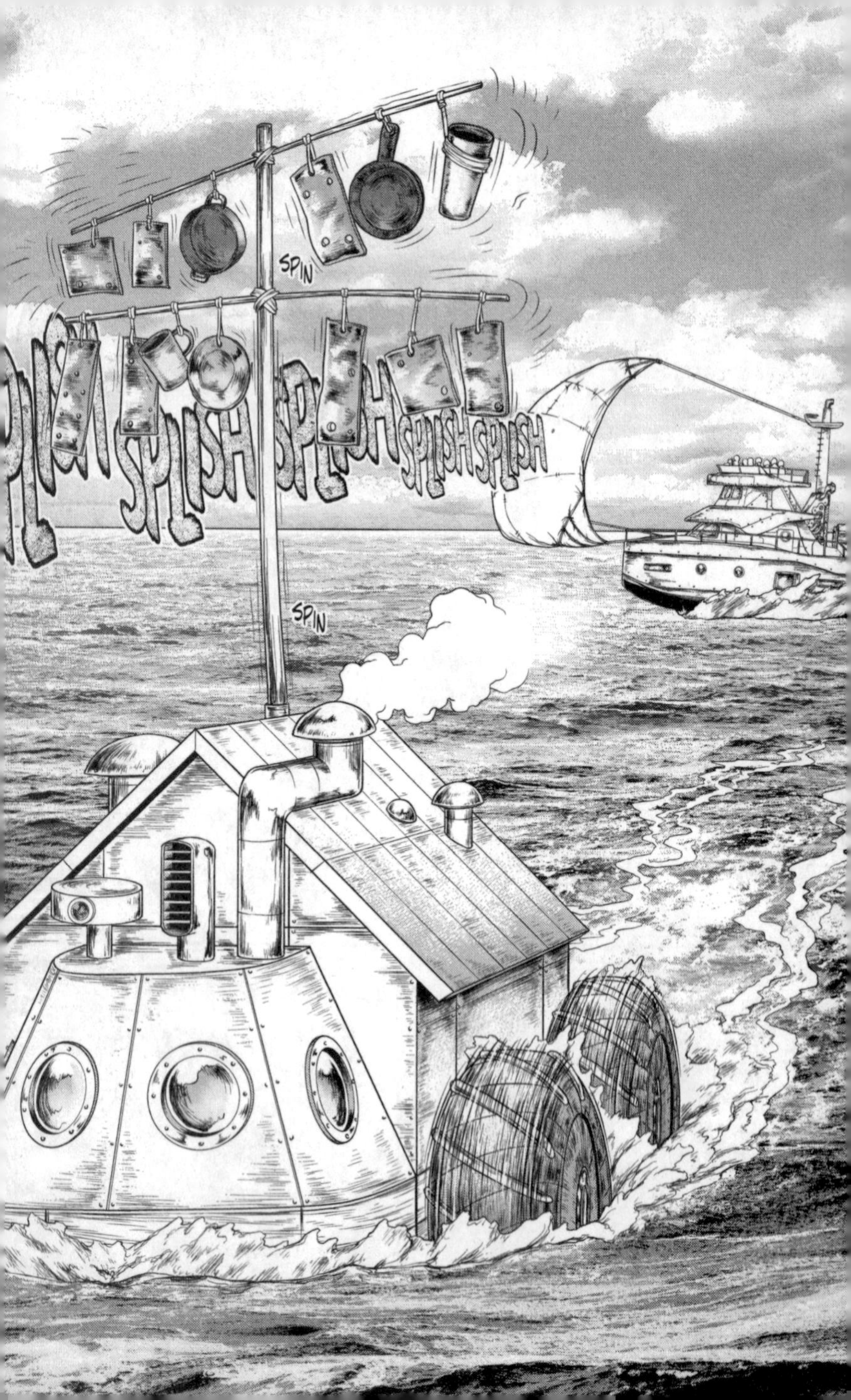
SPIN
SPLISH SPLISH SPLISH SPLISH SPLISH
SPIN

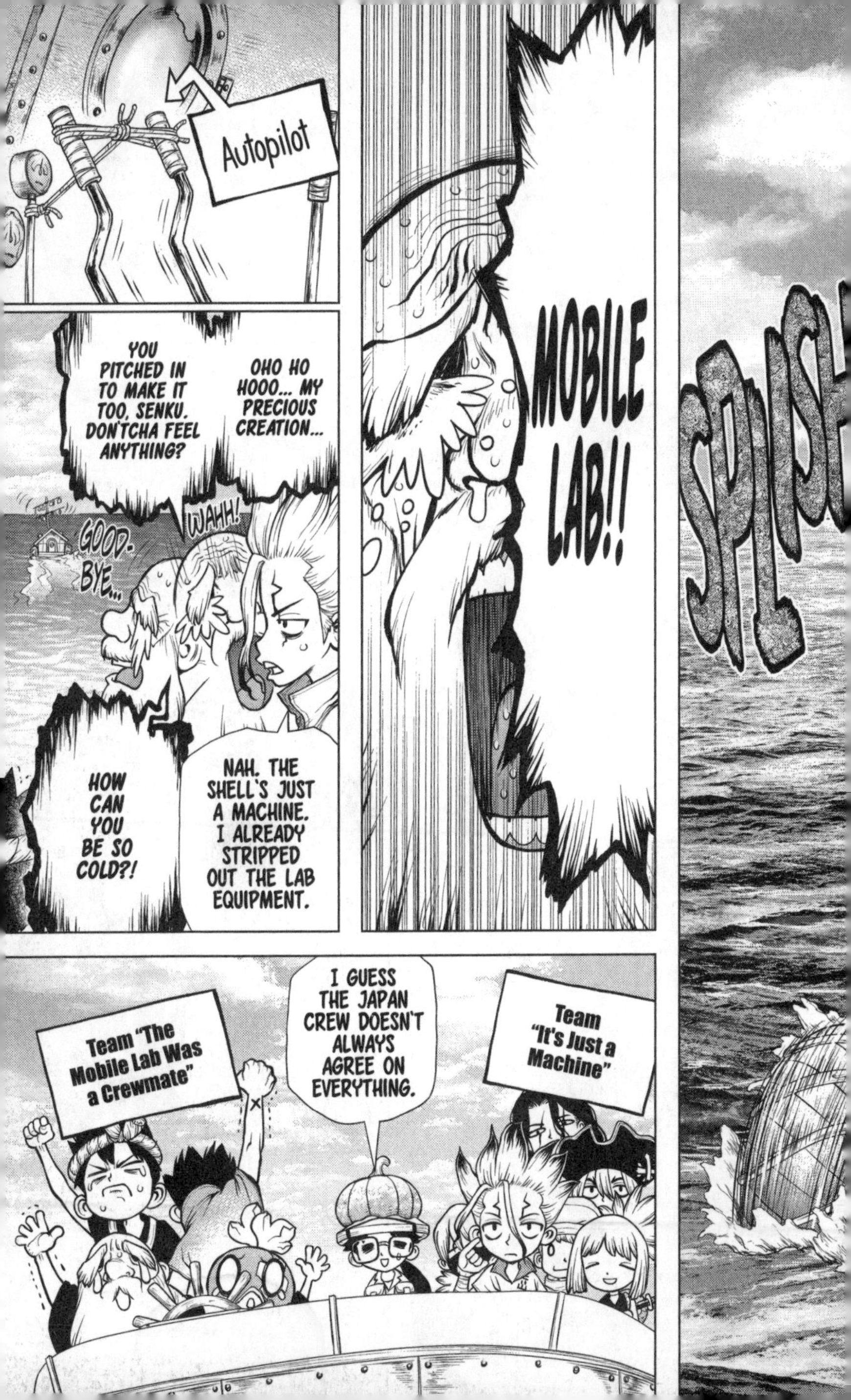
SPLISH
MOBILE LAB!!
Autopilot
OHO HO HOOO... MY PRECIOUS CREATION...
YOU PITCHED IN TO MAKE IT TOO, SENKU. DON'TCHA FEEL ANYTHING?
WAHH!
GOOD-BYE...
NAH. THE SHELL'S JUST A MACHINE. I ALREADY STRIPPED OUT THE LAB EQUIPMENT.
HOW CAN YOU BE SO COLD?!
Team "It's Just a Machine"
I GUESS THE JAPAN CREW DOESN'T ALWAYS AGREE ON EVERYTHING.
Team "The Mobile Lab Was a Crewmate"

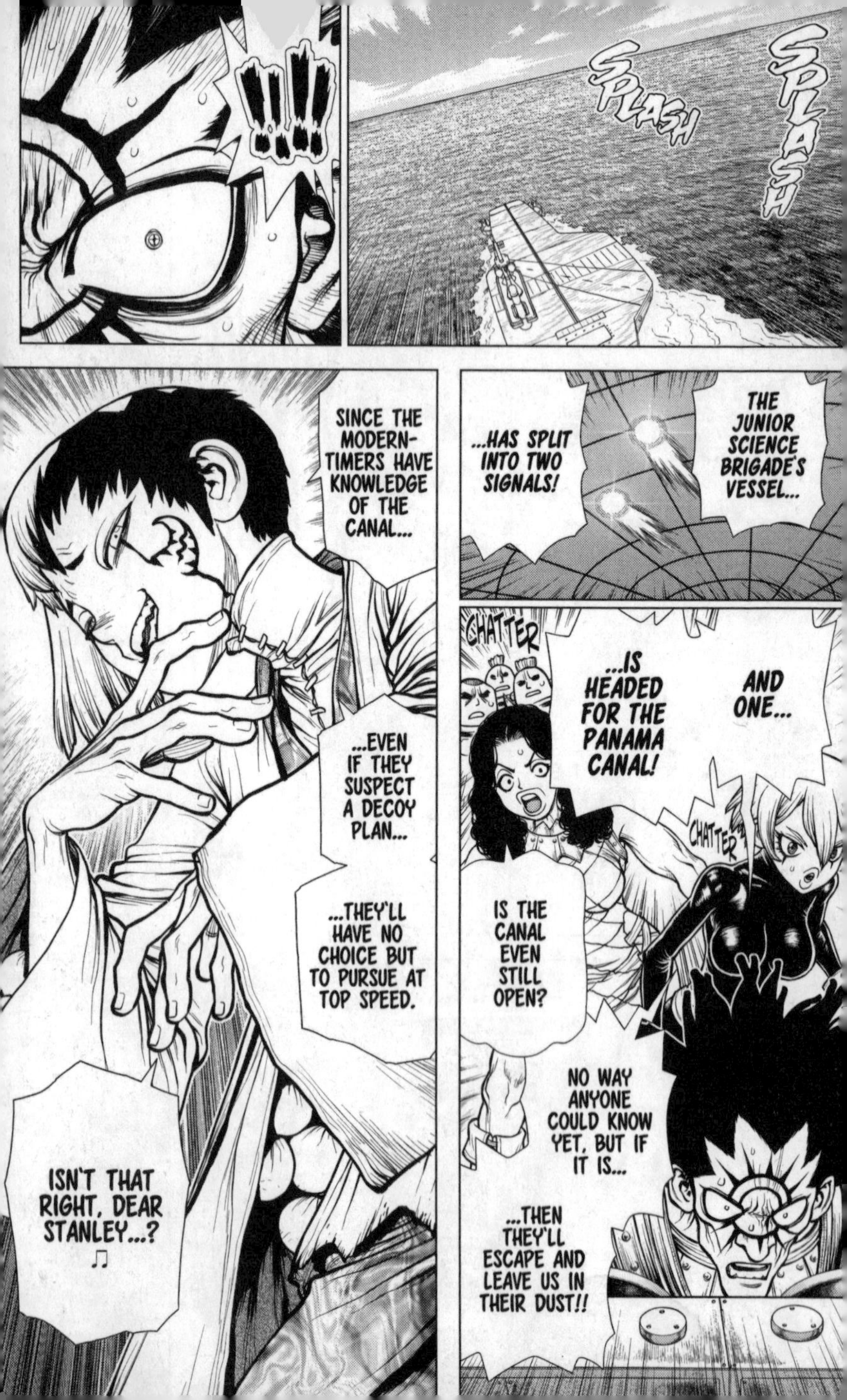
SPLASH
SPLASH
!!!!
THE JUNIOR SCIENCE BRIGADE'S VESSEL...
...HAS SPLIT INTO TWO SIGNALS!
CHATTER
AND ONE...
...IS HEADED FOR THE PANAMA CANAL!
CHATTER
IS THE CANAL EVEN STILL OPEN?
NO WAY ANYONE COULD KNOW YET, BUT IF IT IS...
...THEN THEY'LL ESCAPE AND LEAVE US IN THEIR DUST!!
SINCE THE MODERN-TIMERS HAVE KNOWLEDGE OF THE CANAL...
...EVEN IF THEY SUSPECT A DECOY PLAN...
...THEY'LL HAVE NO CHOICE BUT TO PURSUE AT TOP SPEED.
ISN'T THAT RIGHT, DEAR STANLEY...? ♫

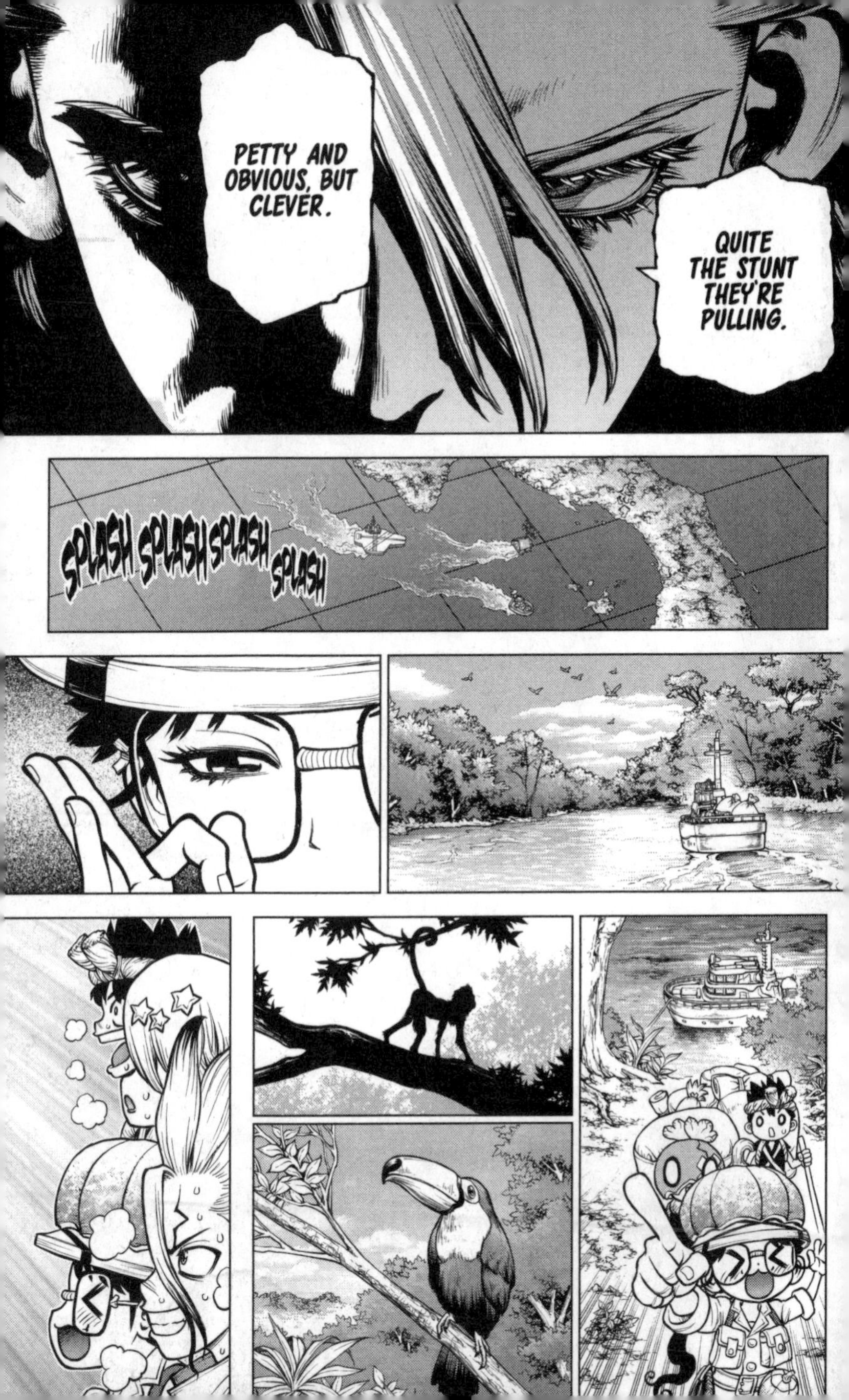
QUITE THE STUNT THEY'RE PULLING.
PETTY AND OBVIOUS, BUT CLEVER.
SPLASH SPLASH SPLASH SPLASH

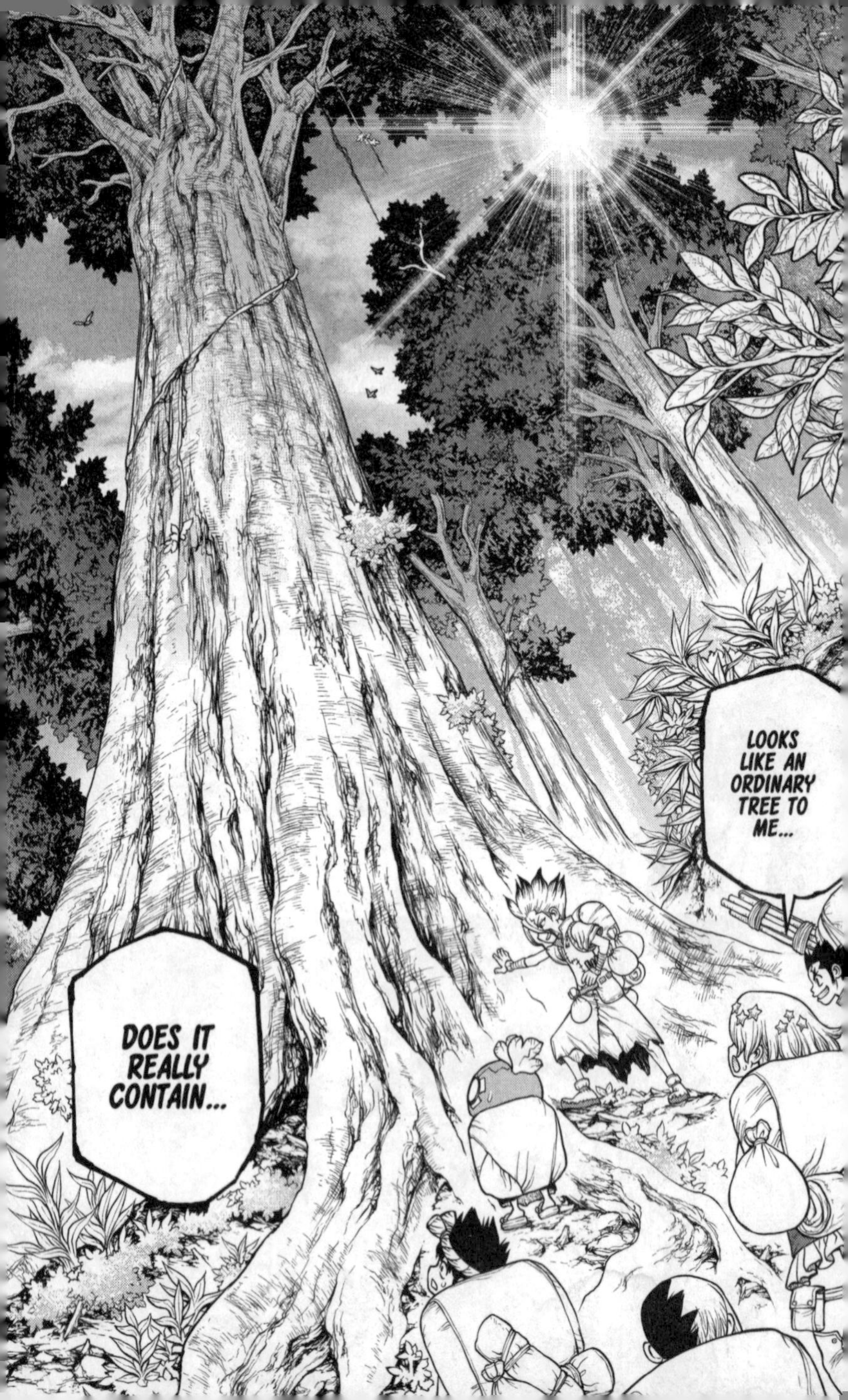
LOOKS LIKE AN ORDINARY TREE TO ME...
DOES IT REALLY CONTAIN...

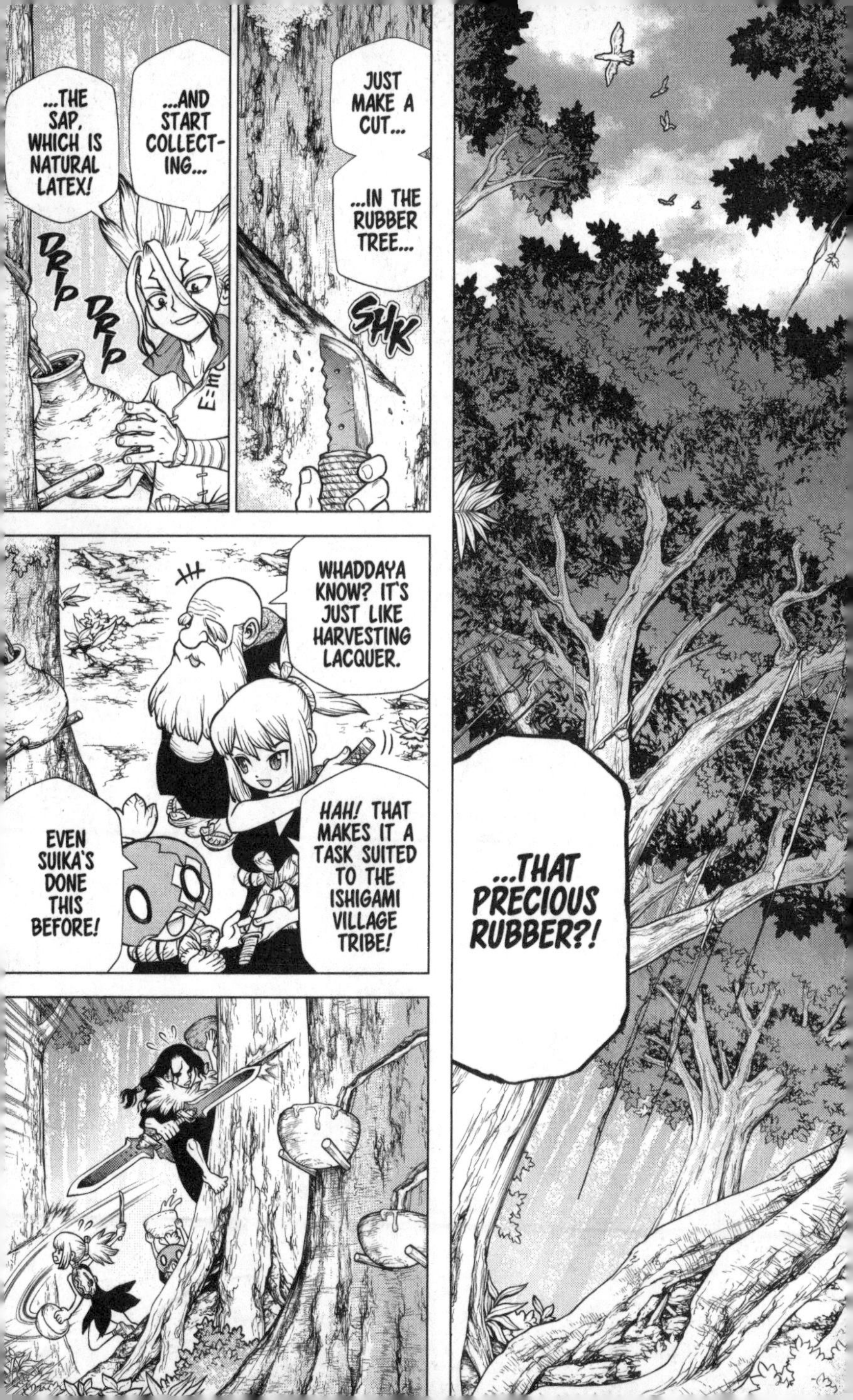
...THAT PRECIOUS RUBBER?!
JUST MAKE A CUT...
...IN THE RUBBER TREE...
SHK
...AND START COLLECTING...
...THE SAP, WHICH IS NATURAL LATEX!
DRIP
DRIP
WHADDAYA KNOW? IT'S JUST LIKE HARVESTING LACQUER.
HAH! THAT MAKES IT A TASK SUITED TO THE ISHIGAMI VILLAGE TRIBE!
EVEN SUIKA'S DONE THIS BEFORE!

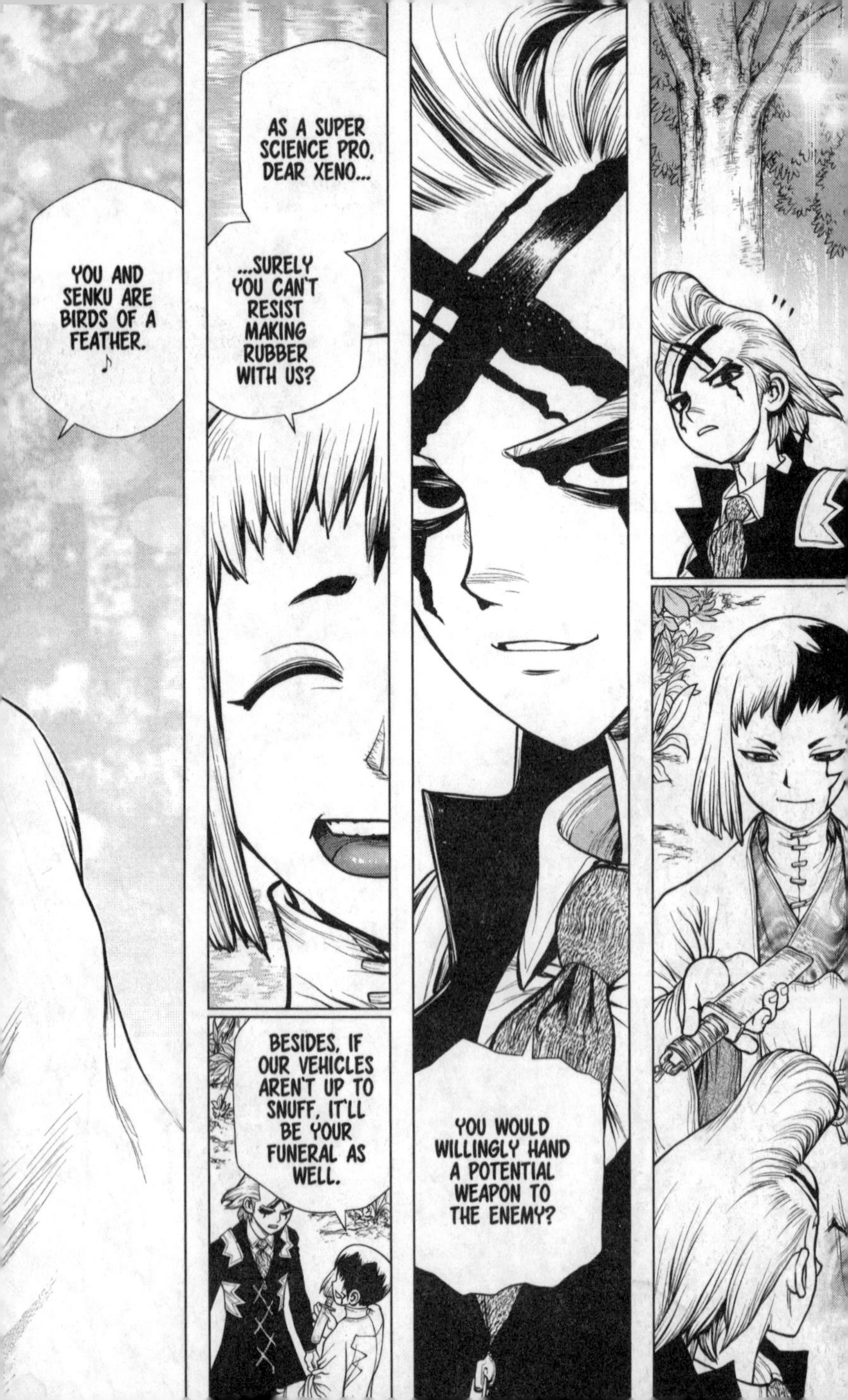
YOU WOULD WILLINGLY HAND A POTENTIAL WEAPON TO THE ENEMY?
AS A SUPER SCIENCE PRO, DEAR XENO...
...SURELY YOU CAN'T RESIST MAKING RUBBER WITH US?
BESIDES, IF OUR VEHICLES AREN'T UP TO SNUFF, IT'LL BE YOUR FUNERAL AS WELL.
YOU AND SENKU ARE BIRDS OF A FEATHER. ♪

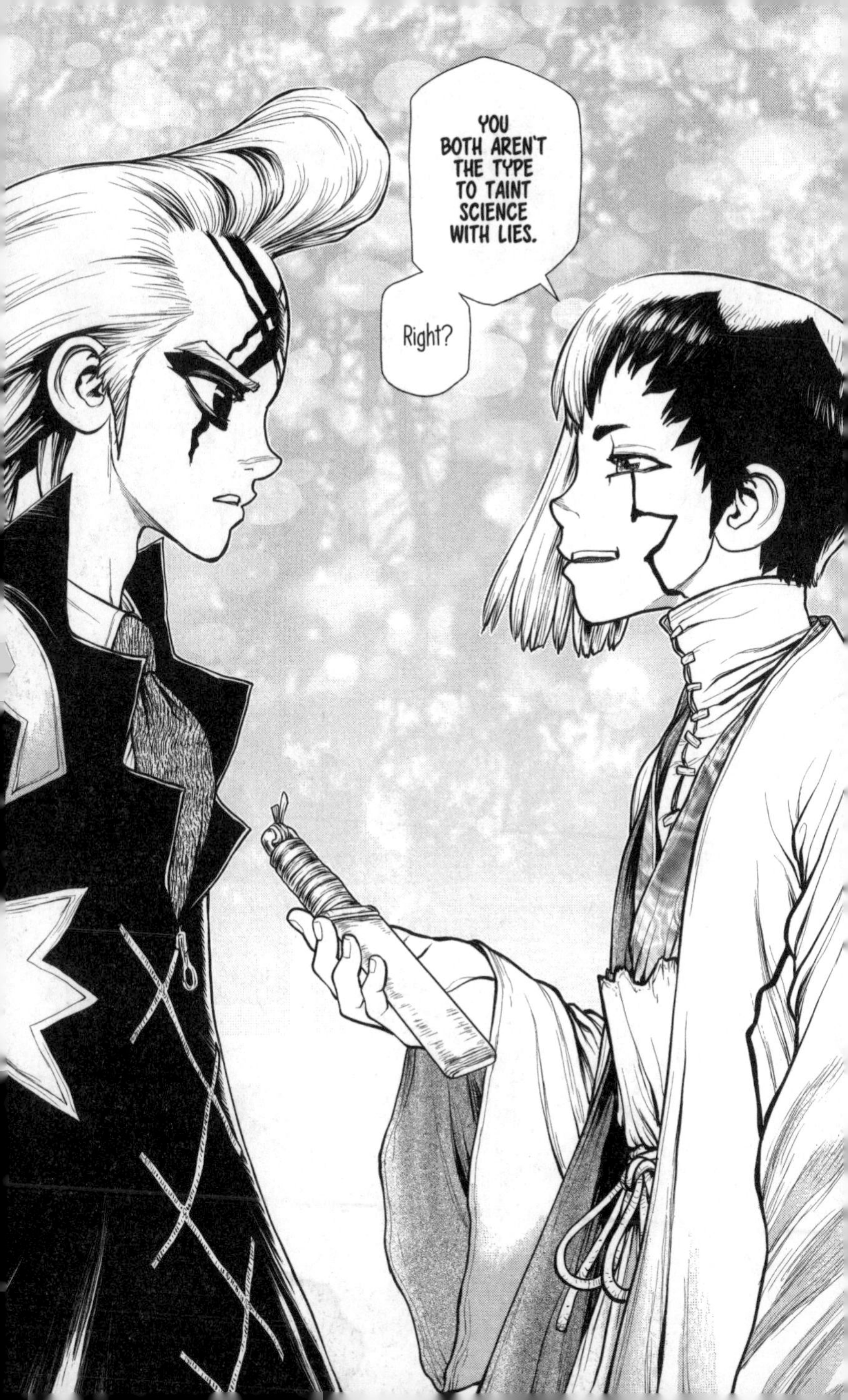
YOU BOTH AREN'T THE TYPE TO TAINT SCIENCE WITH LIES.
Right?

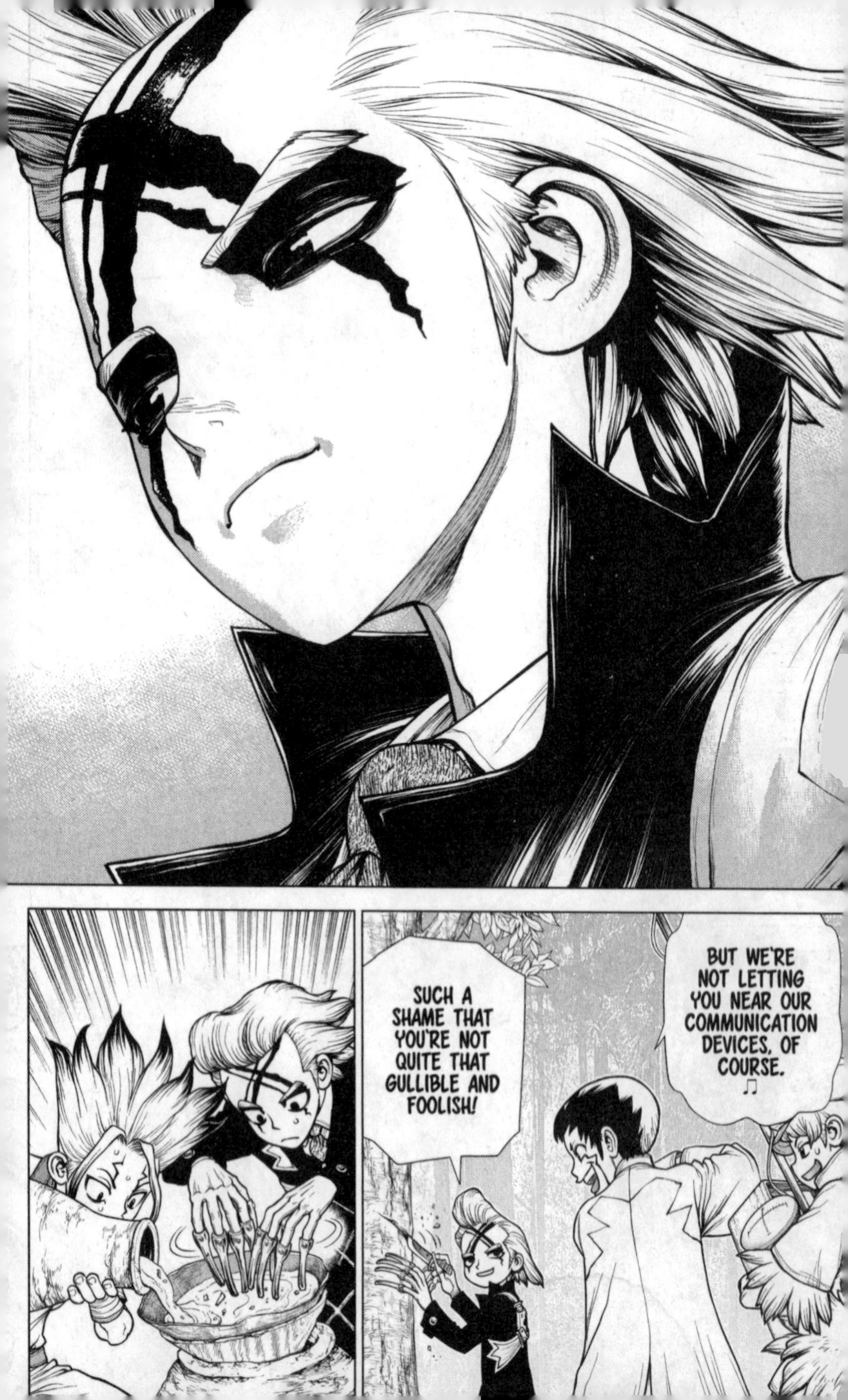
BUT WE'RE NOT LETTING YOU NEAR OUR COMMUNICATION DEVICES, OF COURSE. ♫
SUCH A SHAME THAT YOU'RE NOT QUITE THAT GULLIBLE AND FOOLISH!

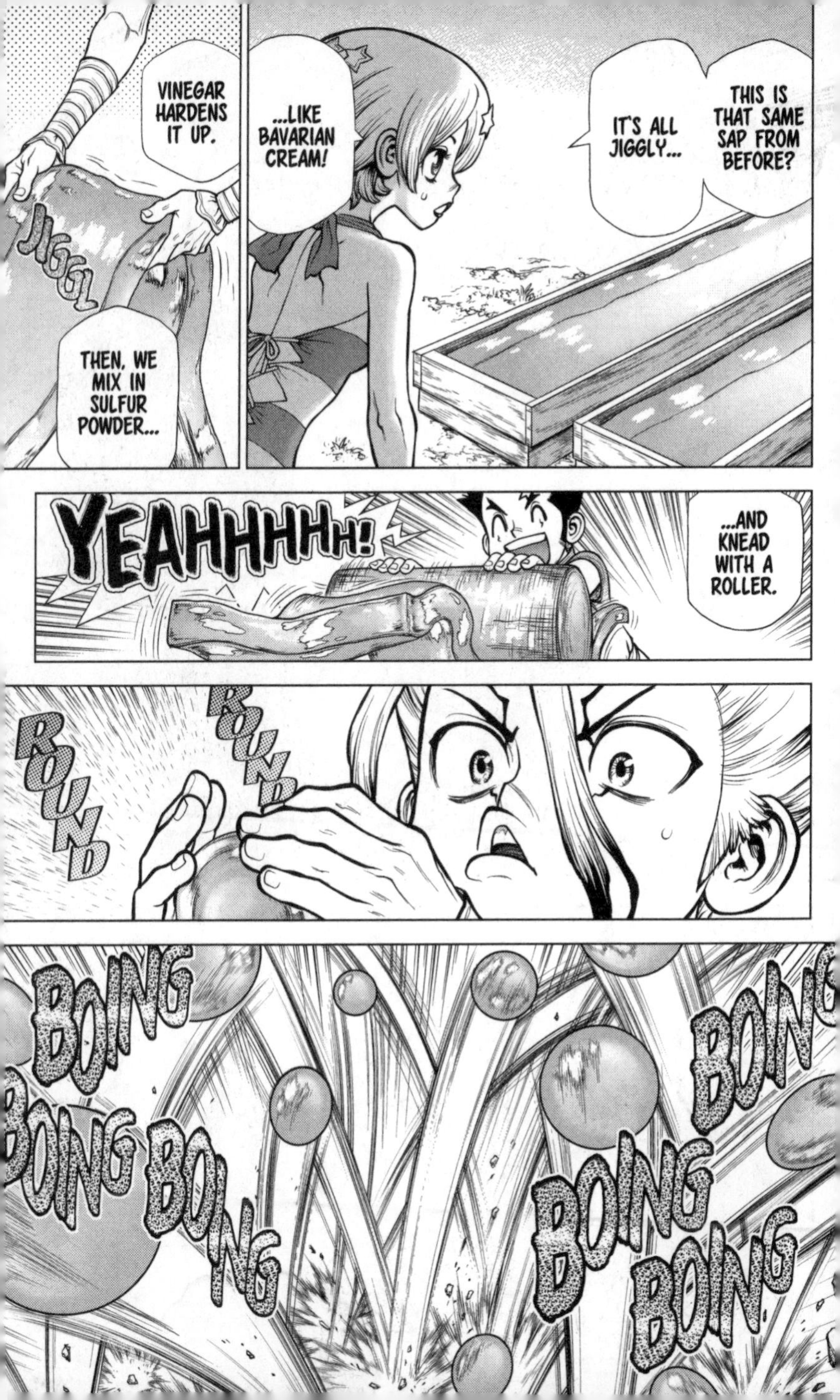
THIS IS THAT SAME SAP FROM BEFORE?
IT'S ALL JIGGLY...
...LIKE BAVARIAN CREAM!
VINEGAR HARDENS IT UP.
JIGGL
THEN, WE MIX IN SULFUR POWDER...
...AND KNEAD WITH A ROLLER.
YEAHHHHH!
ROUND
ROUND
BOING
BOING
BOING
BOING
BOING
BOING
BOING
BOING

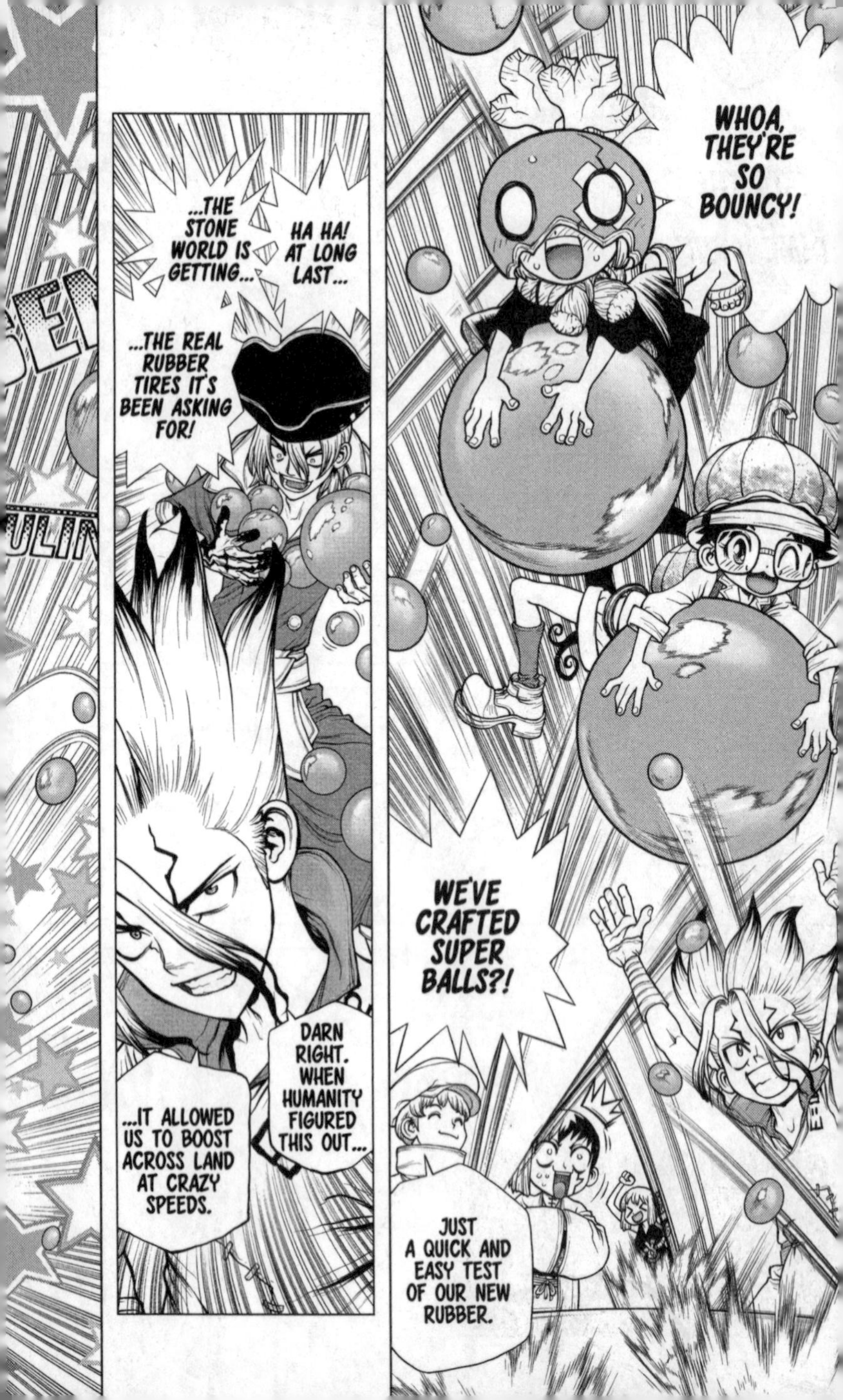
WHOA, THEY'RE SO BOUNCY!
WE'VE CRAFTED SUPER BALLS?!
JUST A QUICK AND EASY TEST OF OUR NEW RUBBER.
HA HA! AT LONG LAST...
...THE STONE WORLD IS GETTING...
...THE REAL RUBBER TIRES IT'S BEEN ASKING FOR!
DARN RIGHT. WHEN HUMANITY FIGURED THIS OUT...
...IT ALLOWED US TO BOOST ACROSS LAND AT CRAZY SPEEDS.

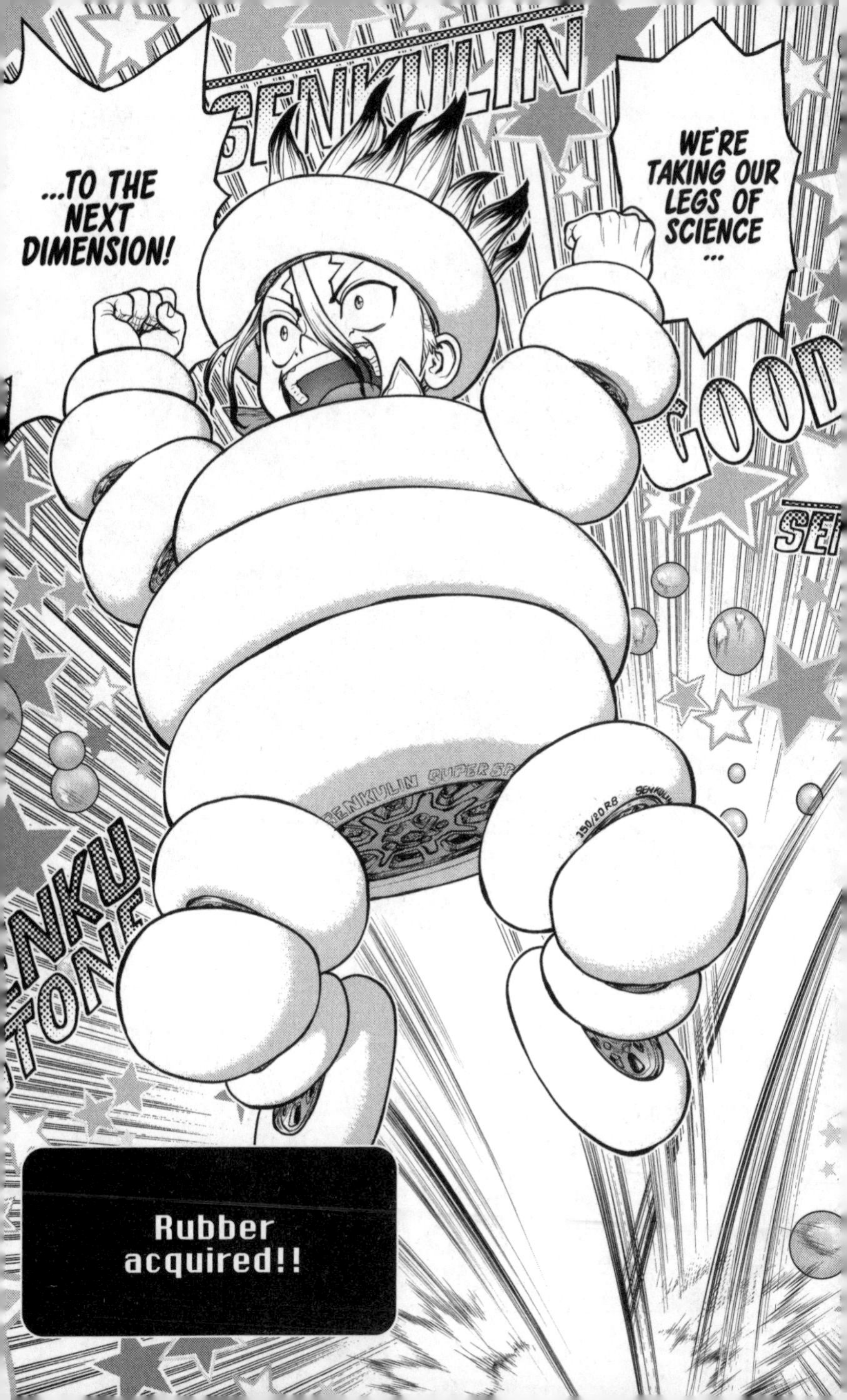
WE'RE TAKING OUR LEGS OF SCIENCE ...
...TO THE NEXT DIMENSION!
SENKULIN
GOOD
Rubber acquired!!

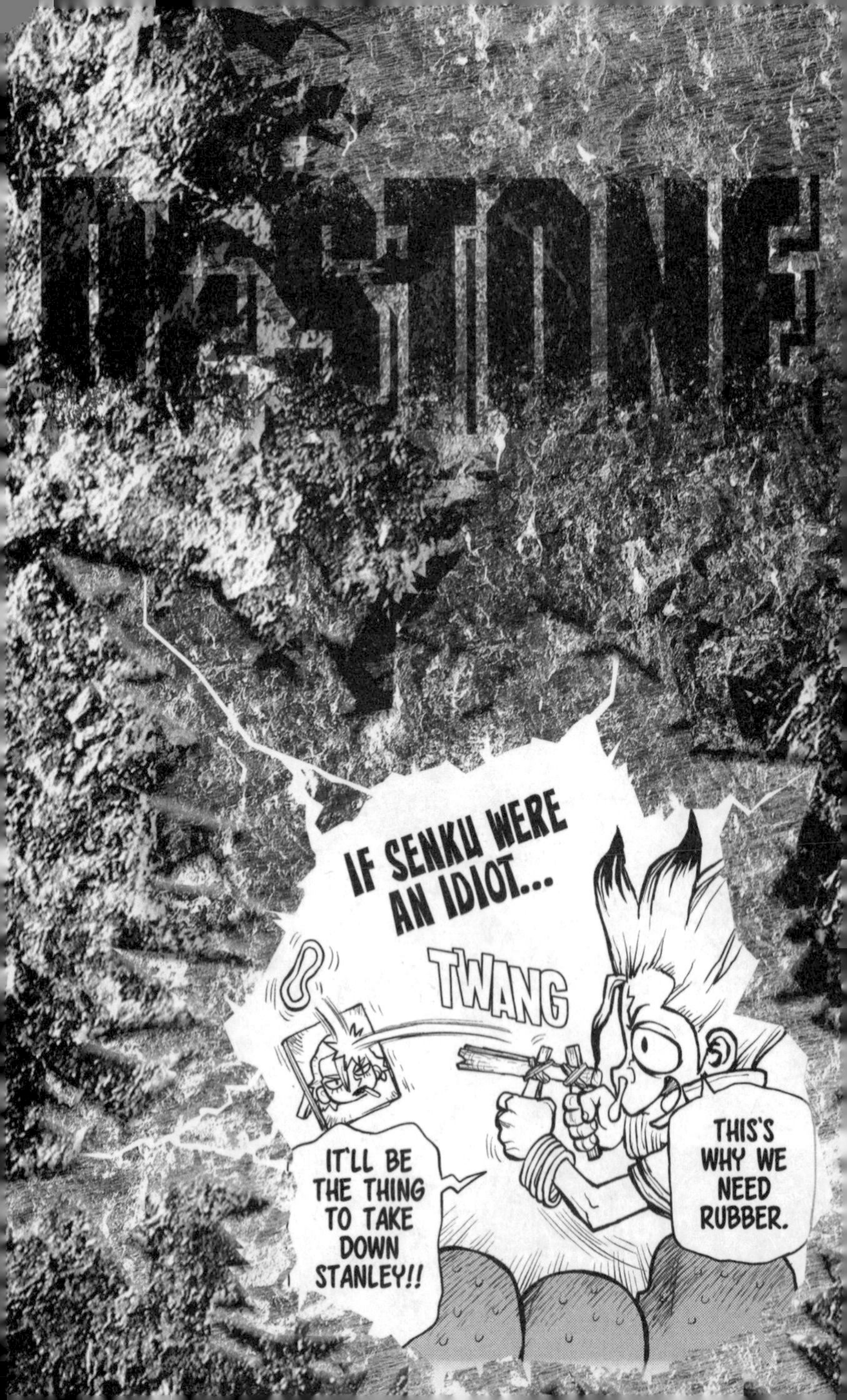
DR.STONE
IF SENKU WERE AN IDIOT...
TWANG
THIS'S WHY WE NEED RUBBER.
IT'LL BE THE THING TO TAKE DOWN STANLEY!!

Z=175: Ultra Race Across South America

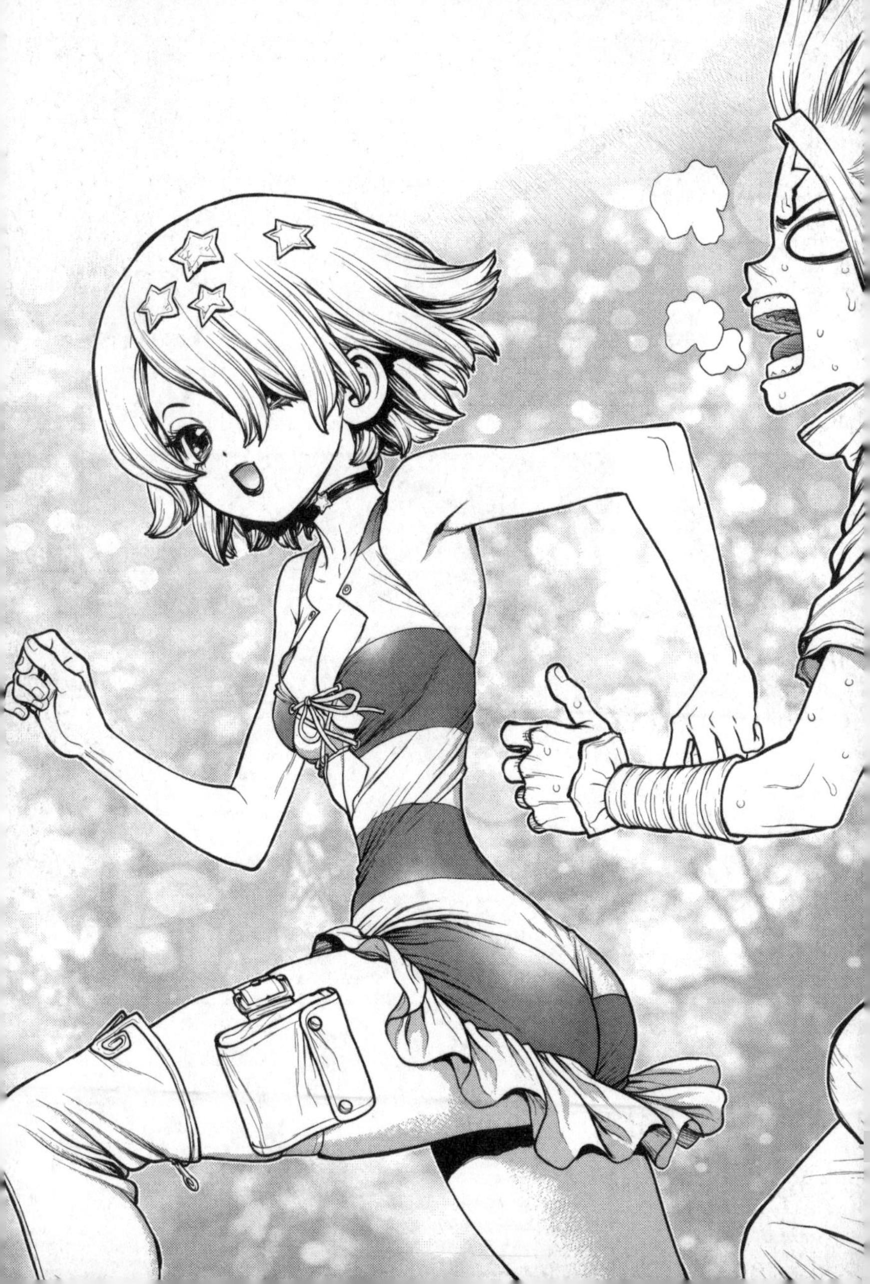

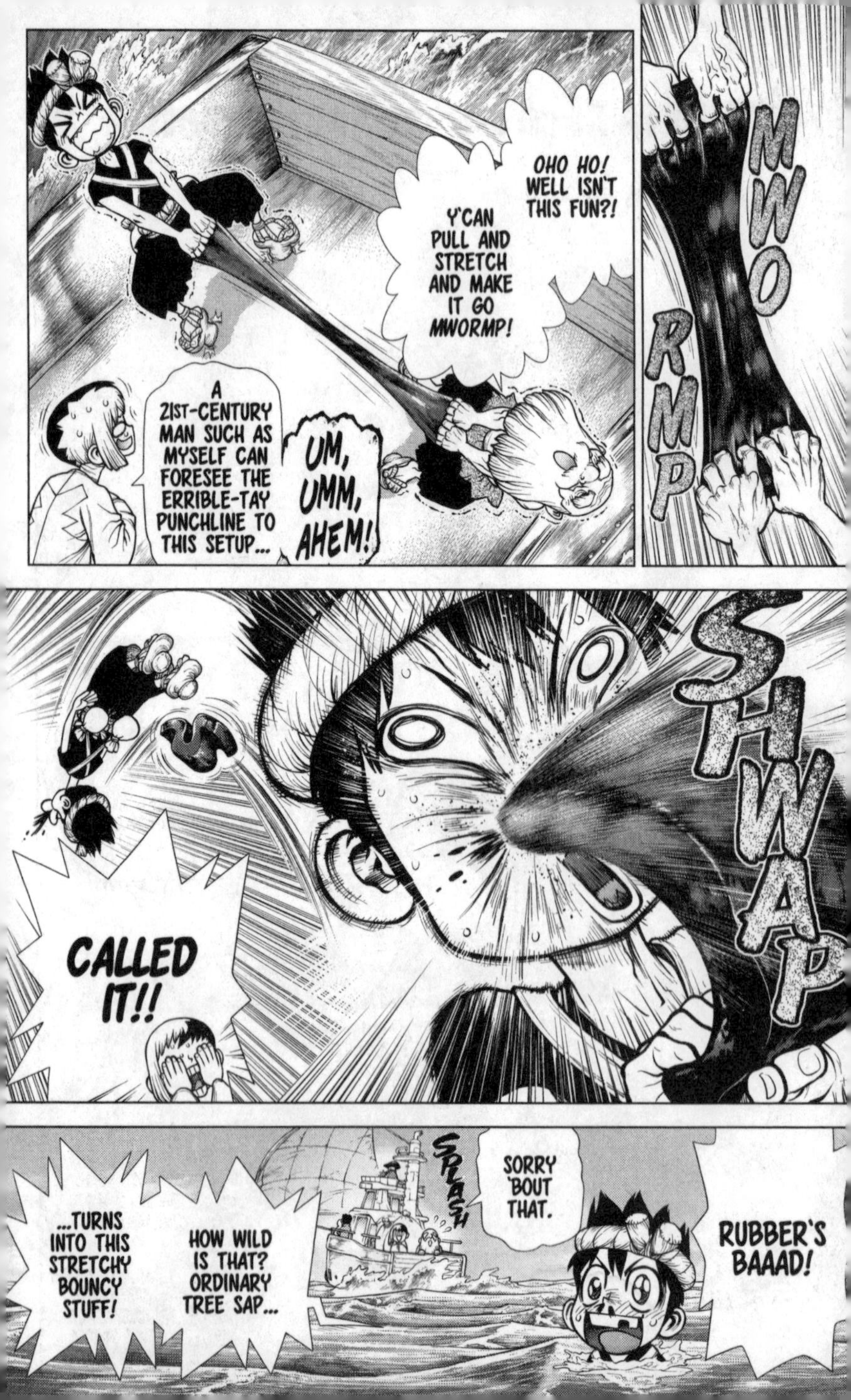
MWORMP
OHO HO! WELL ISN'T THIS FUN?!
Y'CAN PULL AND STRETCH AND MAKE IT GO MWORMP!
UM, UMM, AHEM!
A 21ST-CENTURY MAN SUCH AS MYSELF CAN FORESEE THE ERRIBLE-TAY PUNCHLINE TO THIS SETUP...
SHWAP
CALLED IT!!
RUBBER'S BAAAD!
SORRY 'BOUT THAT.
SPLASH
HOW WILD IS THAT? ORDINARY TREE SAP...
...TURNS INTO THIS STRETCHY BOUNCY STUFF!

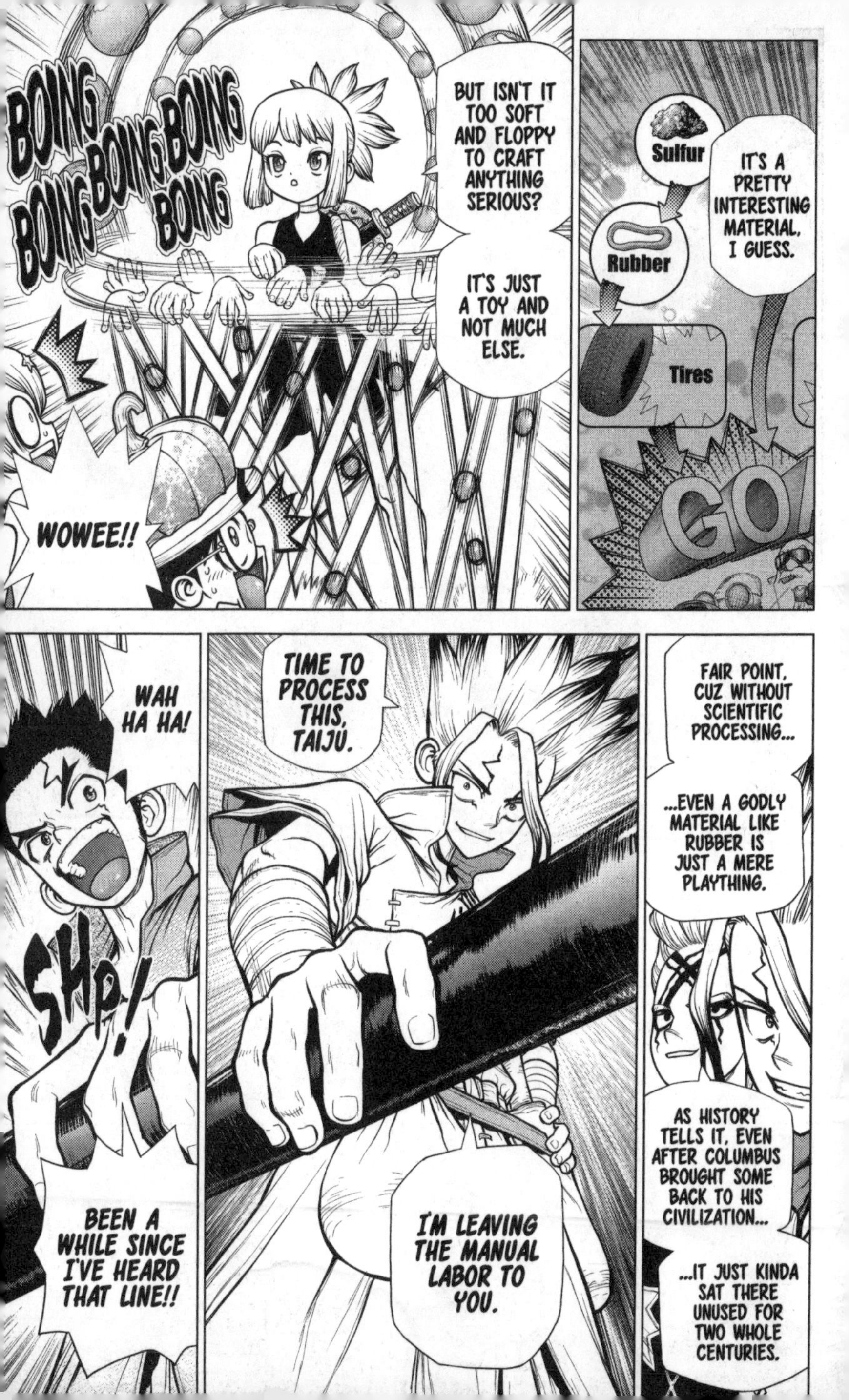
IT'S A PRETTY INTERESTING MATERIAL, I GUESS.
Sulfur
Rubber
Tires
GO
BUT ISN'T IT TOO SOFT AND FLOPPY TO CRAFT ANYTHING SERIOUS?
IT'S JUST A TOY AND NOT MUCH ELSE.
BOING BOING BOING BOING BOING BOING
WOWEE!!
FAIR POINT, CUZ WITHOUT SCIENTIFIC PROCESSING...
...EVEN A GODLY MATERIAL LIKE RUBBER IS JUST A MERE PLAYTHING.
AS HISTORY TELLS IT, EVEN AFTER COLUMBUS BROUGHT SOME BACK TO HIS CIVILIZATION...
...IT JUST KINDA SAT THERE UNUSED FOR TWO WHOLE CENTURIES.
TIME TO PROCESS THIS, TAIJU.
I'M LEAVING THE MANUAL LABOR TO YOU.
WAH HA HA!
SHP!
BEEN A WHILE SINCE I'VE HEARD THAT LINE!!

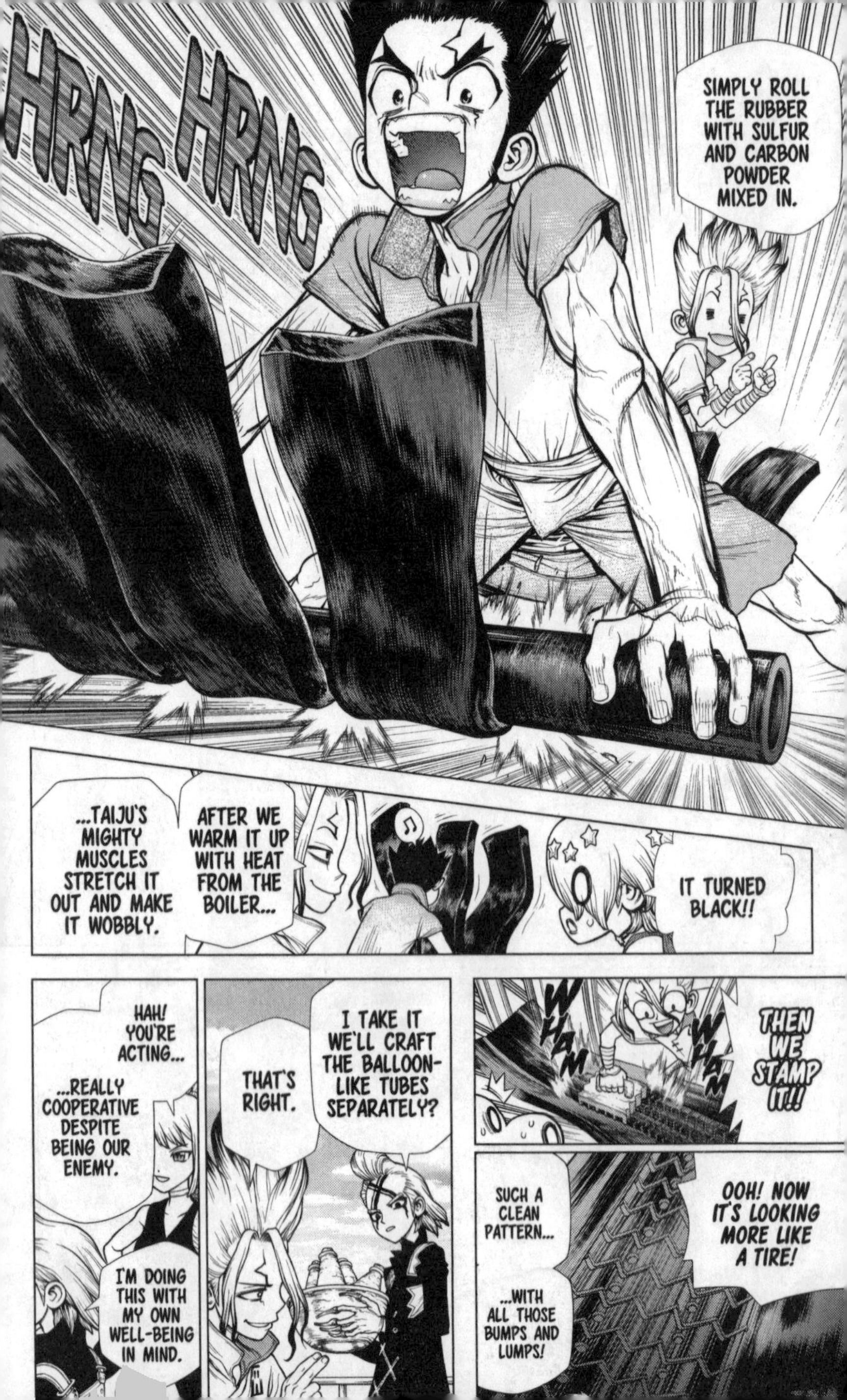
SIMPLY ROLL THE RUBBER WITH SULFUR AND CARBON POWDER MIXED IN.
HRNG HRNG
IT TURNED BLACK!!
AFTER WE WARM IT UP WITH HEAT FROM THE BOILER...
...TAIJU'S MIGHTY MUSCLES STRETCH IT OUT AND MAKE IT WOBBLY.
THEN WE STAMP IT!!
WHAM
WHAM
OOH! NOW IT'S LOOKING MORE LIKE A TIRE!
SUCH A CLEAN PATTERN...
...WITH ALL THOSE BUMPS AND LUMPS!
I TAKE IT WE'LL CRAFT THE BALLOON-LIKE TUBES SEPARATELY?
THAT'S RIGHT.
HAH! YOU'RE ACTING...
...REALLY COOPERATIVE DESPITE BEING OUR ENEMY.
I'M DOING THIS WITH MY OWN WELL-BEING IN MIND.

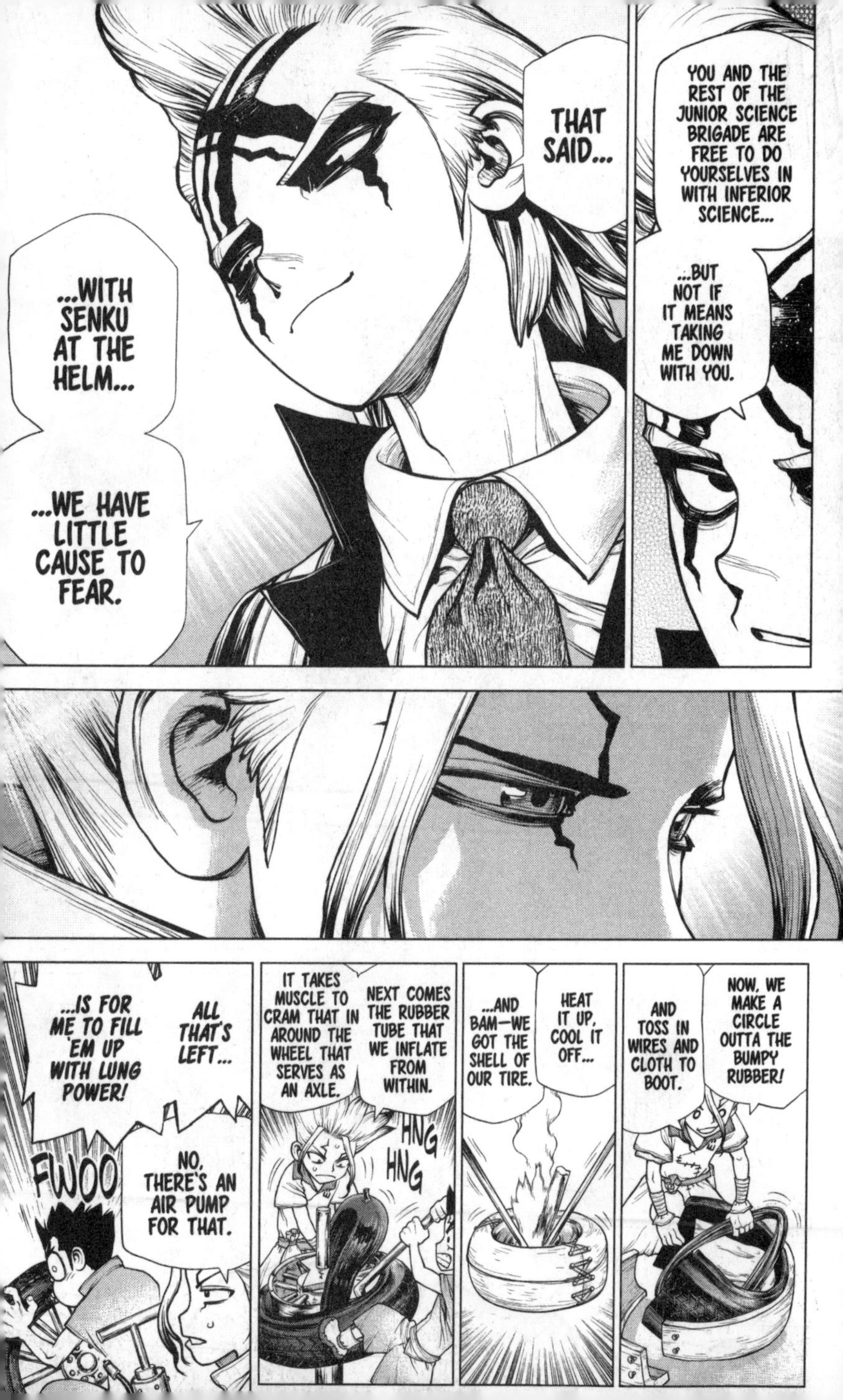
YOU AND THE REST OF THE JUNIOR SCIENCE BRIGADE ARE FREE TO DO YOURSELVES IN WITH INFERIOR SCIENCE...
...BUT NOT IF IT MEANS TAKING ME DOWN WITH YOU.
THAT SAID...
...WITH SENKU AT THE HELM...
...WE HAVE LITTLE CAUSE TO FEAR.
NOW, WE MAKE A CIRCLE OUTTA THE BUMPY RUBBER!
AND TOSS IN WIRES AND CLOTH TO BOOT.
HEAT IT UP, COOL IT OFF...
...AND BAM—WE GOT THE SHELL OF OUR TIRE.
NEXT COMES THE RUBBER TUBE THAT WE INFLATE FROM WITHIN.
IT TAKES MUSCLE TO CRAM THAT IN AROUND THE WHEEL THAT SERVES AS AN AXLE.
HNG HNG
ALL THAT'S LEFT...
...IS FOR ME TO FILL 'EM UP WITH LUNG POWER!
FWOO
NO, THERE'S AN AIR PUMP FOR THAT.

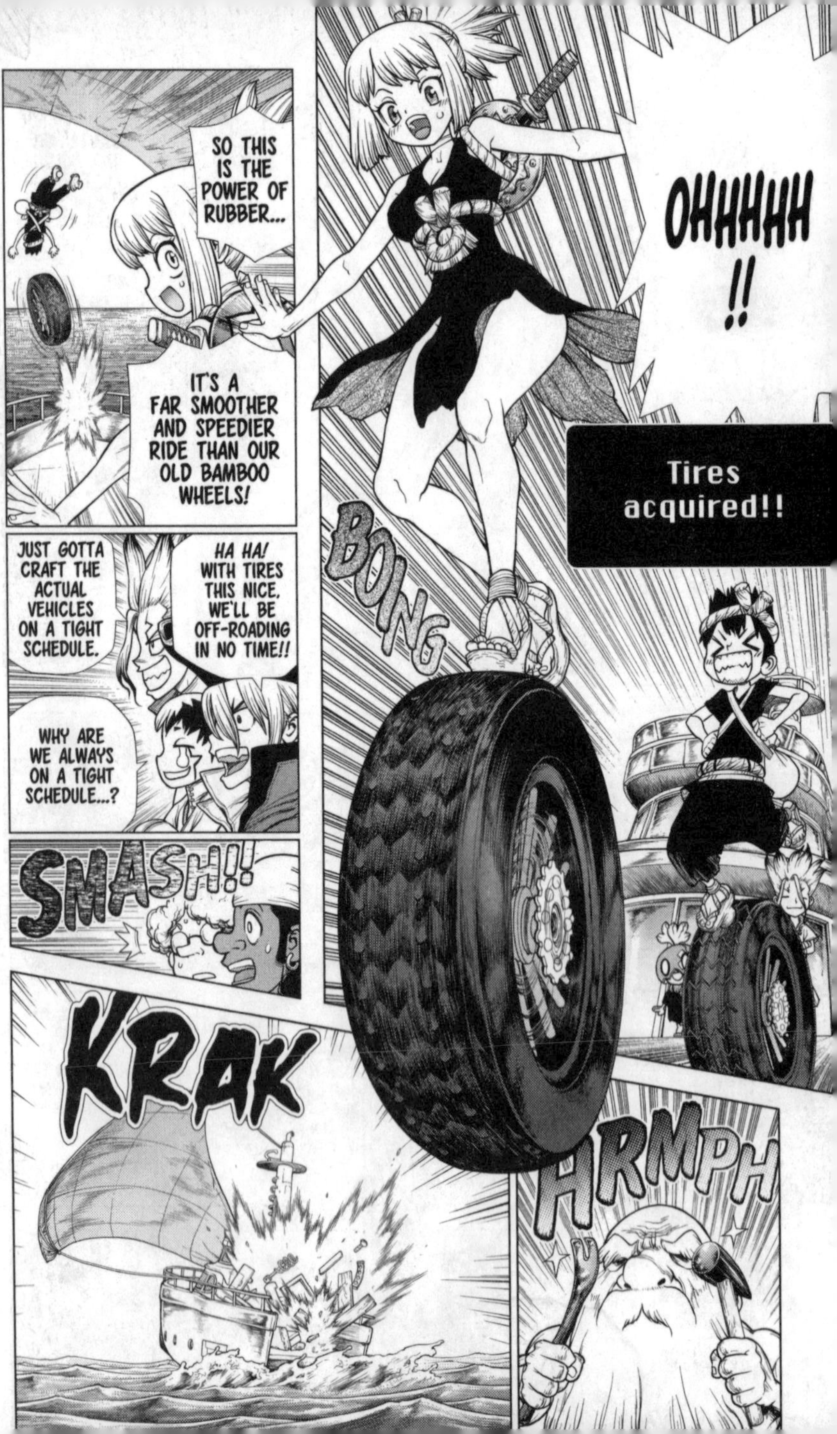
OHHHHH!!
Tires acquired!!
BOING
SO THIS IS THE POWER OF RUBBER...
IT'S A FAR SMOOTHER AND SPEEDIER RIDE THAN OUR OLD BAMBOO WHEELS!
HA HA! WITH TIRES THIS NICE, WE'LL BE OFF-ROADING IN NO TIME!!
JUST GOTTA CRAFT THE ACTUAL VEHICLES ON A TIGHT SCHEDULE.
WHY ARE WE ALWAYS ON A TIGHT SCHEDULE...?
SMASH!!
HRMPH
KRAK

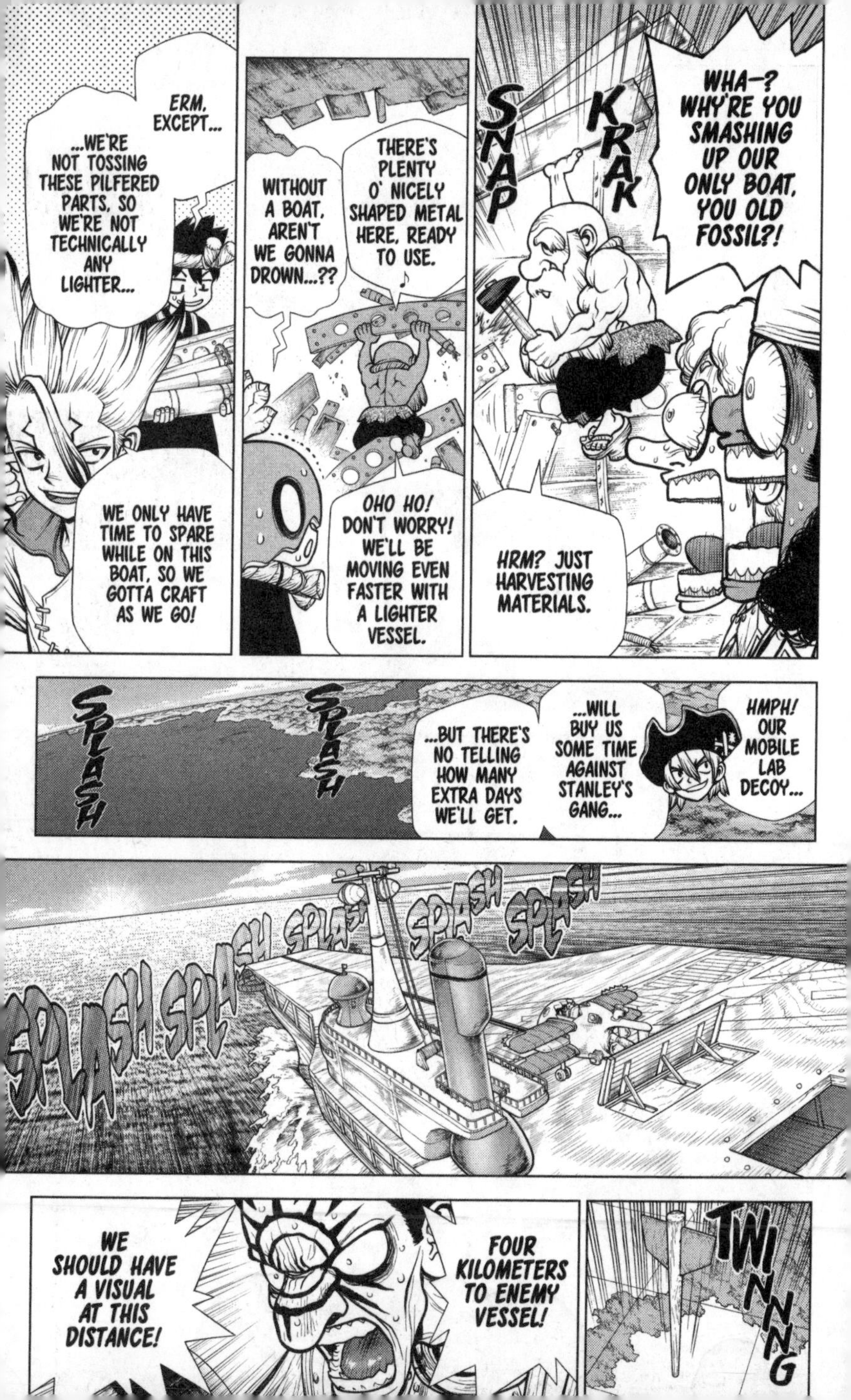
WHA-? WHY'RE YOU SMASHING UP OUR ONLY BOAT, YOU OLD FOSSIL?!
KRAK
SNAP
HRM? JUST HARVESTING MATERIALS.
THERE'S PLENTY O' NICELY SHAPED METAL HERE, READY TO USE. ♪
WITHOUT A BOAT, AREN'T WE GONNA DROWN...??
OHO HO! DON'T WORRY! WE'LL BE MOVING EVEN FASTER WITH A LIGHTER VESSEL.
ERM, EXCEPT...
...WE'RE NOT TOSSING THESE PILFERED PARTS, SO WE'RE NOT TECHNICALLY ANY LIGHTER...
WE ONLY HAVE TIME TO SPARE WHILE ON THIS BOAT, SO WE GOTTA CRAFT AS WE GO!
HMPH! OUR MOBILE LAB DECOY...
...WILL BUY US SOME TIME AGAINST STANLEY'S GANG...
...BUT THERE'S NO TELLING HOW MANY EXTRA DAYS WE'LL GET.
SPLASH
SPLASH
SPLASH SPLASH SPLASH SPLASH SPLASH SPLASH
TWINNNG
FOUR KILOMETERS TO ENEMY VESSEL!
WE SHOULD HAVE A VISUAL AT THIS DISTANCE!

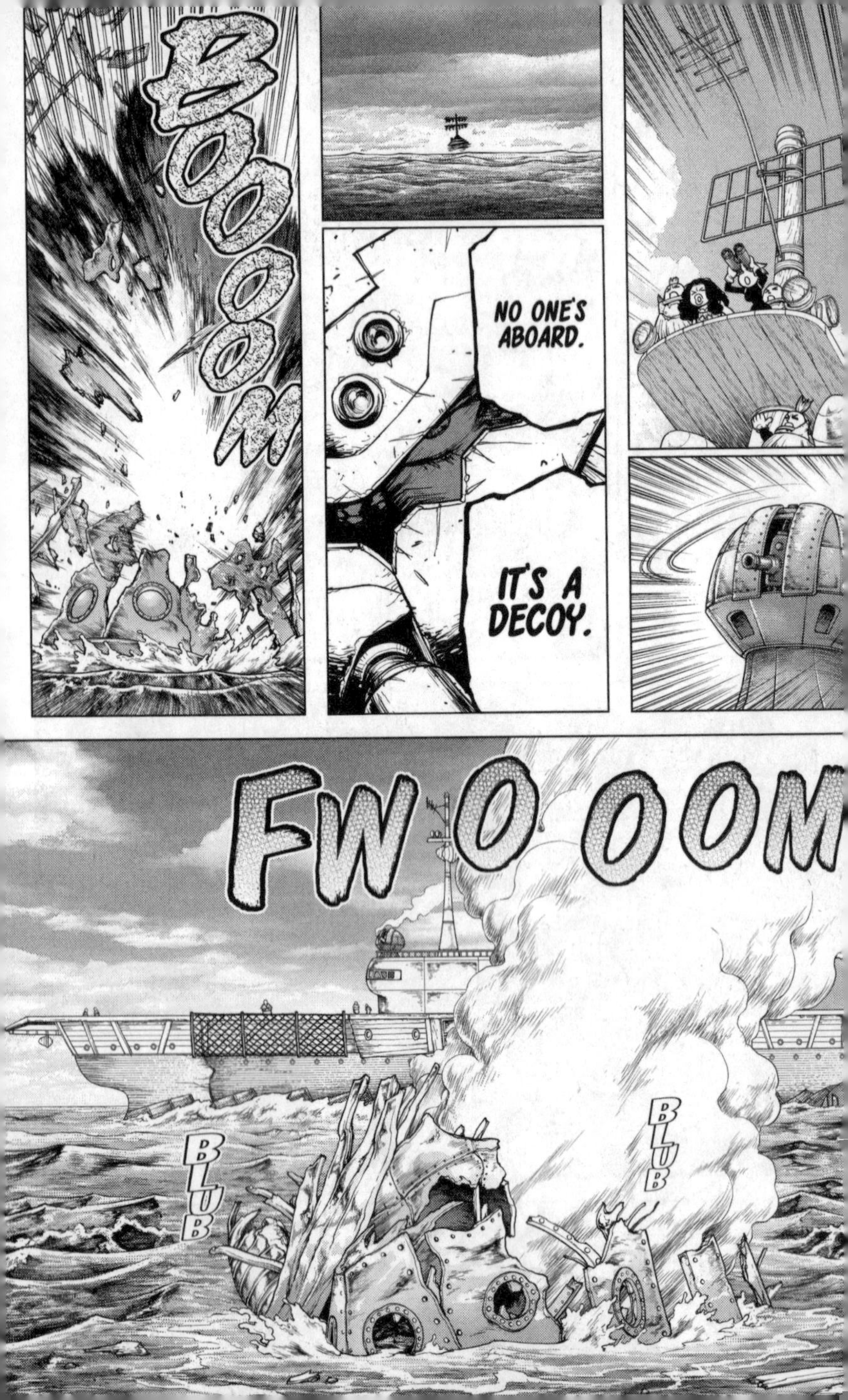
NO ONE'S ABOARD.
IT'S A DECOY.
BOOOOOM
FWOOOM
BLUB
BLUB

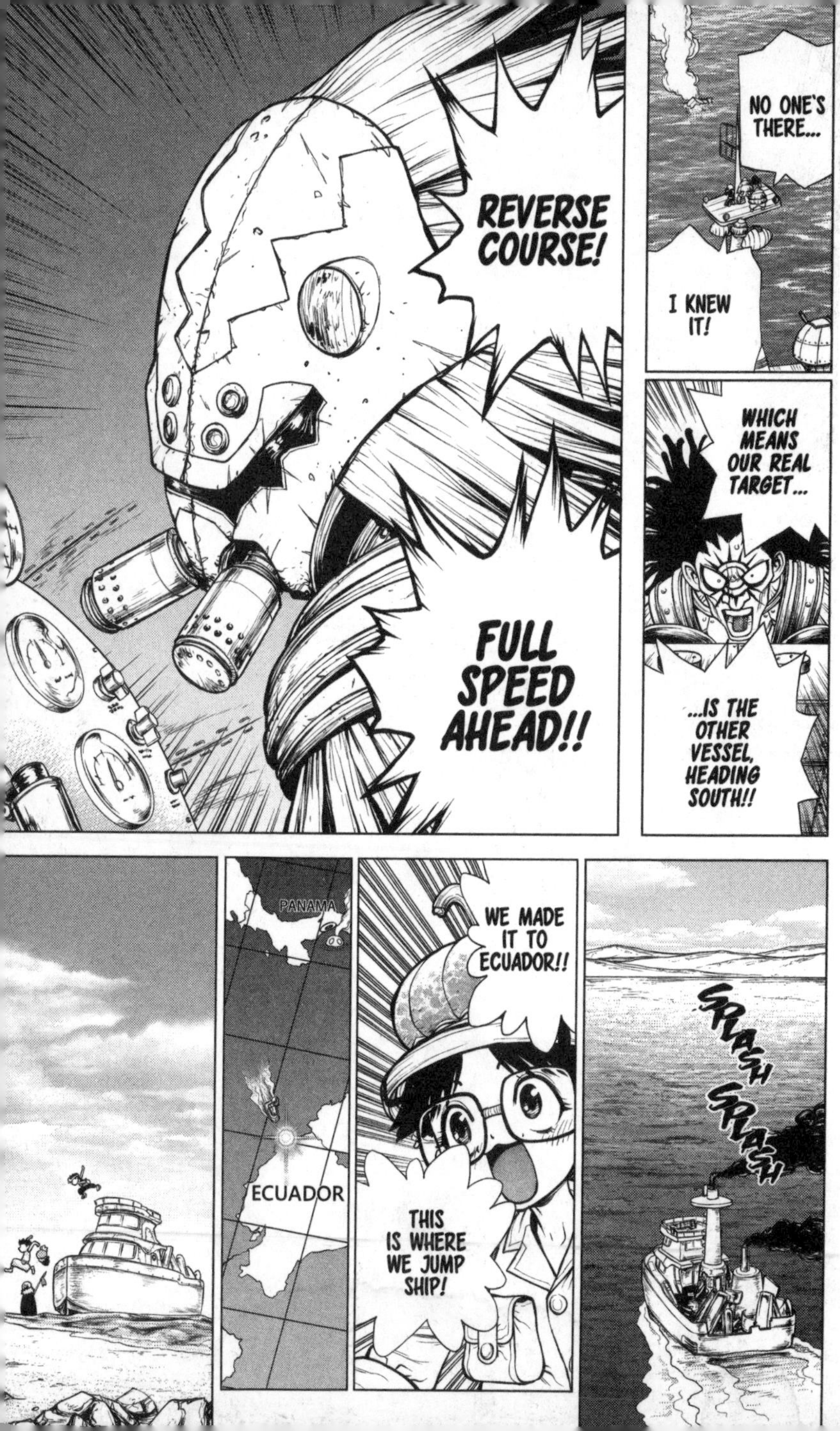
NO ONE'S THERE...
I KNEW IT!
WHICH MEANS OUR REAL TARGET...
...IS THE OTHER VESSEL, HEADING SOUTH!!
REVERSE COURSE!
FULL SPEED AHEAD!!
SPLASH SPLASH
WE MADE IT TO ECUADOR!!
THIS IS WHERE WE JUMP SHIP!
PANAMA
ECUADOR

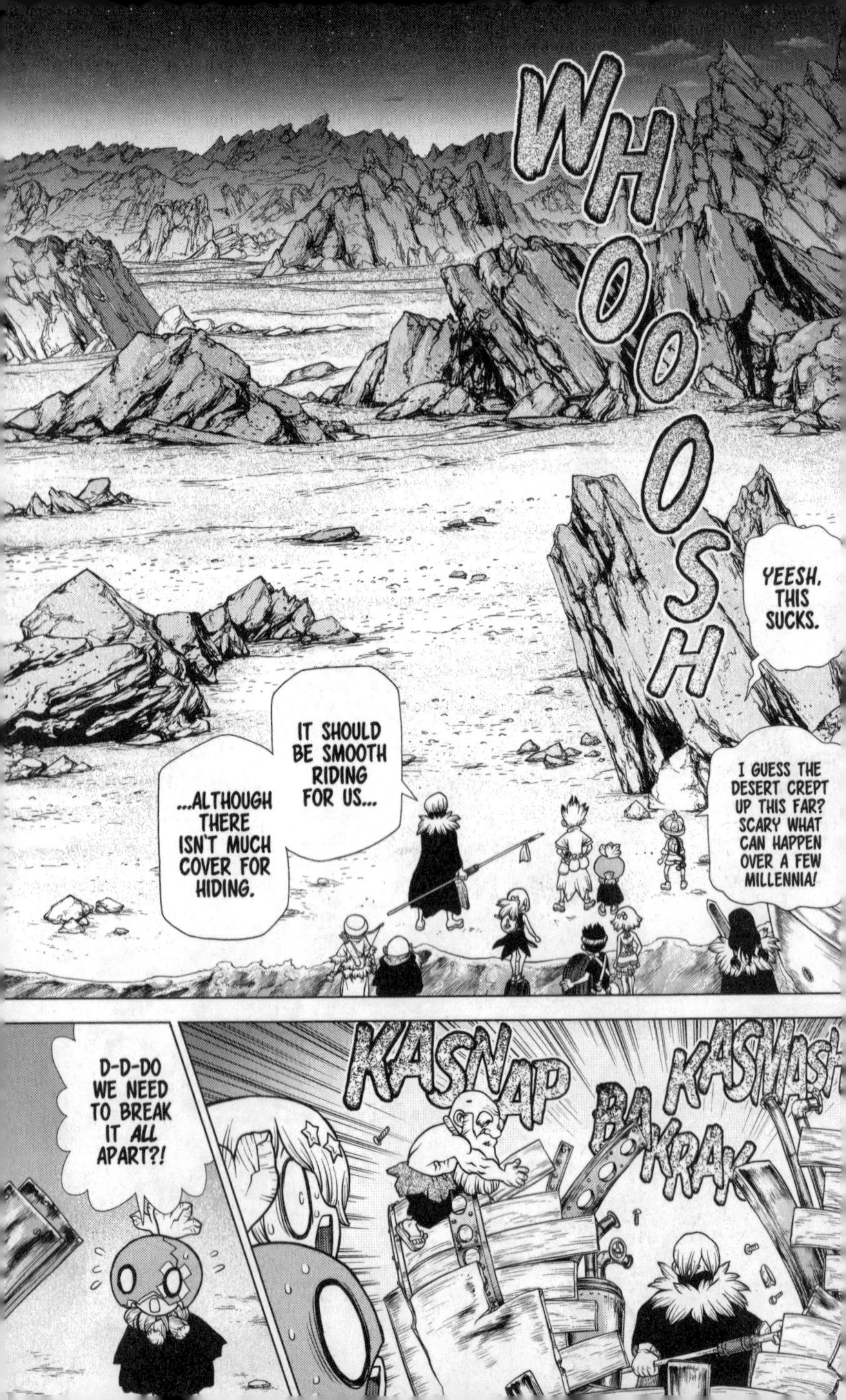
WHOOOOOSH
YEESH. THIS SUCKS.
I GUESS THE DESERT CREPT UP THIS FAR? SCARY WHAT CAN HAPPEN OVER A FEW MILLENNIA!
IT SHOULD BE SMOOTH RIDING FOR US...
...ALTHOUGH THERE ISN'T MUCH COVER FOR HIDING.
KASMASH
BAKRAK
KASNAP
D-D-DO WE NEED TO BREAK IT *ALL* APART?!

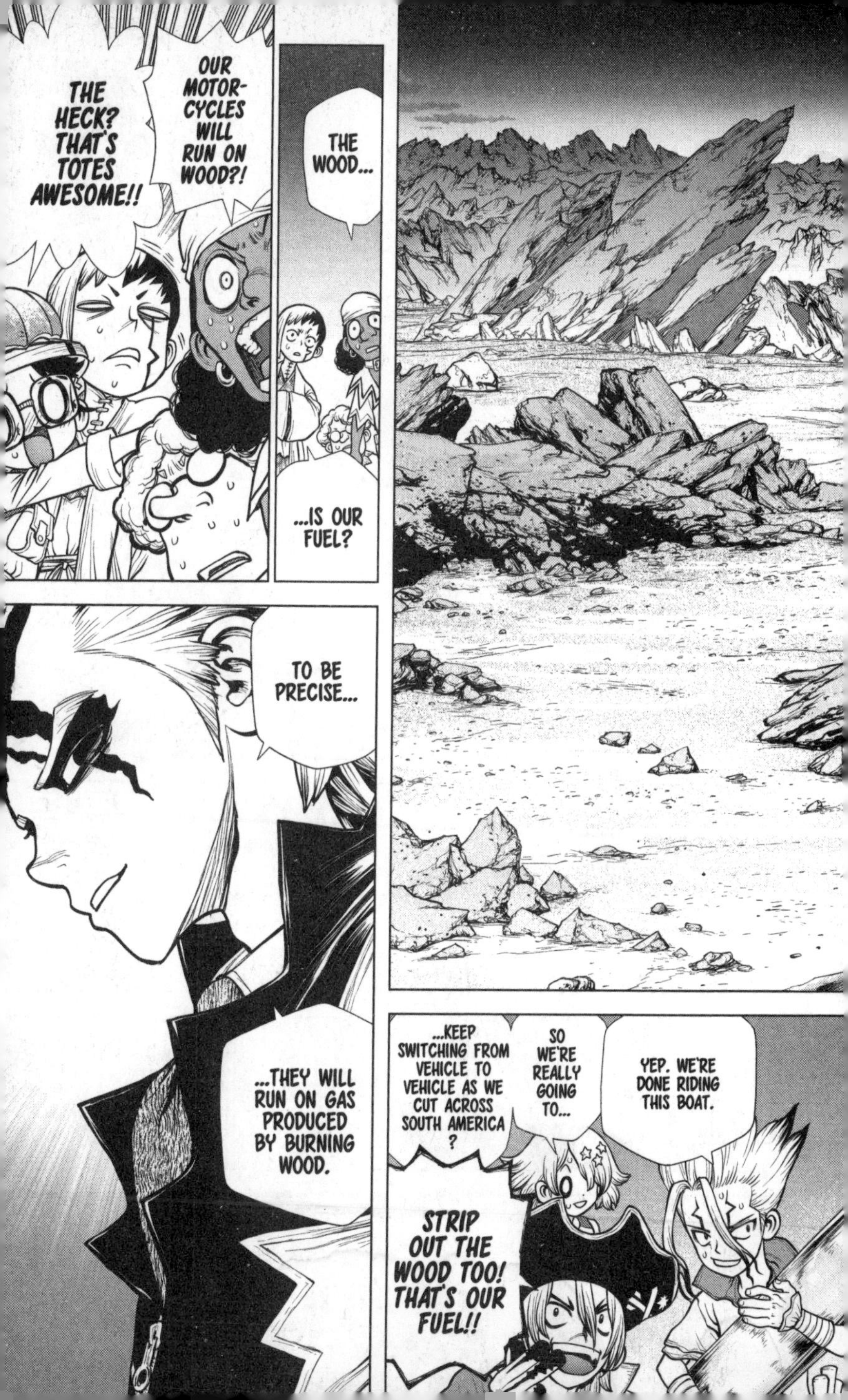
THE WOOD...
...IS OUR FUEL?
OUR MOTOR-CYCLES WILL RUN ON WOOD?!
THE HECK? THAT'S TOTES AWESOME!!
TO BE PRECISE...
...THEY WILL RUN ON GAS PRODUCED BY BURNING WOOD.
YEP. WE'RE DONE RIDING THIS BOAT.
SO WE'RE REALLY GOING TO...
...KEEP SWITCHING FROM VEHICLE TO VEHICLE AS WE CUT ACROSS SOUTH AMERICA ?
STRIP OUT THE WOOD TOO! THAT'S OUR FUEL!!

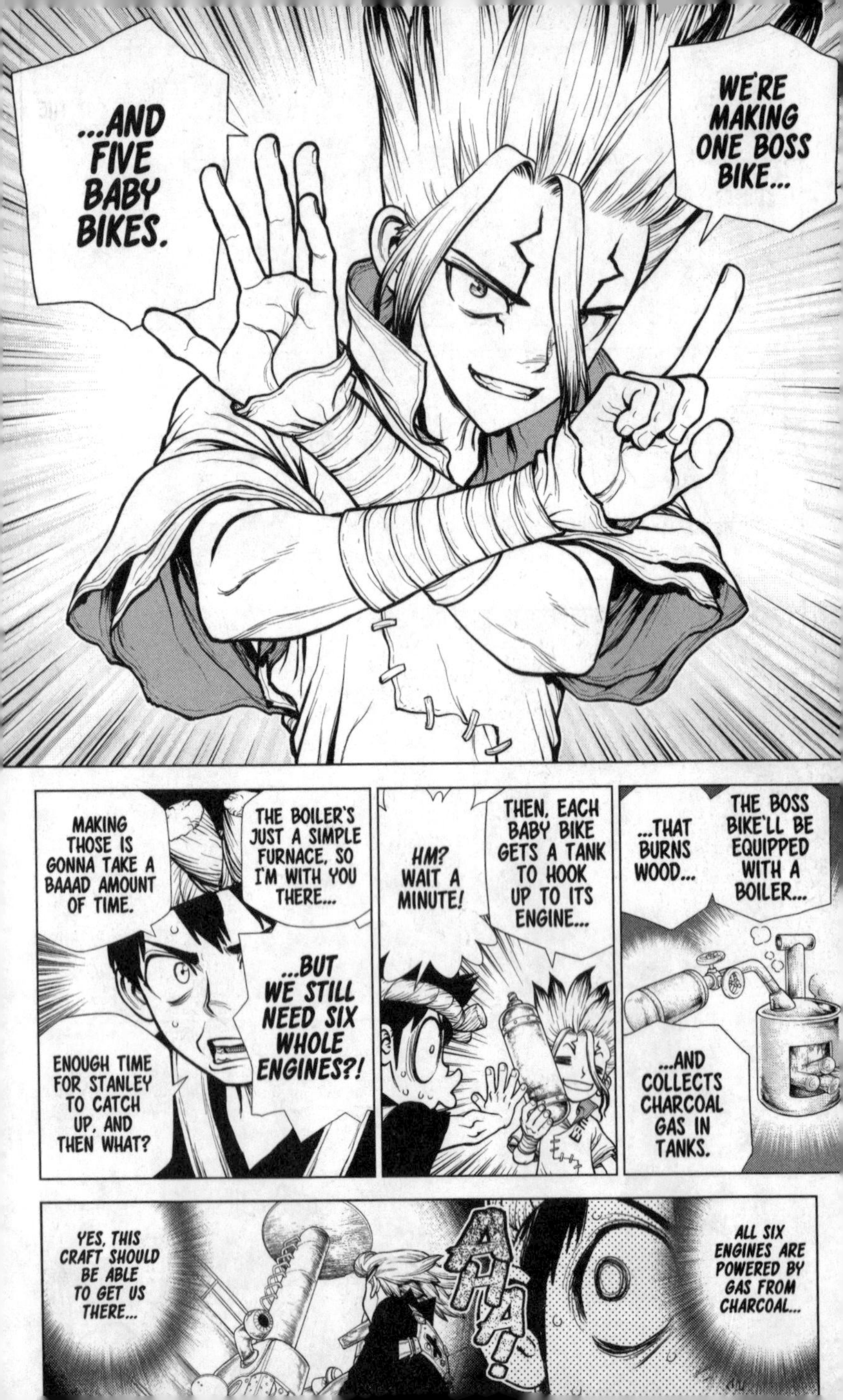
WE'RE MAKING ONE BOSS BIKE...
...AND FIVE BABY BIKES.
THE BOSS BIKE'LL BE EQUIPPED WITH A BOILER...
...THAT BURNS WOOD...
...AND COLLECTS CHARCOAL GAS IN TANKS.
THEN, EACH BABY BIKE GETS A TANK TO HOOK UP TO ITS ENGINE...
HM? WAIT A MINUTE!
THE BOILER'S JUST A SIMPLE FURNACE, SO I'M WITH YOU THERE...
...BUT WE STILL NEED SIX WHOLE ENGINES?!
MAKING THOSE IS GONNA TAKE A BAAAD AMOUNT OF TIME.
ENOUGH TIME FOR STANLEY TO CATCH UP, AND THEN WHAT?
ALL SIX ENGINES ARE POWERED BY GAS FROM CHARCOAL...
AHA!
YES, THIS CRAFT SHOULD BE ABLE TO GET US THERE...

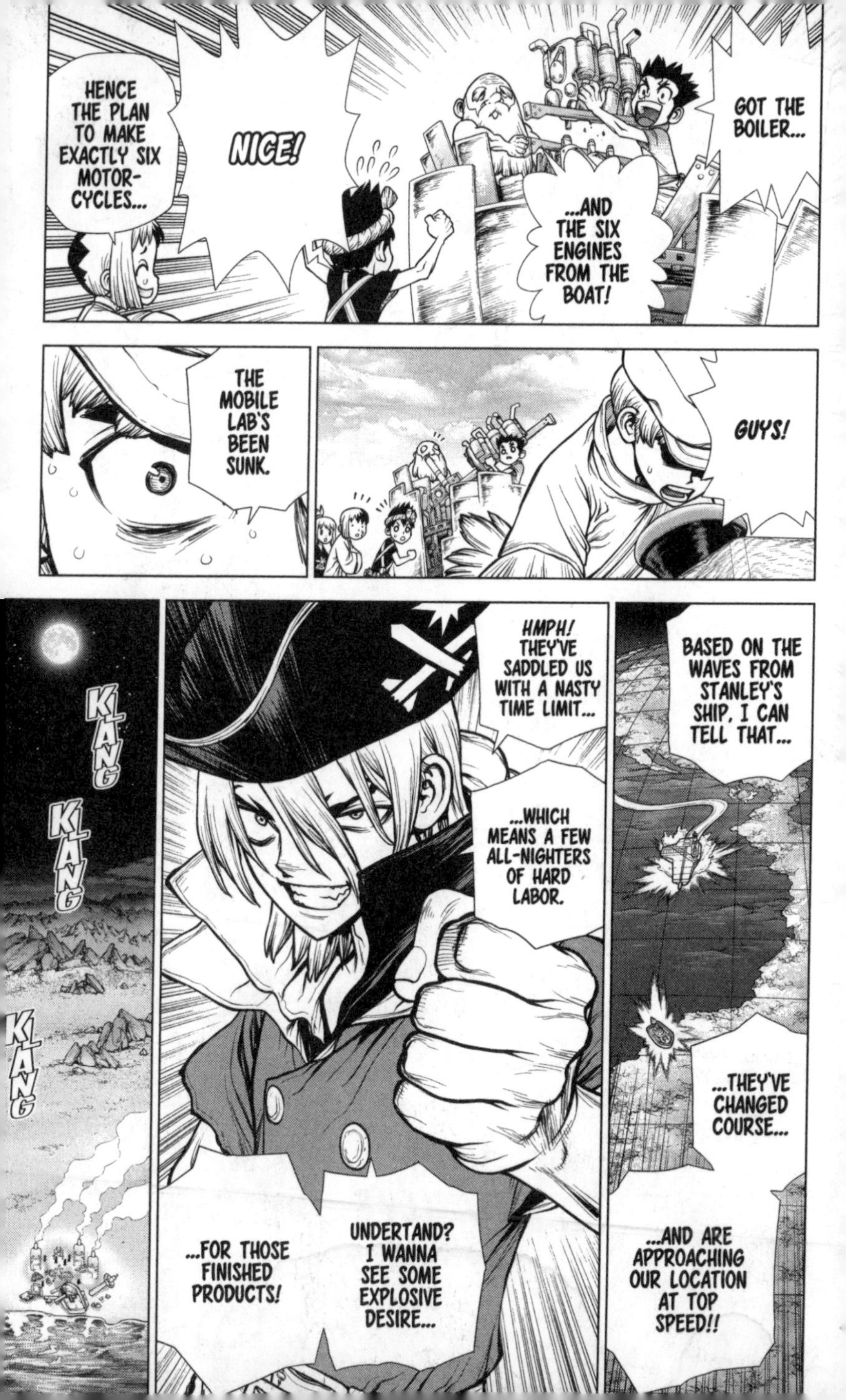
GOT THE BOILER...
...AND THE SIX ENGINES FROM THE BOAT!
NICE!
HENCE THE PLAN TO MAKE EXACTLY SIX MOTOR-CYCLES...
GUYS!
THE MOBILE LAB'S BEEN SUNK.
BASED ON THE WAVES FROM STANLEY'S SHIP, I CAN TELL THAT...
...THEY'VE CHANGED COURSE...
...AND ARE APPROACHING OUR LOCATION AT TOP SPEED!!
HMPH! THEY'VE SADDLED US WITH A NASTY TIME LIMIT...
...WHICH MEANS A FEW ALL-NIGHTERS OF HARD LABOR.
UNDERTAND? I WANNA SEE SOME EXPLOSIVE DESIRE...
...FOR THOSE FINISHED PRODUCTS!
KLANG
KLANG
KLANG

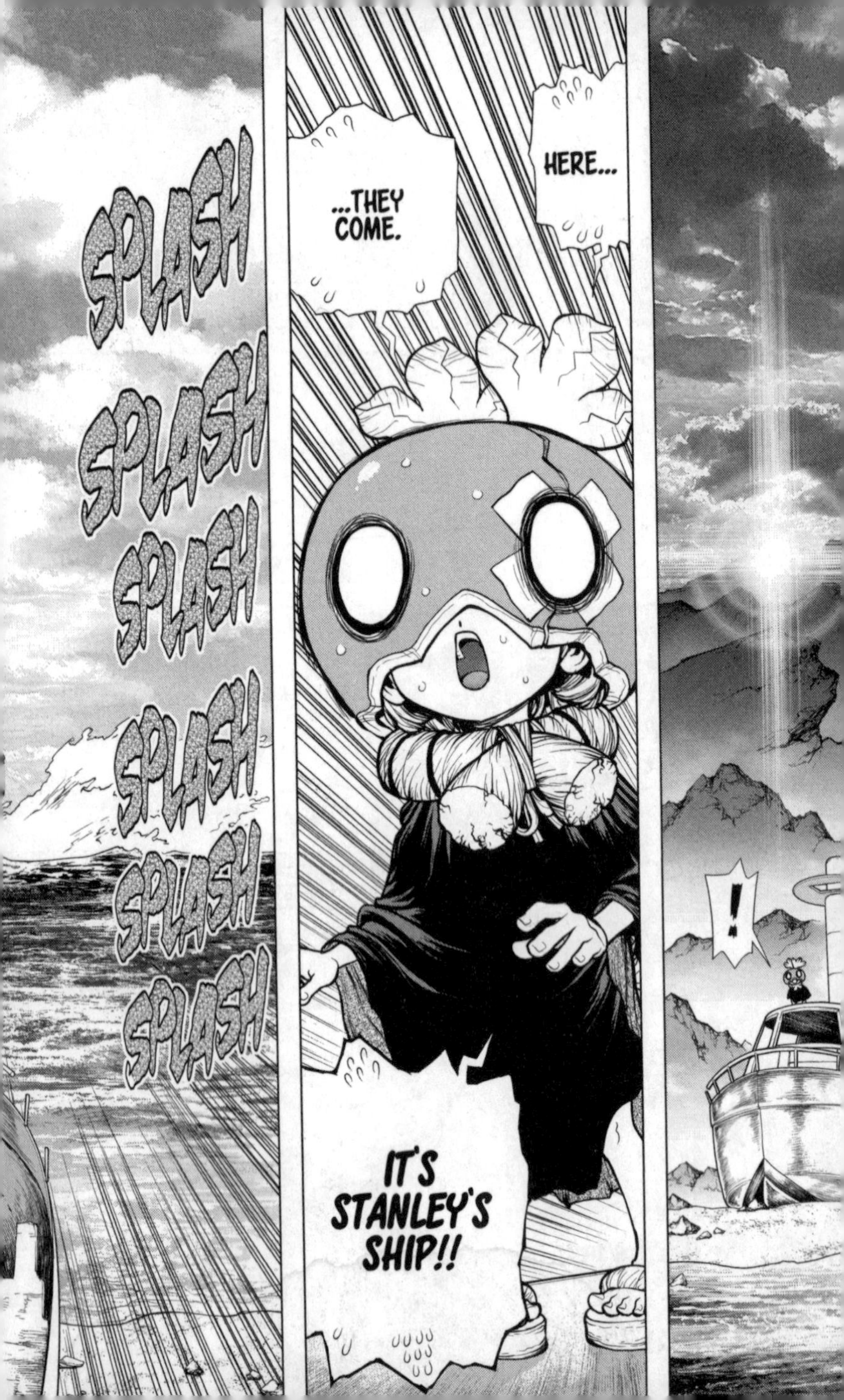
!
HERE...
...THEY COME.
IT'S STANLEY'S SHIP!!
SPLASH
SPLASH
SPLASH
SPLASH
SPLASH
SPLASH

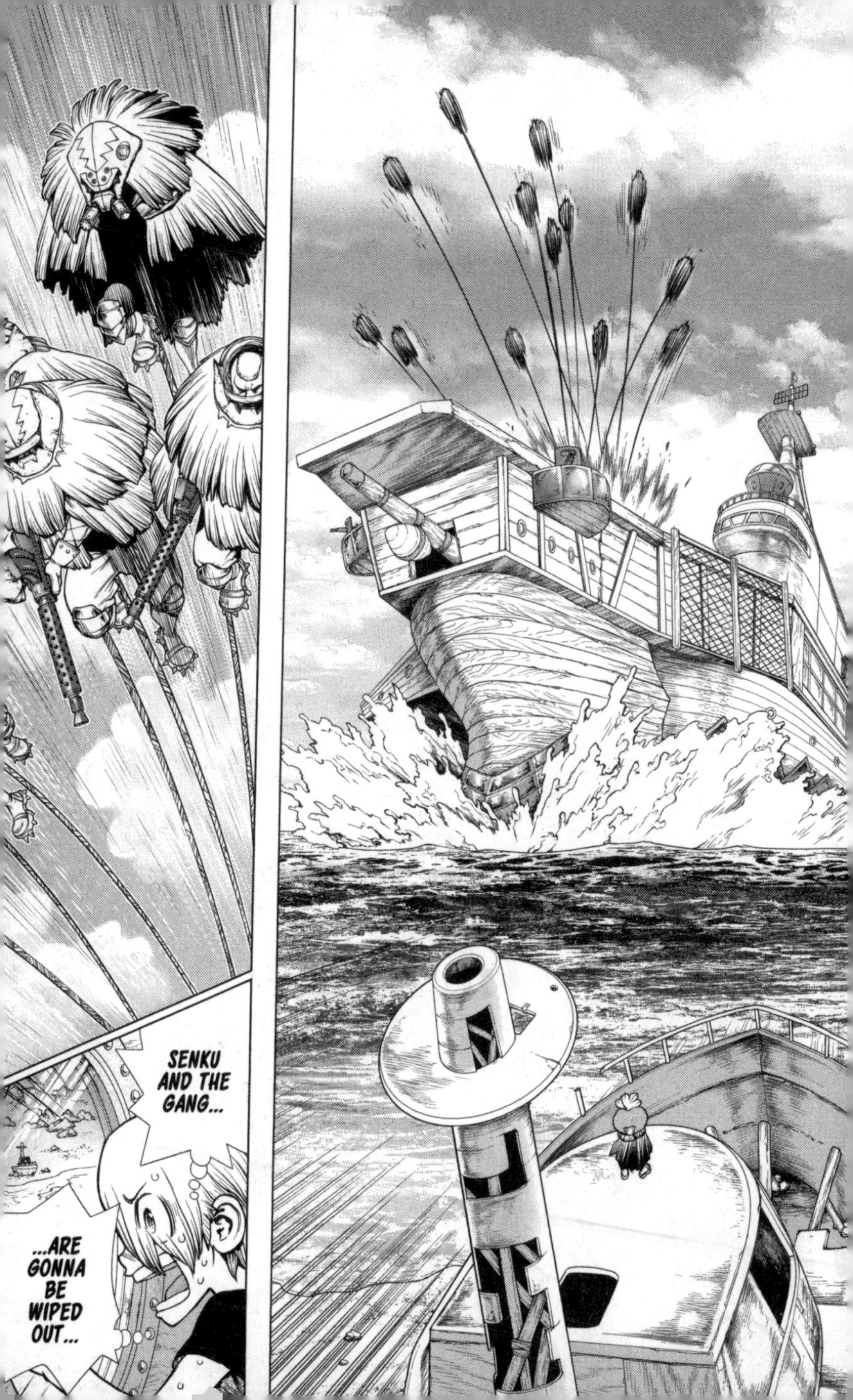
SENKU AND THE GANG...
...ARE GONNA BE WIPED OUT...

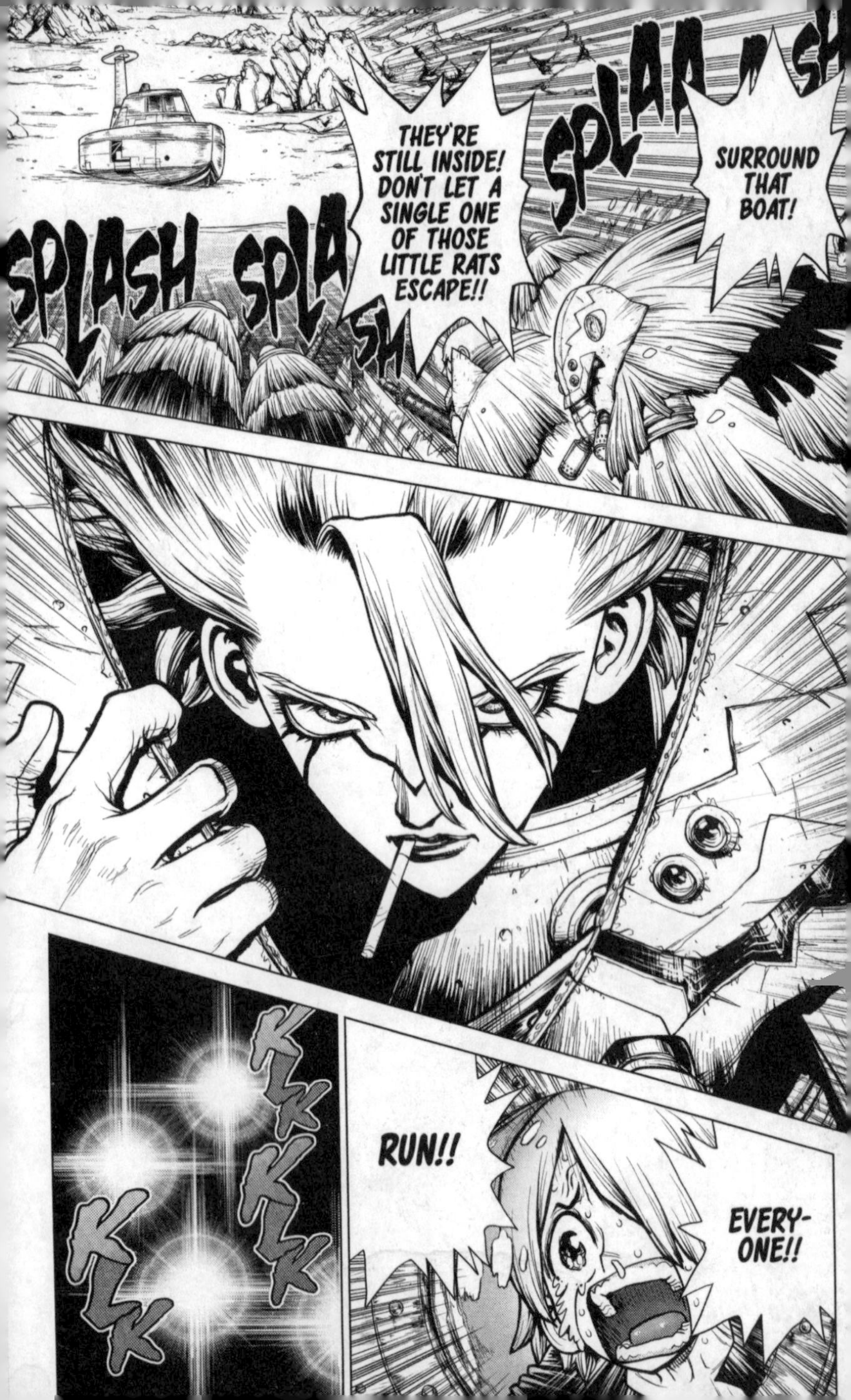
SPLASH
SURROUND THAT BOAT!
SPLASH
THEY'RE STILL INSIDE! DON'T LET A SINGLE ONE OF THOSE LITTLE RATS ESCAPE!!
SPLASH
SPLASH
RUN!!
EVERY-ONE!!

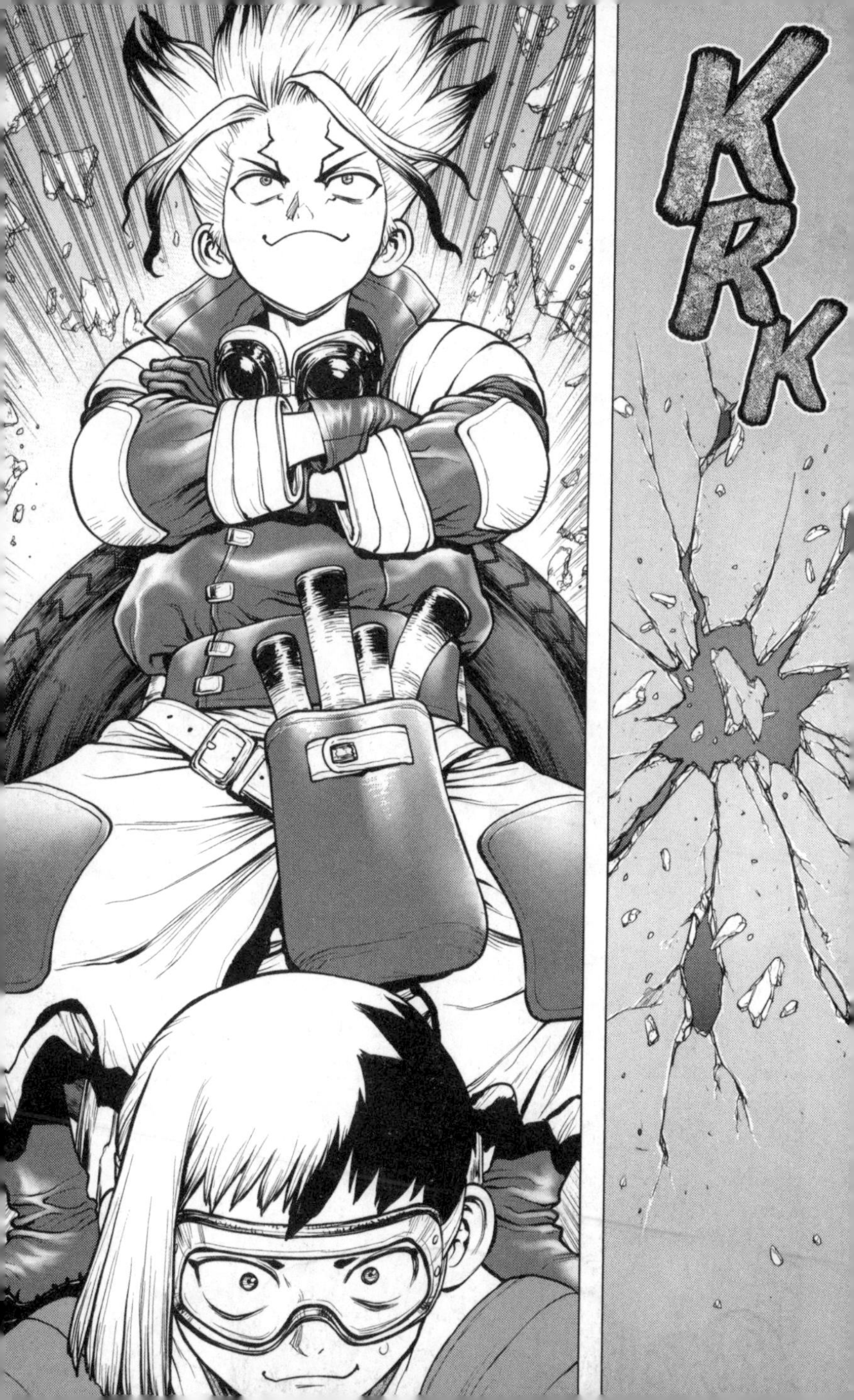
KRK

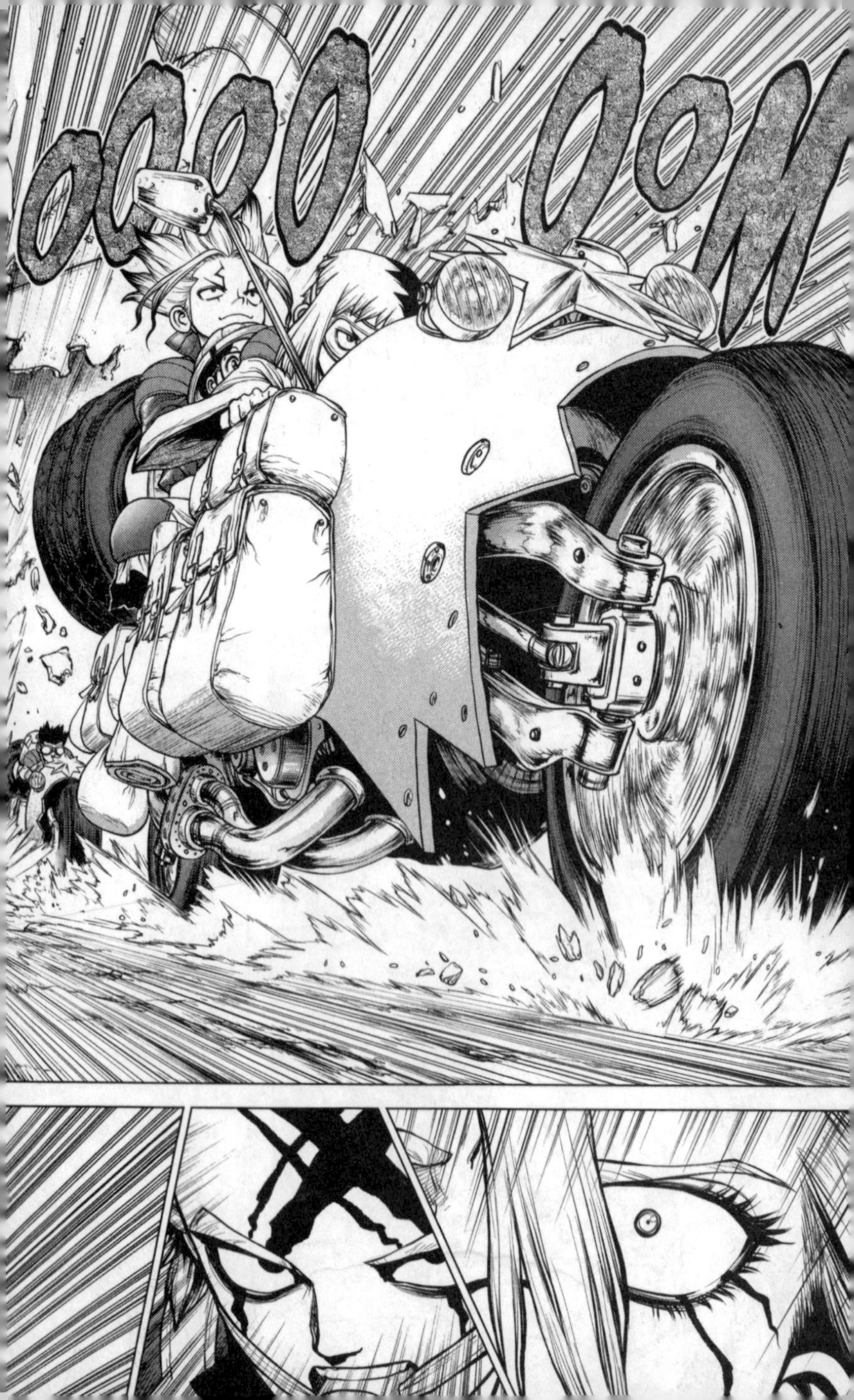
OOOOOOOM

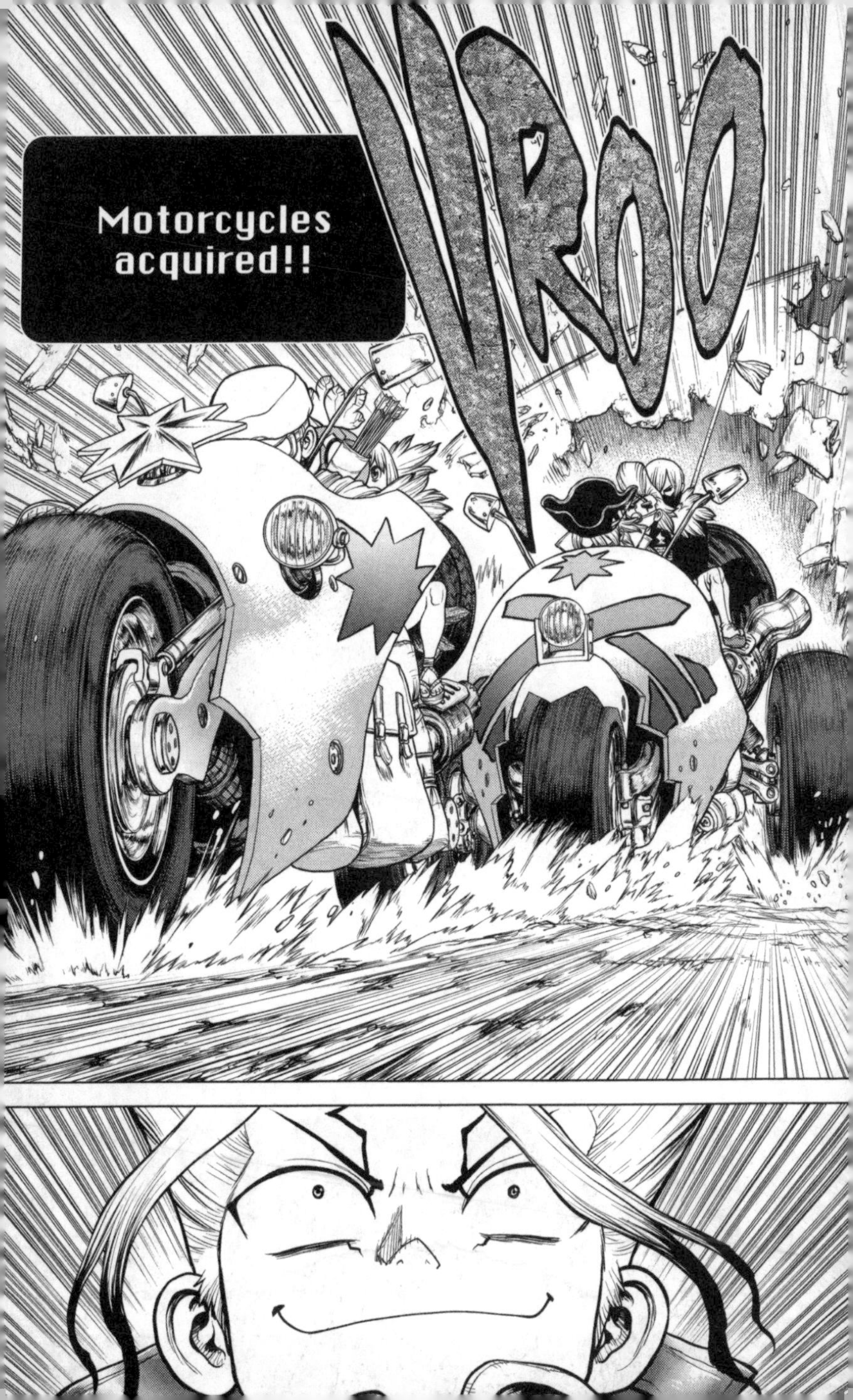
VROO
Motorcycles acquired!!

MECHA SENKU Q&A

SEARCH — Question Corner

Is everyone speaking Japanese to each other? If not, how do they communicate?

M.K. of Shizuoka Prefecture — **SEARCH**

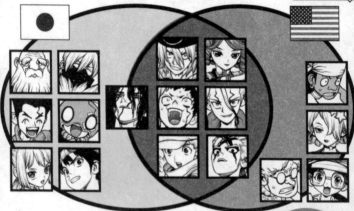

When two people do not share a common tongue. Francois will interpret for them!

Dr.STONE

Z=176: Net-Breaking Battle Plan

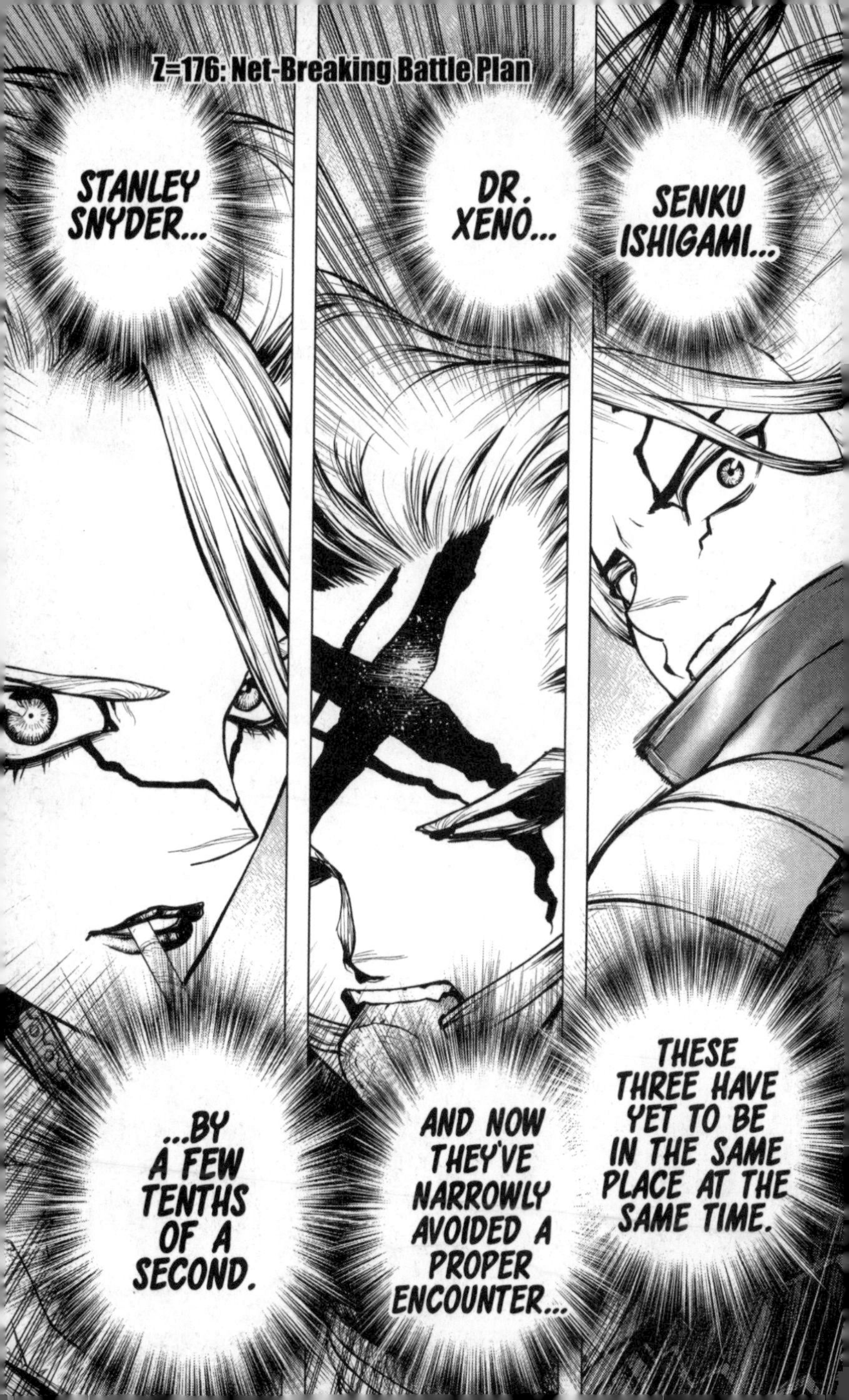
SENKU ISHIGAMI...
DR. XENO...
STANLEY SNYDER...
THESE THREE HAVE YET TO BE IN THE SAME PLACE AT THE SAME TIME.
AND NOW THEY'VE NARROWLY AVOIDED A PROPER ENCOUNTER...
...BY A FEW TENTHS OF A SECOND.

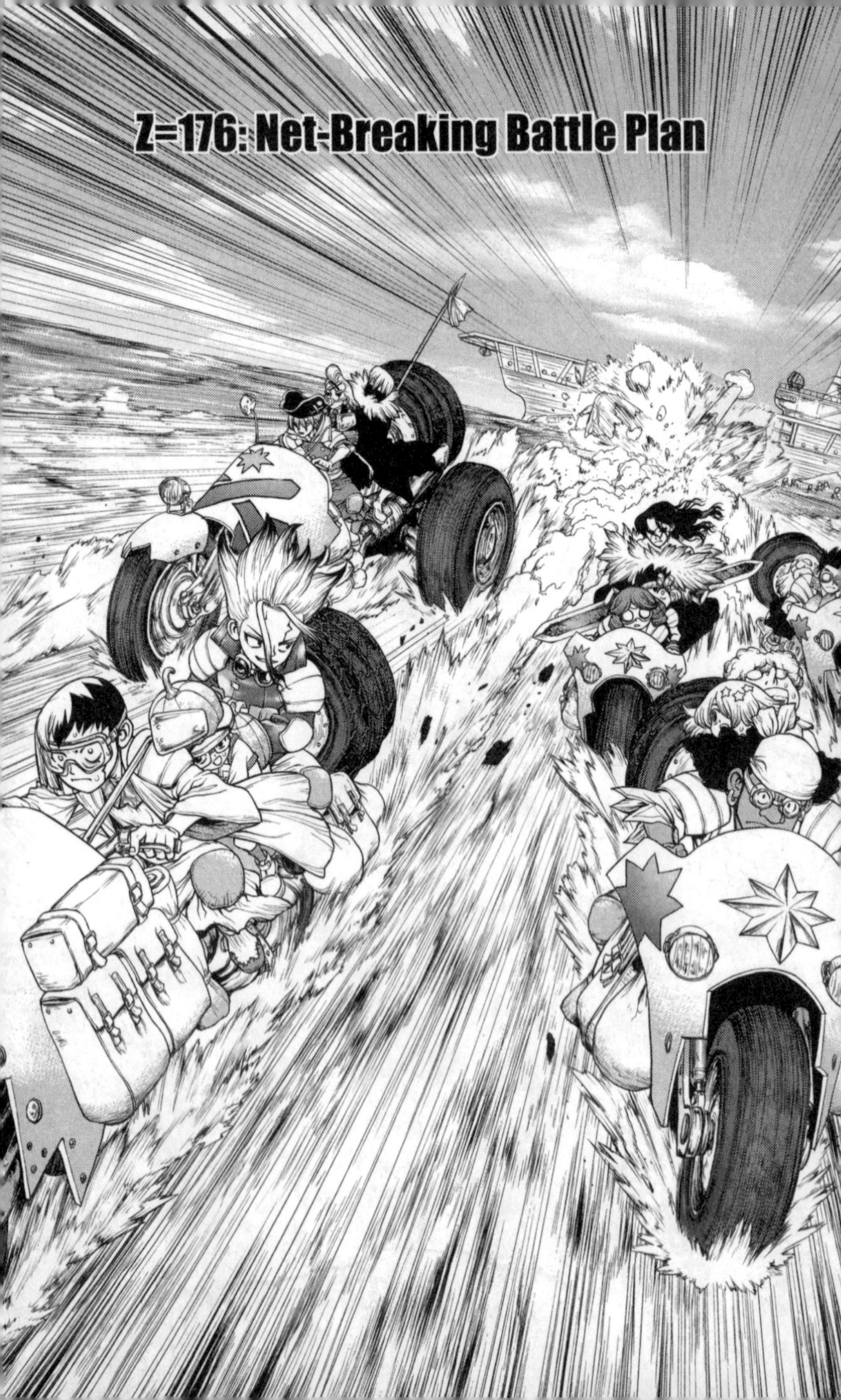
Z=176: Net-Breaking Battle Plan

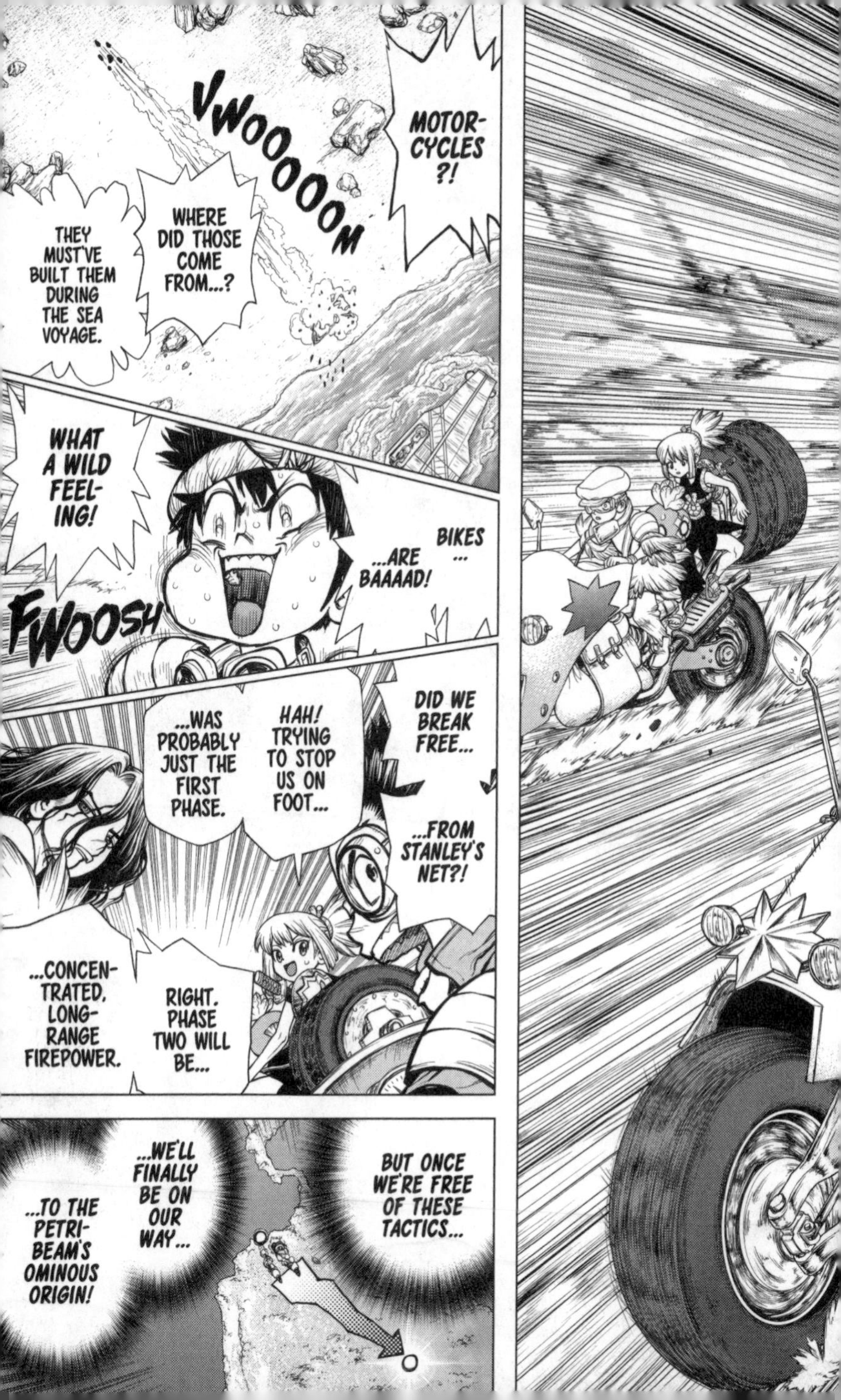
VWOOOOOOM
MOTORCYCLES?!
WHERE DID THOSE COME FROM...?
THEY MUST'VE BUILT THEM DURING THE SEA VOYAGE.
BIKES...
...ARE BAAAAD!
WHAT A WILD FEELING!
FWOOSH
DID WE BREAK FREE...
...FROM STANLEY'S NET?!
HAH! TRYING TO STOP US ON FOOT...
...WAS PROBABLY JUST THE FIRST PHASE.
RIGHT. PHASE TWO WILL BE...
...CONCENTRATED, LONG-RANGE FIREPOWER.
BUT ONCE WE'RE FREE OF THESE TACTICS...
...WE'LL FINALLY BE ON OUR WAY...
...TO THE PETRI-BEAM'S OMINOUS ORIGIN!

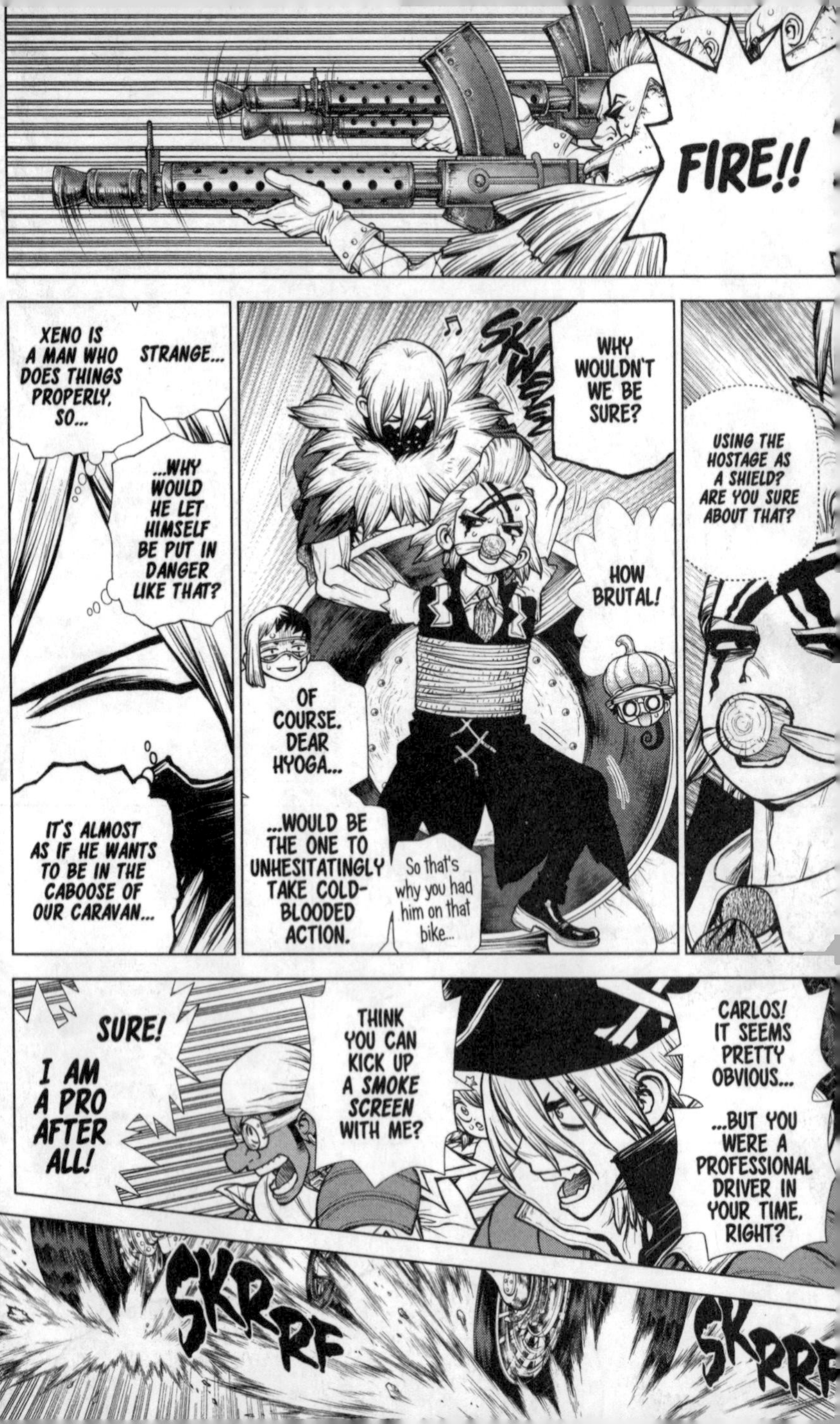
FIRE!!
USING THE HOSTAGE AS A SHIELD? ARE YOU SURE ABOUT THAT?
WHY WOULDN'T WE BE SURE?
HOW BRUTAL!
OF COURSE. DEAR HYOGA...
...WOULD BE THE ONE TO UNHESITATINGLY TAKE COLD-BLOODED ACTION.
So that's why you had him on that bike...
STRANGE...
XENO IS A MAN WHO DOES THINGS PROPERLY, SO...
...WHY WOULD HE LET HIMSELF BE PUT IN DANGER LIKE THAT?
IT'S ALMOST AS IF HE WANTS TO BE IN THE CABOOSE OF OUR CARAVAN...
CARLOS! IT SEEMS PRETTY OBVIOUS...
...BUT YOU WERE A PROFESSIONAL DRIVER IN YOUR TIME, RIGHT?
THINK YOU CAN KICK UP A SMOKE SCREEN WITH ME?
SURE!
I AM A PRO AFTER ALL!
SKRRF
SKRRF

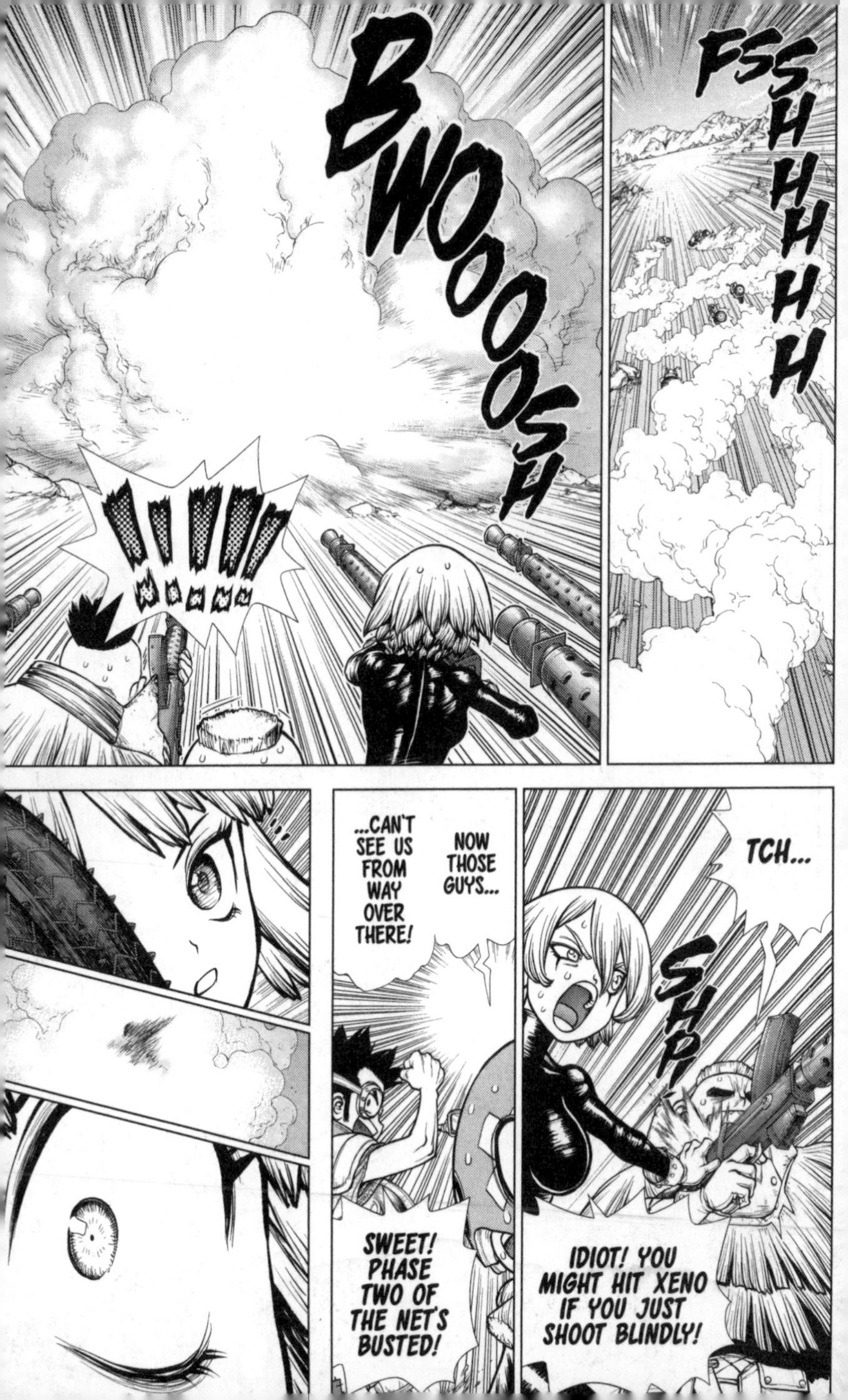
FSSHHHHHH
BWOOOOOSH
!!!!!!
TCH...
SHP
IDIOT! YOU MIGHT HIT XENO IF YOU JUST SHOOT BLINDLY!
NOW THOSE GUYS...
...CAN'T SEE US FROM WAY OVER THERE!
SWEET! PHASE TWO OF THE NET'S BUSTED!

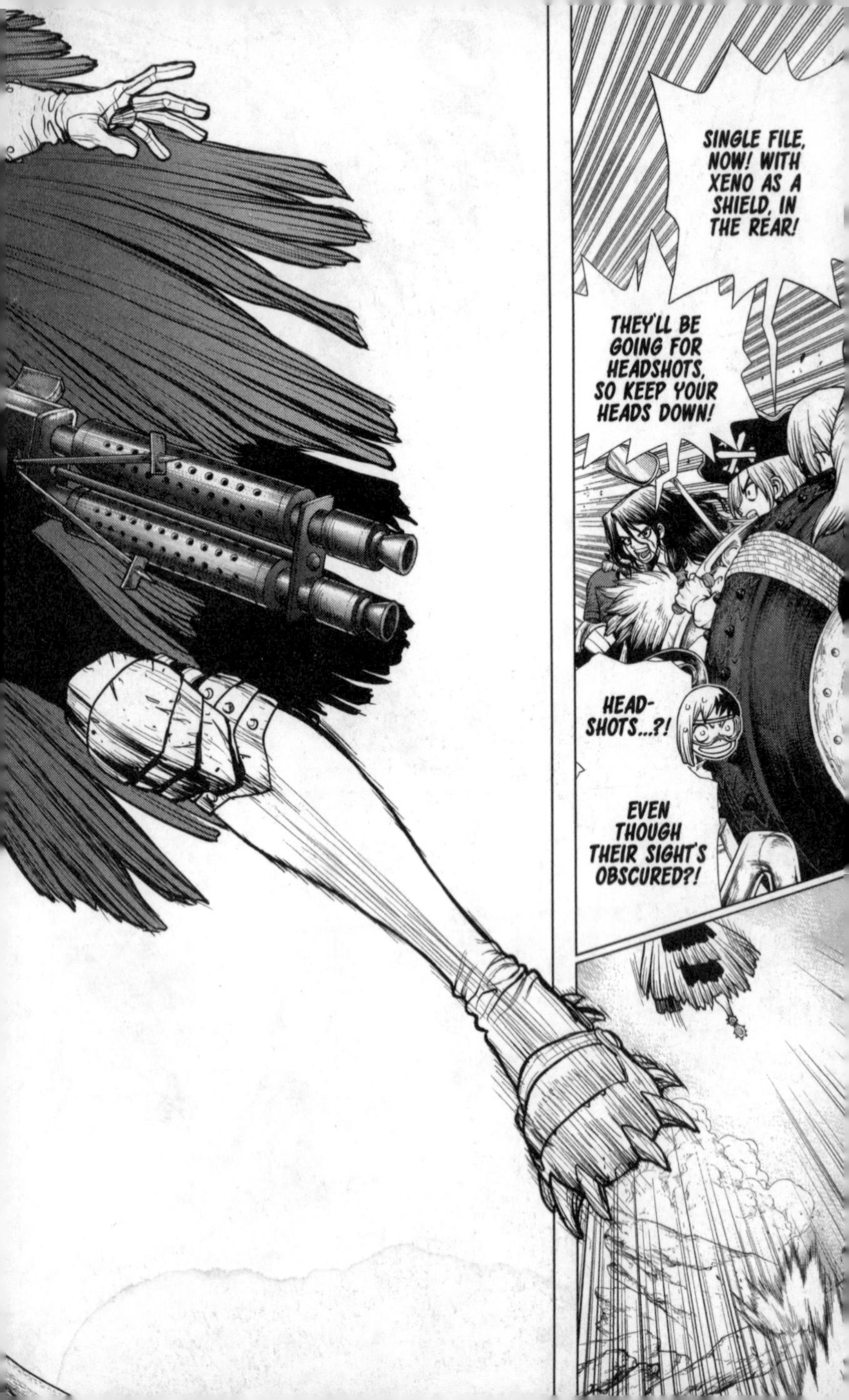
SINGLE FILE, NOW! WITH XENO AS A SHIELD, IN THE REAR!
THEY'LL BE GOING FOR HEADSHOTS, SO KEEP YOUR HEADS DOWN!
HEAD-SHOTS...?!
EVEN THOUGH THEIR SIGHT'S OBSCURED?!

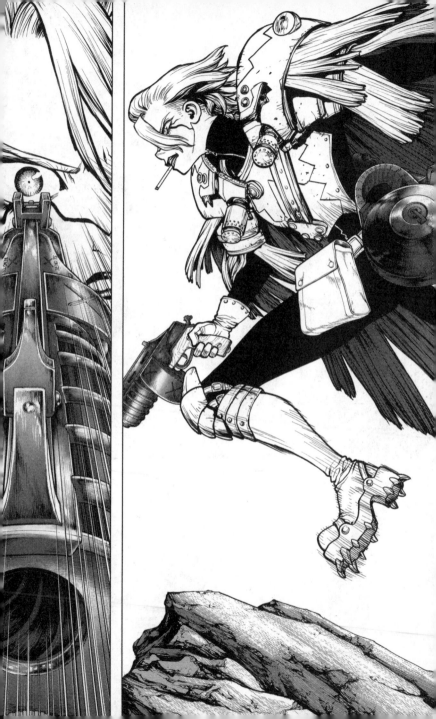

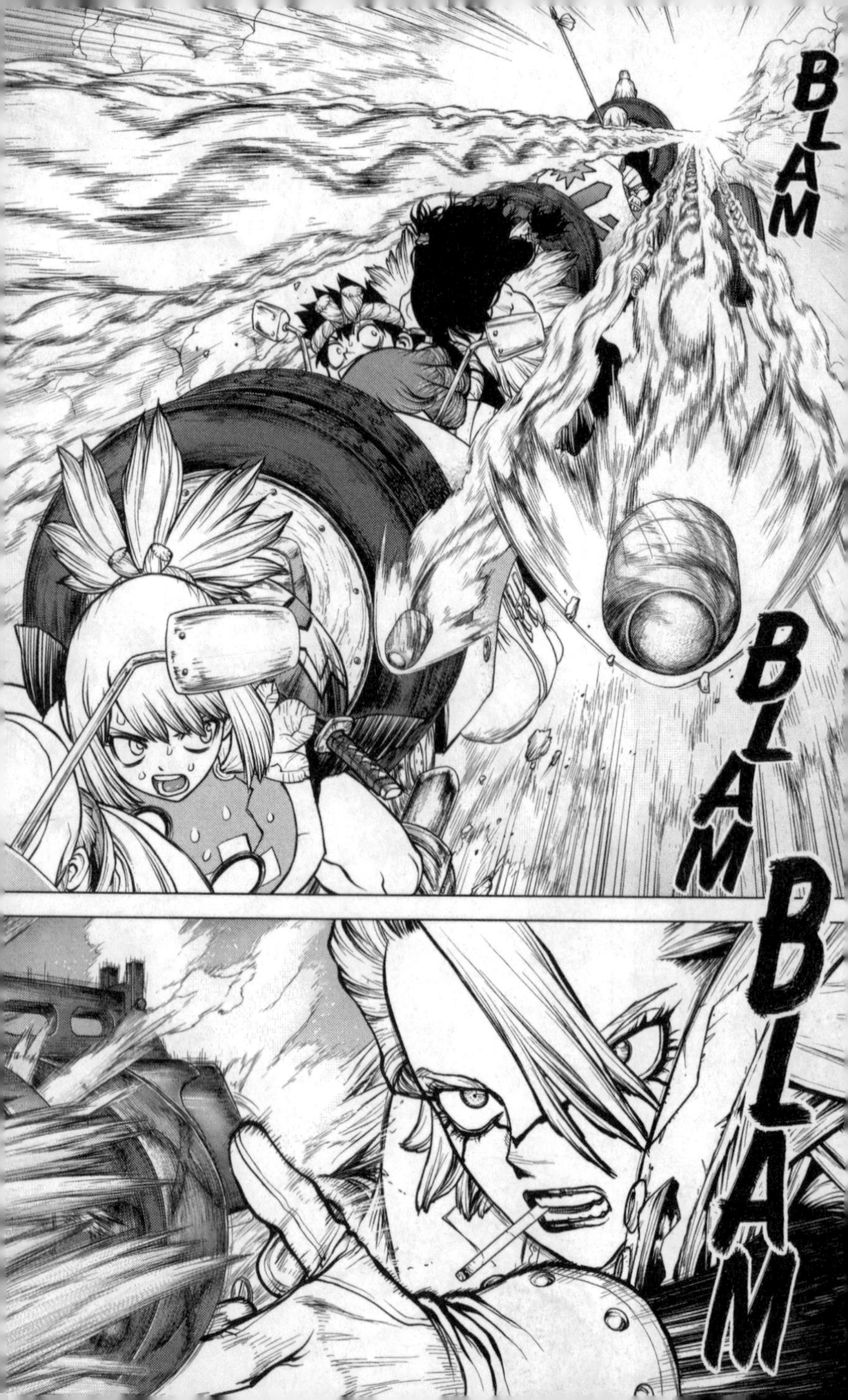
BLAM
BLAM
BLAM

BLAM
BLAM
BLAM

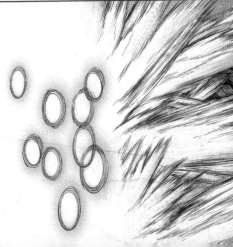

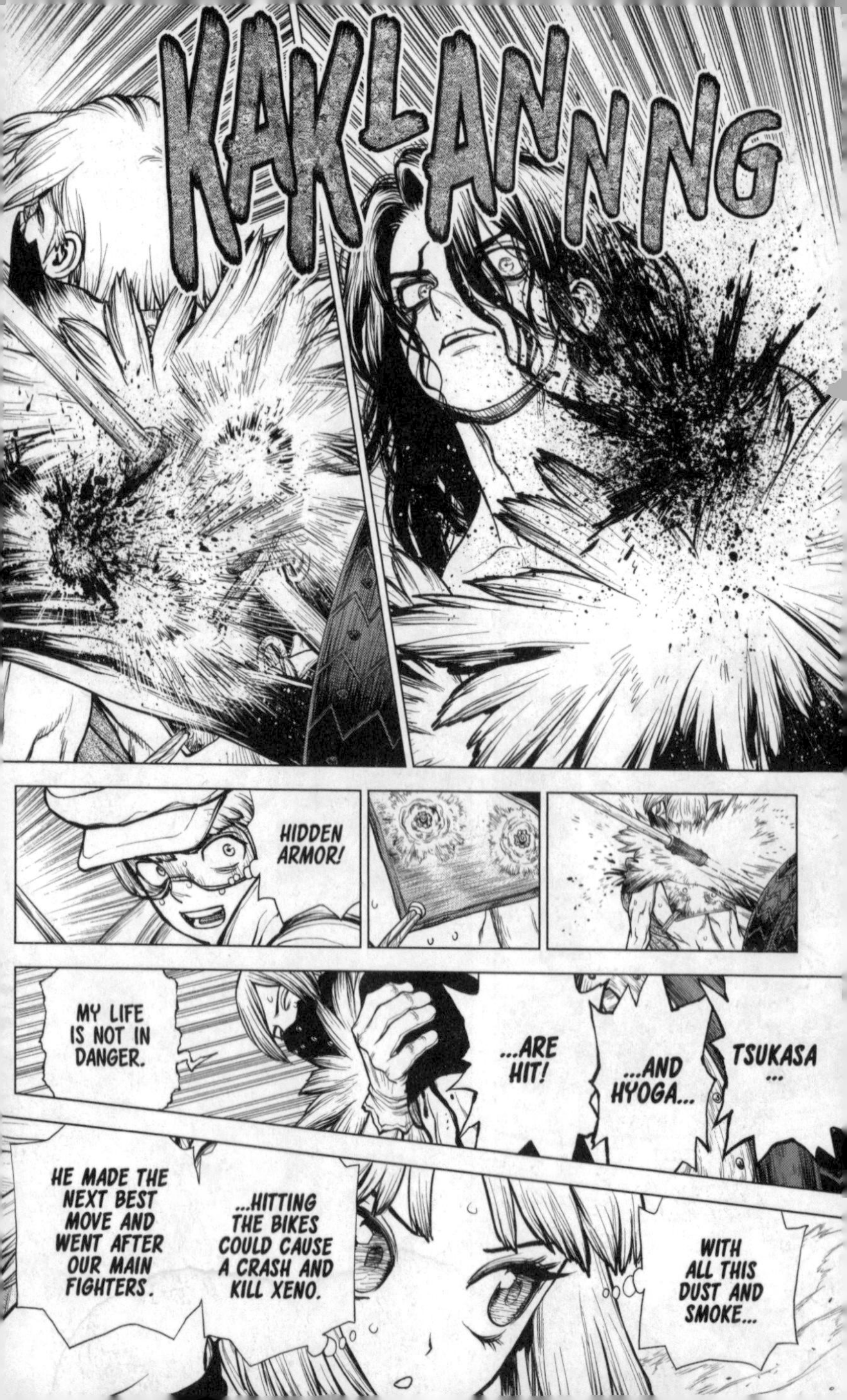
KAKLANNNG
HIDDEN ARMOR!
TSUKASA ...
...AND HYOGA...
...ARE HIT!
MY LIFE IS NOT IN DANGER.
WITH ALL THIS DUST AND SMOKE...
...HITTING THE BIKES COULD CAUSE A CRASH AND KILL XENO.
HE MADE THE NEXT BEST MOVE AND WENT AFTER OUR MAIN FIGHTERS.

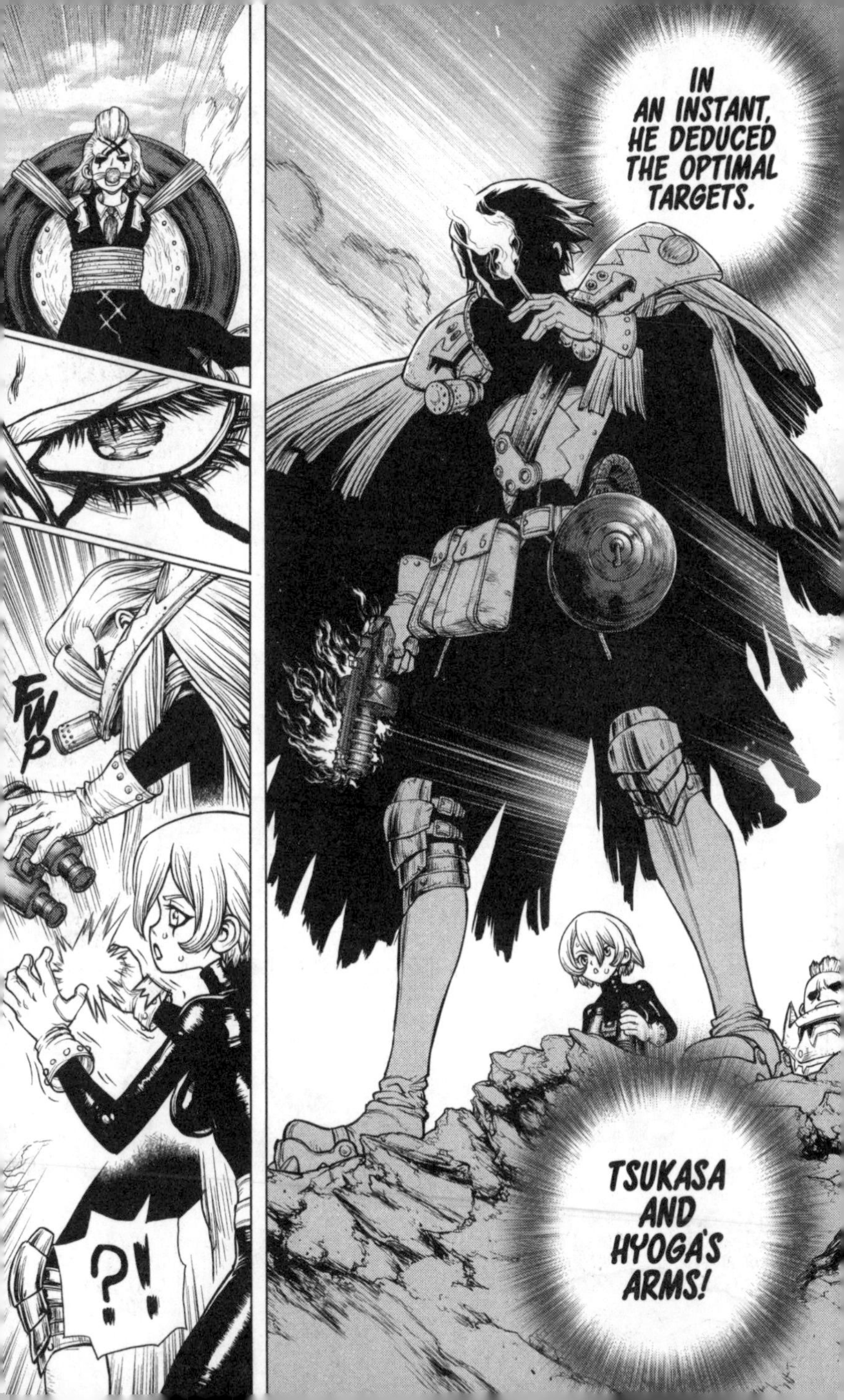
IN AN INSTANT, HE DEDUCED THE OPTIMAL TARGETS.
TSUKASA AND HYOGA'S ARMS!
FWP
?!

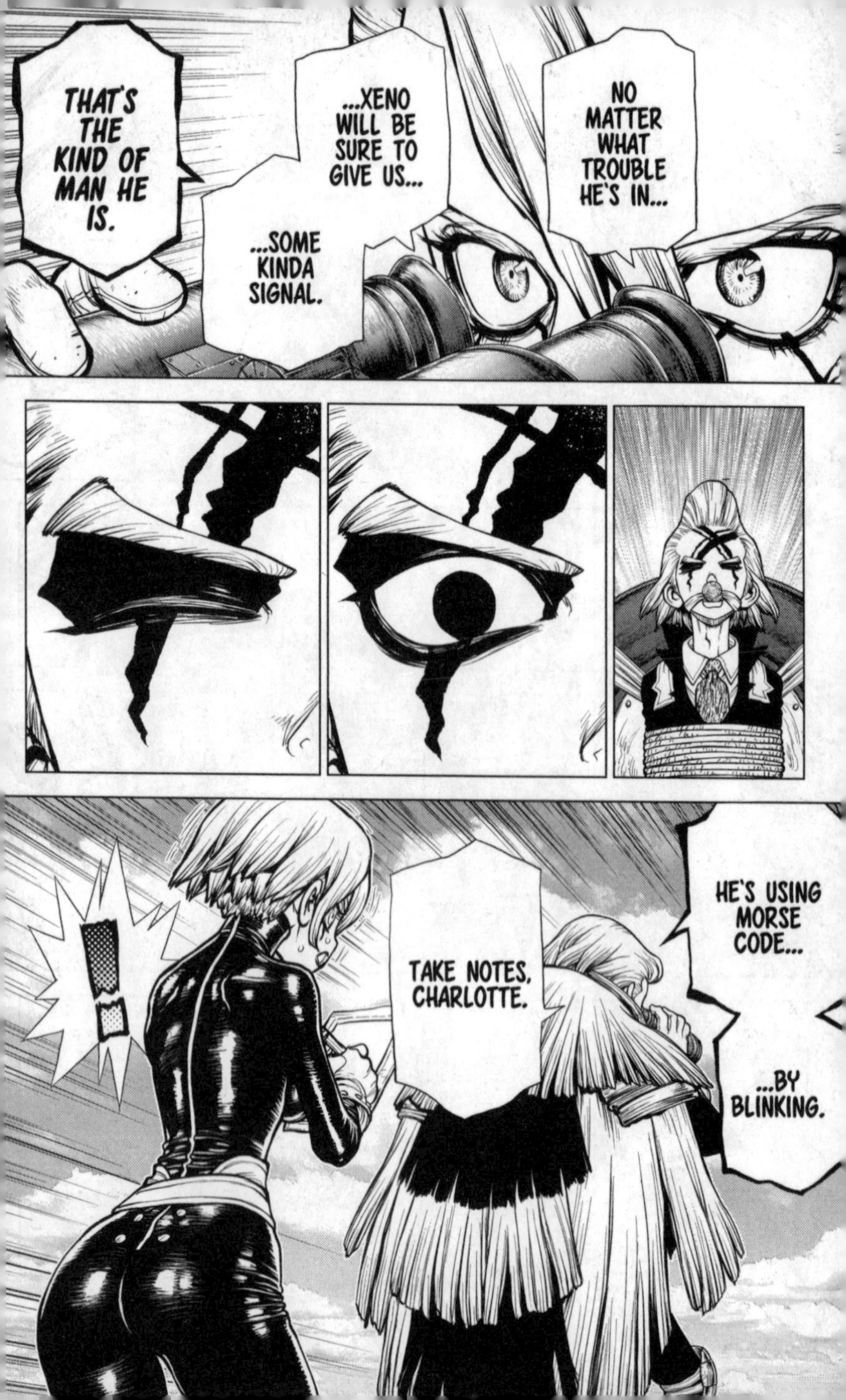
NO MATTER WHAT TROUBLE HE'S IN...
...XENO WILL BE SURE TO GIVE US...
...SOME KINDA SIGNAL.
THAT'S THE KIND OF MAN HE IS.
HE'S USING MORSE CODE...
...BY BLINKING.
TAKE NOTES, CHARLOTTE.
!

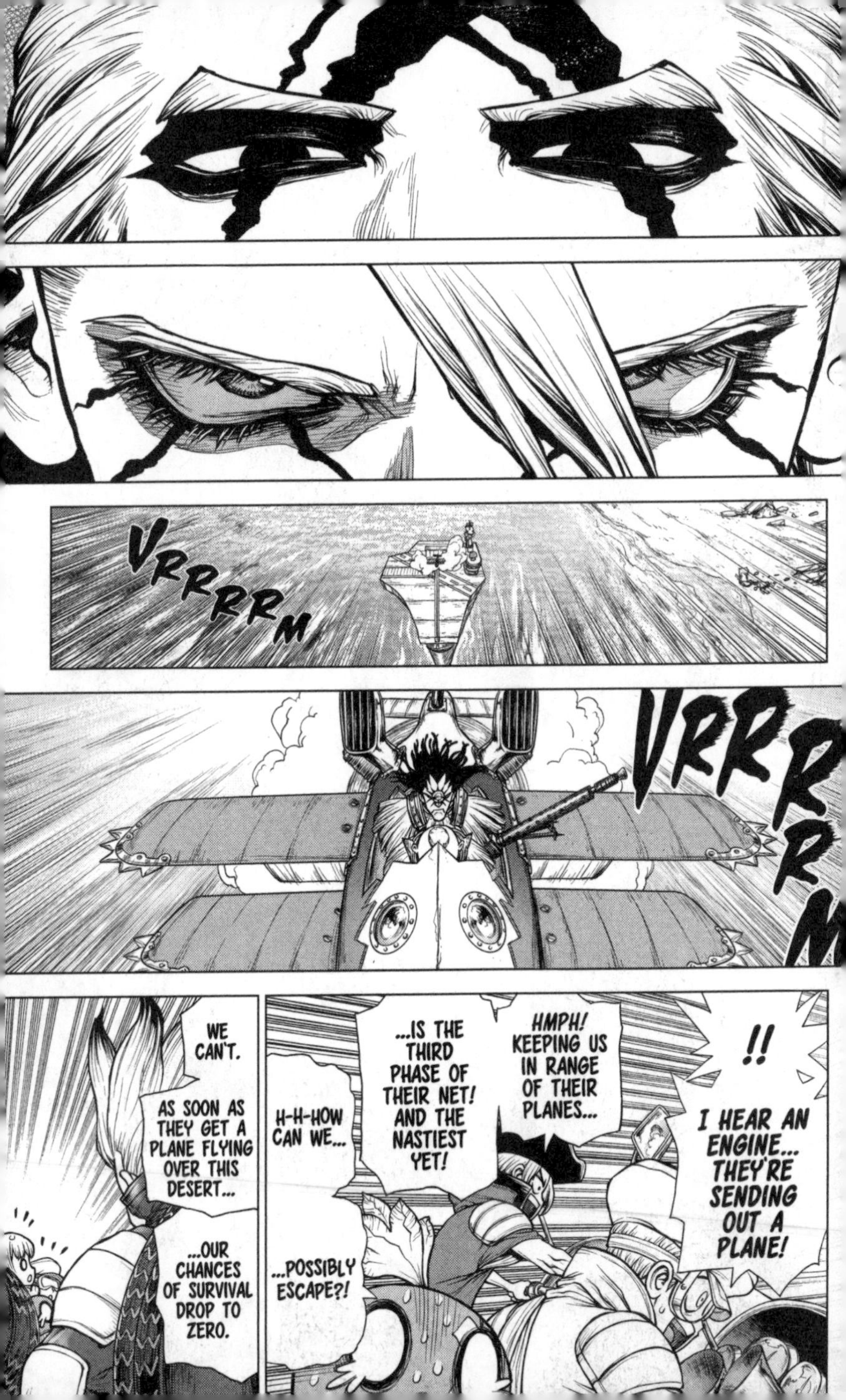
VRRRRM
VRRRRRM
!!
I HEAR AN ENGINE... THEY'RE SENDING OUT A PLANE!
HMPH! KEEPING US IN RANGE OF THEIR PLANES...
...IS THE THIRD PHASE OF THEIR NET! AND THE NASTIEST YET!
H-H-HOW CAN WE...
...POSSIBLY ESCAPE?!
WE CAN'T.
AS SOON AS THEY GET A PLANE FLYING OVER THIS DESERT...
...OUR CHANCES OF SURVIVAL DROP TO ZERO.

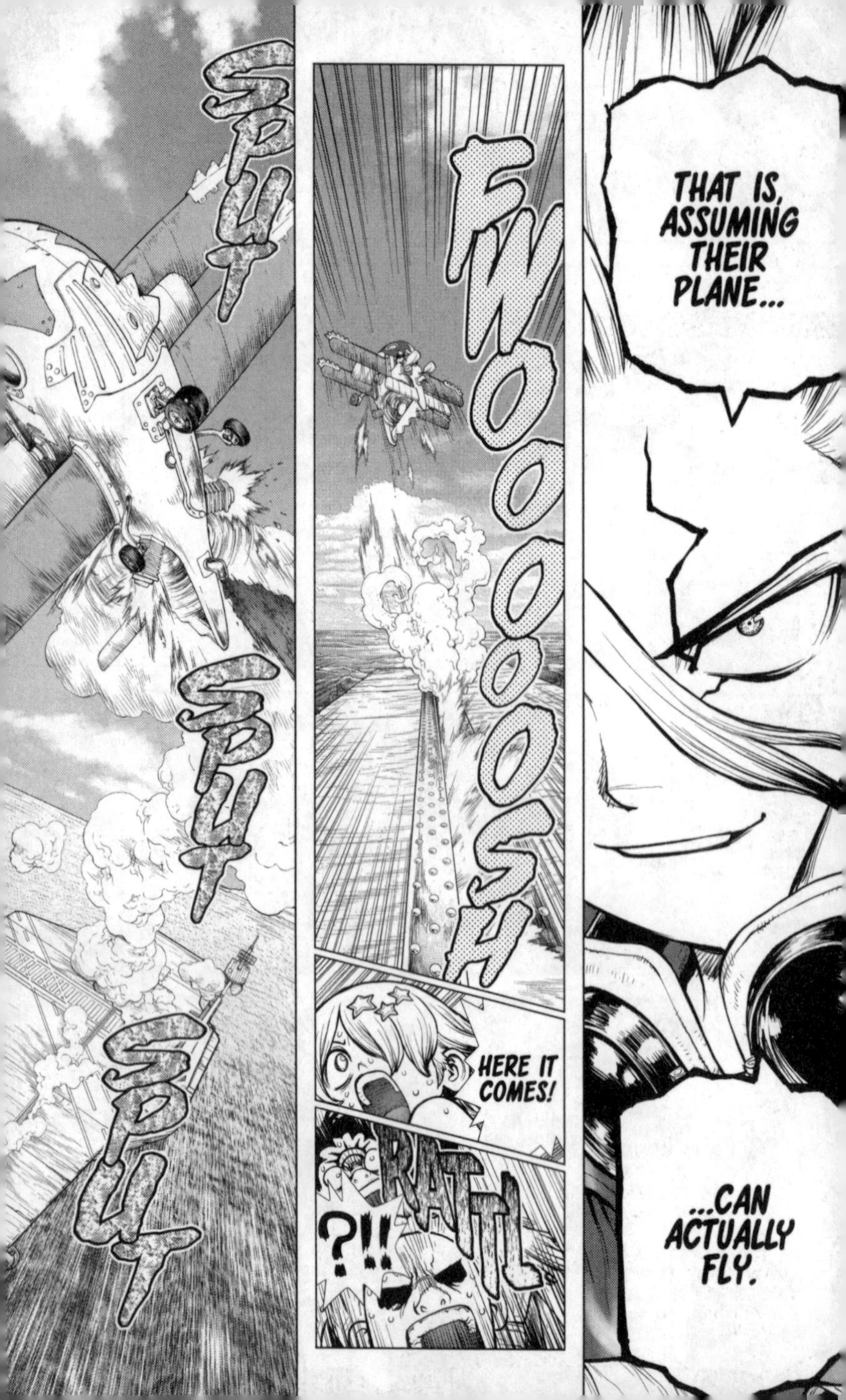
THAT IS, ASSUMING THEIR PLANE...
...CAN ACTUALLY FLY.
FWOOOOOOOSH
HERE IT COMES!
RATTL
?!!
SPUT
SPUT
SPUT

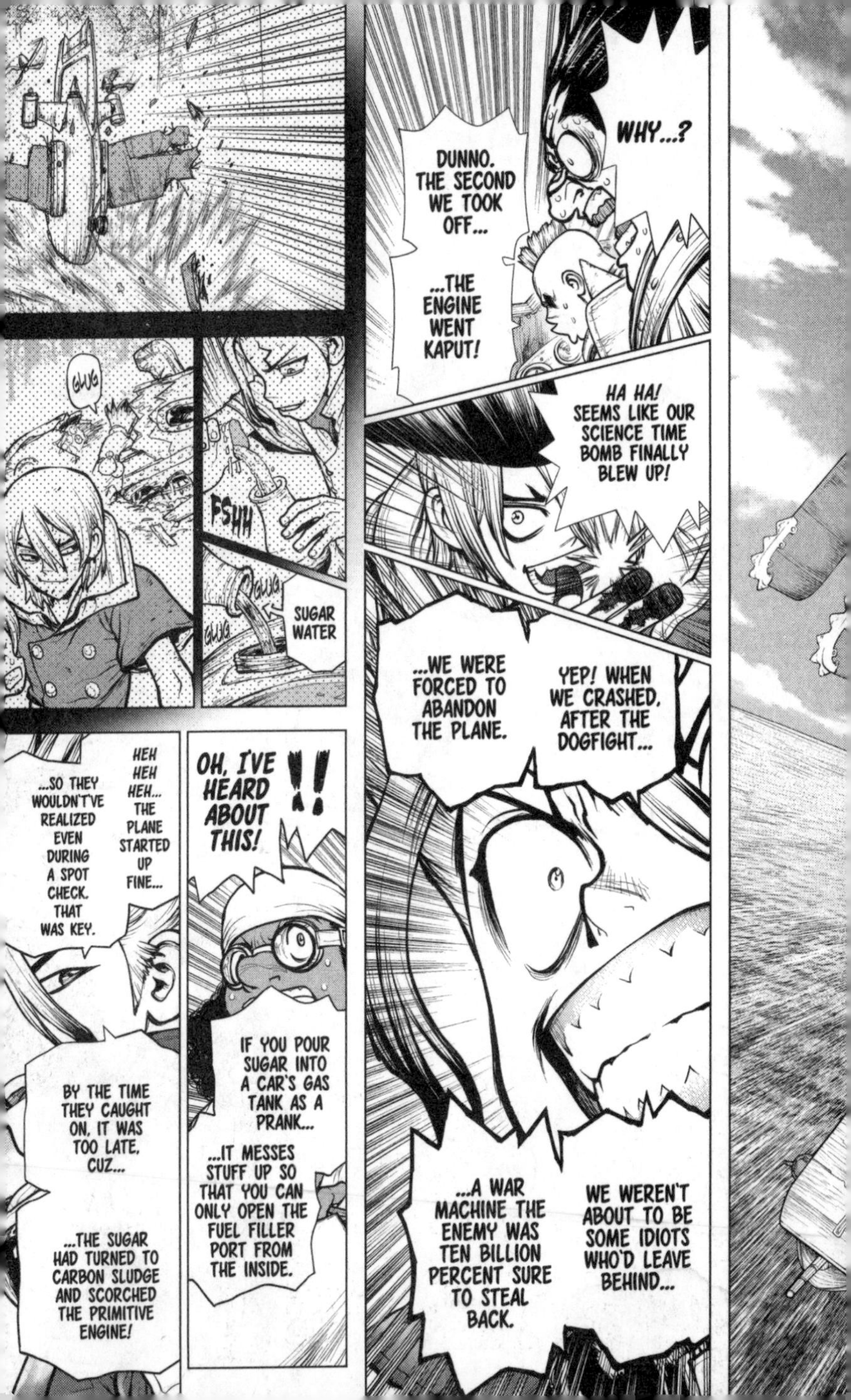
WHY...?
DUNNO. THE SECOND WE TOOK OFF...
...THE ENGINE WENT KAPUT!
HA HA! SEEMS LIKE OUR SCIENCE TIME BOMB FINALLY BLEW UP!
YEP! WHEN WE CRASHED, AFTER THE DOGFIGHT...
...WE WERE FORCED TO ABANDON THE PLANE.
WE WEREN'T ABOUT TO BE SOME IDIOTS WHO'D LEAVE BEHIND...
...A WAR MACHINE THE ENEMY WAS TEN BILLION PERCENT SURE TO STEAL BACK.
FSHH
GLUG
GLUG
SUGAR WATER
GLUG
OH, I'VE HEARD ABOUT THIS!!
IF YOU POUR SUGAR INTO A CAR'S GAS TANK AS A PRANK...
...IT MESSES STUFF UP SO THAT YOU CAN ONLY OPEN THE FUEL FILLER PORT FROM THE INSIDE.
HEH HEH HEH... THE PLANE STARTED UP FINE...
...SO THEY WOULDN'T'VE REALIZED EVEN DURING A SPOT CHECK. THAT WAS KEY.
BY THE TIME THEY CAUGHT ON, IT WAS TOO LATE, CUZ...
...THE SUGAR HAD TURNED TO CARBON SLUDGE AND SCORCHED THE PRIMITIVE ENGINE!

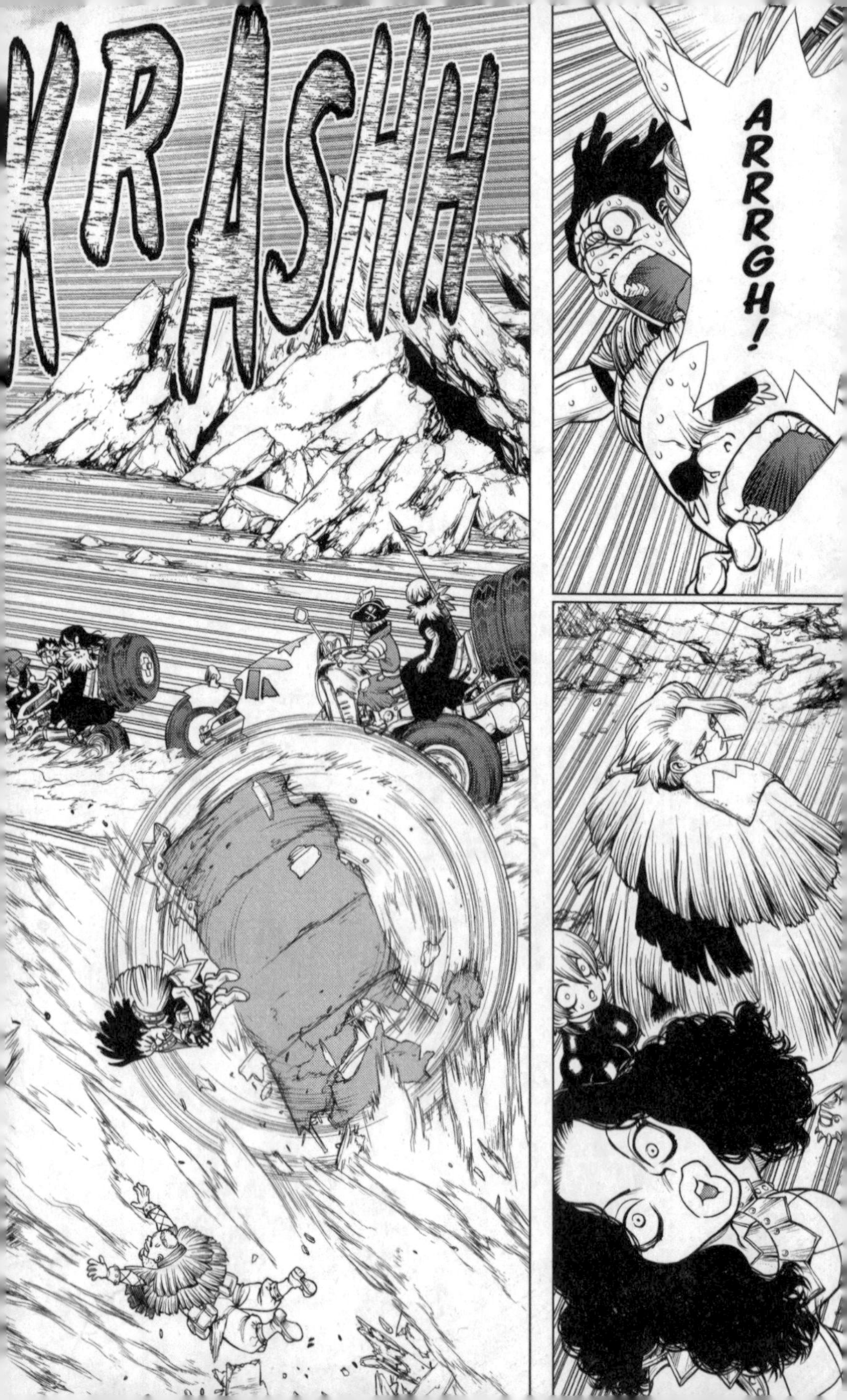
ARRRGH!
KRASHH

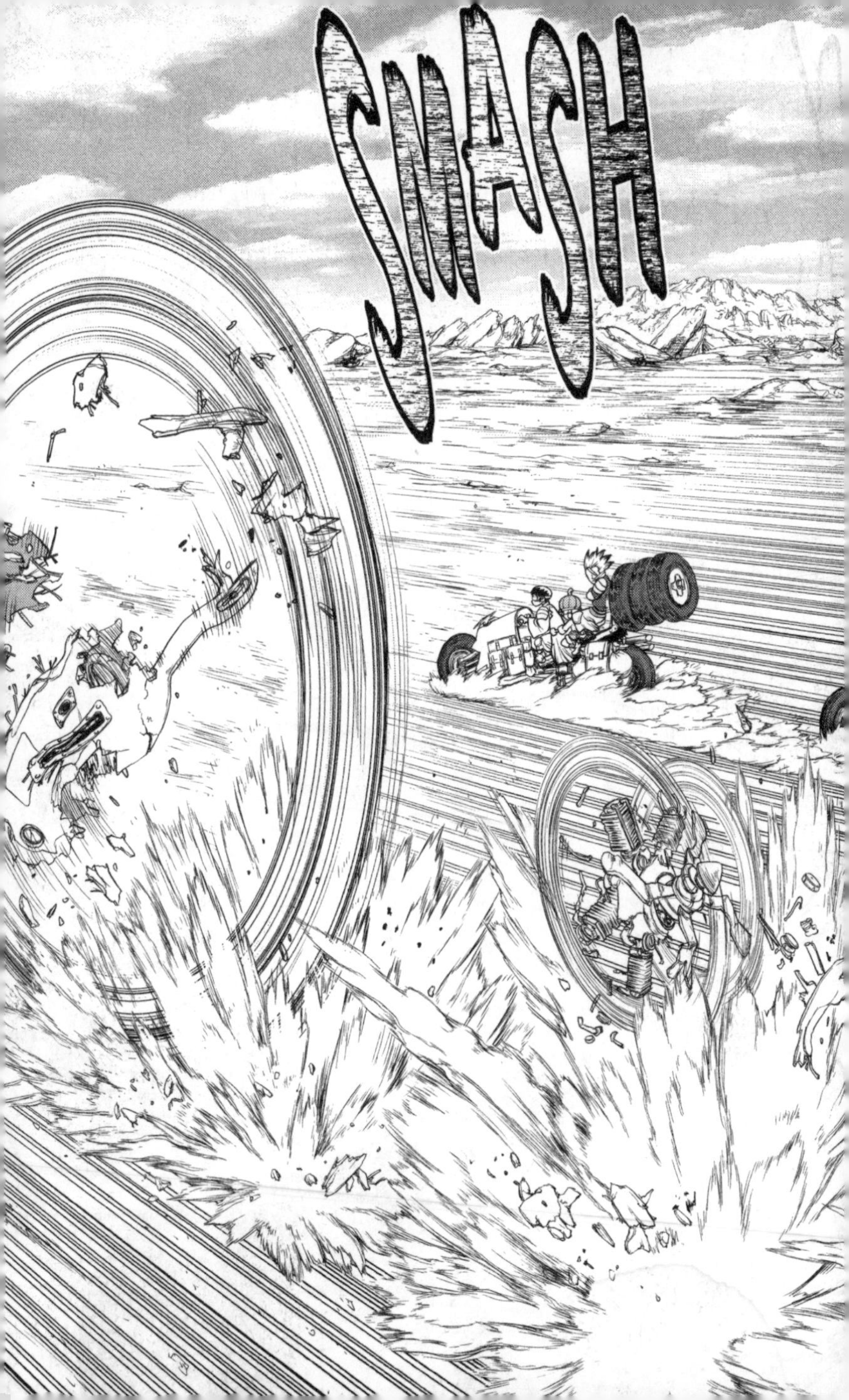
SMASH

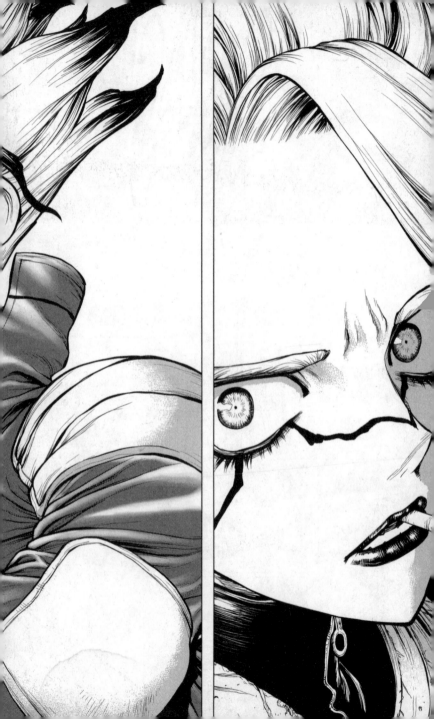

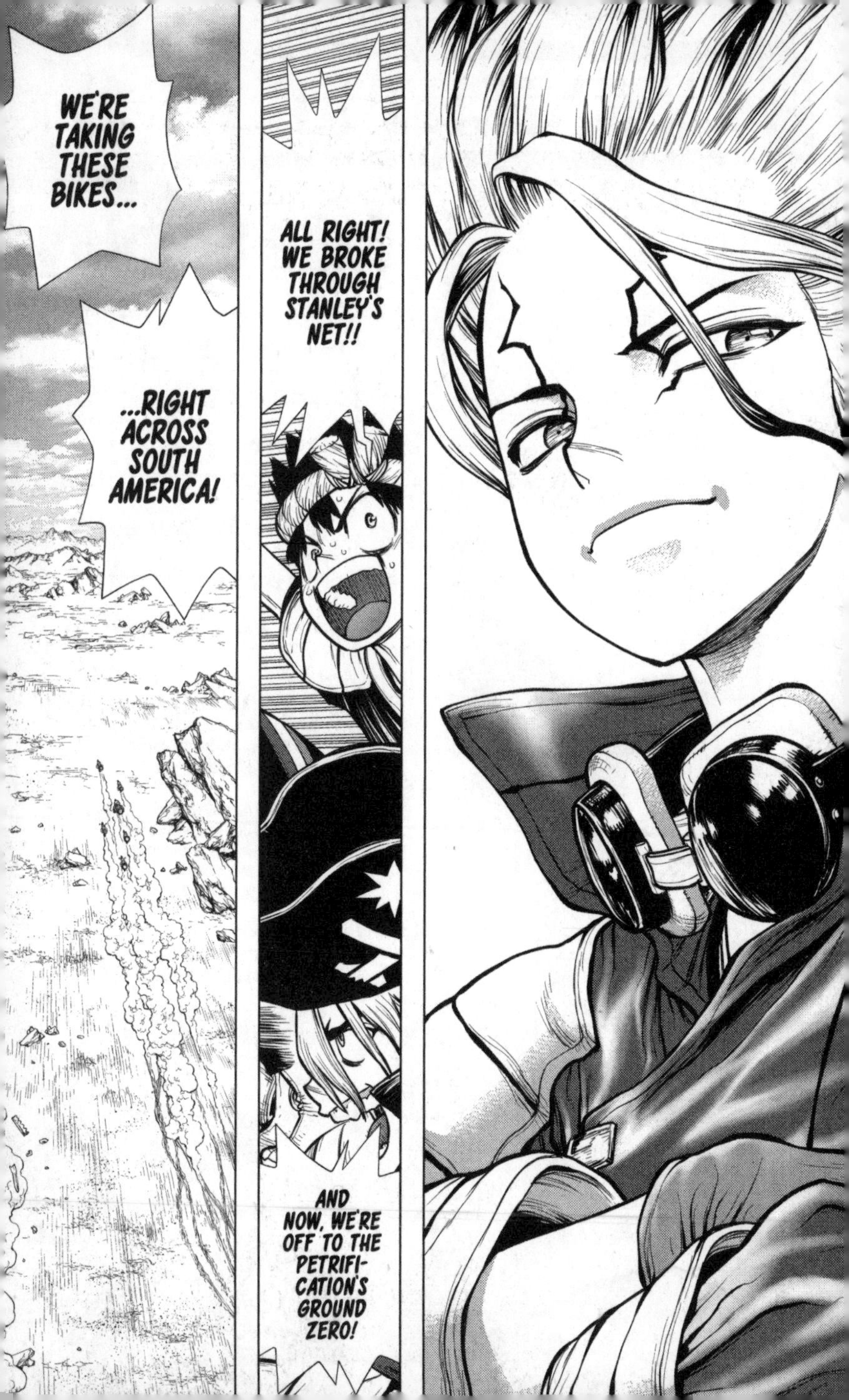
ALL RIGHT! WE BROKE THROUGH STANLEY'S NET!!
AND NOW, WE'RE OFF TO THE PETRIFI-CATION'S GROUND ZERO!
WE'RE TAKING THESE BIKES...
...RIGHT ACROSS SOUTH AMERICA!

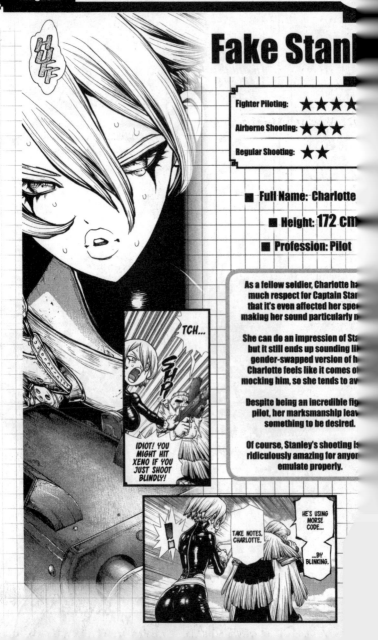

Xeno's Science Kingdom

KNIGHT FILE

Fake Stan

HUFF
TCH...
SHP
IDIOT! YOU MIGHT HIT XENO IF YOU JUST SHOOT BLINDLY!

Fighter Piloting:	★★★★
Airborne Shooting:	★★★
Regular Shooting:	★★

■ Full Name: Charlotte

■ Height: 172 cm

■ Profession: Pilot

As a fellow soldier, Charlotte ha
much respect for Captain Star
that it's even affected her spe
making her sound particularly m

She can do an impression of Sta
but it still ends up sounding li
gender-swapped version of h
Charlotte feels like it comes o
mocking him, so she tends to av

Despite being an incredible fig
pilot, her marksmanship leav
something to be desired.

Of course, Stanley's shooting is
ridiculously amazing for anyon
emulate properly.

HE'S USING MORSE CODE...
...BY BLINKING.
TAKE NOTES, CHARLOTTE.

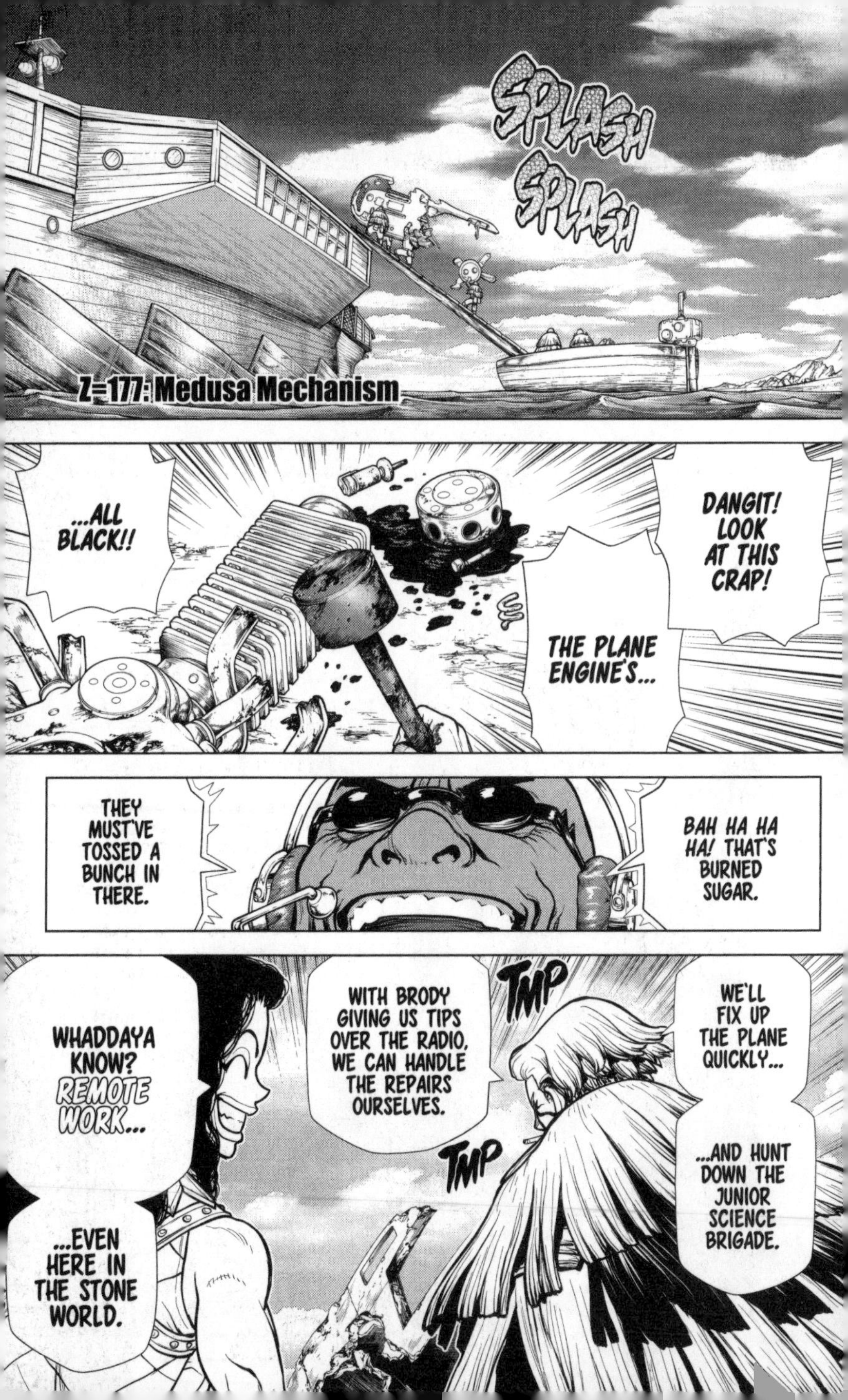
SPLASH
SPLASH
Z=177: Medusa Mechanism
DANGIT! LOOK AT THIS CRAP!
THE PLANE ENGINE'S...
...ALL BLACK!!
BAH HA HA HA! THAT'S BURNED SUGAR.
THEY MUST'VE TOSSED A BUNCH IN THERE.
WE'LL FIX UP THE PLANE QUICKLY...
...AND HUNT DOWN THE JUNIOR SCIENCE BRIGADE.
TMP
TMP
WITH BRODY GIVING US TIPS OVER THE RADIO, WE CAN HANDLE THE REPAIRS OURSELVES.
WHADDAYA KNOW? REMOTE WORK...
...EVEN HERE IN THE STONE WORLD.

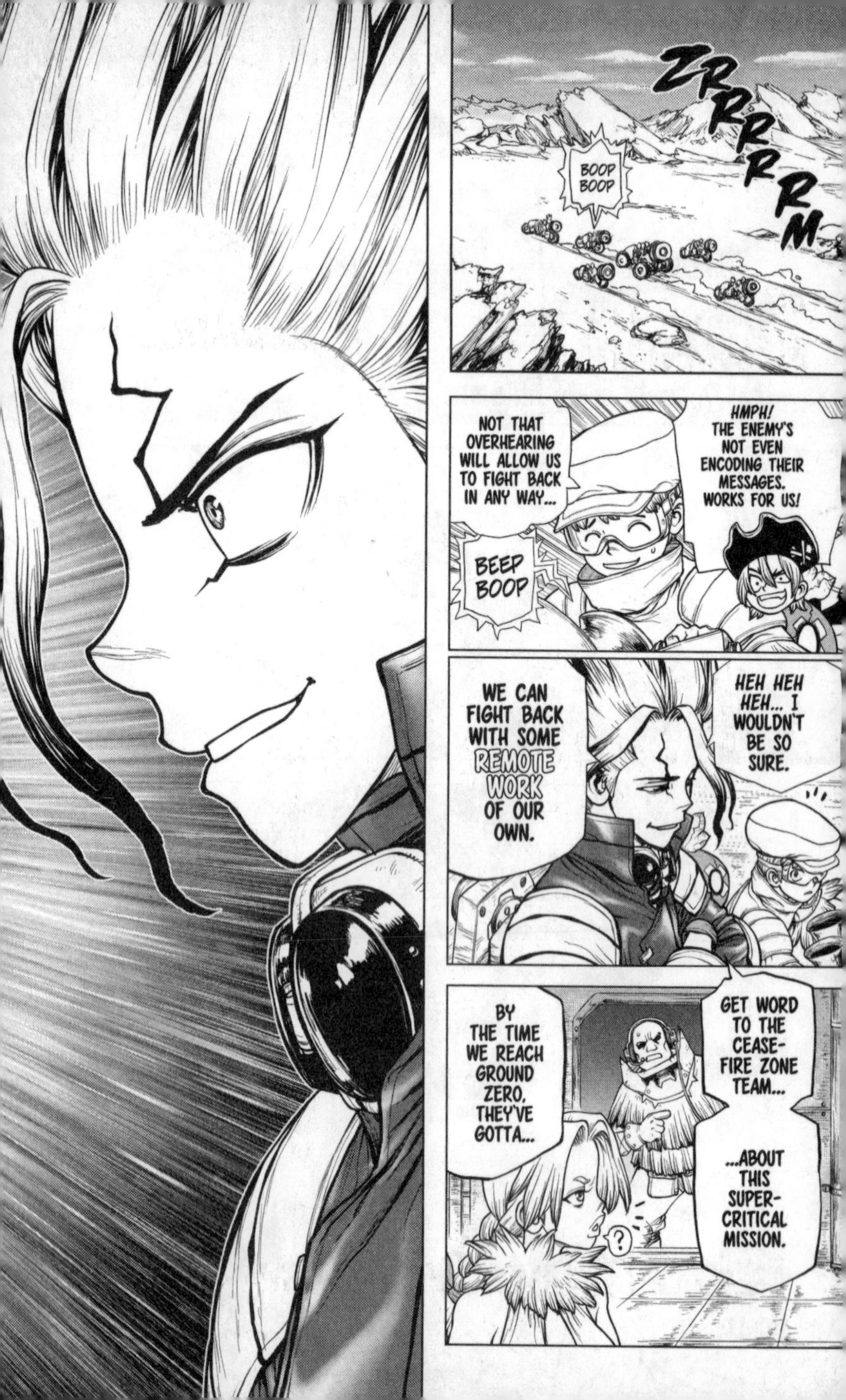
ZRRRRRM
BOOP BOOP
HMPH! THE ENEMY'S NOT EVEN ENCODING THEIR MESSAGES. WORKS FOR US!
NOT THAT OVERHEARING WILL ALLOW US TO FIGHT BACK IN ANY WAY...
BEEP BOOP
HEH HEH HEH... I WOULDN'T BE SO SURE.
WE CAN FIGHT BACK WITH SOME REMOTE WORK OF OUR OWN.
GET WORD TO THE CEASE-FIRE ZONE TEAM...
...ABOUT THIS SUPER-CRITICAL MISSION.
BY THE TIME WE REACH GROUND ZERO, THEY'VE GOTTA...
?

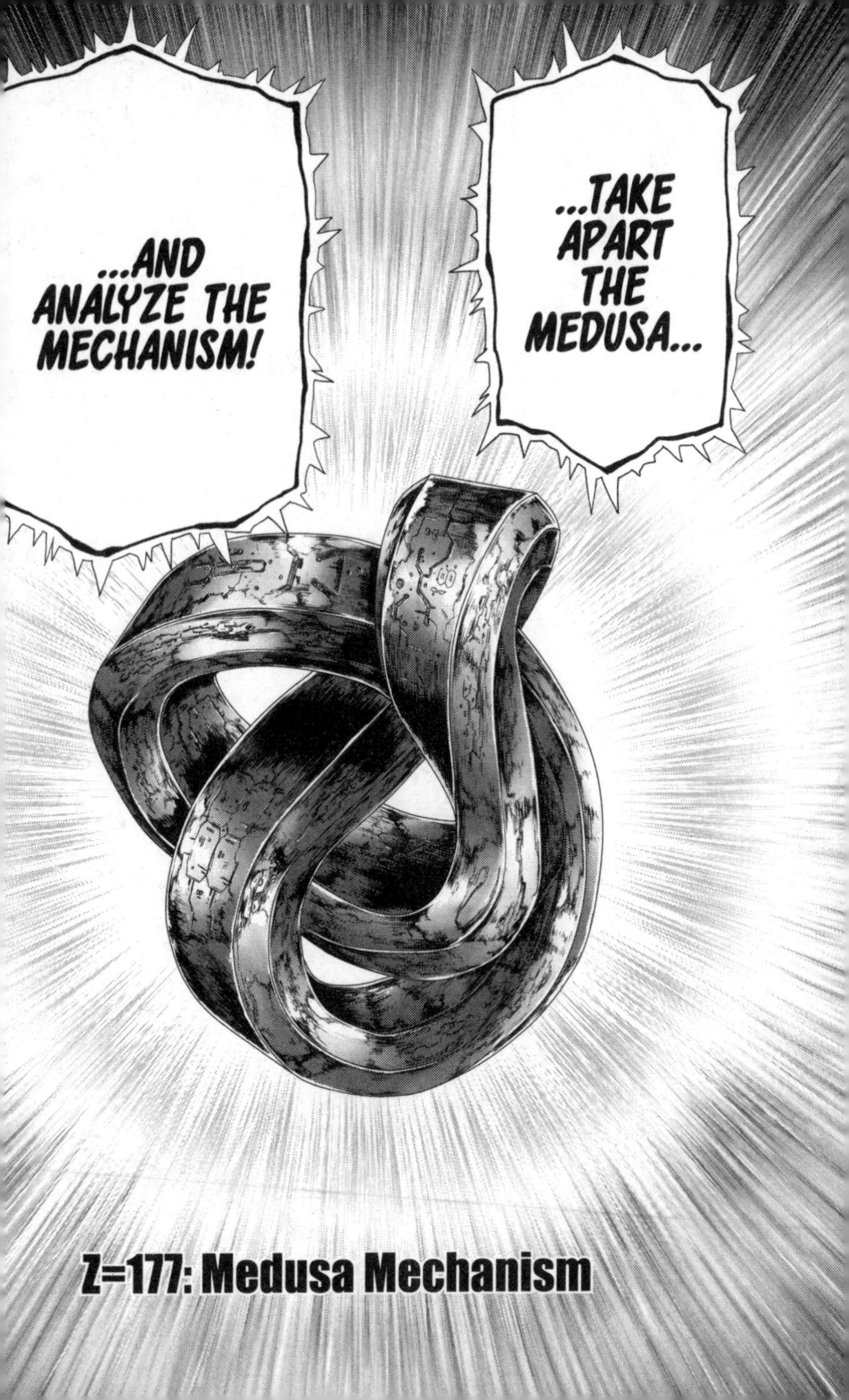
...TAKE APART THE MEDUSA...
...AND ANALYZE THE MECHANISM!
Z=177: Medusa Mechanism

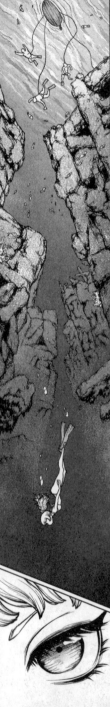

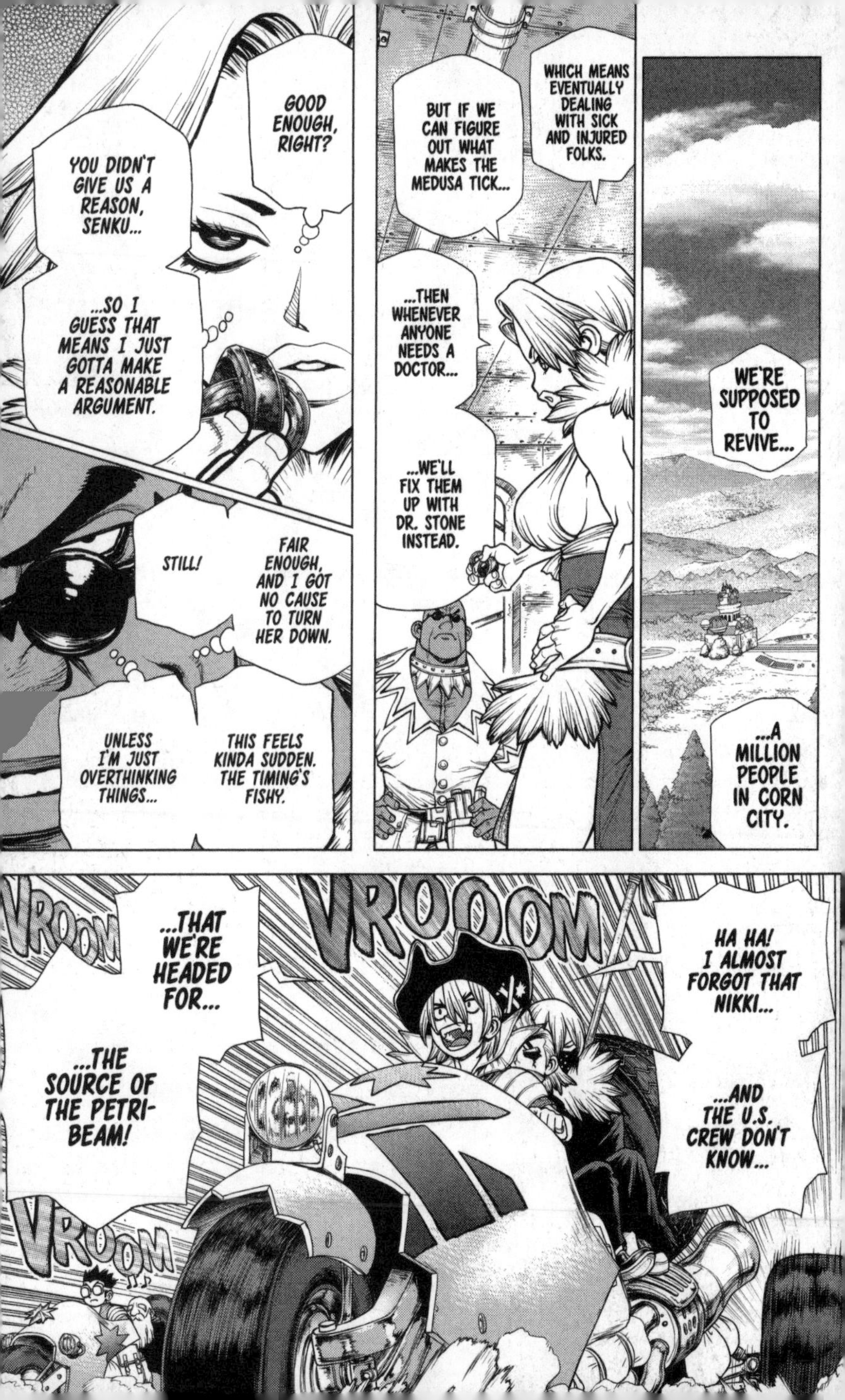
WE'RE SUPPOSED TO REVIVE...
...A MILLION PEOPLE IN CORN CITY.
WHICH MEANS EVENTUALLY DEALING WITH SICK AND INJURED FOLKS.
BUT IF WE CAN FIGURE OUT WHAT MAKES THE MEDUSA TICK...
...THEN WHENEVER ANYONE NEEDS A DOCTOR...
...WE'LL FIX THEM UP WITH DR. STONE INSTEAD.
GOOD ENOUGH, RIGHT?
YOU DIDN'T GIVE US A REASON, SENKU...
...SO I GUESS THAT MEANS I JUST GOTTA MAKE A REASONABLE ARGUMENT.
FAIR ENOUGH, AND I GOT NO CAUSE TO TURN HER DOWN.
STILL!
THIS FEELS KINDA SUDDEN. THE TIMING'S FISHY.
UNLESS I'M JUST OVERTHINKING THINGS...
HA HA! I ALMOST FORGOT THAT NIKKI...
...AND THE U.S. CREW DON'T KNOW...
VROOOM
...THAT WE'RE HEADED FOR...
...THE SOURCE OF THE PETRI-BEAM!
VROOM
VROOM

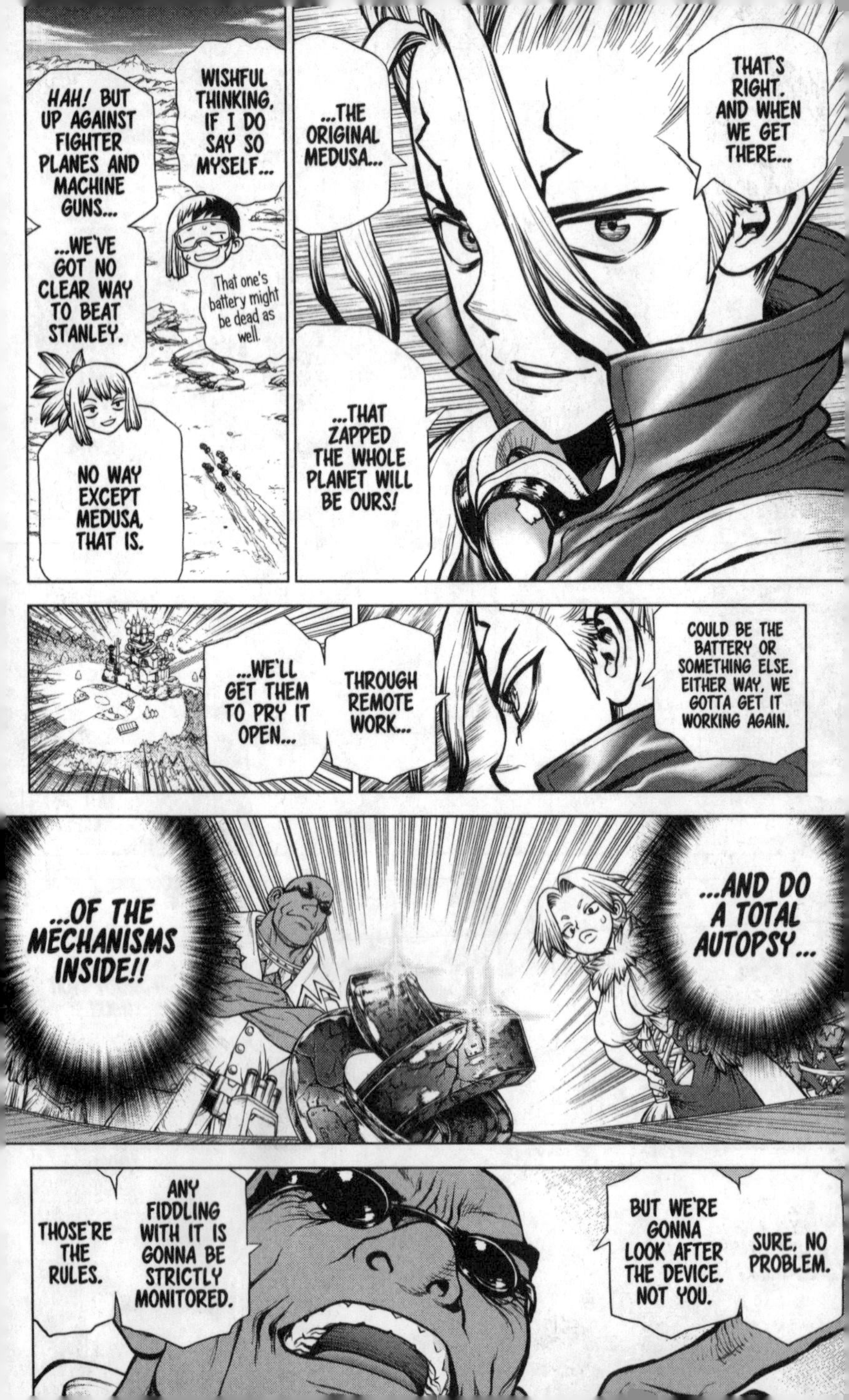
THAT'S RIGHT. AND WHEN WE GET THERE...
...THE ORIGINAL MEDUSA...
...THAT ZAPPED THE WHOLE PLANET WILL BE OURS!
WISHFUL THINKING, IF I DO SAY SO MYSELF...
HAH! BUT UP AGAINST FIGHTER PLANES AND MACHINE GUNS...
...WE'VE GOT NO CLEAR WAY TO BEAT STANLEY.
That one's battery might be dead as well.
NO WAY EXCEPT MEDUSA, THAT IS.
COULD BE THE BATTERY OR SOMETHING ELSE. EITHER WAY, WE GOTTA GET IT WORKING AGAIN.
THROUGH REMOTE WORK...
...WE'LL GET THEM TO PRY IT OPEN...
...AND DO A TOTAL AUTOPSY...
...OF THE MECHANISMS INSIDE!!
SURE, NO PROBLEM.
BUT WE'RE GONNA LOOK AFTER THE DEVICE. NOT YOU.
ANY FIDDLING WITH IT IS GONNA BE STRICTLY MONITORED.
THOSE'RE THE RULES.

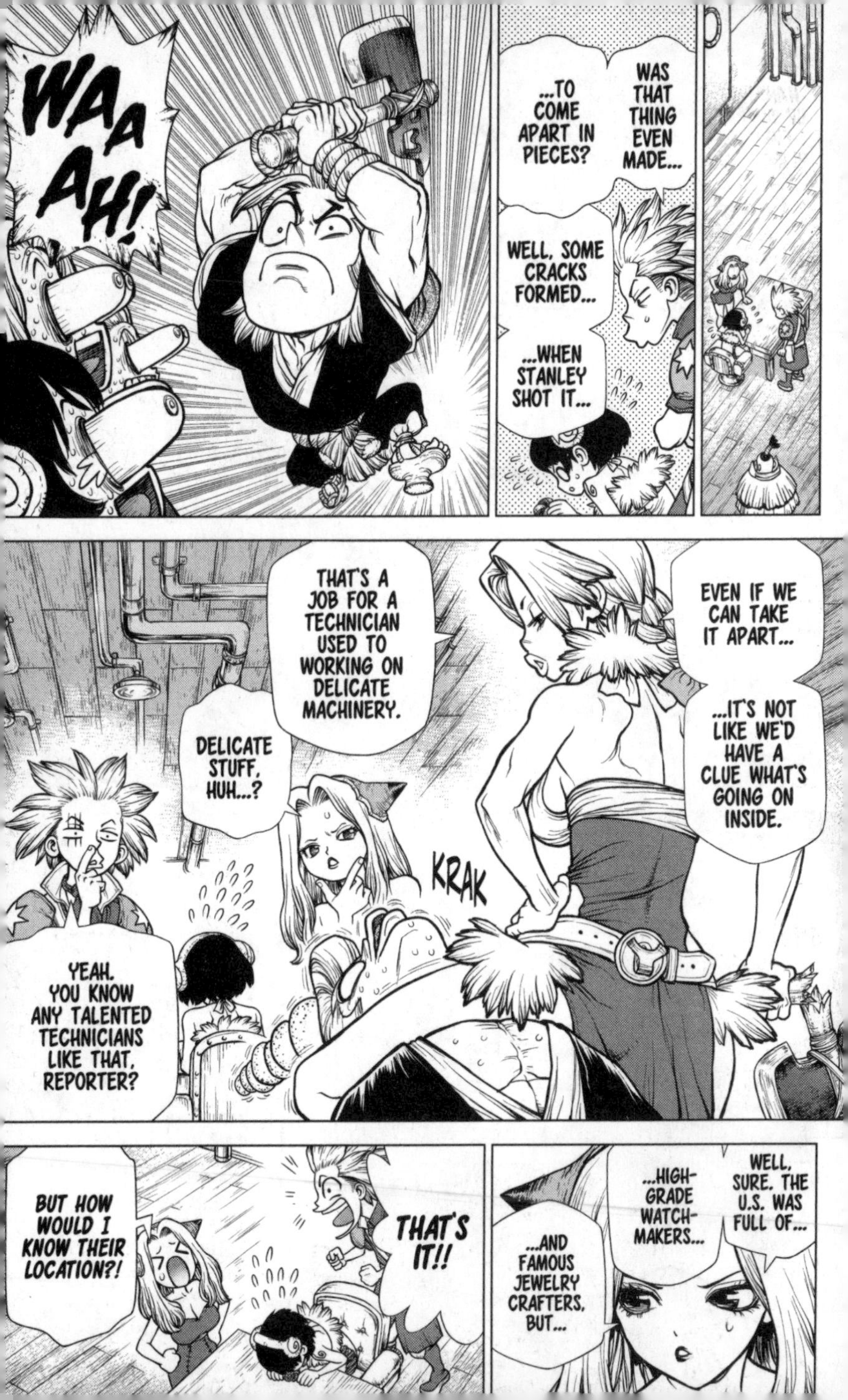
WAS THAT THING EVEN MADE...
...TO COME APART IN PIECES?
WELL, SOME CRACKS FORMED...
...WHEN STANLEY SHOT IT...
WAAAAH!
EVEN IF WE CAN TAKE IT APART...
...IT'S NOT LIKE WE'D HAVE A CLUE WHAT'S GOING ON INSIDE.
THAT'S A JOB FOR A TECHNICIAN USED TO WORKING ON DELICATE MACHINERY.
KRAK
DELICATE STUFF, HUH...?
YEAH. YOU KNOW ANY TALENTED TECHNICIANS LIKE THAT, REPORTER?
WELL, SURE. THE U.S. WAS FULL OF...
...HIGH-GRADE WATCH-MAKERS...
...AND FAMOUS JEWELRY CRAFTERS, BUT...
THAT'S IT!!
BUT HOW WOULD I KNOW THEIR LOCATION?!

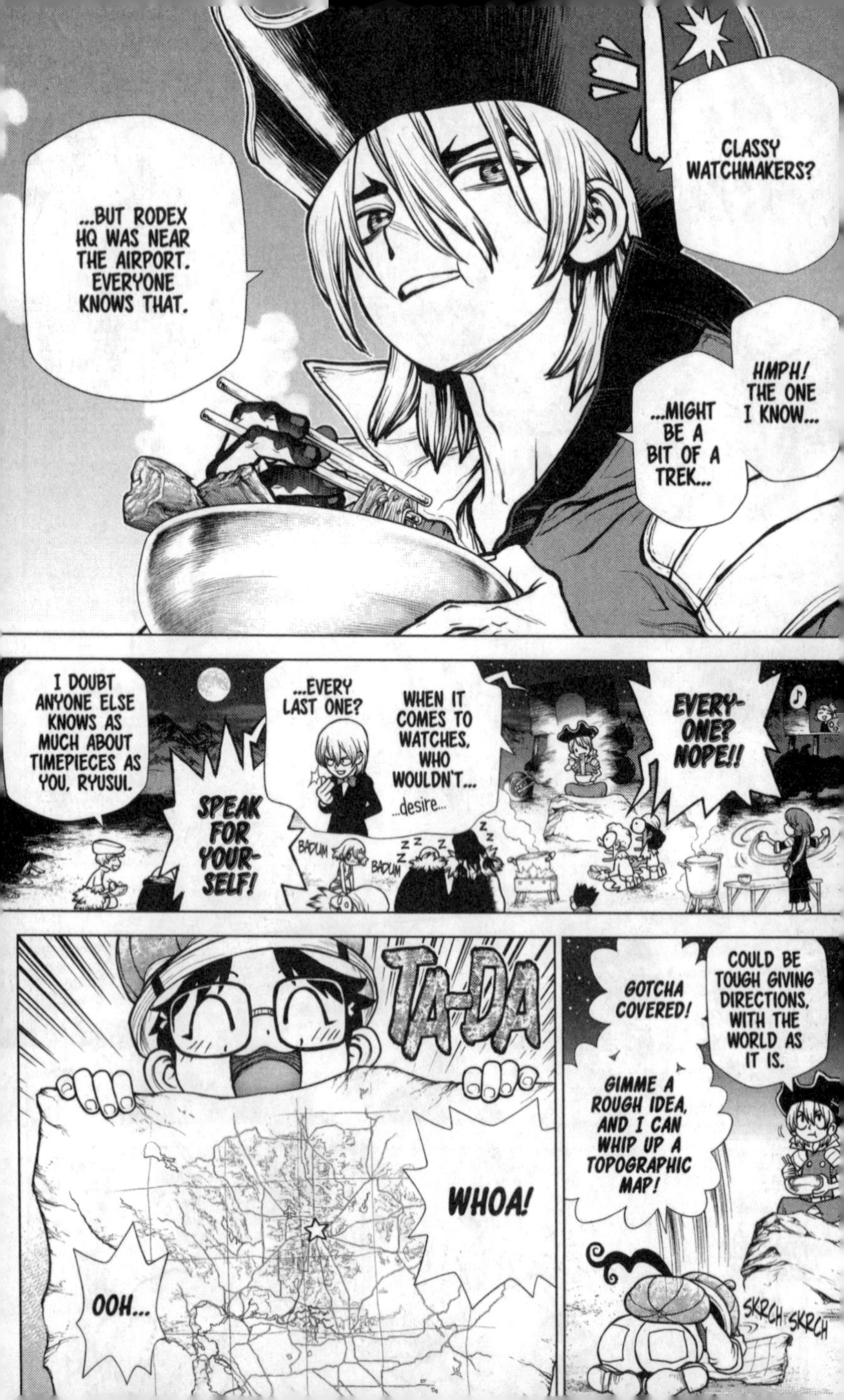
CLASSY WATCHMAKERS?
HMPH! THE ONE I KNOW...
...MIGHT BE A BIT OF A TREK...
...BUT RODEX HQ WAS NEAR THE AIRPORT. EVERYONE KNOWS THAT.
EVERY-ONE? NOPE!!
WHEN IT COMES TO WATCHES, WHO WOULDN'T...
...desire...
...EVERY LAST ONE?
SPEAK FOR YOUR-SELF!
I DOUBT ANYONE ELSE KNOWS AS MUCH ABOUT TIMEPIECES AS YOU, RYUSUI.
BADUM
BADUM
Z Z Z
Z Z
COULD BE TOUGH GIVING DIRECTIONS, WITH THE WORLD AS IT IS.
GOTCHA COVERED!
GIMME A ROUGH IDEA, AND I CAN WHIP UP A TOPOGRAPHIC MAP!
SKRCH SKRCH
TA-DA
WHOA!
OOH...

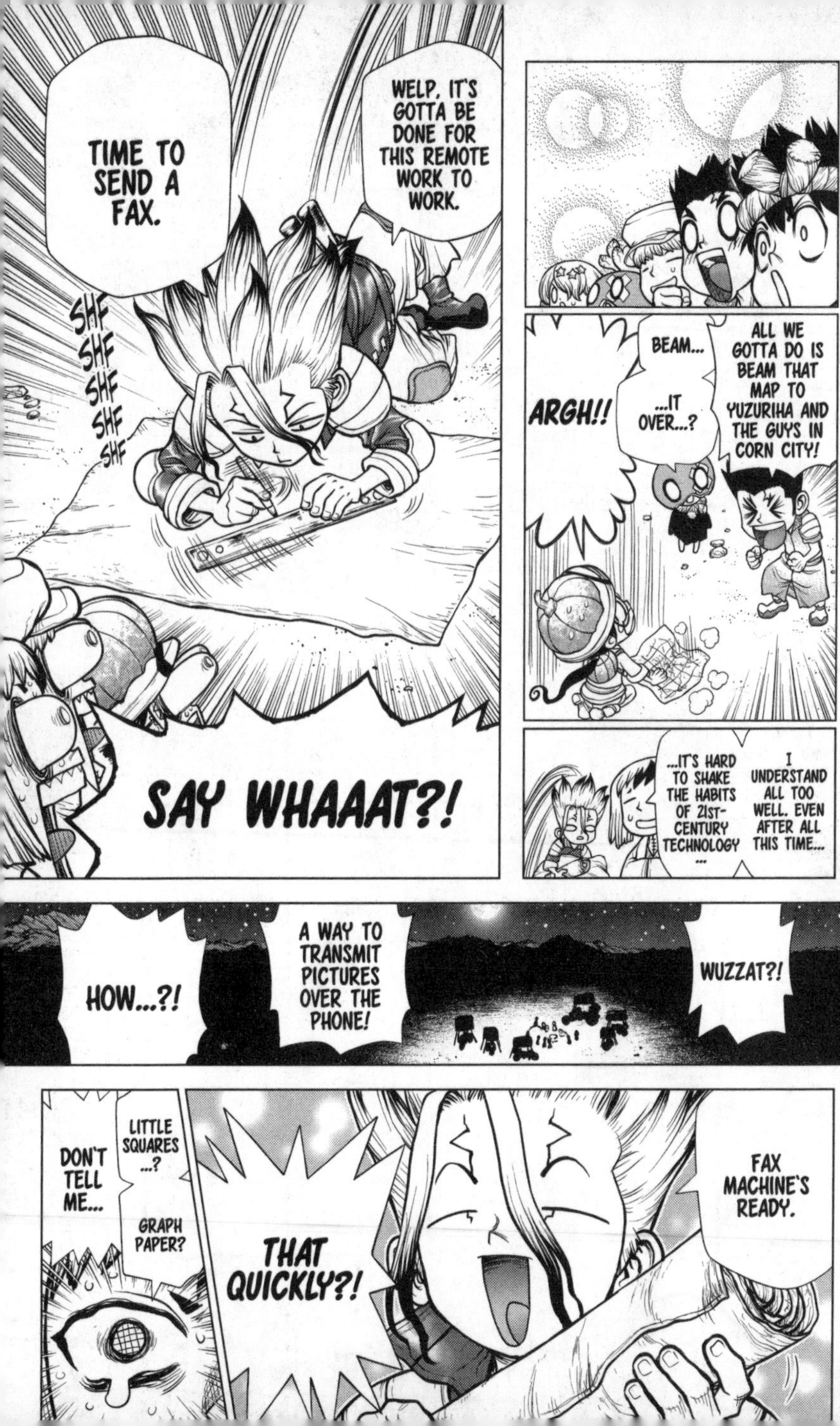
ALL WE GOTTA DO IS BEAM THAT MAP TO YUZURIHA AND THE GUYS IN CORN CITY!
BEAM... ...IT OVER...?
ARGH!!
I UNDERSTAND ALL TOO WELL. EVEN AFTER ALL THIS TIME...
...IT'S HARD TO SHAKE THE HABITS OF 21ST-CENTURY TECHNOLOGY...
WELP, IT'S GOTTA BE DONE FOR THIS REMOTE WORK TO WORK.
TIME TO SEND A FAX.
SHF SHF SHF SHF SHF
SAY WHAAAT?!
WUZZAT?!
A WAY TO TRANSMIT PICTURES OVER THE PHONE!
HOW...?!
FAX MACHINE'S READY.
THAT QUICKLY?!
LITTLE SQUARES...?
DON'T TELL ME...
GRAPH PAPER?

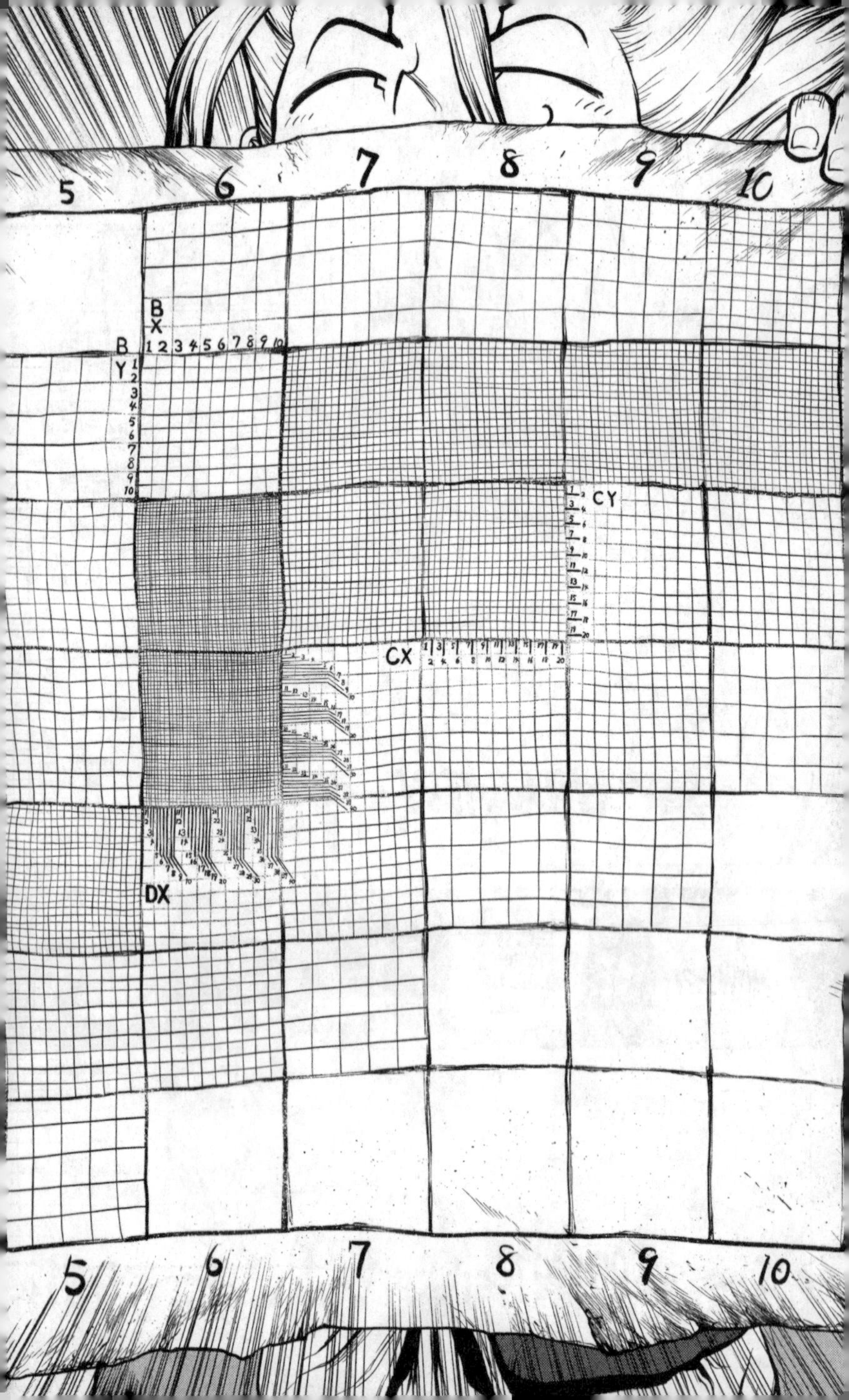
5 6 7 8 9 10
B X
1 2 3 4 5 6 7 8 9 10
B Y
CY
CX
DX
5 6 7 8 9 10

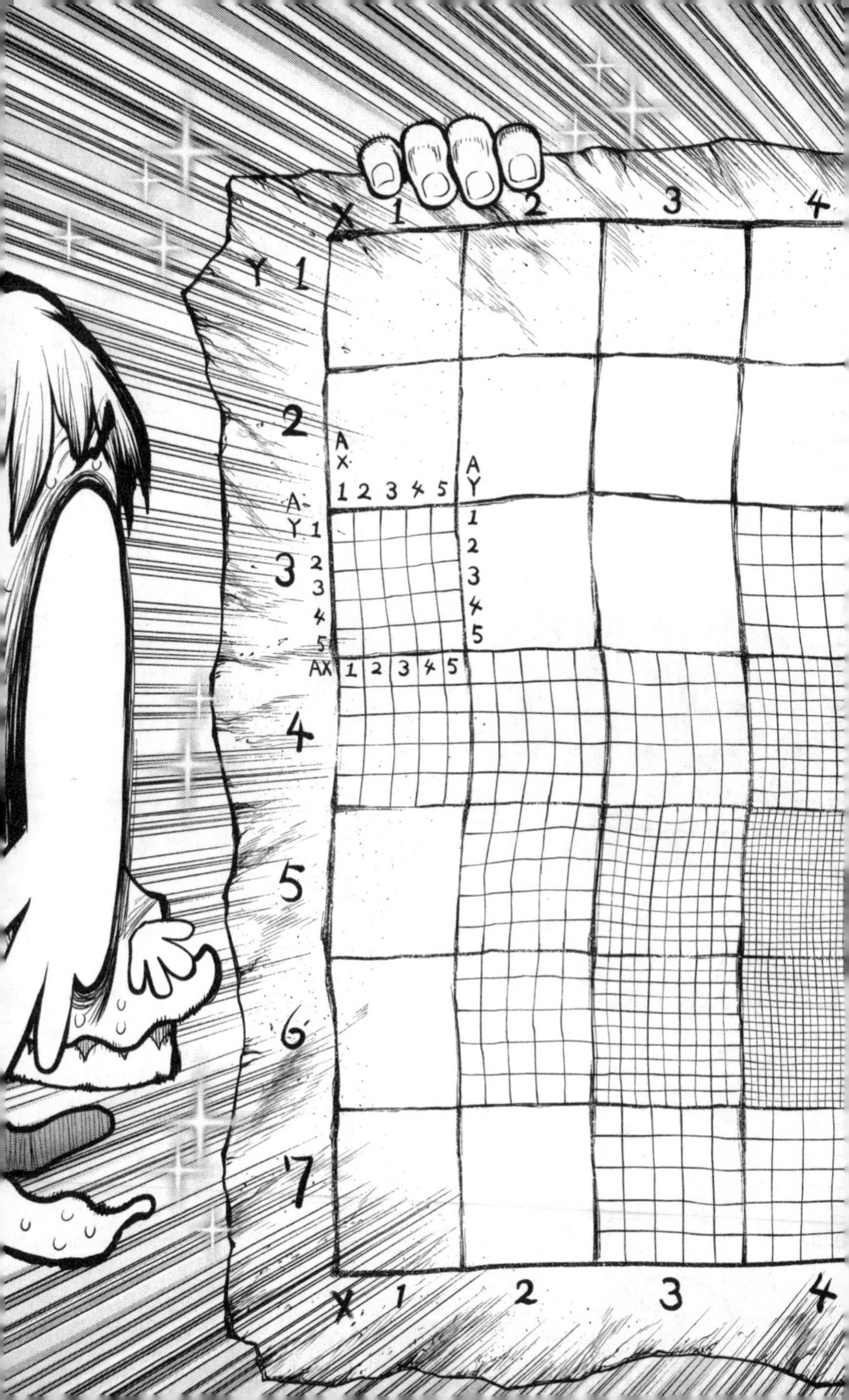
X 1 2 3 4
Y 1
2
A X 1 2 3 4 5
A Y 1 2 3 4 5
3
A Y 1 2 3 4 5
AX 1 2 3 4 5
4
5
6
7
X 1 2 3 4

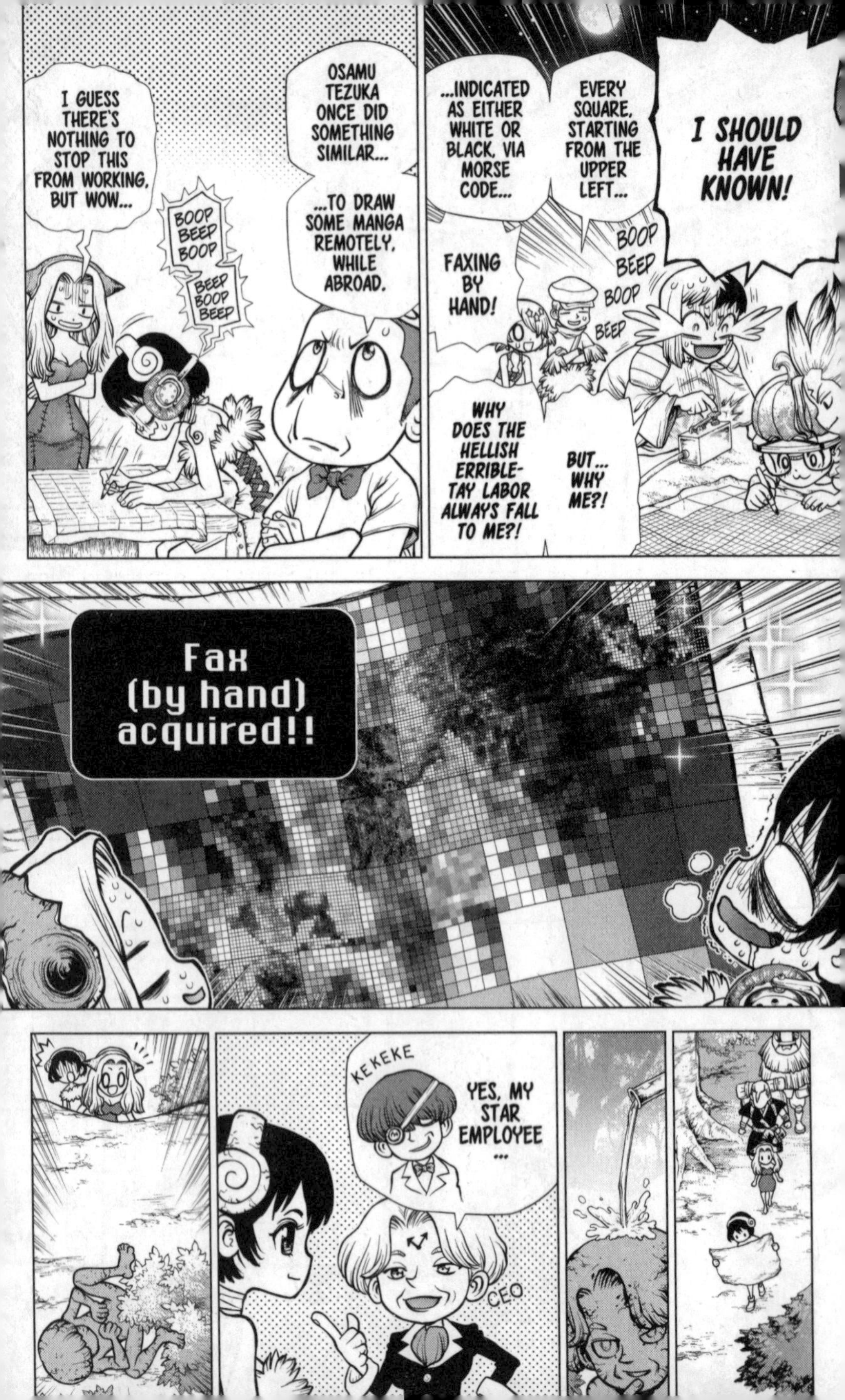
I SHOULD HAVE KNOWN!
EVERY SQUARE, STARTING FROM THE UPPER LEFT...
...INDICATED AS EITHER WHITE OR BLACK, VIA MORSE CODE...
BOOP BEEP BOOP BEEP
FAXING BY HAND!
BUT... WHY ME?!
WHY DOES THE HELLISH ERRIBLE-TAY LABOR ALWAYS FALL TO ME?!
OSAMU TEZUKA ONCE DID SOMETHING SIMILAR...
...TO DRAW SOME MANGA REMOTELY, WHILE ABROAD.
BOOP BEEP BOOP
BEEP BOOP BEEP
I GUESS THERE'S NOTHING TO STOP THIS FROM WORKING, BUT WOW...
Fax (by hand) acquired!!
KEKEKE
YES, MY STAR EMPLOYEE ...
CEO

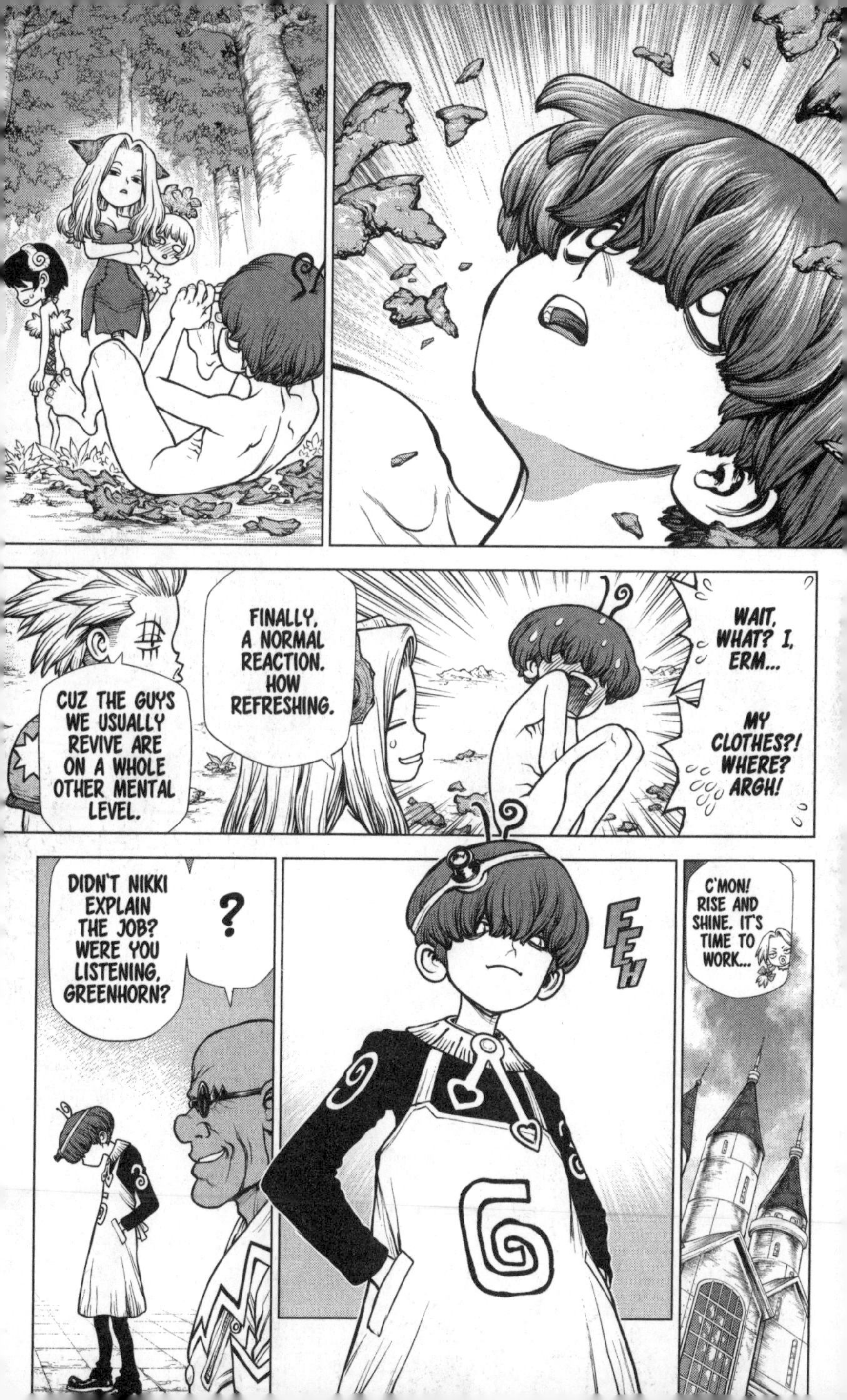
WAIT, WHAT? I, ERM...
MY CLOTHES?! WHERE? ARGH!
FINALLY, A NORMAL REACTION. HOW REFRESHING.
CUZ THE GUYS WE USUALLY REVIVE ARE ON A WHOLE OTHER MENTAL LEVEL.
C'MON! RISE AND SHINE. IT'S TIME TO WORK...
FEH
?
DIDN'T NIKKI EXPLAIN THE JOB? WERE YOU LISTENING, GREENHORN?

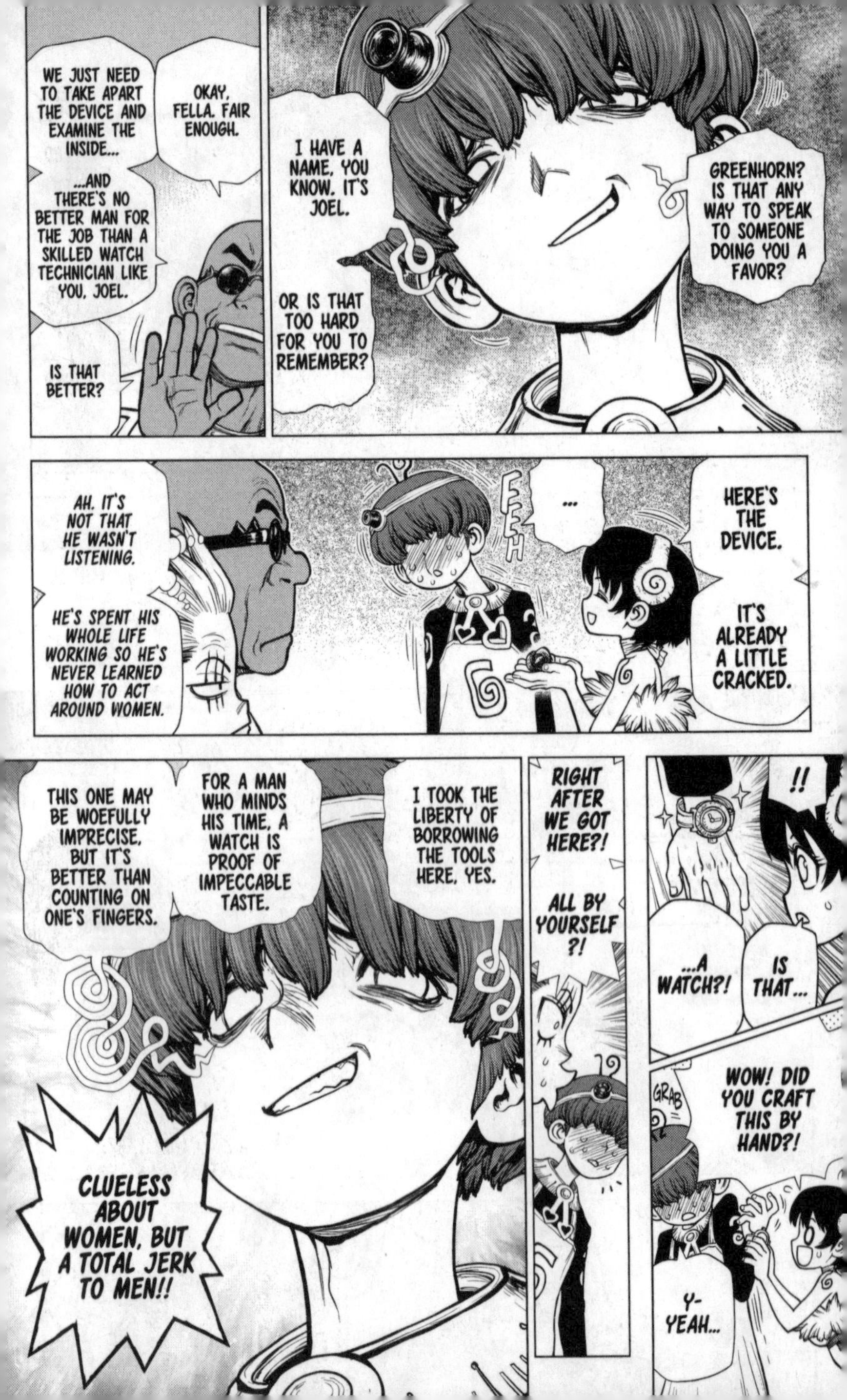
GREENHORN? IS THAT ANY WAY TO SPEAK TO SOMEONE DOING YOU A FAVOR?
I HAVE A NAME, YOU KNOW. IT'S JOEL.
OR IS THAT TOO HARD FOR YOU TO REMEMBER?
OKAY, FELLA. FAIR ENOUGH.
WE JUST NEED TO TAKE APART THE DEVICE AND EXAMINE THE INSIDE...
...AND THERE'S NO BETTER MAN FOR THE JOB THAN A SKILLED WATCH TECHNICIAN LIKE YOU, JOEL.
IS THAT BETTER?
HERE'S THE DEVICE.
IT'S ALREADY A LITTLE CRACKED.
...
FEEH
AH. IT'S NOT THAT HE WASN'T LISTENING.
HE'S SPENT HIS WHOLE LIFE WORKING SO HE'S NEVER LEARNED HOW TO ACT AROUND WOMEN.
!!
IS THAT...
...A WATCH?!
GRAB
WOW! DID YOU CRAFT THIS BY HAND?!
Y-YEAH...
RIGHT AFTER WE GOT HERE?!
ALL BY YOURSELF?!
I TOOK THE LIBERTY OF BORROWING THE TOOLS HERE, YES.
FOR A MAN WHO MINDS HIS TIME, A WATCH IS PROOF OF IMPECCABLE TASTE.
THIS ONE MAY BE WOEFULLY IMPRECISE, BUT IT'S BETTER THAN COUNTING ON ONE'S FINGERS.
CLUELESS ABOUT WOMEN, BUT A TOTAL JERK TO MEN!!

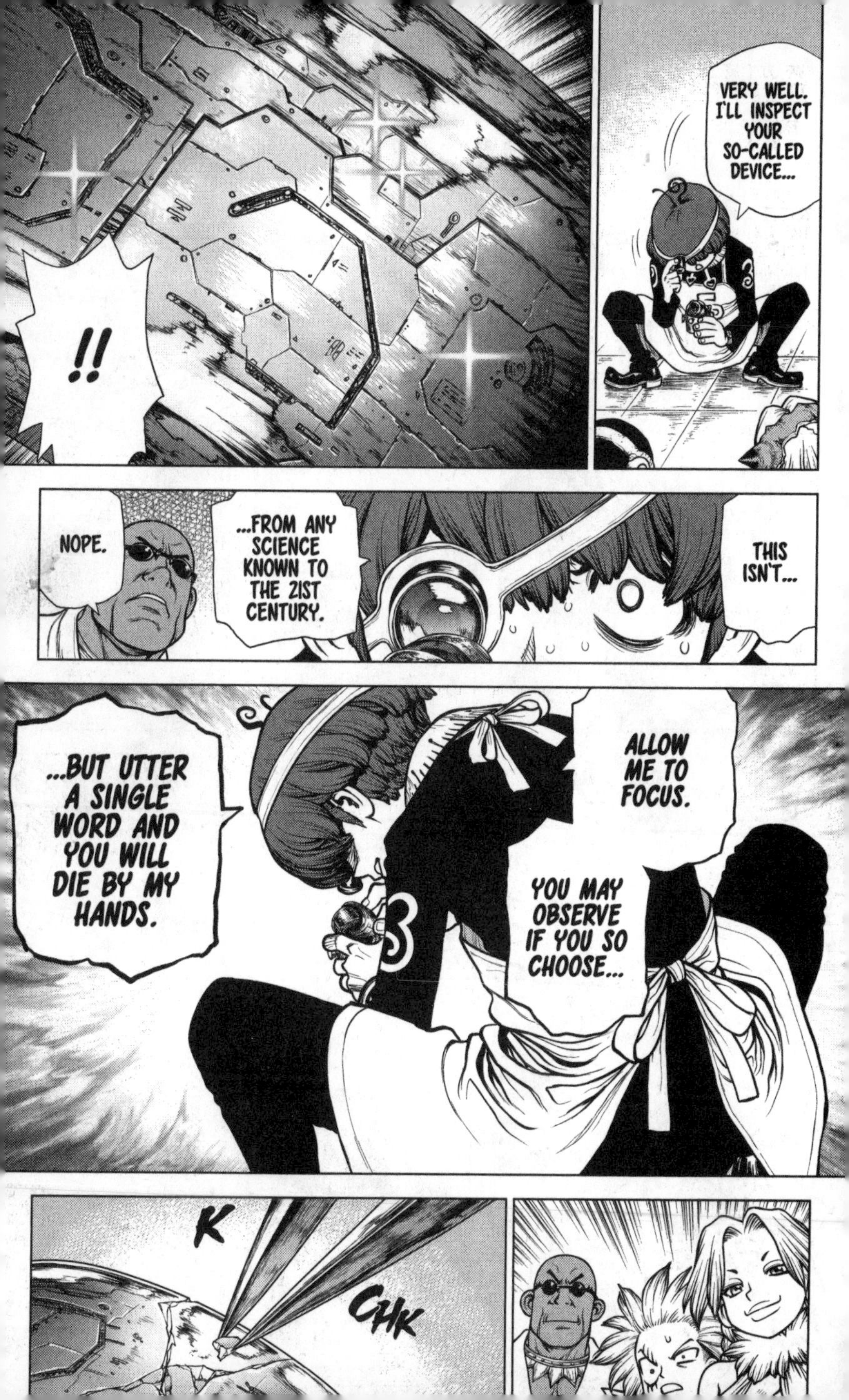
VERY WELL. I'LL INSPECT YOUR SO-CALLED DEVICE...
!!
THIS ISN'T...
...FROM ANY SCIENCE KNOWN TO THE 21ST CENTURY.
NOPE.
ALLOW ME TO FOCUS.
YOU MAY OBSERVE IF YOU SO CHOOSE...
...BUT UTTER A SINGLE WORD AND YOU WILL DIE BY MY HANDS.
K
CHK

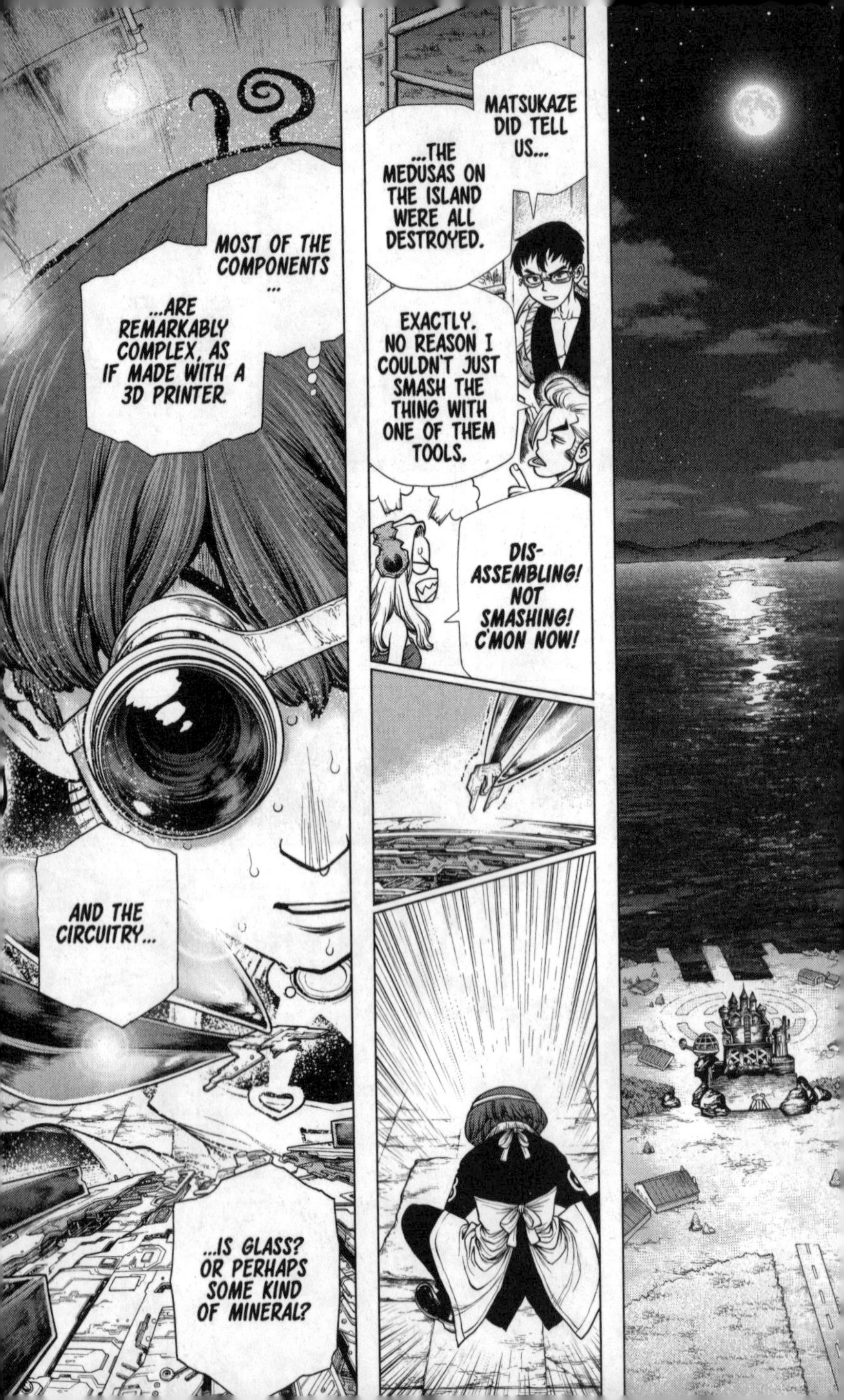
MATSUKAZE DID TELL US...
...THE MEDUSAS ON THE ISLAND WERE ALL DESTROYED.
EXACTLY. NO REASON I COULDN'T JUST SMASH THE THING WITH ONE OF THEM TOOLS.
DIS-ASSEMBLING! NOT SMASHING! C'MON NOW!
MOST OF THE COMPONENTS...
...ARE REMARKABLY COMPLEX, AS IF MADE WITH A 3D PRINTER.
AND THE CIRCUITRY...
...IS GLASS? OR PERHAPS SOME KIND OF MINERAL?

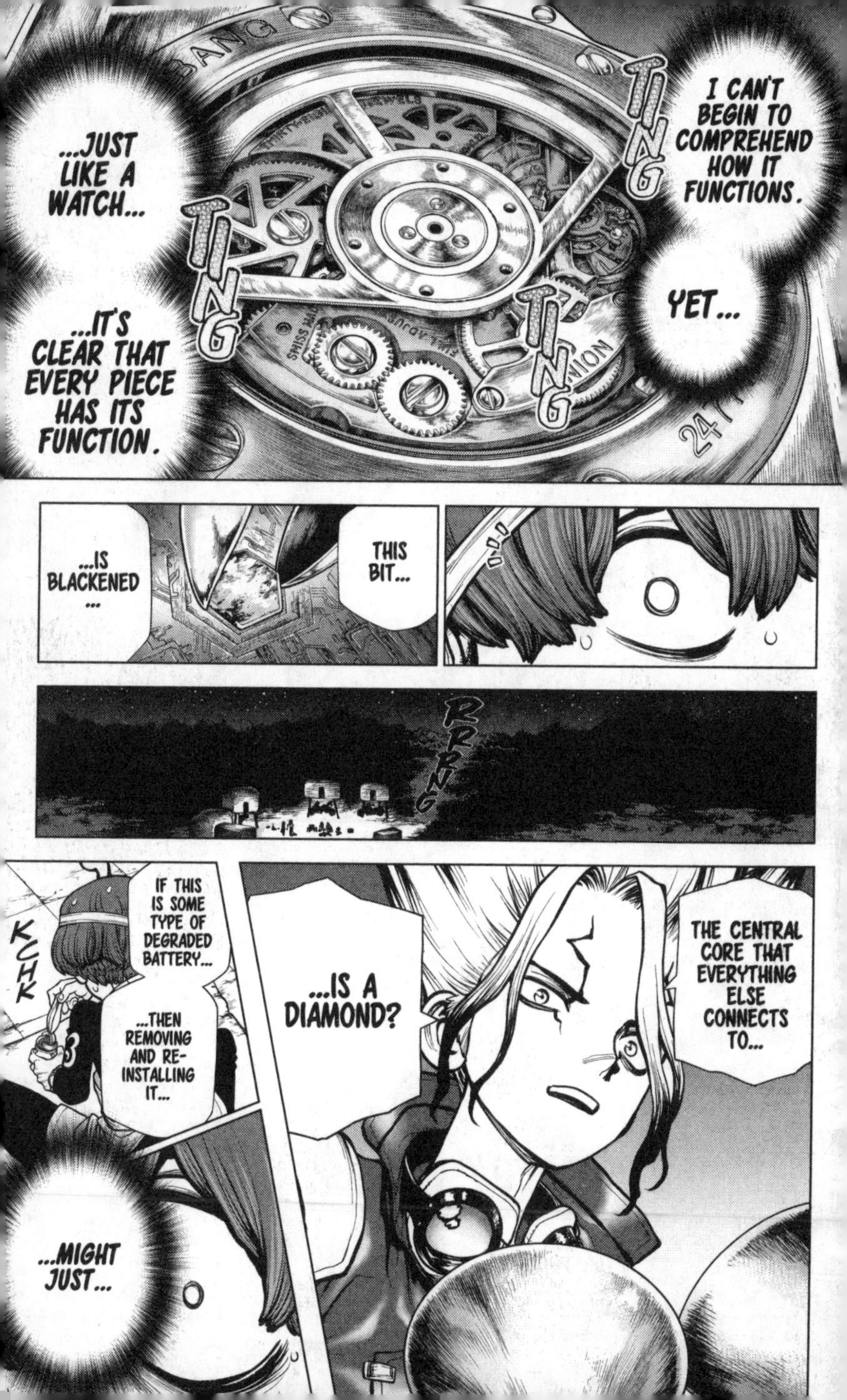

I CAN'T BEGIN TO COMPREHEND HOW IT FUNCTIONS.
TING
...JUST LIKE A WATCH...
TING
YET...
TING
...IT'S CLEAR THAT EVERY PIECE HAS ITS FUNCTION.
THIS BIT...
...IS BLACKENED ...
RRRNG
THE CENTRAL CORE THAT EVERYTHING ELSE CONNECTS TO...
...IS A DIAMOND?
IF THIS IS SOME TYPE OF DEGRADED BATTERY...
...THEN REMOVING AND RE-INSTALLING IT...
KCHK
...MIGHT JUST...

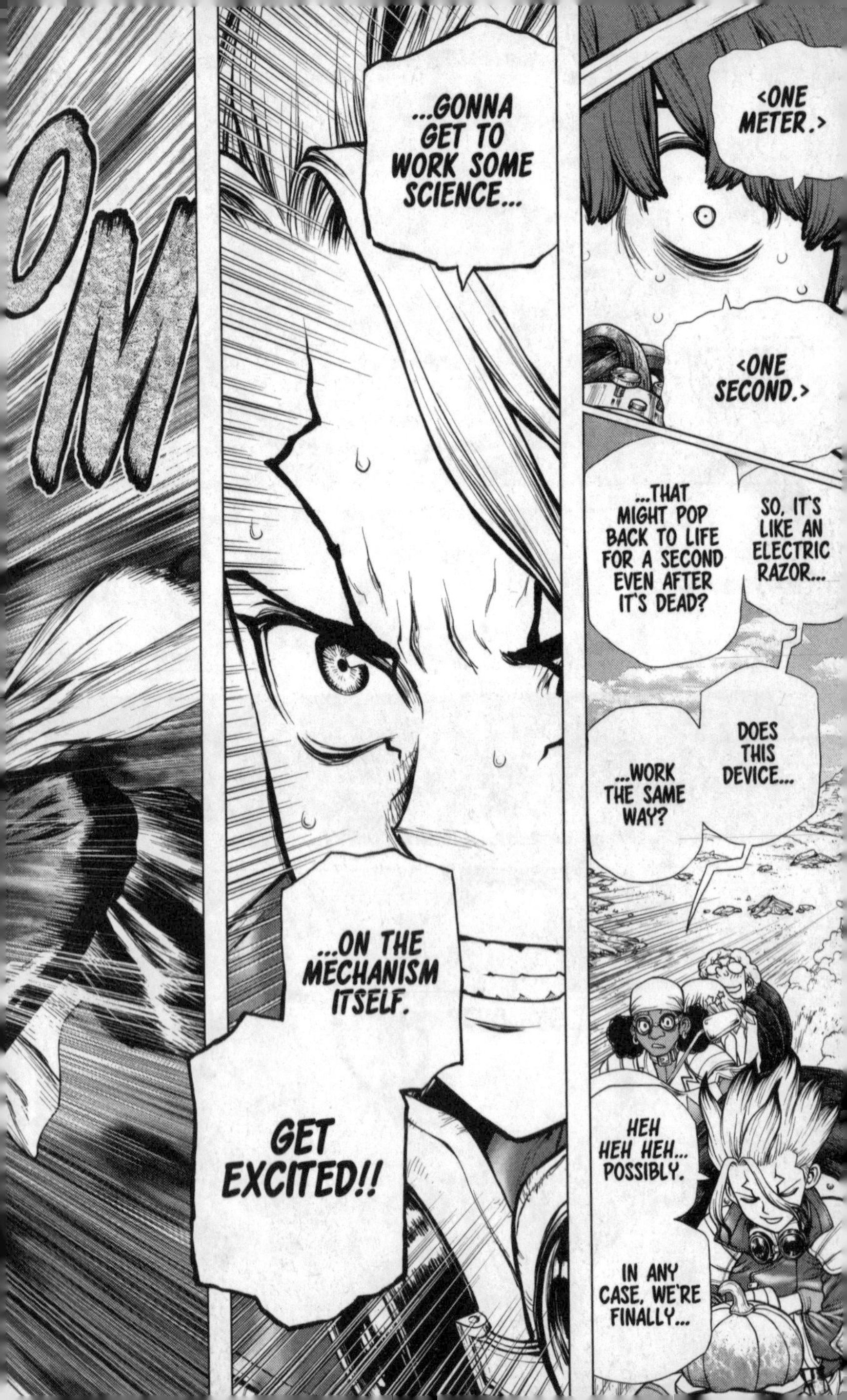
<ONE METER.>
<ONE SECOND.>
SO, IT'S LIKE AN ELECTRIC RAZOR...
...THAT MIGHT POP BACK TO LIFE FOR A SECOND EVEN AFTER IT'S DEAD?
DOES THIS DEVICE...
...WORK THE SAME WAY?
HEH HEH HEH... POSSIBLY.
IN ANY CASE, WE'RE FINALLY...
...GONNA GET TO WORK SOME SCIENCE...
...ON THE MECHANISM ITSELF.
GET EXCITED!!
OM

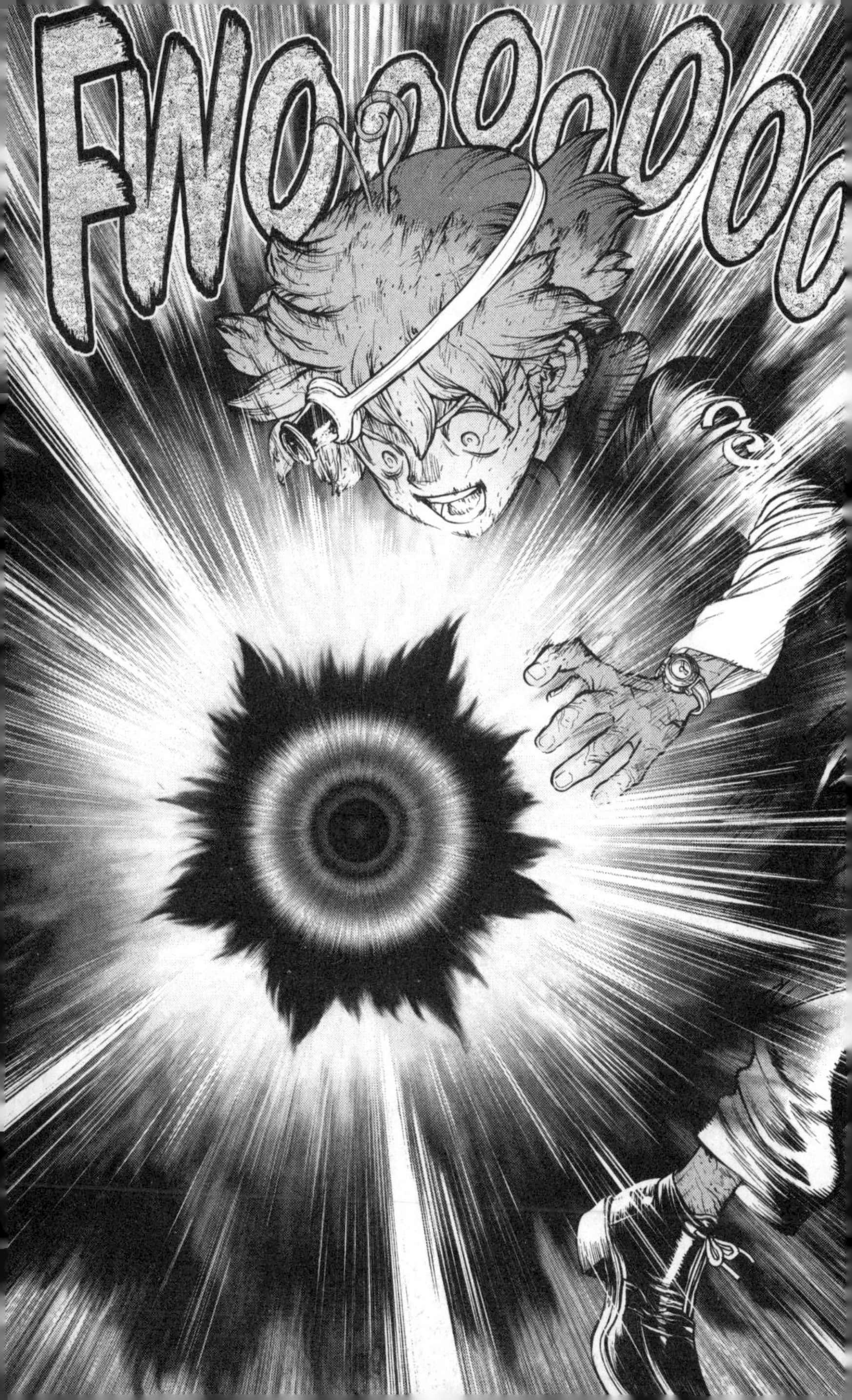
FWOOOOOOOOO

Xeno's Science Kingdom

KNIGHT FILE 9

Brody

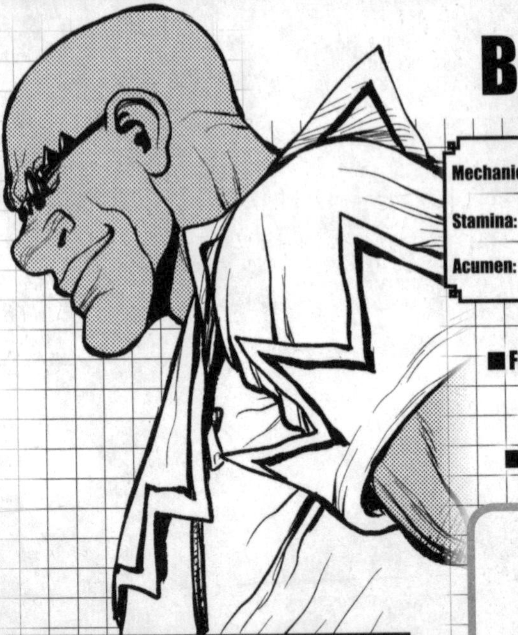

Mechanical Skills: ★★★★★

Stamina: ★★★★

Acumen: ★★★

■ Full Name: Brody Dudley

■ Height: 822 cm

■ Profession: Mechanic

Even as a child, Brody was a gearhead who loved tinkering with cars.

He's not much for the theoretical...so he doesn't sweat the details too much when putting together massive projects!

Which is why Brody is so grateful to Xeno. He's willing to follow Captain Stanley's orders and do all he can to see Xeno's vision fulfilled.

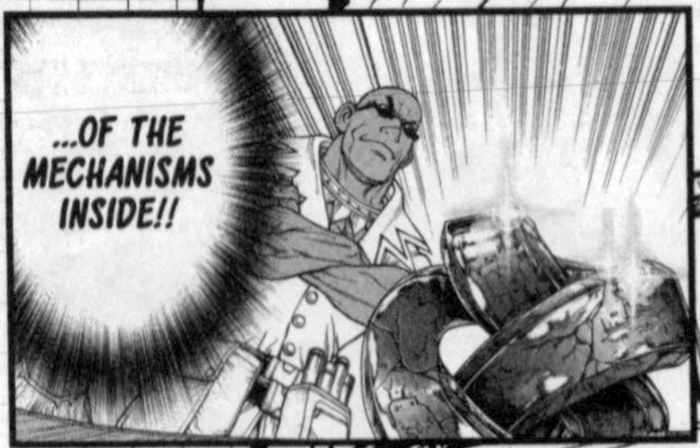
...OF THE MECHANISMS INSIDE!!

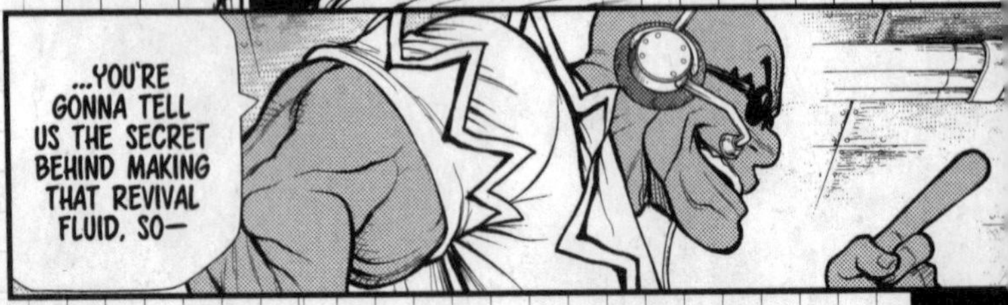
...YOU'RE GONNA TELL US THE SECRET BEHIND MAKING THAT REVIVAL FLUID, SO—

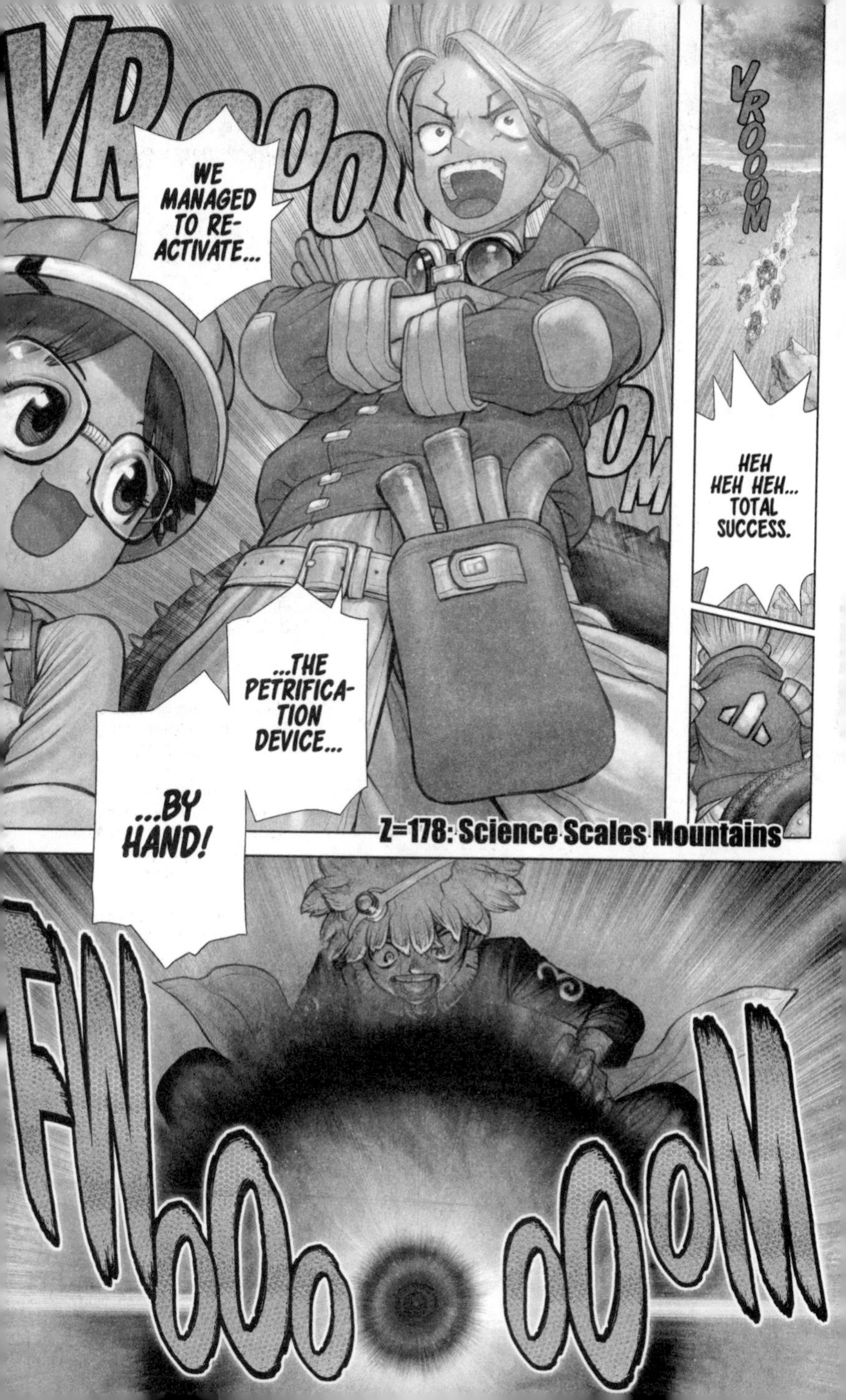
VROOOM
HEH HEH HEH... TOTAL SUCCESS.
VROOOOOOM
WE MANAGED TO RE-ACTIVATE...
...THE PETRIFICATION DEVICE...
...BY HAND!
Z=178: Science Scales Mountains
FWOOOOOOOOM

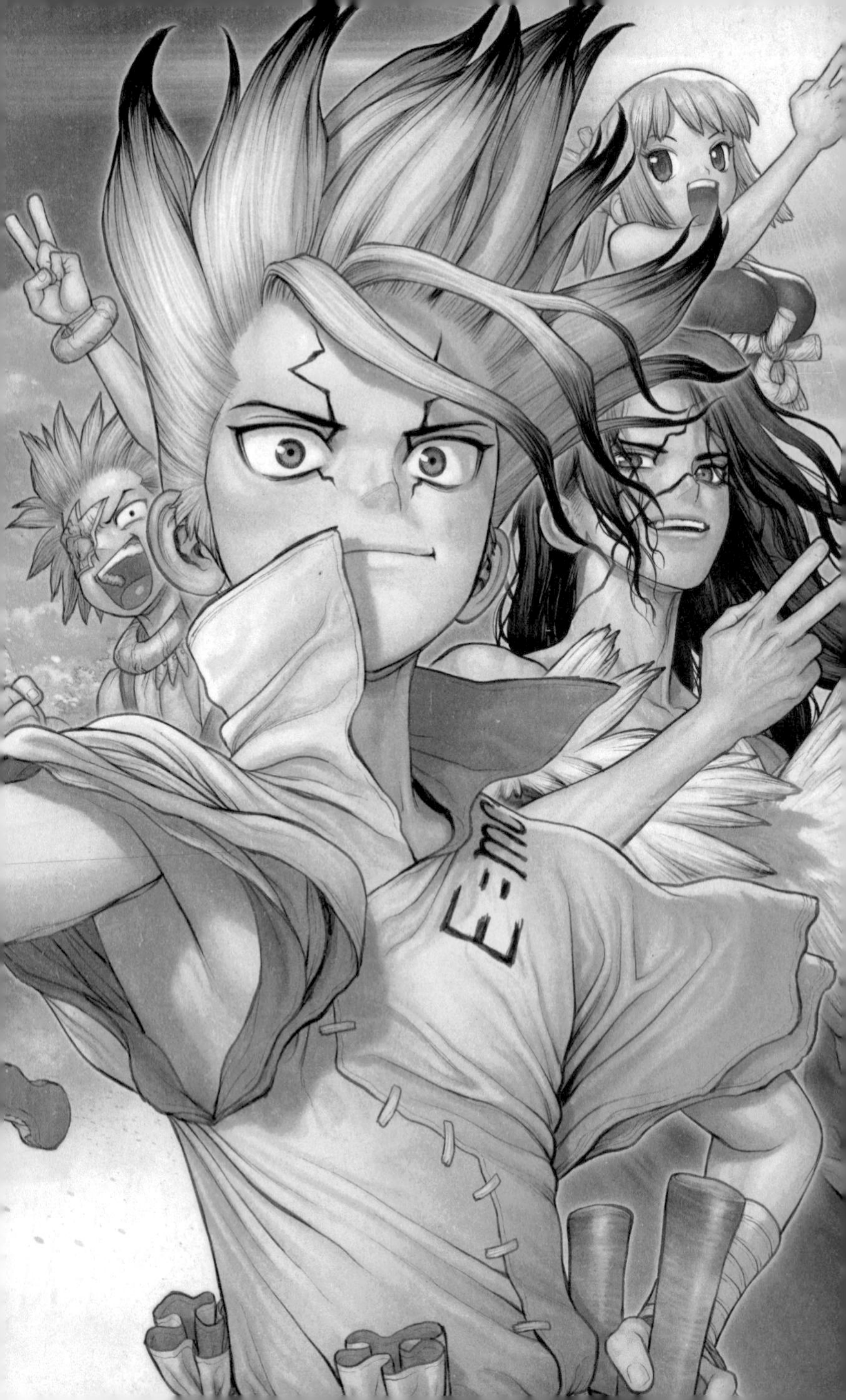

Z=178: Science Scales Mountains

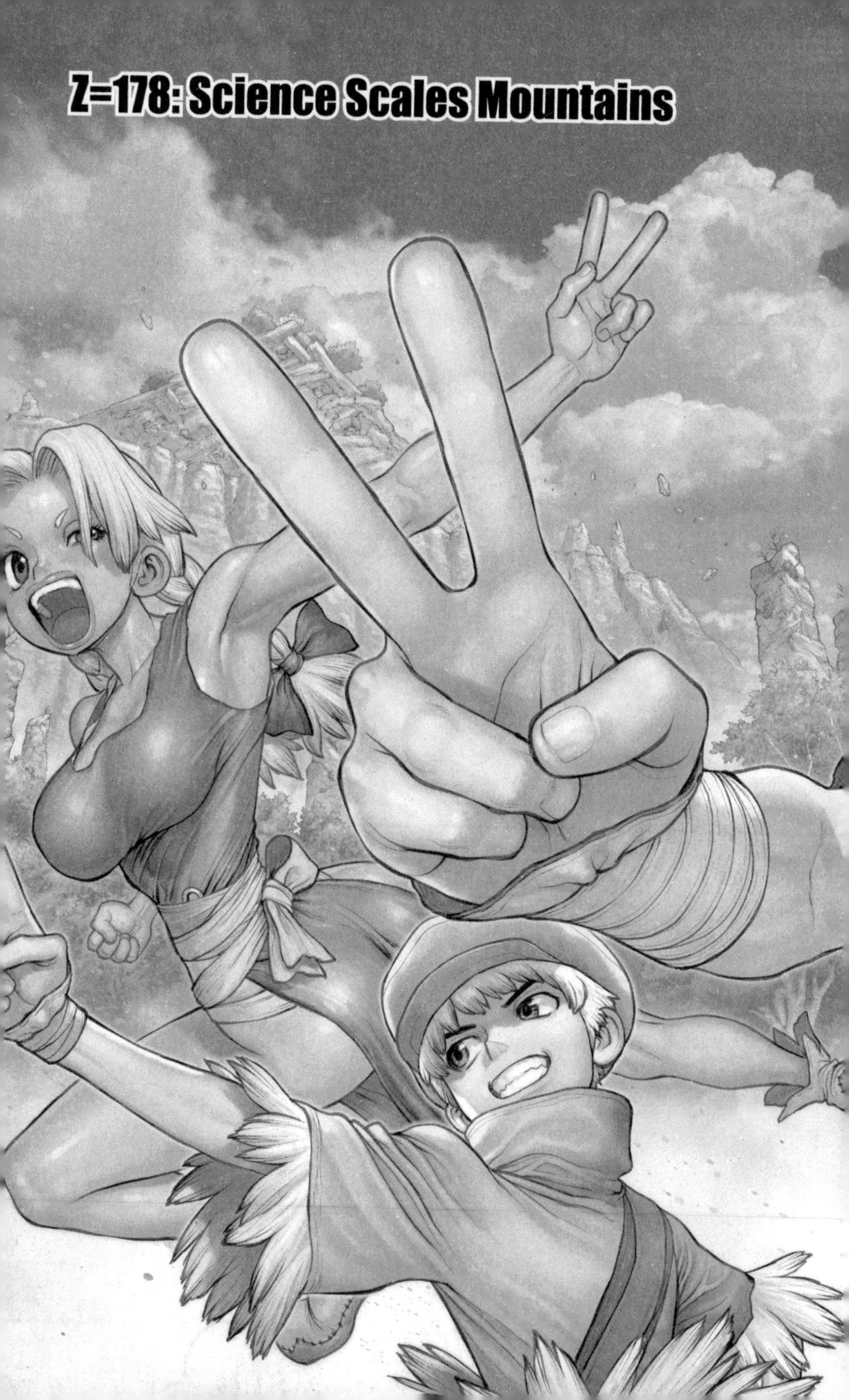

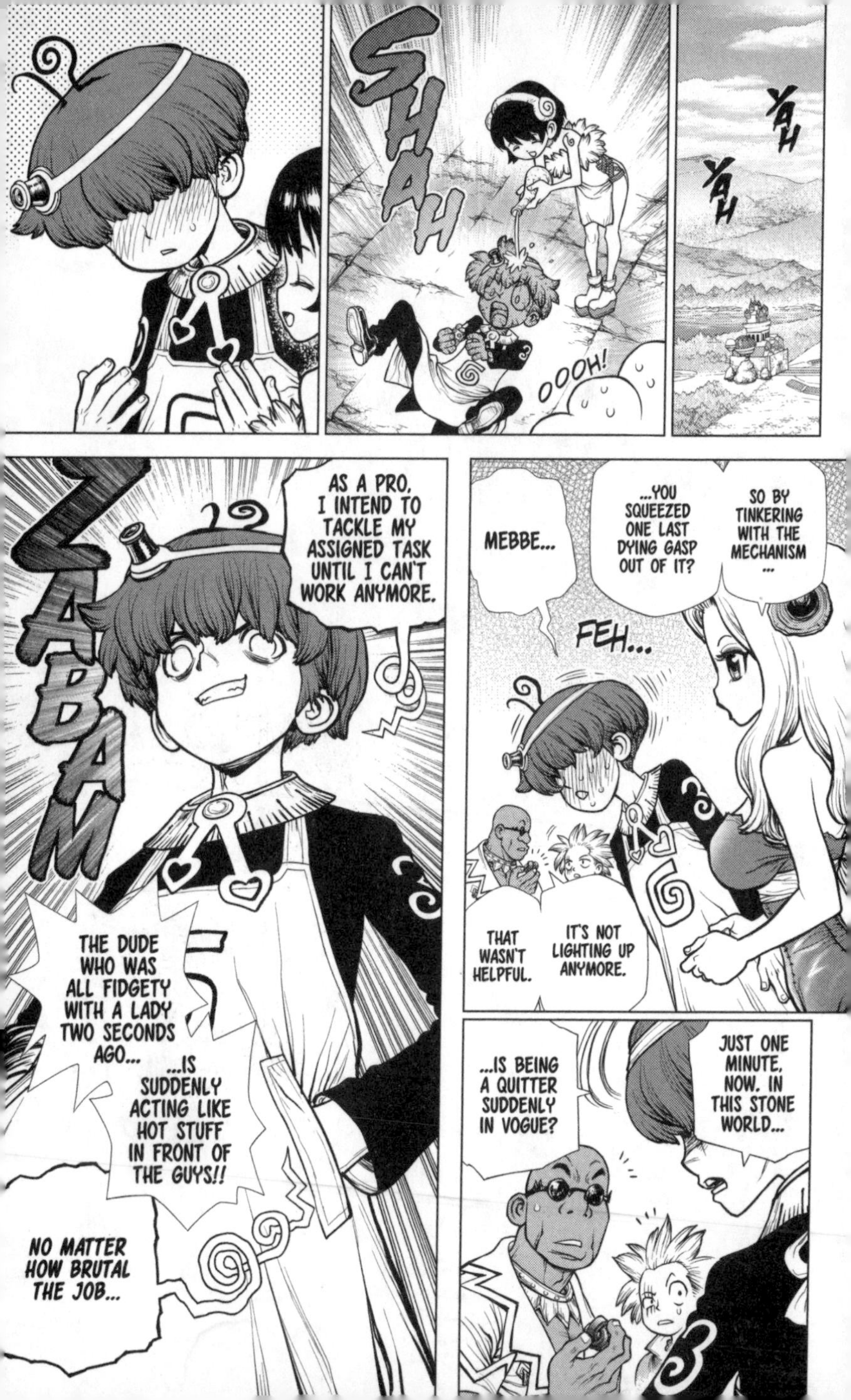
YAH
YAH
SHAH
OOOH!
SO BY TINKERING WITH THE MECHANISM...
...YOU SQUEEZED ONE LAST DYING GASP OUT OF IT?
MEBBE...
FEH...
IT'S NOT LIGHTING UP ANYMORE.
THAT WASN'T HELPFUL.
JUST ONE MINUTE, NOW. IN THIS STONE WORLD...
...IS BEING A QUITTER SUDDENLY IN VOGUE?
AS A PRO, I INTEND TO TACKLE MY ASSIGNED TASK UNTIL I CAN'T WORK ANYMORE.
ZABAM
THE DUDE WHO WAS ALL FIDGETY WITH A LADY TWO SECONDS AGO...
...IS SUDDENLY ACTING LIKE HOT STUFF IN FRONT OF THE GUYS!!
NO MATTER HOW BRUTAL THE JOB...

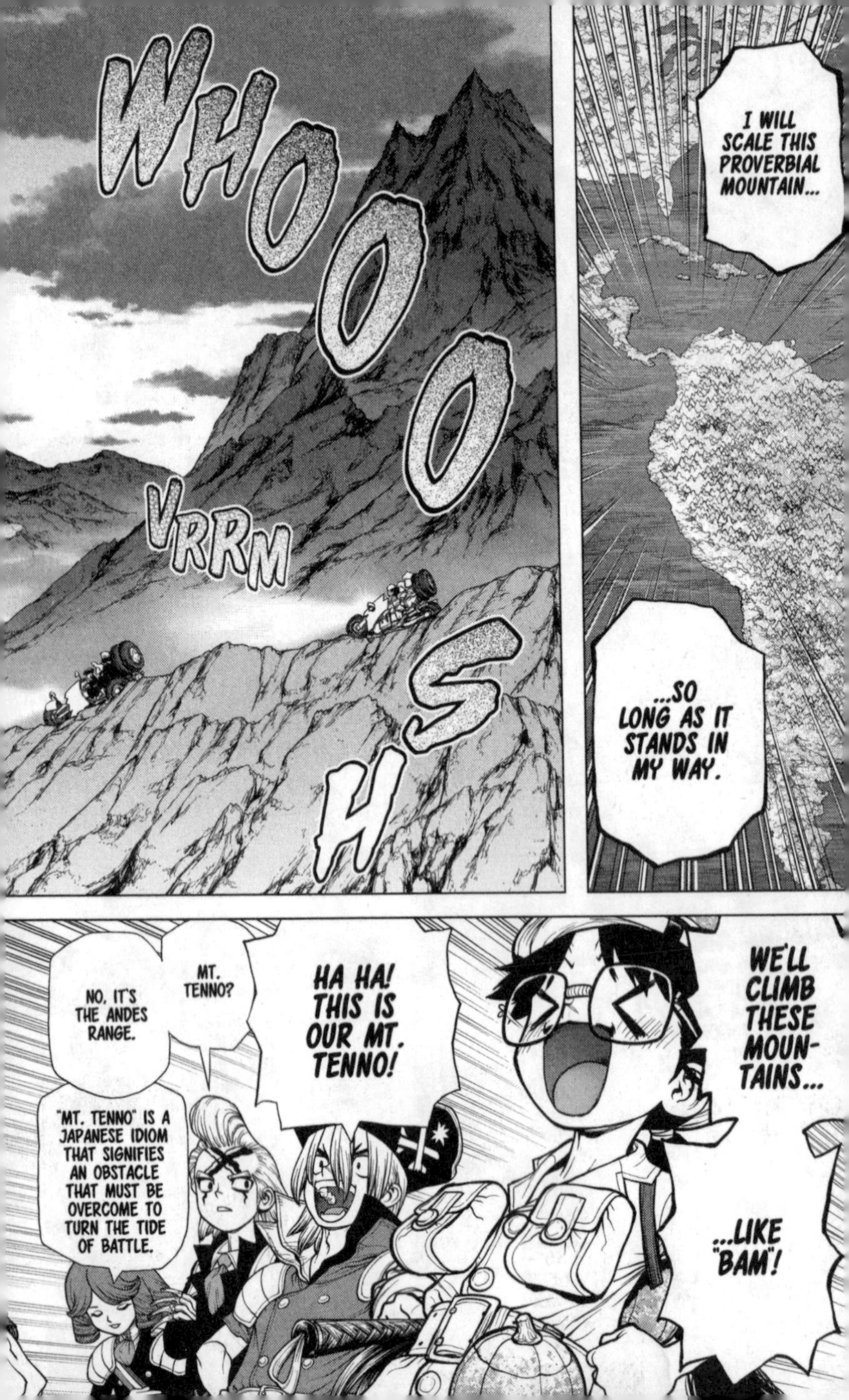
I WILL SCALE THIS PROVERBIAL MOUNTAIN...
...SO LONG AS IT STANDS IN MY WAY.
WHOOOOSH
VRRM
WE'LL CLIMB THESE MOUN-TAINS...
...LIKE "BAM"!
HA HA! THIS IS OUR MT. TENNO!
MT. TENNO?
NO, IT'S THE ANDES RANGE.
"MT. TENNO" IS A JAPANESE IDIOM THAT SIGNIFIES AN OBSTACLE THAT MUST BE OVERCOME TO TURN THE TIDE OF BATTLE.

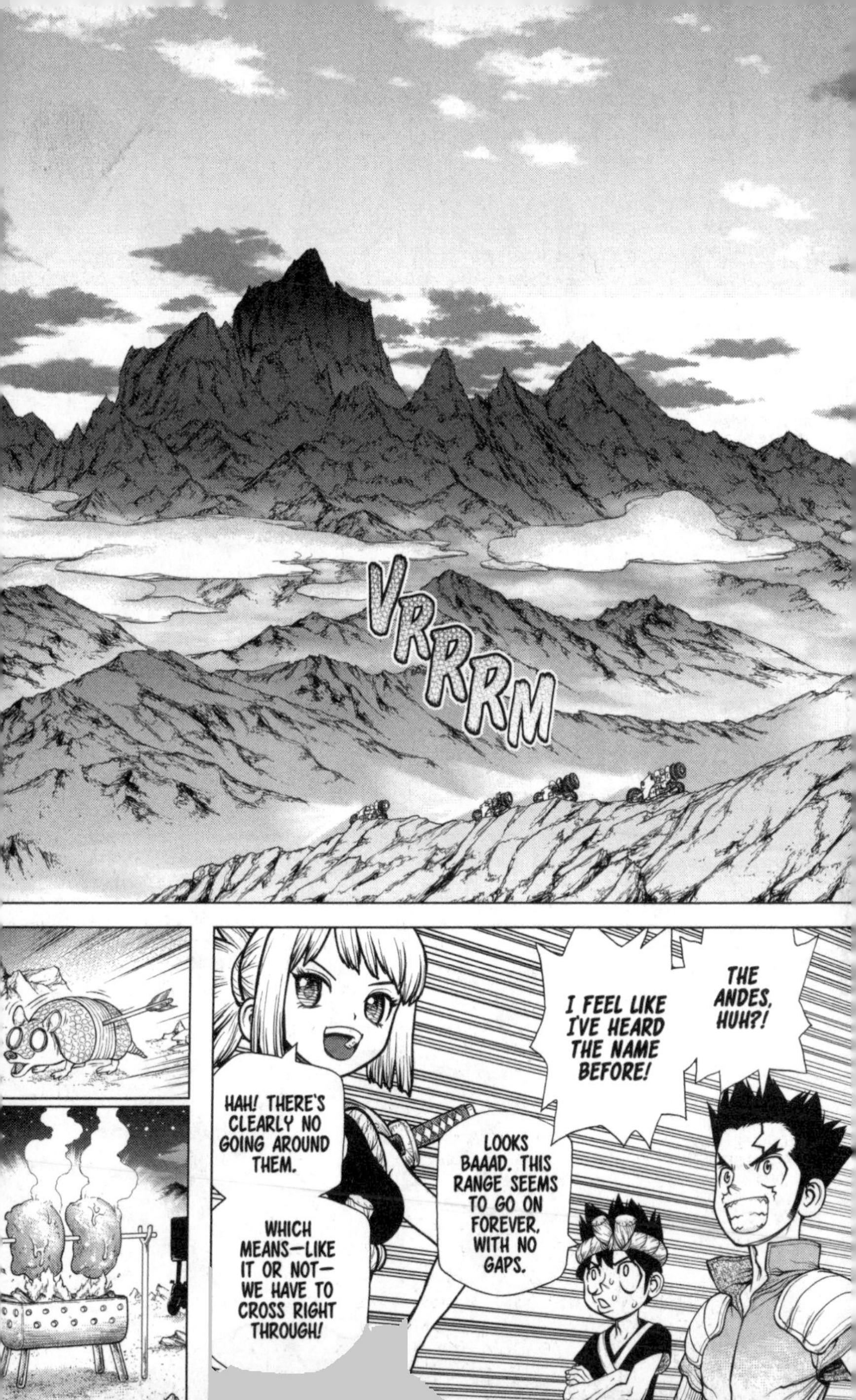
VRRRM
THE ANDES, HUH?!
I FEEL LIKE I'VE HEARD THE NAME BEFORE!
LOOKS BAAAD. THIS RANGE SEEMS TO GO ON FOREVER, WITH NO GAPS.
HAH! THERE'S CLEARLY NO GOING AROUND THEM.
WHICH MEANS—LIKE IT OR NOT—WE HAVE TO CROSS RIGHT THROUGH!

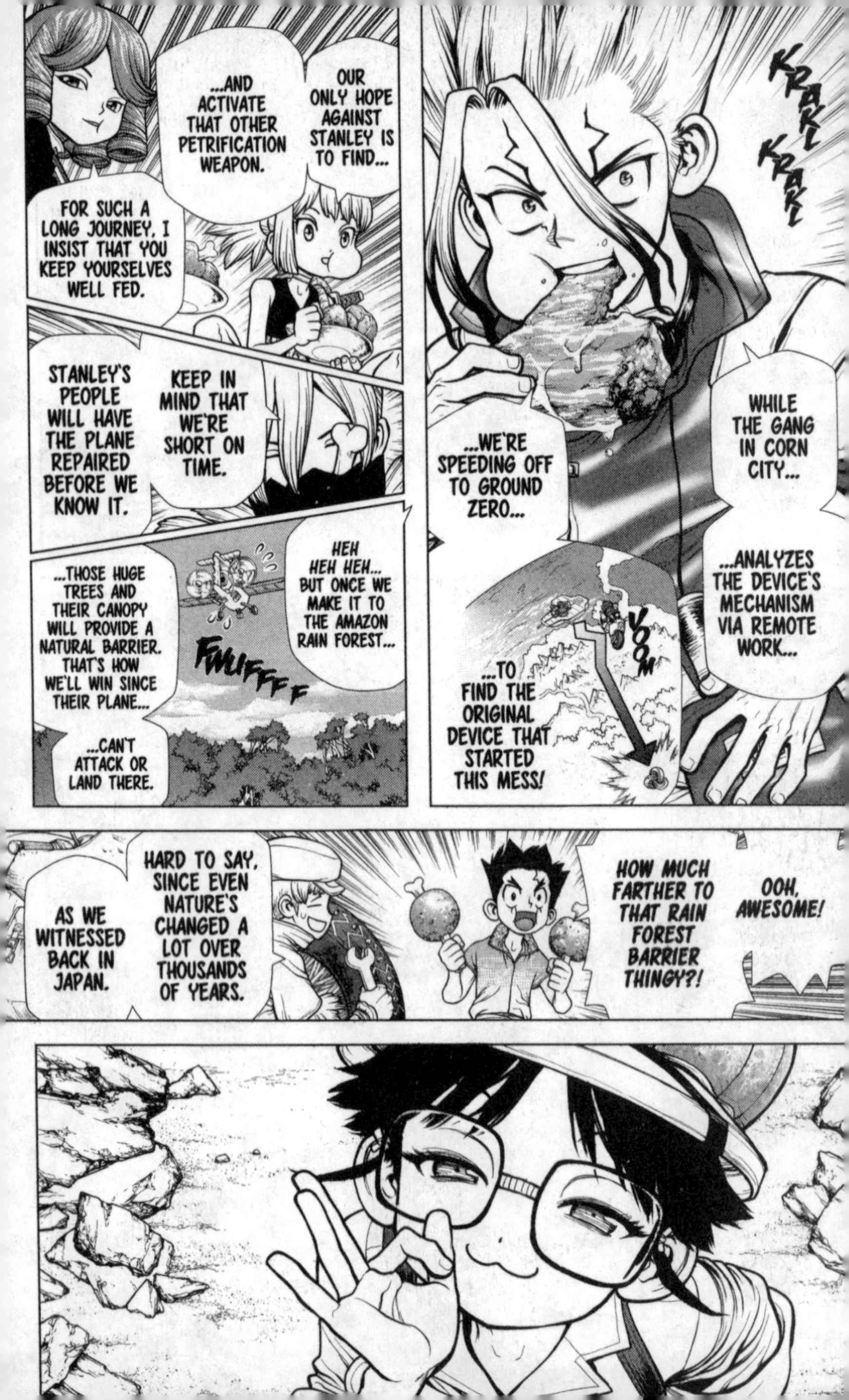
KRAKL KRAKL
WHILE THE GANG IN CORN CITY...
...ANALYZES THE DEVICE'S MECHANISM VIA REMOTE WORK...
...WE'RE SPEEDING OFF TO GROUND ZERO...
VOOM
...TO FIND THE ORIGINAL DEVICE THAT STARTED THIS MESS!
OUR ONLY HOPE AGAINST STANLEY IS TO FIND...
...AND ACTIVATE THAT OTHER PETRIFICATION WEAPON.
FOR SUCH A LONG JOURNEY, I INSIST THAT YOU KEEP YOURSELVES WELL FED.
KEEP IN MIND THAT WE'RE SHORT ON TIME.
STANLEY'S PEOPLE WILL HAVE THE PLANE REPAIRED BEFORE WE KNOW IT.
HEH HEH HEH... BUT ONCE WE MAKE IT TO THE AMAZON RAIN FOREST...
FWUFFFFF
...THOSE HUGE TREES AND THEIR CANOPY WILL PROVIDE A NATURAL BARRIER. THAT'S HOW WE'LL WIN SINCE THEIR PLANE...
...CAN'T ATTACK OR LAND THERE.
OOH, AWESOME!
HOW MUCH FARTHER TO THAT RAIN FOREST BARRIER THINGY?!
HARD TO SAY, SINCE EVEN NATURE'S CHANGED A LOT OVER THOUSANDS OF YEARS.
AS WE WITNESSED BACK IN JAPAN.

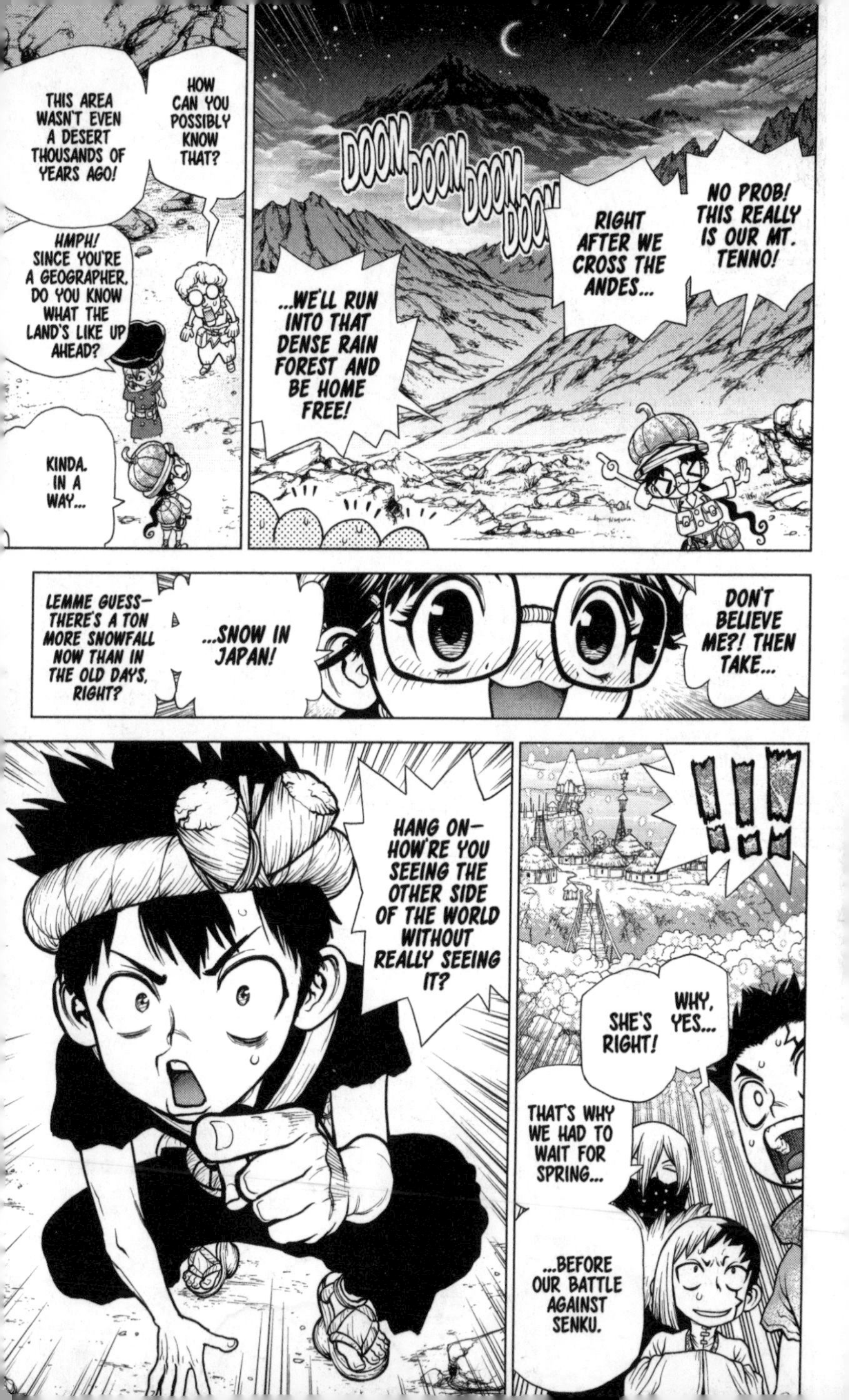
DOOM DOOM DOOM DOOM
NO PROB! THIS REALLY IS OUR MT. TENNO!
RIGHT AFTER WE CROSS THE ANDES...
...WE'LL RUN INTO THAT DENSE RAIN FOREST AND BE HOME FREE!
HOW CAN YOU POSSIBLY KNOW THAT?
THIS AREA WASN'T EVEN A DESERT THOUSANDS OF YEARS AGO!
HMPH! SINCE YOU'RE A GEOGRAPHER, DO YOU KNOW WHAT THE LAND'S LIKE UP AHEAD?
KINDA. IN A WAY...
DON'T BELIEVE ME?! THEN TAKE...
...SNOW IN JAPAN!
LEMME GUESS—THERE'S A TON MORE SNOWFALL NOW THAN IN THE OLD DAYS, RIGHT?
!!!
WHY, YES...
SHE'S RIGHT!
THAT'S WHY WE HAD TO WAIT FOR SPRING...
...BEFORE OUR BATTLE AGAINST SENKU.
HANG ON—HOW'RE YOU SEEING THE OTHER SIDE OF THE WORLD WITHOUT REALLY SEEING IT?

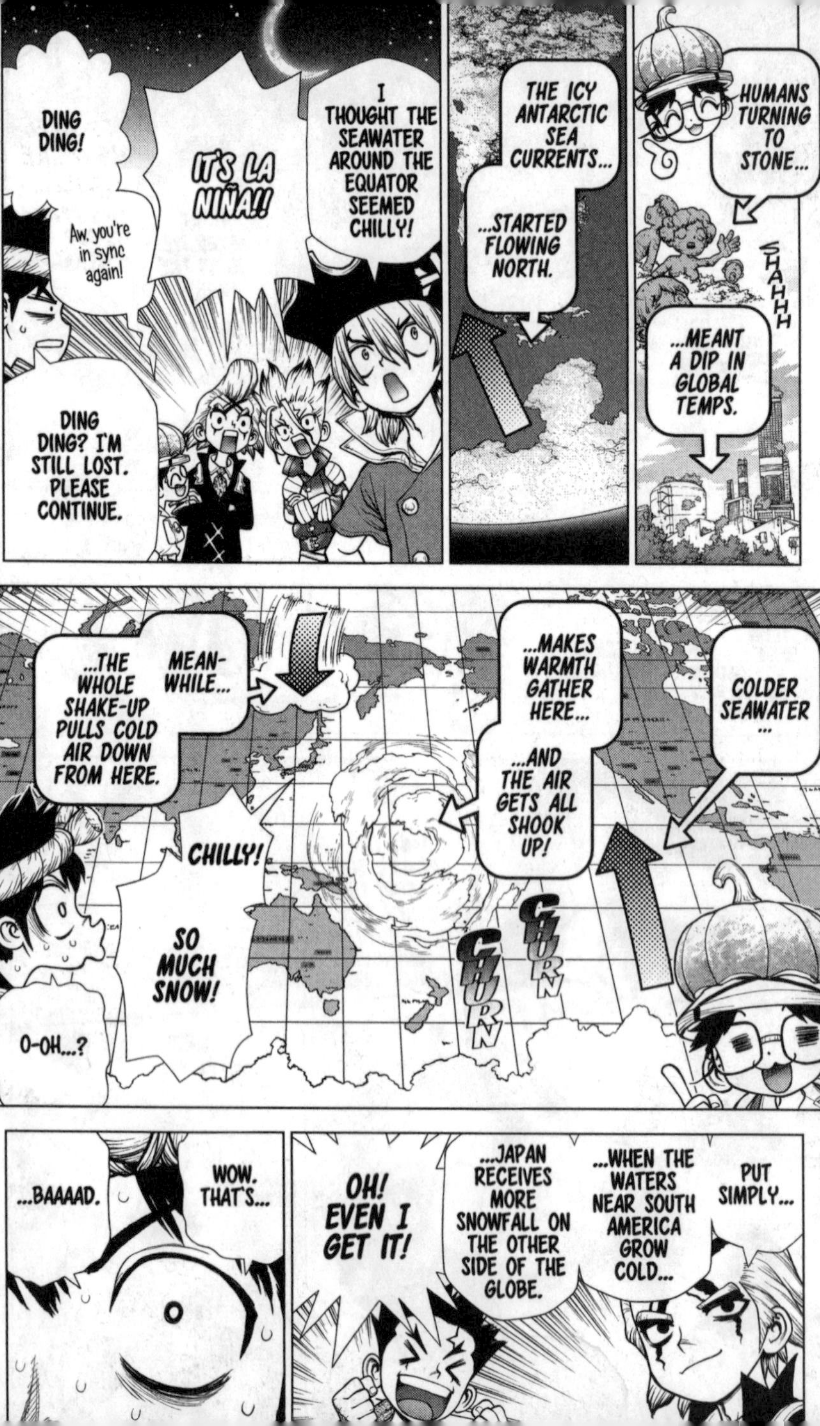
HUMANS TURNING TO STONE...
SHAHHH
...MEANT A DIP IN GLOBAL TEMPS.
THE ICY ANTARCTIC SEA CURRENTS...
...STARTED FLOWING NORTH.
I THOUGHT THE SEAWATER AROUND THE EQUATOR SEEMED CHILLY!
IT'S LA NIÑA!!
DING DING!
Aw, you're in sync again!
DING DING? I'M STILL LOST. PLEASE CONTINUE.
COLDER SEAWATER...
...MAKES WARMTH GATHER HERE...
...AND THE AIR GETS ALL SHOOK UP!
CHURN
CHURN
MEAN-WHILE...
...THE WHOLE SHAKE-UP PULLS COLD AIR DOWN FROM HERE.
CHILLY!
SO MUCH SNOW!
O-OH...?
PUT SIMPLY...
...WHEN THE WATERS NEAR SOUTH AMERICA GROW COLD...
...JAPAN RECEIVES MORE SNOWFALL ON THE OTHER SIDE OF THE GLOBE.
OH! EVEN I GET IT!
WOW. THAT'S...
...BAAAAD.

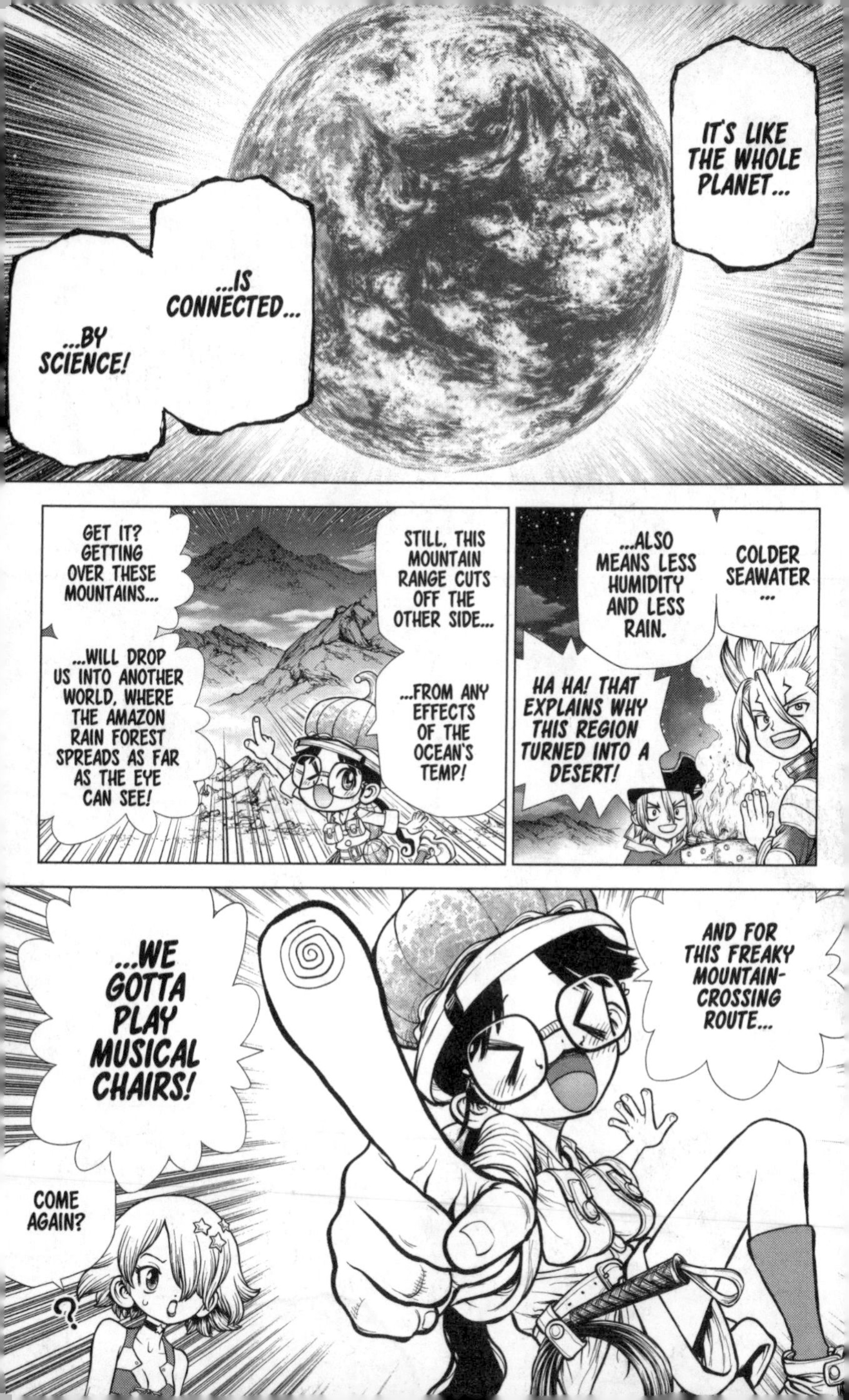
IT'S LIKE THE WHOLE PLANET...
...IS CONNECTED...
...BY SCIENCE!
COLDER SEAWATER ...
...ALSO MEANS LESS HUMIDITY AND LESS RAIN.
HA HA! THAT EXPLAINS WHY THIS REGION TURNED INTO A DESERT!
STILL, THIS MOUNTAIN RANGE CUTS OFF THE OTHER SIDE...
...FROM ANY EFFECTS OF THE OCEAN'S TEMP!
GET IT? GETTING OVER THESE MOUNTAINS...
...WILL DROP US INTO ANOTHER WORLD, WHERE THE AMAZON RAIN FOREST SPREADS AS FAR AS THE EYE CAN SEE!
AND FOR THIS FREAKY MOUNTAIN-CROSSING ROUTE...
...WE GOTTA PLAY MUSICAL CHAIRS!
COME AGAIN?
?

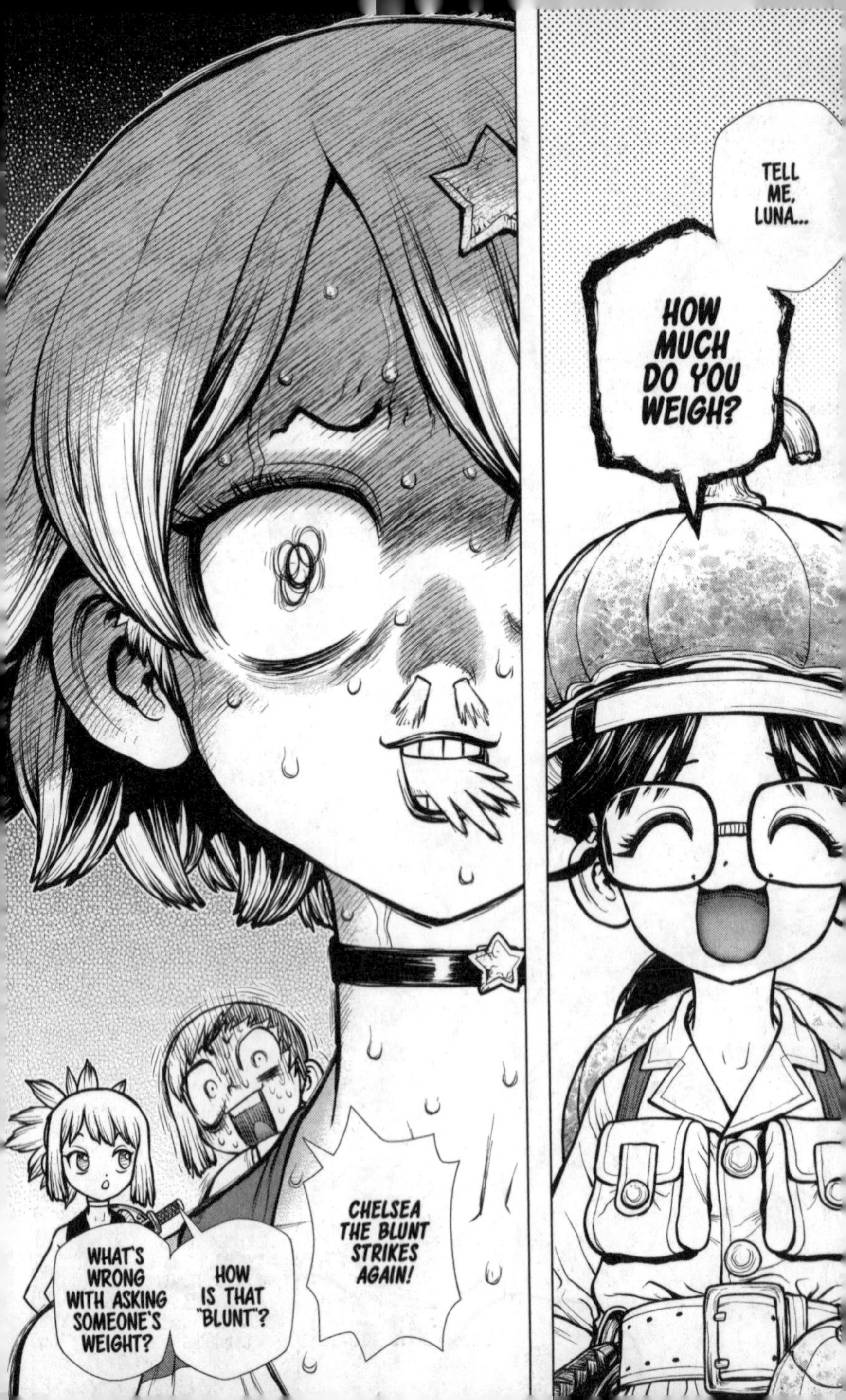
TELL ME, LUNA...
HOW MUCH DO YOU WEIGH?
CHELSEA THE BLUNT STRIKES AGAIN!
HOW IS THAT "BLUNT"?
WHAT'S WRONG WITH ASKING SOMEONE'S WEIGHT?

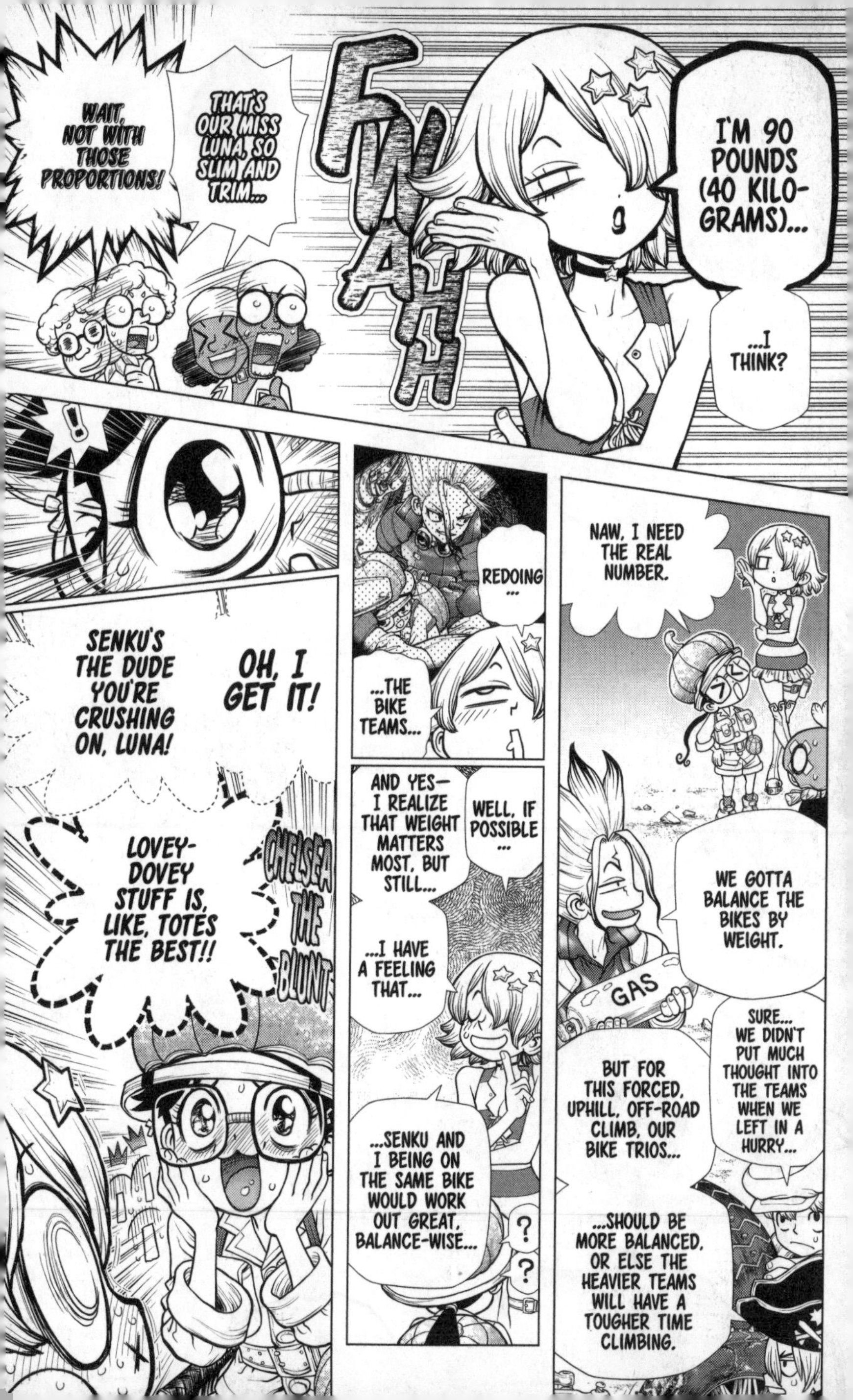
I'M 90 POUNDS (40 KILOGRAMS)...
...I THINK?
FWAH
THAT'S OUR MISS LUNA, SO SLIM AND TRIM...
WAIT, NOT WITH THOSE PROPORTIONS!
NAW, I NEED THE REAL NUMBER.
WE GOTTA BALANCE THE BIKES BY WEIGHT.
GAS
SURE... WE DIDN'T PUT MUCH THOUGHT INTO THE TEAMS WHEN WE LEFT IN A HURRY...
BUT FOR THIS FORCED, UPHILL, OFF-ROAD CLIMB, OUR BIKE TRIOS...
...SHOULD BE MORE BALANCED, OR ELSE THE HEAVIER TEAMS WILL HAVE A TOUGHER TIME CLIMBING.
REDOING...
...THE BIKE TEAMS...
WELL, IF POSSIBLE...
AND YES— I REALIZE THAT WEIGHT MATTERS MOST, BUT STILL...
...I HAVE A FEELING THAT...
...SENKU AND I BEING ON THE SAME BIKE WOULD WORK OUT GREAT, BALANCE-WISE...
?
?
!
OH, I GET IT!
SENKU'S THE DUDE YOU'RE CRUSHING ON, LUNA!
CHELSEA THE BLUNT
LOVEY-DOVEY STUFF IS, LIKE, TOTES THE BEST!!

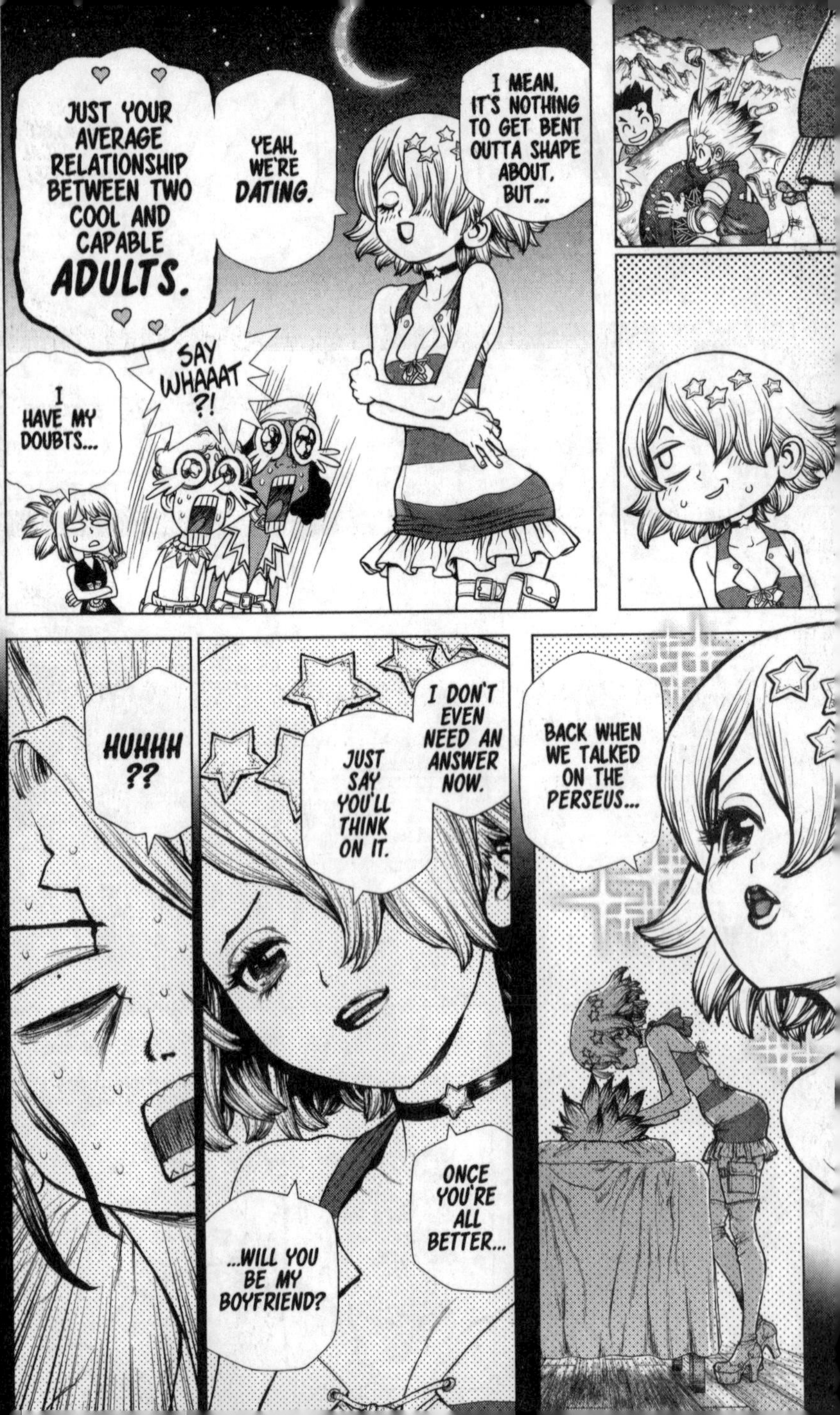
I MEAN, IT'S NOTHING TO GET BENT OUTTA SHAPE ABOUT, BUT...
YEAH, WE'RE DATING.
JUST YOUR AVERAGE RELATIONSHIP BETWEEN TWO COOL AND CAPABLE ADULTS.
SAY WHAAAT?!
I HAVE MY DOUBTS...
BACK WHEN WE TALKED ON THE PERSEUS...
I DON'T EVEN NEED AN ANSWER NOW.
JUST SAY YOU'LL THINK ON IT.
ONCE YOU'RE ALL BETTER...
...WILL YOU BE MY BOYFRIEND?
HUHHH??

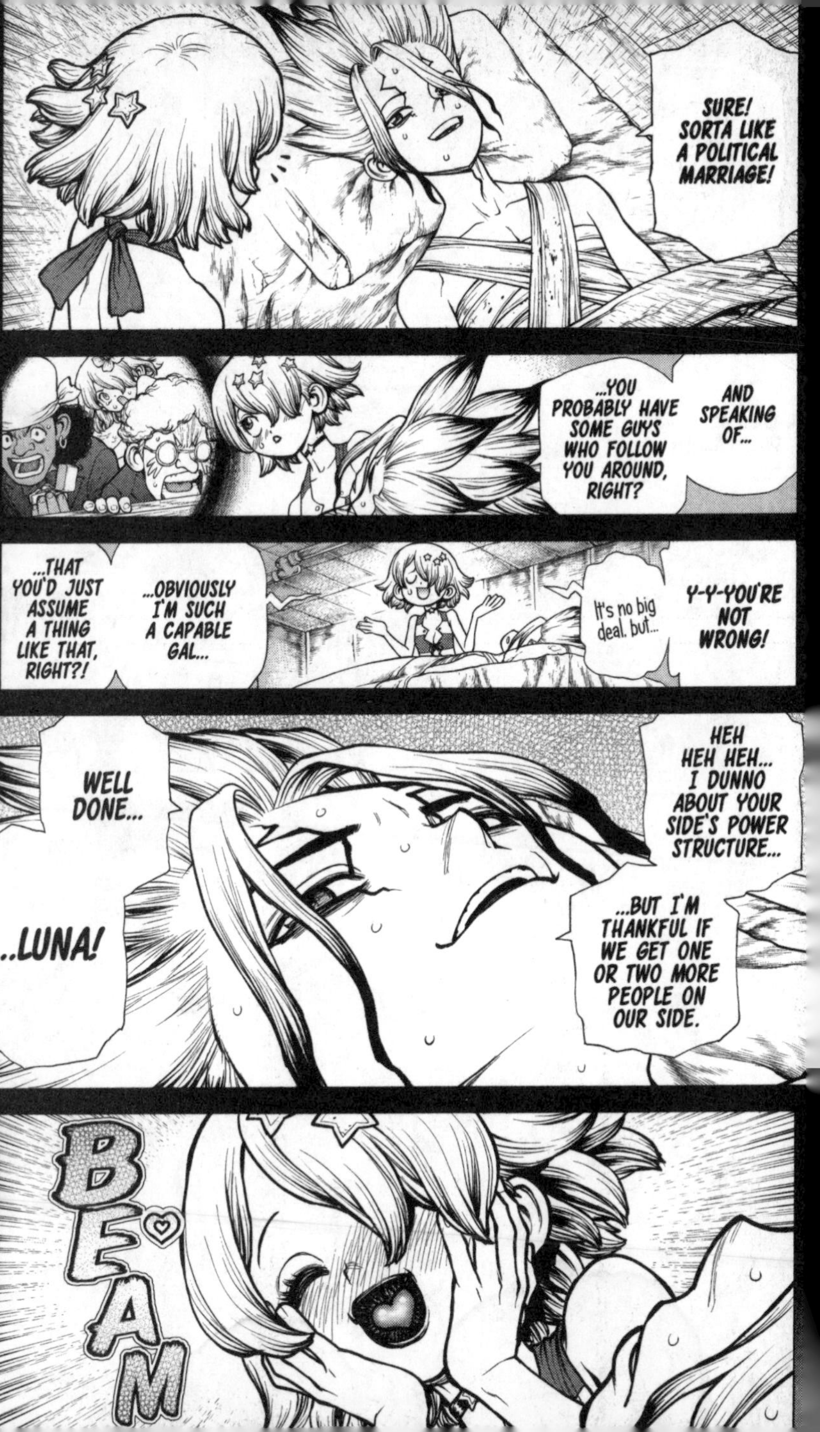
SURE! SORTA LIKE A POLITICAL MARRIAGE!
AND SPEAKING OF...
...YOU PROBABLY HAVE SOME GUYS WHO FOLLOW YOU AROUND, RIGHT?
Y-Y-YOU'RE NOT WRONG!
It's no big deal, but...
...OBVIOUSLY I'M SUCH A CAPABLE GAL...
...THAT YOU'D JUST ASSUME A THING LIKE THAT, RIGHT?!
HEH HEH HEH... I DUNNO ABOUT YOUR SIDE'S POWER STRUCTURE...
...BUT I'M THANKFUL IF WE GET ONE OR TWO MORE PEOPLE ON OUR SIDE.
WELL DONE...
...LUNA!
BEAM

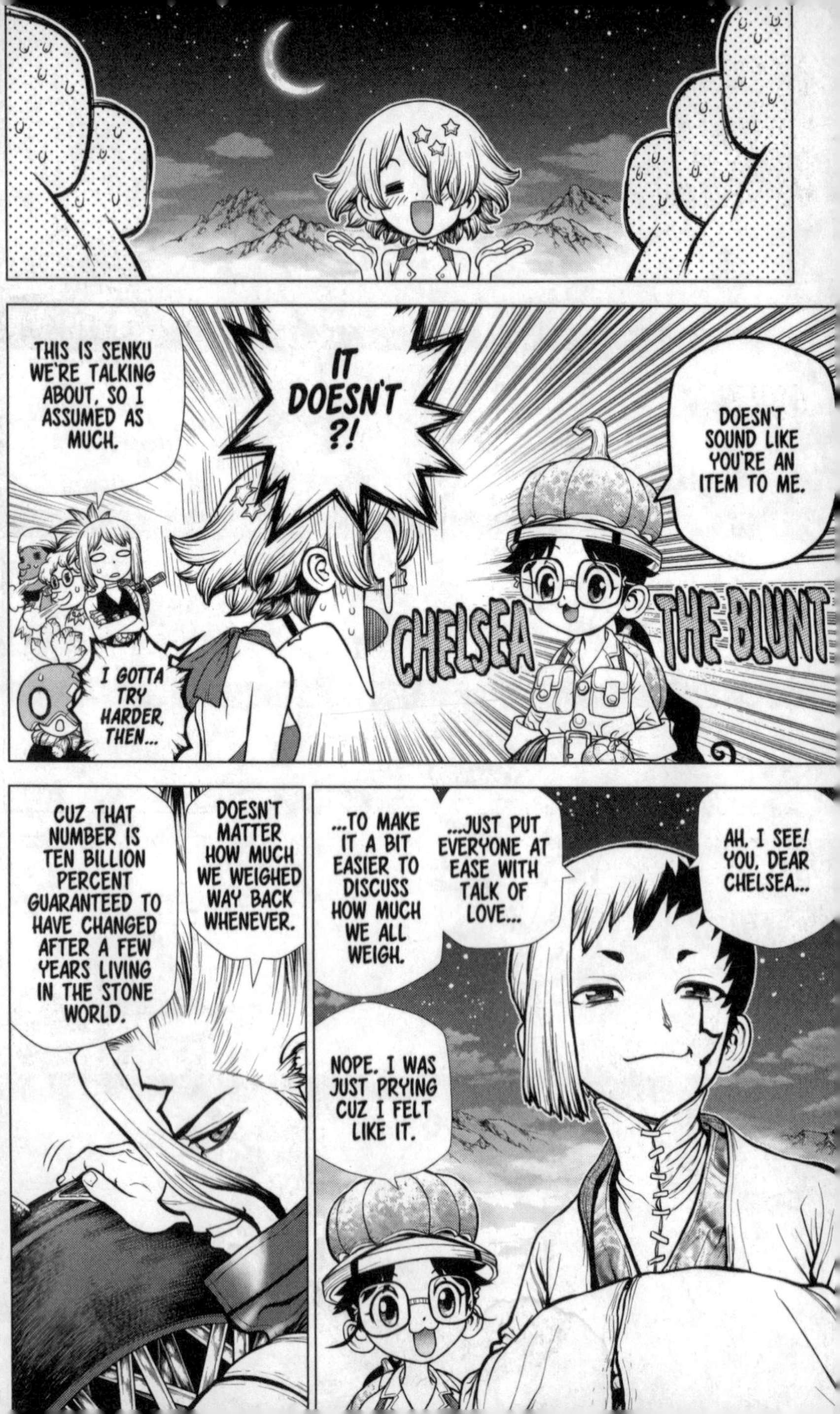
DOESN'T SOUND LIKE YOU'RE AN ITEM TO ME.
IT DOESN'T ?!
CHELSEA THE BLUNT
THIS IS SENKU WE'RE TALKING ABOUT, SO I ASSUMED AS MUCH.
I GOTTA TRY HARDER, THEN...
AH, I SEE! YOU, DEAR CHELSEA...
...JUST PUT EVERYONE AT EASE WITH TALK OF LOVE...
...TO MAKE IT A BIT EASIER TO DISCUSS HOW MUCH WE ALL WEIGH.
NOPE. I WAS JUST PRYING CUZ I FELT LIKE IT.
DOESN'T MATTER HOW MUCH WE WEIGHED WAY BACK WHENEVER.
CUZ THAT NUMBER IS TEN BILLION PERCENT GUARANTEED TO HAVE CHANGED AFTER A FEW YEARS LIVING IN THE STONE WORLD.

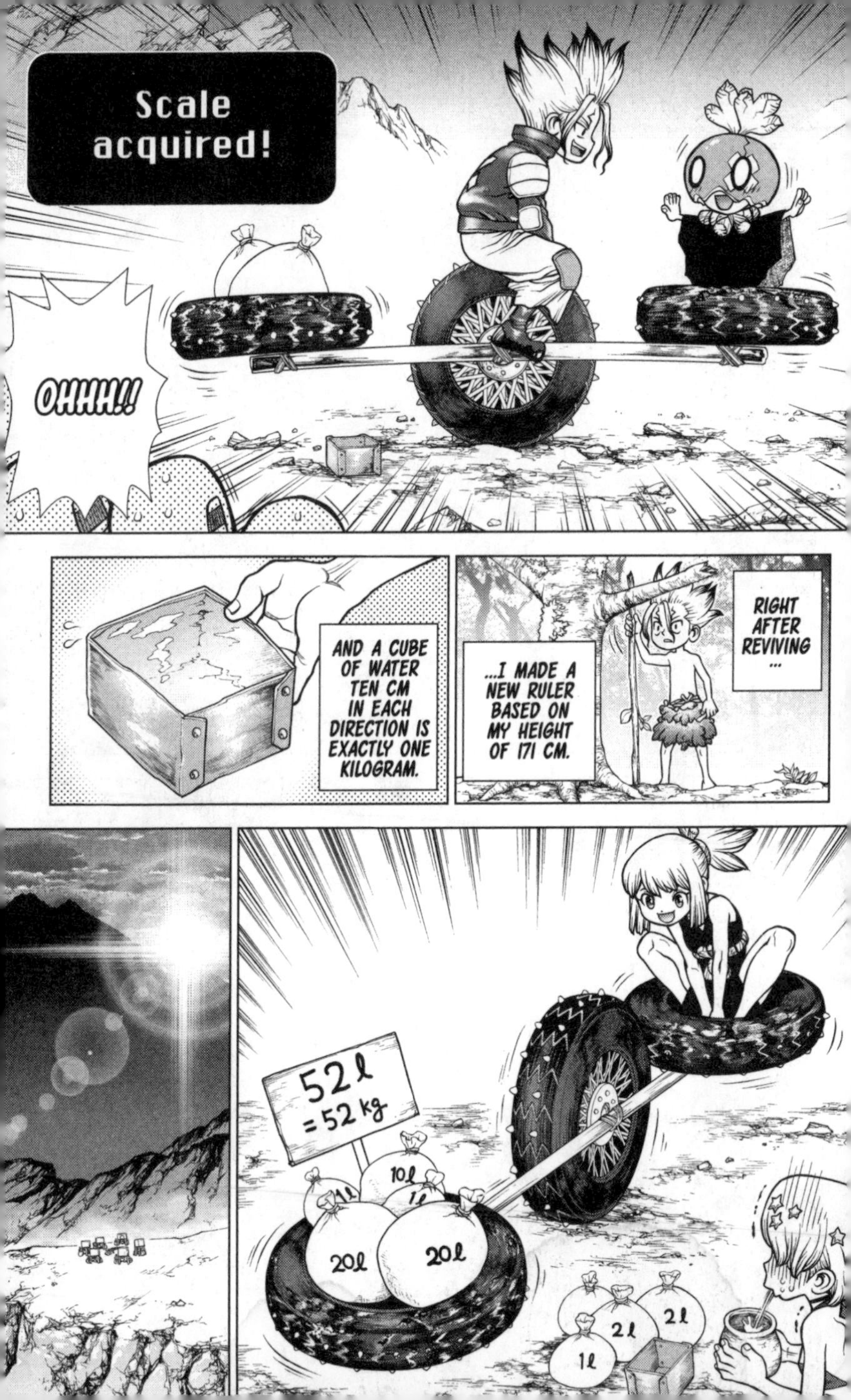
Scale acquired!
OHHHH!!
RIGHT AFTER REVIVING ...
...I MADE A NEW RULER BASED ON MY HEIGHT OF 171 CM.
AND A CUBE OF WATER TEN CM IN EACH DIRECTION IS EXACTLY ONE KILOGRAM.
52 l = 52 kg
10l
1l
1l
20l
20l
2l
2l
1l

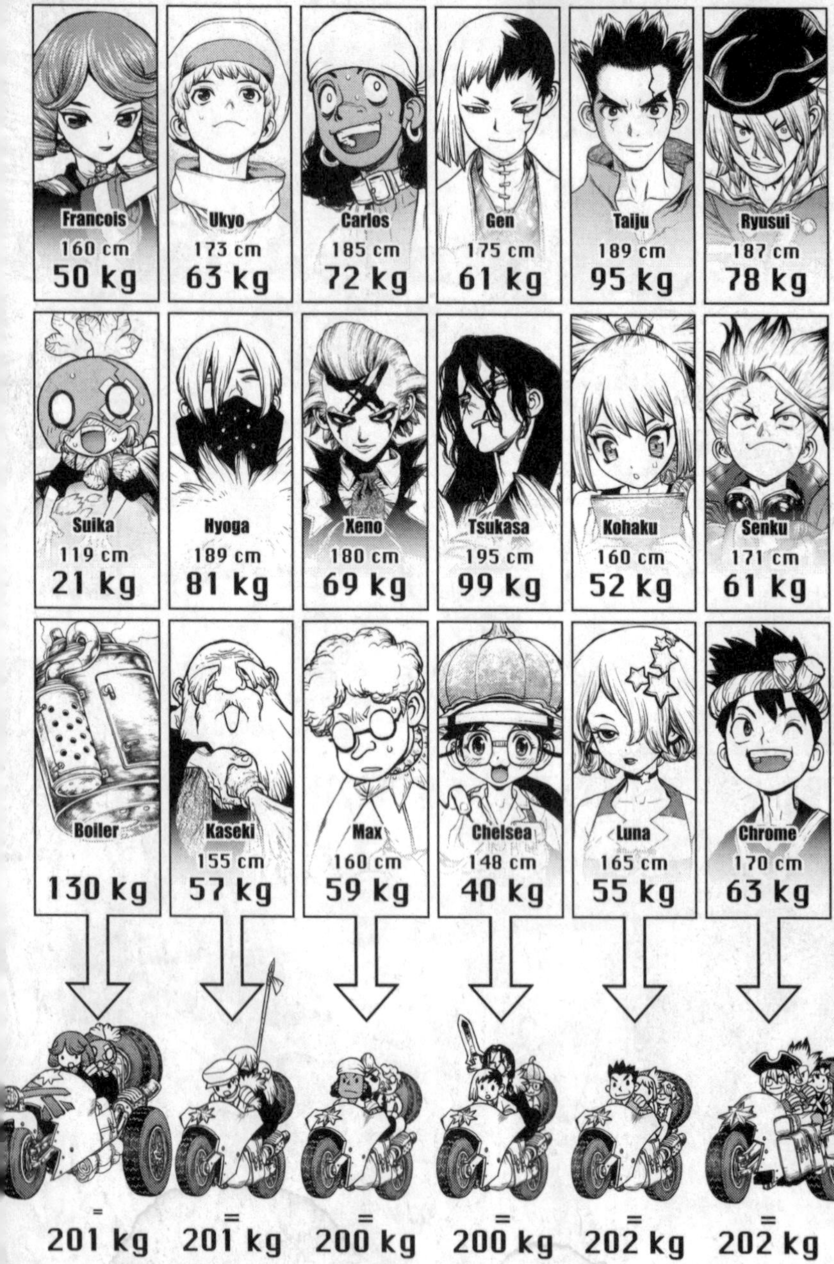
Francois
160 cm
50 kg
Ukyo
173 cm
63 kg
Carlos
185 cm
72 kg
Gen
175 cm
61 kg
Taiju
189 cm
95 kg
Ryusui
187 cm
78 kg
Suika
119 cm
21 kg
Hyoga
189 cm
81 kg
Xeno
180 cm
69 kg
Tsukasa
195 cm
99 kg
Kohaku
160 cm
52 kg
Senku
171 cm
61 kg
Boiler
130 kg
Kaseki
155 cm
57 kg
Max
160 cm
59 kg
Chelsea
148 cm
40 kg
Luna
165 cm
55 kg
Chrome
170 cm
63 kg
= 201 kg
= 201 kg
= 200 kg
= 200 kg
= 202 kg
= 202 kg

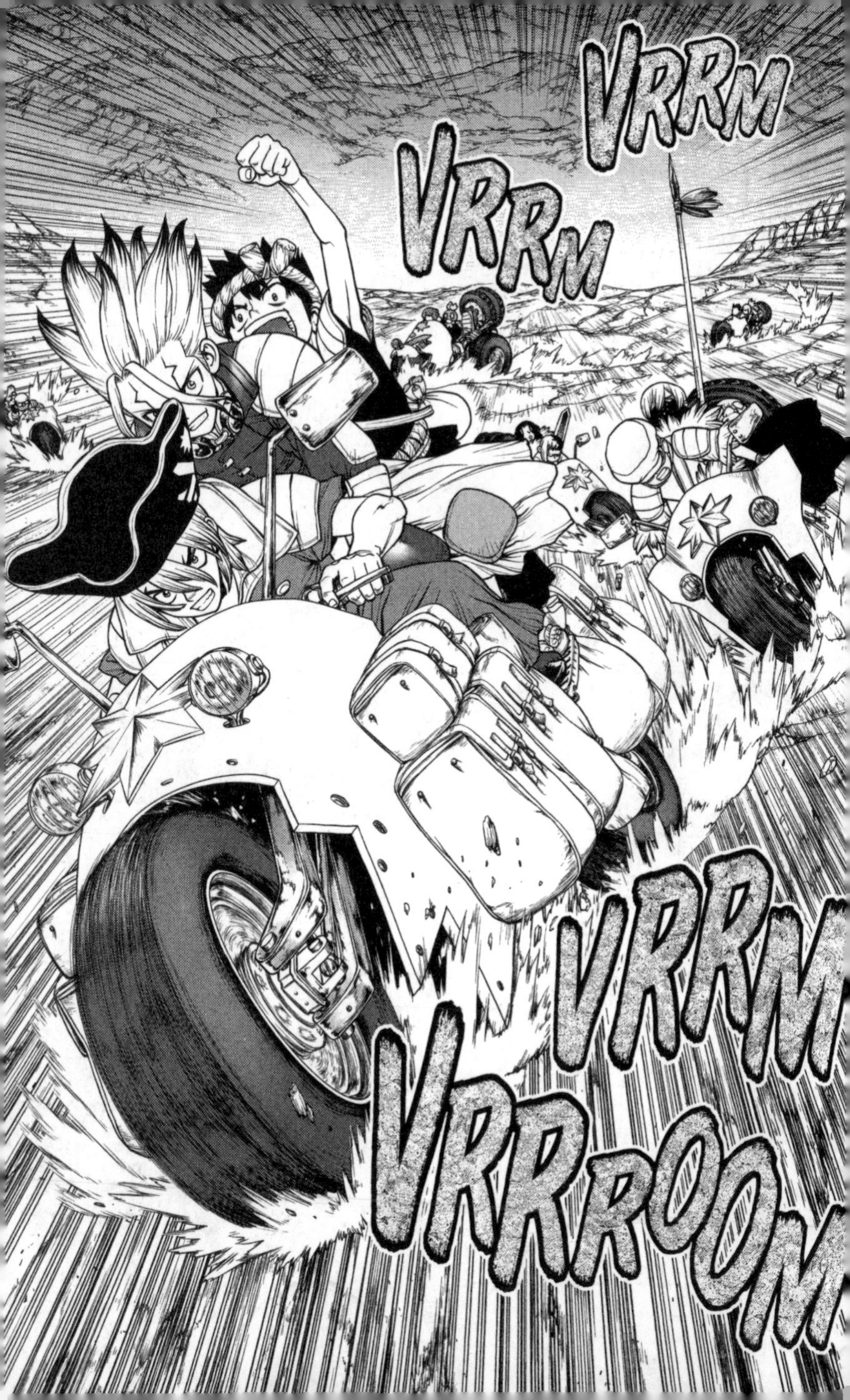
VRRM
VRRM
VRRM
VRRROOM

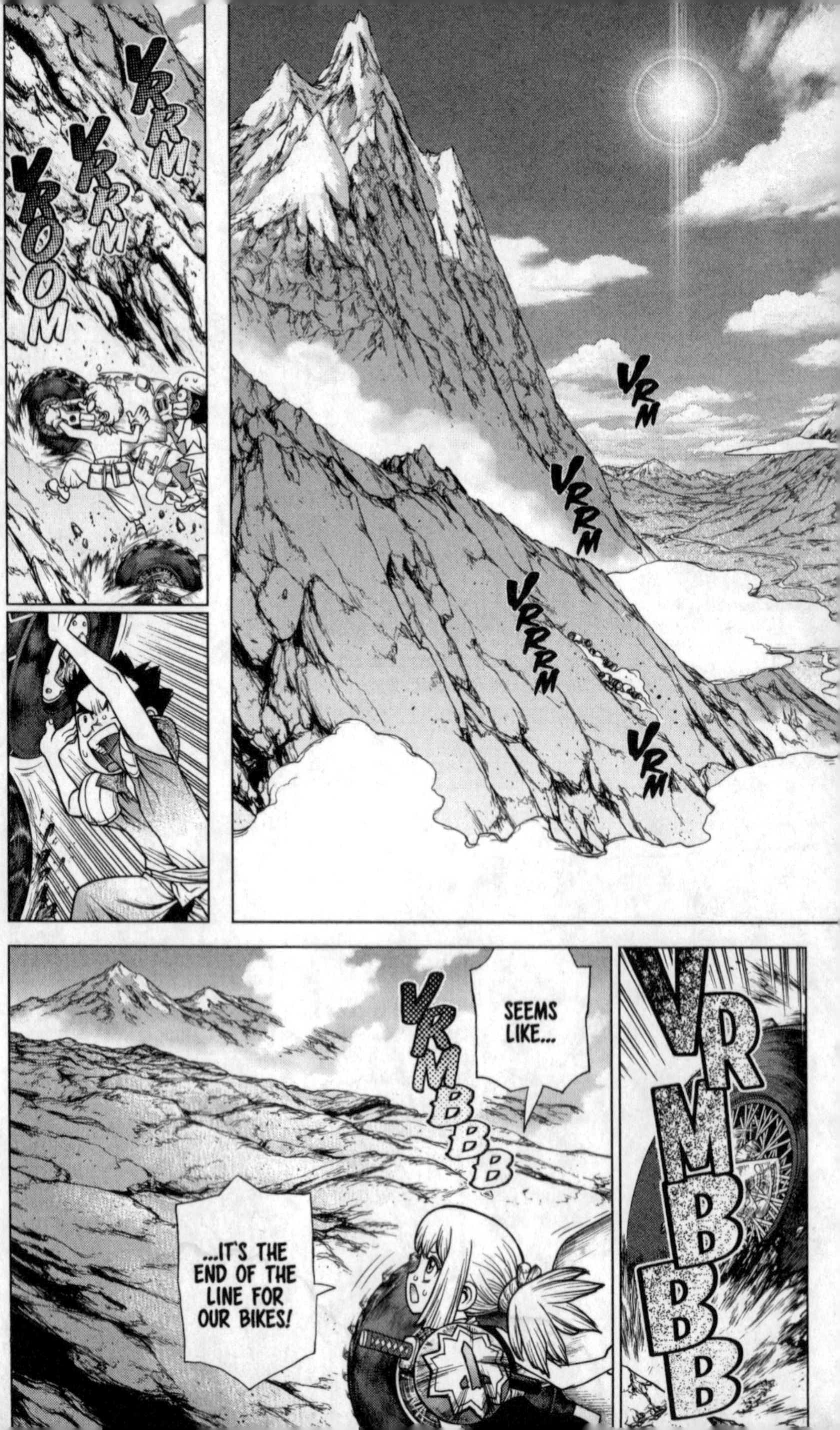
VRM
VRRM
VRRRM
VRM
VRRM
VRRRM
VROOOM
VRMBBBB
VRMBBB
SEEMS LIKE...
...IT'S THE END OF THE LINE FOR OUR BIKES!

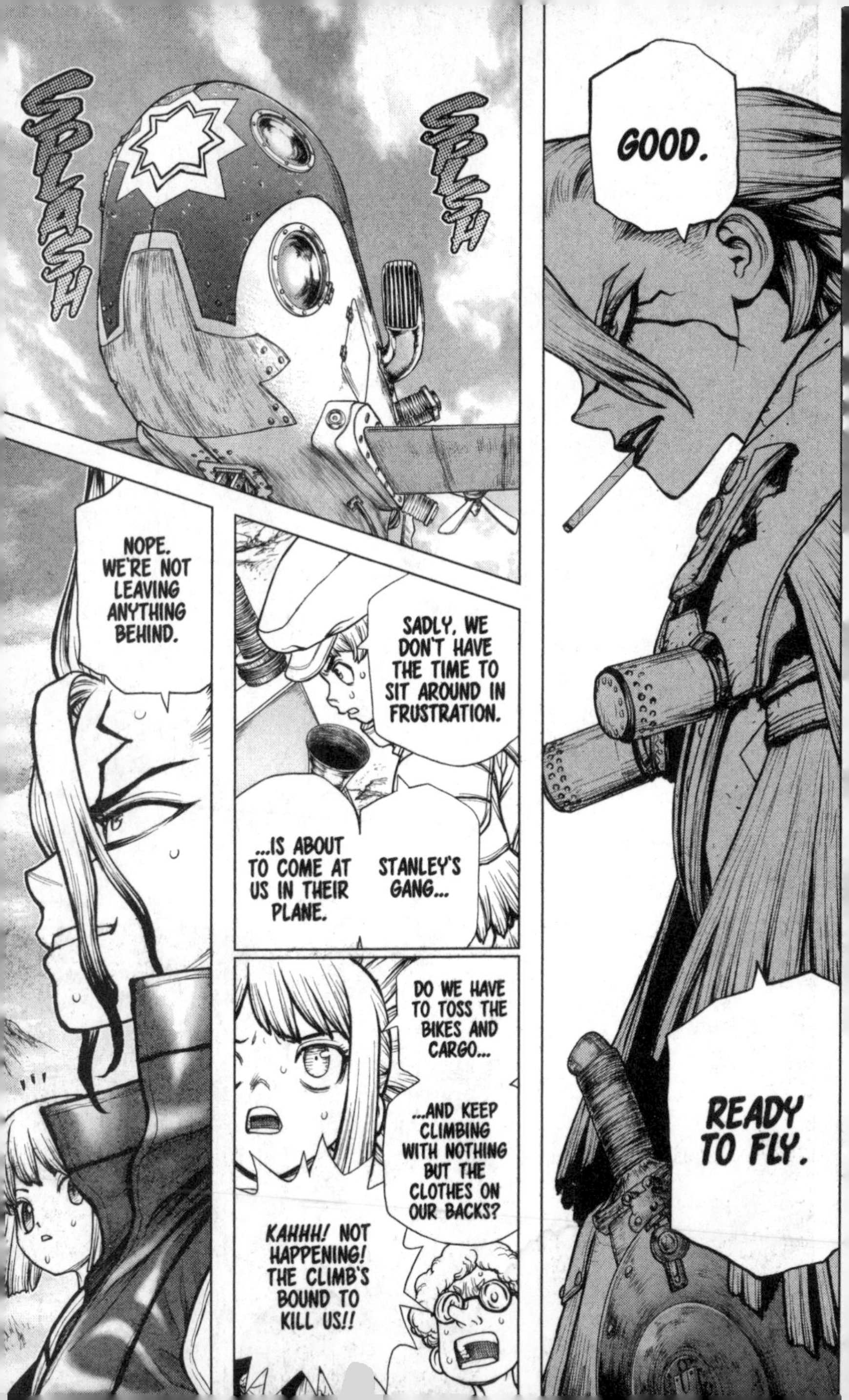
GOOD.
READY TO FLY.
SPLASH
SPLASH
SADLY, WE DON'T HAVE THE TIME TO SIT AROUND IN FRUSTRATION.
STANLEY'S GANG...
...IS ABOUT TO COME AT US IN THEIR PLANE.
DO WE HAVE TO TOSS THE BIKES AND CARGO...
...AND KEEP CLIMBING WITH NOTHING BUT THE CLOTHES ON OUR BACKS?
KAHHH! NOT HAPPENING! THE CLIMB'S BOUND TO KILL US!!
NOPE. WE'RE NOT LEAVING ANYTHING BEHIND.

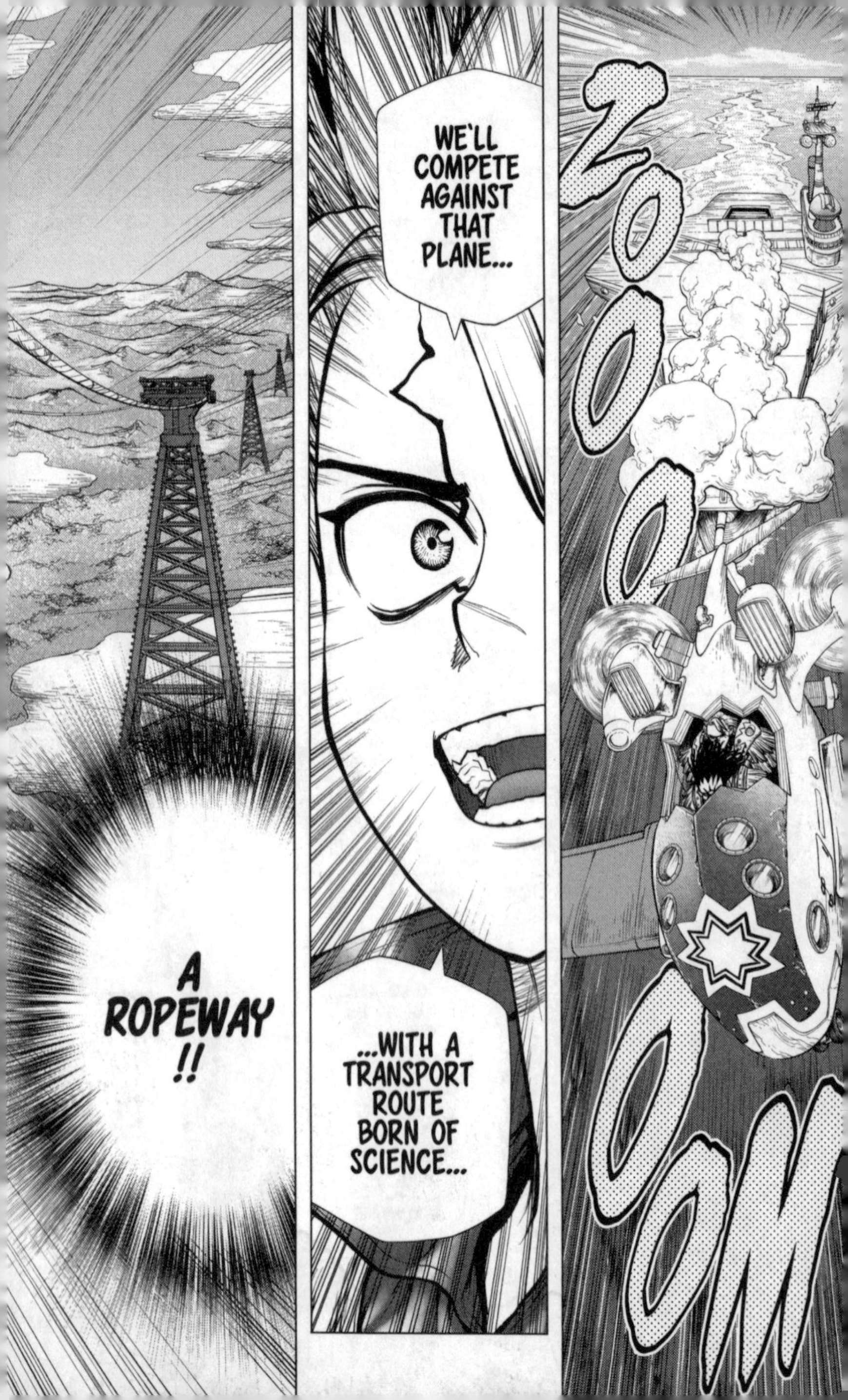
ZOOOOOM
WE'LL COMPETE AGAINST THAT PLANE...
...WITH A TRANSPORT ROUTE BORN OF SCIENCE...
A ROPEWAY!!

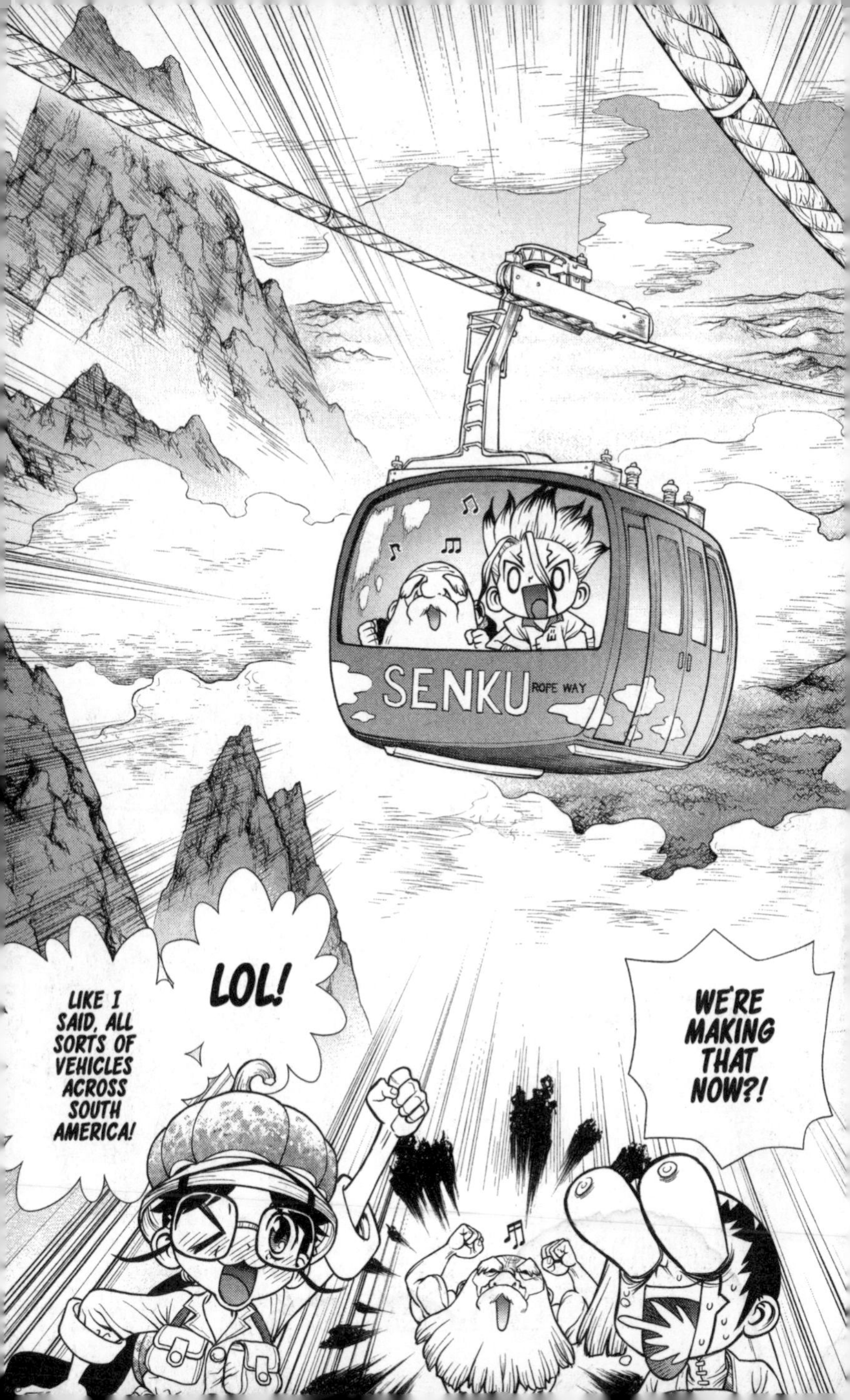
SENKU ROPE WAY
WE'RE MAKING THAT NOW?!
LOL!
LIKE I SAID, ALL SORTS OF VEHICLES ACROSS SOUTH AMERICA!

BOICHI

For a while now, I've been thinking we need to start viewing the comic arts as a singular, unified concept under an umbrella term. I've suggested "toon," which is what I've used personally for years now.

Because of these differentiated labels, we can't seem to see each other as being similar (even though we are all basically family) because of fundamental industry concerns. But the future we're headed for has no need of that. Try to imagine an era in which Western comics, manga, graphic novels, and webtoons are distributed to everyone regardless of territory. We can learn from each other, grow together, and share in our mutual successes. Authors, editors, and fans can meet, interact, laugh, and debate. There will be a distinct feeling that deep down, we are all one.

I believe that's the grand future in store for us. I've been saying that the 21st century will be the era of manga. This is that moment. That's why the industry that ties us together needs a single name. Those of us who speak through our art are already united.

RIICHIRO INAGAKI

I made some of Senku and Xeno's super soap bubble formula in real life, and my kids and I played with it in the bathroom.

Instead of blowing the bubbles with your mouth, I recommend using a big hoop.

The one in the picture is just a coat hanger twisted into a circle and taped together.

How'd the bubbles turn out? Extra gigantic!

The kids loved it!!

Boichi is a Korean-born artist currently living and working in Japan. His previous works include *Sun-Ken Rock* and *Terra Formars Asimov*.

Riichiro Inagaki is a Japanese manga writer from Tokyo. He is the writer for the sports manga series *Eyeshield 21*, which was serialized in *Weekly Shonen Jump*.

Dr.STONE

20

SHONEN JUMP Manga Edition

Story **RIICHIRO INAGAKI**
Art **BOICHI**

Science Consultant/**KURARE** **with Yakuri Classroom of Doom: Aruma Zirou, Cyrano, POKA**
Translation/**CALEB COOK**
Touch-Up Art & Lettering/**STEPHEN DUTRO**
Design/**JULIAN [JR] ROBINSON**
Editor/**JOHN BAE**

Consulted Works:

- Dartnell, Lewis, *The Knowledge: How to Rebuild Civilization in the Aftermath of a Cataclysm* Translated by Erika Togo, Kawade Shobo Shinsha, 2015
- Diamond, Jared, *Guns, Germs, and Steel: The Fates of Human Societies* Translated by Akira Kurahone, Soshisha Publishing Co., 2012
- Harari, Yuval Noah, *Sapiens: A Brief History of Humankind* Translated by Hiroyuki Shibata, Kawade Shobo Shinsha, 2016
- Weisman, Alan, *The World Without Us*, Translated by Shinobu Onizawa, Hayakawa Publishing, 2009

Printed in Canada

Published by VIZ Media, LLC
P.O. Box 77010
San Francisco, CA 94107

10 9 8 7 6 5 4 3 2 1
First printing, February 2022

VIZ MEDIA
viz.com

SHONEN JUMP

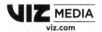

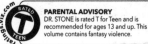

YOU'RE READING THE WRONG WAY

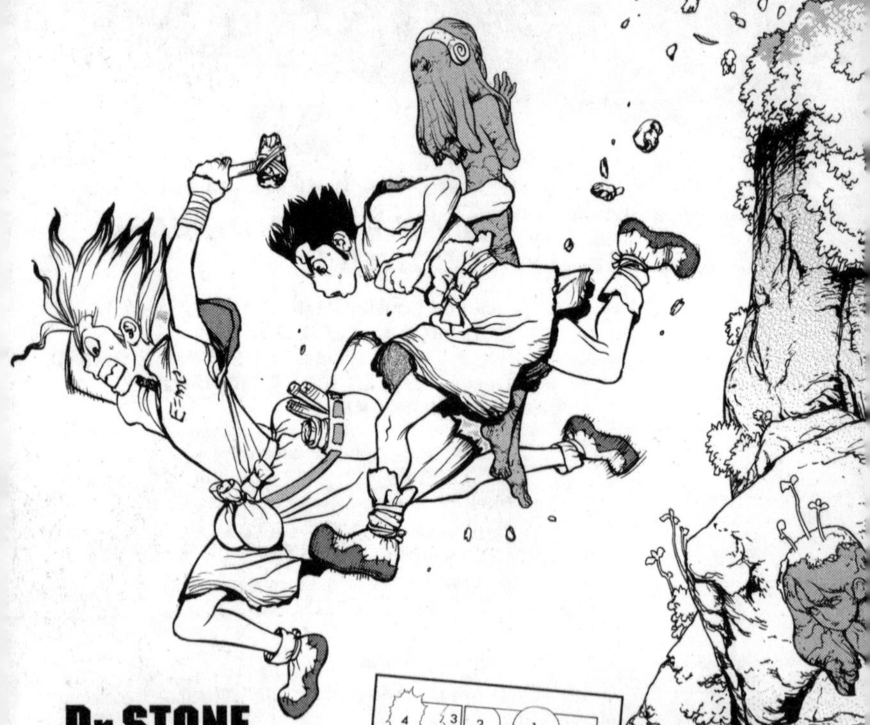

Dr.STONE

reads from right to left, starting in the upper-right corner. Japanese is read from right to left, meaning that action, sound effects, and word-balloon order are completely reversed from English order.

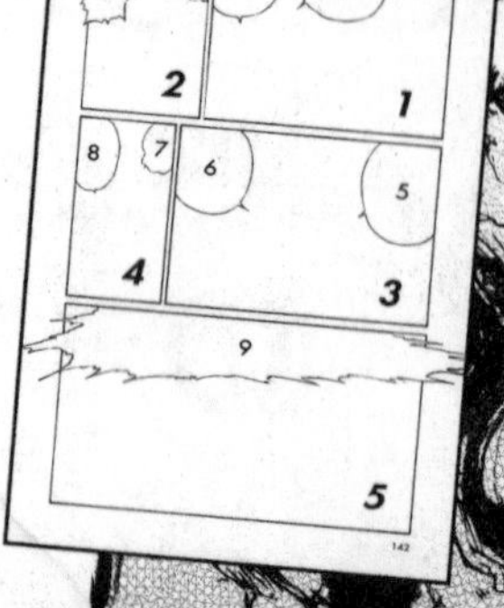